7/ 9/ 0 8

GENERALS IN GRAY

GENERALS

IN GRAY

Lives of the Confederate Commanders

BY EZRA J. WARNER

Louisiana State University Press

BATON ROUGE AND LONDON

ISBN 0-8071-0823-5
LIBRARY OF CONGRESS CATALOG CARD NUMBER 58-7551
COPYRIGHT © 1959, 1987 BY DOROTHY P. WARNER
ALL RIGHTS RESERVED
MANUFACTURED IN THE UNITED STATES OF AMERICA
DESIGNED BY THEO JUNG
1995 printing

The paper in this book meets the guidelines for permanence and durability of the
Committee on Production Guidelines for Book Longevity of the Council on Library Resources. ∞

PREFACE

THE GENESIS of this book goes back many years. My interest in the idea was probably first aroused by reading the late Douglas Southall Freeman's *Lee's Lieutenants*. I returned to this great work again and again, with a growing curiosity about the lives of Dr. Freeman's subjects and of their contemporaries in the other armies of the Confederacy. Some desultory research followed. I discovered that published accounts of the Confederate commanders were often erroneous, and in many cases, altogether lacking; and from a friend of my family whose father had been a Confederate brigadier, I learned that even the family records of the generals could be extremely meager.

After a slow start, I finally determined in 1951, with the encouragement of my friend Ralph Newman, to work seriously on the book. The need for it became more than ever apparent to me after I had checked the *Dictionary of American Biography*. This was the only readily available biographical dictionary which boasted any pretense to accuracy and fullness, and it was compiled after the deaths of all the 425 generals. Yet, exactly 200 (or 47 per cent) of the officers did not appear in it. Further research showed that at least fifty of the generals did not appear in any published source, however recondite.

My purpose, then, was two-fold: To present a concise biography of every Confederate general officer, correcting errors in and adding to the accounts in standard reference works and other published sources, as well as resurrecting the many men whose lives had never before been sketched; and secondly, to reproduce an authentic likeness of each officer. Every effort has been made—through the writing of literally thousands of letters and extensive travel from Maine to California—to verify or establish the exact places and dates of birth and death, and the present place of burial, of each general; and also to set down a reliable outline of his career, before, during, and after the war. As for the likenesses, I have been able to find pictures of all the officers with the single exception of John Breckinridge Grayson.

Thus a great part of the research for *Generals in Gray* has been done not so much in books as in the field—in a long chase after humble, but elusive, facts. For the reader who wishes to go beyond the narrow confines of this work, the Bibliography at the end of the volume may be suggestive.

In bringing this work to completion I have placed myself in the debt of several institutions and of scores of persons, who have contributed information, pictures, and critical counsel. I have tried to thank as many of these as possible in the Acknowledgments on a later page; to all those whom I may have omitted, my apologies and best gratitude.

E. J. W.

Aboard *Prairie Belle*
South Pass Range Rear Light Station
Mississippi River Delta, Louisiana
May 13, 1959

ACKNOWLEDGMENTS

A MAJORITY of the photographs in this book have appeared in *Confederate Military History: A Library of Confederate States History,* edited by C. E. Evans, and in *The Photographic History of the Civil War,* edited by F. T. Miller and R. S. Lanier (I would point out that wrong identification of the subjects is not uncommon in these otherwise splendid works). Other principal source books are *Battles and Leaders of the Civil War,* edited by R. U. Johnson and C. C. Buel; and *The Confederate Veteran* magazine. Special thanks and acknowledgments are due to certain institutions for making available photographs for reproduction: The Confederate Museum, Richmond, Va.; The Library of Congress, Washington, D. C.; and The Valentine Museum, Richmond, Va. I am also especially grateful to Mr. Hirst D. Milhollen, Alexandria, Va., and to Mr. John R. Peacock, High Point, N. C. for their generous co-operation in making many pictures available to me.

Without the assistance of almost countless individuals and institutions many of the photographs and much of the factual data in this book would have been impossible to obtain, since substantially more than half of the generals are not sketched in detail in any standard reference work. Considerations of space render it impossible to give credit to everyone who has been helpful in these matters. Also, a number of Civil War scholars have read the text and offered excellent suggestions for improving it. I am much indebted to these men for detecting errors and for giving constructive advice, though they are, of course, not responsible for the imperfections that remain. My cordial thanks must go specifically to the following:

Mrs. Martha Rivers Adams, Lynchburg, Va.; Mr. Rucker Agee, Birmingham, Ala.; Mrs. William T. Bailey, Nashville, Tenn.; Mr. Thomas J. Barnes, McMinnville, Tenn.; Mr. Lewis H. Beck, Griffin, Ga.; Dr. Virgil Bedsole, Head, Department of Archives, Louisiana State University, Baton Rouge, La; Major General K. L. Berry, The Adjutant General, Austin, Tex.; Mrs. W. Elmer Bomar, Alexandria, La.; Mr. Palmer Bradley, Houston, Tex.; Mr. Peter A. Brannon, State Archivist, Montgomery, Ala.; Mrs. Mary G. Bryan, Director, Department of Archives and History, Atlanta, Ga.; Miss Mattie Lee Buchanan, Okolona, Miss.; Mrs. Randolph Buck, St. Augustine, Fla.; Miss Charlotte Capers, Director, Department of Archives and History, Jackson, Miss.; Mr. H. Bailey Carroll, Director, Texas State Historical Association, Austin, Tex.; Mr. Louis S. Chamberlin, Burnet, Tex.; Mr. G. Glenn Clift, Assistant Secretary, Kentucky Historical Society, Frankfort, Ky.; Mr. Monroe F. Cockrell, Evanston, Ill.; Mrs. J. L. Copeland, Magnolia, Ark.; Colonel William Couper, Virginia Military Institute, Lexington, Va.; Miss Pollyanna Creekmore, Lawson McGhee Library, Knoxville, Tenn.; Mrs. L. A. Davis, Starke, Fla.; Dr. Nora M. Davis, Troy, S. C.; Mr. William H. Dean, Shenandoah Junction, W. Va.; Mr. and Mrs. Clifton E. Denny, Fayette, Mo.; Mrs. John H. DeWitt, Secretary, Tennessee Historical Commission, Nashville, Tenn.; Dr. Dorothy Dodd, State Librarian, Tallahassee, Fla.; Mr. Charles L. Dufour, New Orleans, La.; Dr. John P. Dyer, New Orleans, La.; Mr. J. H. Easterby, Director, Historical Commission of South Carolina, Columbia, S. C.; Dr. Otto Eisenschiml, Chicago, Ill.; Mr. Howell C. Erwin, Athens, Ga.; Mr. O. H. Felton, Lyons, Ill.; Mr. George O. Ferguson, Jr., Registrar, University of Virginia, Charlottesville, Va; Miss Llerena Friend, Librarian, Barker Texas History Center, University of Texas Library, Austin, Tex.; Mr. Franklin Garrett, Atlanta, Ga.; Mr. John W. Garrott, Houston, Tex.; Mr. James M. Goggin, El Paso, Tex.; Mrs. Elsie D. Hand, Librarian, Oklahoma Historical Society, Oklahoma City, Okla.; Professor Guy B. Harrison, Jr., Baylor University, Waco, Tex.; Mrs. Lilla M. Hawes, Director, Georgia Historical Society, Savannah, Ga.; Mr. Thomas R. Hay, Locust Valley, N. Y.; Mr. Robert T. Head, San Francisco, Calif.; Mr. Basil Duke Henning, New Haven, Conn.; Mr. Dallas T. Herndon, Executive Secretary, Arkansas History Commission, Little Rock, Ark.; Miss Lillian Hill, Tuscaloosa, Ala.; Miss Geraldine C. Hope, Ohio University

Alumni Association, Athens, O.; Mr. Stanley F. Horn, Nashville, Tenn.; Miss Barbara Kell, Reference Librarian, Missouri Historical Society, St. Louis, Mo.; Mrs. Maud McLure Kelly, Montgomery, Ala.; Mr. Wilbur G. Kurtz, Atlanta, Ga.; Mr. Ned Lee, Eupora, Miss.; Dr. Lawrence T. Lowrey, Blue Mountain, Miss.; Dr. Neill W. Macaulay, Columbia, S. C.; Colonel John A. McComsey, Secretary, Association of Graduates, West Point, N. Y.; Mrs. Dan McDonald, Pine Bluff, Ark.; Mr. Kenneth W. Mackall, Cicero, N. Y.; Mr. W. F. G. McMurry, St. Charles, Mo.; Dr. R. Gerald McMurtry, Fort Wayne, Ind.; Mr. Craig Mathews, Dalton, Ga.; Miss M. B. Meriwether, South Caroliniana Library, University of South Carolina, Columbia, S. C.; Mr. Hirst D. Milhollen, Alexandria, Va.; Mr. C. Moffett Moore, Cossitt Library, Memphis, Tenn.; Mrs. Mary T. Moore, Librarian, Kentucky Collection, Western Kentucky State College, Bowling Green, Ky.; Mrs. Maurice Moore, Lynchburg, Va.; Mrs. W. Bedford Moore, Jr., Columbia, S. C.; Colonel W. J. Morton, former Librarian, United States Military Academy, West Point, N. Y.; Dr. Ralph G. Newman, Chicago, Ill.; Mr. Lowell Niebuhr, Chicago, Ill.; Mrs. Courtenay Stovall North and Mrs. Earnest M. North, Savannah, Ga.; Mr. Walter C. N. Norton, London, England; Office of the Adjutant General, United States Army, Washington, D. C.; Mrs. Marie B. Owen, former Director, Department of Archives and History, Montgomery, Ala.; Mr. John R. Peacock, High Point, N. C.; Miss Isabelle M. Perrault, Natchez, Miss.; Mr. John L. Perrin, Jr., Abbeville, S. C.; Mrs. W. A. Porter, Richmond, Va.; Mr. W. Brooke Price, Lawrenceville, Va.; Mr. Robert Quarles, State Archivist, Nashville, Tenn.; Mr. Carol H. Quenzel, Librarian, Mary Washington College, Fredericksburg, Va.; Mrs. R. W. Reynolds, Lake Village, Ark.; Mr. Robert E. Richardson, DeValls Bluff, Ark.; Mrs. G. Price Russ, Jr., Mobile, Ala.; Mr. Milton C. Russell, Virginia State Library, Richmond, Va.; Dr. Henry L. Savage, Archivist, Princeton University Library, Princeton, N. J.; Miss Mahala Saville, Reference Librarian, University of Mississippi Library, University, Miss.; Mr. J. A. Sharp, Sevierville, Tenn.; Mr. Bert Sheldon, Washington, D. C.; Mr. Fred Shelley, Librarian, Maryland Historical Society, Baltimore, Md.; Mr. Floyd C. Shoemaker, Secretary, State Historical Society of Missouri, Columbia, Mo.; Mrs. Walter Sillers, Sr., Rosedale, Miss.; Mrs. George Smith, Bisbee, Ariz.; Mr. Hugh W. Smith, New Orleans, La.; Mr. and Mrs. LeSueur G.

Smith, Pelham Manor, N. Y.; Miss Harriet Smither, State Archivist, Austin, Tex.; Colonel Thomas Spencer, Atlanta, Ga.; Mrs. Walter Stokes, Jr., Nashville, Tenn.; Mrs. W. W. Taylor, Signal Mountain, Tenn.; Miss Margaret Lynn Templeton, Staunton, Va.; Miss India W. Thomas, House Regent, Confederate Museum, Richmond, Va.; Mr. Kenneth T. Urquhart, New Orleans, La.; Dr. Frank E. Vandiver, Houston, Tex.; Mr. Samuel Anderson Weakley, Nashville, Tenn.; Professor Manly Wade Wellman, Chapel Hill, N. C.; Miss Margaret A. Whalen, Research Librarian, Maine State Library, Augusta, Me.; Mr. William N. Wilkins, Baltimore, Md.; Dr. T. Harry Williams, Baton Rouge, La.; Mrs. Catherine N. Wilson, Granbury, Tex.; Mrs. William B. Wingo, Norfolk, Va.; Mrs. C. S. Woodward, Little Rock, Ark.; Mr. John C. Wyllie, Alderman Library, University of Virginia, Charlottesville, Va.

E. J. W.

CONTENTS

INTRODUCTION

T H E S O U T H E R N C O N F E D E R A C Y was carried for four long years on the bayonets of its armies. This is a common enough observation but a true one. Although the South's effort to achieve independence partook of the nature of a revolution—and was recognized as such, then and now—yet the Confederacy had no administrators and statesmen comparable to those in our earlier common War for Independence. The South produced no Jeffersons, no Franklins, no Patrick Henrys, no Richard Henry Lees; nor yet any Robert Morrises or Silas Deanes. With few exceptions her civil officials were mediocrities; and in many respects the President himself was but ill-adapted to the gigantic problems with which he was confronted. (1) Thus, in large measure, the story of that long-ago nation—and it was indubitably a nation —is the story of its military leaders; and not of its President, its Cabinet, its Congress, nor of its dissident state governors and legislatures. The South was at war, and the flower of its manhood embraced the profession of arms. Hence, the present book may claim to be, in some measure, the abstract of an age.

Sixty-three years had passed since Robert E. Lee had entered the red brick dwelling at Appomattox Court House, since Generals Joseph E. Johnston and W. T. Sherman had conferred at a way station in North Carolina, and since Edmund Kirby Smith had entered into a convention to surrender all the Confederate forces west of the Mississippi. In the interval fourteen presidents had occupied the White House; two wars had been fought and three major economic depressions had been weathered; and some few Americans were contending that World War II was in prospect, though no one, naturally, paid much attention to these alarmists.

In this same year, 1928, a news story from the Southwest reported the death of a Confederate officer. It was not surprising that the obituary attracted little notice. And yet, the event had its symbolic importance. For this man was one of the last principal witnesses of the Civil War—of a struggle that involved the American people more radically than any before or since, and that altered the whole course of their economics, politics, and history.

As the sun reached meridian over Waco, Texas, on April 20, 1928, Brigadier General Felix Huston Robertson "crossed over the river"—the final surviving general officer of the armies of the Confederacy. (2) He had outlived by some fourteen years, Simon Bolivar Buckner, the last of the lieutenant generals, who had died on his Kentucky estate on January 8, 1914. (3) Buckner was preceded in death by Major General Prince de Polignac of France on November 15, 1913; (4) and death had taken earlier the last of the full generals when Kirby Smith succumbed at Sewanee, Tennessee, on March 28, 1893. (5) In April 1959 only one man survives from the hosts of the American Civil War—the redoubtable Confederate private, Walter Washington Williams, now in his 117th year.

Except in the homes of their descendants and on the bookshelves of scholars of the period, the Confederate generals now exist as an almost mythical group. Many of them marched from the points where they gave their paroles into almost total obscurity. But some who had been well-known figures in the ante-bellum South, and other younger men, who made their mark in the War, became leaders of the New South for a generation and more after Appomattox.

Almost from the closing days of the War, controversies have raged about who was and who was not entitled to be called "General" in the armies of the Confederate States. Through ignorance, prejudice, or sentiment many officers have been promoted to grades to which they themselves would not have laid claim. It is also true that some officers, as old men, in the shimmering haze of retrospect, have indulged in self-promotions. Southern writers, and especially Southern newspapers, have been loath to dispute such claims, however tenuous their basis. The result has been the attribution in otherwise excellent biographies of totally unverifiable rank. Too, the policy adopted by the United Confederate Veterans of according high military rank to its officials during the post-bellum period created a whole hierarchy of "generals," the majority of whom were actually rank and file during the War. Confusion has been further compounded by the publication of lists "compiled from official records"—all of them exhibiting a want of accurate research.

This fact should be established at the outset: All laws which were enacted by the Confederate Congress regarding the creation of general officers, required appointment by the President; and all but one (that of May 21, 1861) provided for confirmation by the Senate. (6) Therefore, by strict construction, only officers confirmed by the Senate or holding rank under the act of May 21, 1861, were entitled to the three stars and wreath of a general. The procedure was customarily as follows: If the Senate was in session, the President, upon the recommendation of the Secretary of War, would nominate to that body an officer to one of the four grades of general. The Senate would then either confirm or reject the nomination, or as happened in a few cases, take no action. Upon confirmation, the officer was formally appointed. If the Senate was not in session, the appointment was of necessity made first, and the nomination was sent over at the next session. Exceptions to this procedure were, however, not uncommon.

The foregoing, of course, resulted in some officers' having appointments without being confirmed, and in their exercising command for longer or shorter periods at the grade to which they were appointed. Examples are D. H. Hill, whom the President declined to nominate to the grade of lieutenant general, after having appointed him while the Senate was not in session; William W. Allen, whose nomination to the grade of major general was not acted upon by the Senate; and Theodore W. Brevard, whose appointment to the grade of brigadier general was made after the Senate had adjourned for the last time. (7)

Still other officers were promoted in orders by General E. Kirby Smith in the Trans-Mississippi Department, but not appointed by the President nor confirmed by the Senate. There was also an extensive list of officers referred to in the *Official Records* as "Acting Brigadier General," "General," and so on; and others nowhere officially referred to as "General," but who at one time or another acted in that capacity.

To sum up—we have the following groups of officers, all of whom appear on one or another list of Confederate generals, and would seem to have a claim to the grade:

1. Officers regularly appointed and nominated, and confirmed by the Senate.
2. Officers regularly appointed and nominated, but whose nominations were either rejected or not acted upon by the Senate; and officers regularly appointed, but not nominated, or whose nominations were withdrawn.
3. Officers "assigned to command" by General E. K. Smith and others, but neither appointed by the President nor confirm.d by the Senate.
4. Officers sometimes referred to in official reports and correspondence as "General," but not so appointed; and others who exercised brigade command at times, and who have reached posterity as generals.

So far as the individuals in category 1 are concerned, there can exist no question as to their rank. Because of the personal prejudices known to have existed in the Confederate Senate and the strained relations between Congress and the Executive, particularly toward the latter part of the war, the individuals in category 2 have a very positive claim to their respective ranks. Moreover, not a few officers, duly appointed, were killed or died before they could be nominated, simply because the Congress was not in session.

Category 3 presents a special problem. Owing to the almost complete absence of ready communication between Richmond and the Trans-Mississippi after the fall of Vicksburg, General Smith made repeated application to Richmond for authority to make promotions to the grades of brigadier and major general. Although this authority was never forthcoming, Smith made several such promotions in orders, some "subject to the approval of the President," and others not. In some cases the officers in question were subsequently appointed by Davis and confirmed by the Senate. In at least ten instances, however, such appointment did not follow. Although these officers manifestly were not the recipients of legal appointments, they were paroled at the grades assigned them by General Smith, and are accordingly listed in the Appendix.

Category 4, in the author's opinion, must be excluded from consideration. This category embraces officers who commanded either brigades or other organizations larger than regiments, but whose official rank was not higher than colonel. Many of these officers signed themselves, were referred to, and have been accepted by competent historians as generals, and are so cited in such admirable works as *Confederate Military History, Dictionary of American Biography,* and so on. To include them in a definitive list of general officers of the Confederacy is to do injustice to the many other gallant officers who discharged identical responsibilities, but who everywhere appear at their official rank. The returns of the Army of Northern Virginia for February 28, 1865 list thirty-nine brigades of infantry. Of these no more than twenty were under the command of officers of commensurate rank, seventeen being commanded by colonels, one by a lieutenant colonel, and one by a major. (8) Similarly, the returns of the forces under General Joseph E. Johnston for March 31, 1865 show that thirteen of the thirty-six infantry brigades were led by colonels, six by lieutenant colonels, two by majors, and four by captains. Here we have a total of forty-four officers below the grade of brigadier in command of brigades. (9) Yet only one (George P. Harrison, Jr., Colonel of the 32nd Georgia) is often cited as having been a brigadier; and this officer uniformly signed himself and was addressed as "Colonel, Commanding Brigade." (10)

Some readers may also take issue with the grade herein assigned to certain officers. It has been almost always taken for granted, for example, that Major Generals John B. Gordon of Georgia and Joseph Wheeler of Alabama were lieutenant generals, despite the fact that no conclusive evidence exists to support such assumptions. Unofficial lists of Confederate generals usually cite both officers as lieutenant generals. The biographical sketch of Wheeler in *Confederate Military History* even cites a date of appointment (February 28, 1865). In point of fact, Wheeler's nomination as major general was debated in the Senate for over a year; confirmation was finally voted, 12 to 9, only by Davis's appealing to the distinctly unfriendly Joseph E. Johnston for assistance in persuading certain recalcitrant senators. (11) It is entirely probable that Johnston, who was partial to Wheeler, recommended the latter for promotion; there are indications in the *Official Records* which can be construed to mean that he gave Wheeler assurances of a forthcoming commission at that grade. No evidence of such, however, can be found.

In the case of Gordon, the strength of the 2nd Corps at the time he was assigned to command had declined to less than that of a good-sized division in 1862. (12) Gordon's own autobiography is significantly silent on the subject, although he recites the occasions of his promotion to brigadier and major general. In his old age Gordon alleged he had been verbally promoted by John C. Breckinridge, then Confederate Secretary of War. (13)

The principal authority upon which rank and grade are herein based is the *Journal of the Congress of the Confederate States of America, 1861-1865*. This record contains all nominations and confirmations of officers as provided for by law. As stated previously, from a strict legal standpoint it can be said that no officer not appearing therein as having been confirmed by the Senate or as holding rank under the act of May 21, 1861 was a general officer in the Confederate service. Certain officers appointed by the President but not nominated to the Senate are contained in *Memorandum Relative to the General Officers Appointed by the President in the Armies of the Confederate States, 1861-1865*. This work was probably compiled by General Wright and is incorporated almost verbatim into Wright's *General Officers of the Confederate Army*. Research in the *Official Records* has provided the names of officers promoted in orders by General E. K. Smith.

A word should be said in regard to state militia officers, whose names are not infrequently found in lists of Confederate generals. General Thomas T. Fauntleroy is a case in point. Resigning his commission as Colonel of the 1st Dragoons, U.S.A., he was appointed a brigadier general in the provisional army of Virginia, from which he was relieved at his own request on August 25, 1861. He never held rank in the Confederate service. (14) Similarly, John V. Harris was a general of Mississippi militia and M. Jeff Thompson of the Missouri State Guard; both sometimes appear as Confederate brigadiers. (15)

The reader will recognize that the line of demarcation in many individual cases is not readily discernible. Circumstances alter cases, and Confederate records of all kinds are deplorably incomplete. The author has reached his conclusions after exhaustive research on the subject; and for the omission of a cherished name, he can only offer his apologies. Every effort has been made to include in the following pages all discoverable officers whose claim to one of the four grades of general in the armies of the Confederacy rests on reasonable grounds.

In this connection, *intent*—whether stated or implied—on the part of the controlling authority has been the criterion for inclusion. Unfortunately, this same criterion has operated to exclude such gallant officers as Colonels David B. Harris, Thomas T. Munford, and Lieutenant Colonel Henry Kyd Douglas, (16) to name only a few. In their cases it was the obvious wish of their superior officers that they receive promotion to brigadier—but apparently *not* the intention of President Davis.

The records exhibit that 425 individuals received appointment by the President to one of the four grades of general, of whom 299 were in grade at the end of the war. (17) The attrition is accounted for as follows:

Killed in action or died of wounds	77
Resigned	19
Died by accident or from natural causes	15
Appointments cancelled	5
Declined appointment	3
Killed in "personal encounters"	2
Assassinated	1
Committed suicide	1
Dropped	1
Retired by reason of wounds	1
Reverted to rank of colonel	1
Total	126

The recognized necessity (perhaps partaking to some extent of the Napoleonic tradition) of making the faint-hearted stand up to their work by personal example is reflected in the seventy-seven general officers who were killed outright or mortally wounded. This number is approximately one-fifth of the generals "for duty," and an enormously larger fraction of the field commanders. Unfortunately, more than a few excellent officers were lost to the Confederacy by a compulsive rashness, which was attributable to this need for personal valor. Instances were so numerous as to make specific mention invidious.

The adjective "faint-hearted" perhaps deserves some explanation. In the early months of the war officers were confronted with levies of raw, untrained, and undisciplined recruits totally unaccustomed to hostile fire. Whole commands were known to panic and retire quite unnecessarily, a phenomenon by no means confined to the Confederates. During the closing scenes many Southern soldiers, wise in the ways of warfare from long experience, could sense when they were whipped. Not infrequently they would dissolve when it became apparent to them that a position was untenable, irrespective of the tactical considerations determined by superiors. This naturally threw the entire burden on their officers—and particularly on the "Old Man"—to show the way and carry out the orders received. All this, of course, does not apply to the many commands who fought to the last cartridge.

It may also be of interest that 22 per cent of the "casualties" resulted from resignations, declination and cancellation of appointments, and so forth. In other words, 61 per cent were killed in action or died of wounds; 13 per cent died of disease or other ostensibly natural causes (some at least of these superinduced by the effects of campaigning); and 4 per cent by virtue of non-service-connected causes.

There is a common misconception that the War was fought largely by armed mobs and officered by lawyers, politicians, and tradesmen wholly ignorant of even the elements of drill. The facts do not bear out any such theory; the great preponderance of officers in the higher echelons were professionals. In detail—of the 425 individuals who attained the grade of brigadier or higher, no less than 146 were graduates of the United States Military Academy, while at least ten others completed one or more years as a cadet there. In addition, nineteen of the generals had been officers of the ante-bellum U. S. Army, though they did not attend West Point. Mexican War veterans accounted for fifty-one others; five, if not more, had commanded troops against the Creeks and Seminoles. The Virginia Military Institute gave seventeen former students; the South Carolina Military Academy, four; and other military schools, not less than two. The ascertainable number of former state militia officers who secured general's rank is ten; there were doubtless others. Two generals had fought in the Texas War for Independence, while three had been officers of the United States Navy. Two veterans of the British Army and one graduate of L'Ecole Militaire in Paris afford a demonstrable total of

272 with previous military training, slightly less than two-thirds of the Confederate higher command. Were it possible to know more intimately the ante-bellum careers of the less prominent officers, this preponderance of professional over nonprofessional would perhaps be measurably increased. In the highest grades, officers with nonmilitary backgrounds were few indeed. All eight of the generals of full rank were West Point graduates; as were fourteen of the seventeen lieutenant generals. Of the remaining three, Richard Taylor had served as secretary to his father, Zachary, in Mexico and had had side experience in the military field. Of the seventy-two major generals, only nine had uninterruptedly engaged in civilian pursuits prior to 1861.

In the following table the generals have been classified according to their principal ante-bellum occupations. The classification has tended to be somewhat arbitrary, since many of the individuals failed to fall readily into one or another of the vocations listed. For example, most of the "politicians" had been trained in the law; whereas, many of the "lawyers and jurists" owned plantations. By the same token, thirty-nine of the men included in groupings other than "professional soldier" were graduates of West Point and had served one or more years in the United States Army. Each individual has been labeled according to what seems to have been his own preferred calling, even though he may have had more than one occupation before the war. Thus, Harvey Hill and Stonewall Jackson have been classified as "educators," for instance, and Simon B. Buckner and Joseph R. Anderson as "businessmen," although all four were alumni of the Military Academy and had honorable records of varying length in the regular service. Whether Robert Toombs and Howell Cobb were more politicians than lawyers is a moot point. Actually, of course, they were both; but they have here been considered as politicians because of their services in Washington.

Lawyers, jurists	129
Professional soldiers	125
Businessmen (including bankers, manufacturers, and merchants)	55
Farmers, planters	42
Politicians	24
Educators	15

Civil Engineers	13
Students	6*
Doctors	4
Ministers	3
Frontiersmen, peace officers	3
Indian agents	2
Naval officers	2
Editor	1
Soldier of fortune	1 (18)
Total	425

* In school or college at the time of their enlistment in the Confederate Army. Does not include West Point cadets who resigned at the outbreak of war; these men are classified as "Professional soldiers."

It is interesting to see that the exclusively landowner class, who might be presumed to have had the most substantial interest in the perpetuation of slavery, represents but 10 per cent of the total; whereas, military and professional men constitute the overwhelming majority.

A favorite premise of Civil War authors, particularly in years gone by, is that the United States Army prior to the outbreak of hostilities was largely officered by Southerners possessing not only open affection for their "peculiar institution" but every sort of secession proclivity as well. This is variously attributed to favoritism on the part of Winfield Scott—Commander in Chief of the Army in 1861, and a Virginian by birth; to calculated villainy fostered by Secretary of War John B. Floyd (another Virginian), and his predecessor in office, Jefferson Davis; and to a certain apathy on the part of Northern youth, who manifested no interest in military life. An analysis of the *Army Register of 1860* will hardly bear out any such inference. The two factors of slow promotion and the enormous relative increase in population of the free states after 1840 must be reckoned with.

According to the Census of 1860 the population of the free states was approximately nineteen million and that of the slave states twelve million (including three and a half million slaves); or percentages of the whole of 61 and 39, respectively. As noted above, much of the disproportion in population between the two sections had occurred since 1840. During this period officer personnel of the Regular Army had remained virtually fixed. To cite a few examples: the

Quartermaster General and the Commissary General had held their posts continuously since 1818; the Chief Engineer and Chief Topographical Engineer, since 1838; and two of the four generals of the line, since 1841. Eleven of the nineteen colonels of the line were veterans of the War of 1812; Colonel Whistler of the 4th Infantry was, in fact, too old to have attended West Point, having been commissioned a 2nd lieutenant the year before the academy opened its doors in 1802.

With promotion obstructed in this way, it would appear that the officers of the army were as representative of the nation as a whole as was practicable under the circumstances, even after making deductions for the four millions of blacks in the slave areas. To be specific: there were somewhat over 1,000 officers on the roster as of June 30, 1860, including both line and staff. Excluding the Medical Department and Military Storekeepers, a figure of 950 is arrived at. Of these, 555 were appointed from free states and 395 from slave states, the latter including nonseceding Missouri, Kentucky, Maryland, Delaware, and the Federal District. Accordingly, the percentages were 58.4 as against 41.6, hardly an overwhelming preponderance in favor of the South.

Further examination reveals some interesting statistics. The mounted arm of the service alone had a majority of Southern officers, there being 104 against 72 Northerners. On the other hand, there were 142 artillerists from the North to 67 from below Mason and Dixon's line; and similarly with infantrymen and staff officers—the North outnumbered the South by 200 to 139, and 141 to 85, respectively. (Staff officers included both engineer and ordnance departments.) The field grade officers of the line appointed from Dixie numbered but 30 from a total of 76.

Another interesting fact is that of 239 officers of the Regular Army who resigned in 1861 to cast their lot with the Confederacy, 26 (or approximately 11 per cent) were appointed originally from Northern states. In several of these cases no plausible reason for the decision can be ascertained. One officer, Frank C. Armstrong of the 2nd Dragoons, participated in the battle of First Manassas on the Union side, but later resigned and distinguished himself as a brigadier in Forrest's cavalry corps. What is perhaps more important is the fact that more Southern-born officers of the old army adhered to the Union than resigned. Outstanding examples are Brevet Lieutenant General Scott and Major Generals George H. Thomas and John Gibbon. General Gibbon, in fact, was reared in North Carolina and had two brothers in the Confederate Army. (19)

As in the United States since the earliest days of the Republic, the founders of the Confederacy envisaged two separate military forces: one a "peacetime" regular organization of professionals to be known as the Confederate States Army (C. S. A.), the other a volunteer force to be designated Provisional Army, Confederate States (P. A. C. S.). The regular service never progressed beyond the blueprint stage; and only six members of its officer corps as appointed by the President were ultimately confirmed by the Senate. These were the generals of full rank: Samuel Cooper, Albert Sidney Johnston, Robert Edward Lee, Joseph Eggleston Johnston, Pierre Gustave Toutant Beauregard, and Braxton Bragg. Edmund Kirby Smith was a full general in the Provisional Army, as was John Bell Hood, the latter being appointed with temporary rank only, and not being confirmed as such. (20) As a consequence, with the exceptions noted, all of the generals sketched in this book derived their rank from the Provisional Army, and were "Lieutenant-General Early, P. A. C. S.," "Major-General Cleburne, P. A. C. S.," and so on. In the pages which follow certain prior appointments to lower grades in the Regular Army are mentioned for the sake of information; however, it should be understood that such appointments were of a theoretical nature, inasmuch as they were not confirmed. (21) Nor were any "regular" regiments recruited or mustered into service during the war.

First and last it was a young man's war, though extant photographs are in many cases misleading. As a result of the hirsute facial adornments just then coming into vogue, no generation since the cave dwellers has given such an erroneous impression of its age. In point of fact, probably no war in history has advanced so many young men to high rank. Examining the well-nigh invisible features of John B. Hood, of Fitzhugh Lee, and of Stephen D. Lee, it is difficult to realize that the first was appointed a full general at the age of thirty-three, the second, major general at the age of twenty-seven, and the third, lieutenant general at the age of thirty.

When the first shell exploded over Fort Sumter on the misty morning of April 12, 1861, there were 425 men living north and south who would become general officers of the

Confederacy in the ensuing four years. Eight of these would attain the grade of full general in either the Regular or Provisional Army. All of these eight were (or had been) professional soldiers in the military establishment of the United States; their average age that day was forty-eight years, seven months. The eldest was Samuel Cooper, sixty-two, lately Adjutant General, U. S. A., whose future duties were not to include field command; the youngest, John Bell Hood, a tall raw-boned 1st lieutenant of the 2nd U. S. Cavalry, age twenty-nine.

Of the seventeen who would become lieutenant generals, Leonidas Polk, Missionary Bishop of the Southwest, and a graduate of West Point in the class of 1827, was fifty-four; Stephen D. Lee, lately resigned as a 1st lieutenant of the 4th Artillery (and who was at Sumter that day) lacked five months of attaining his twenty-eighth birthday; their average age was just over forty-one.

Seventy-two were to become major generals, ranging from the venerable David E. Twiggs, age seventy-one, lately dismissed from the United States Army as a brigadier of the line, to Robert E. Lee's second son, William Henry Fitzhugh, age twenty-three, for two years a 2nd lieutenant of the 6th Infantry, but since 1859 a Virginia farmer. Again youth predominated; the average was slightly over thirty-seven.

In the course of the war, 328 men would be appointed to the grade of brigadier by Jefferson Davis. The eldest of these and the only one over sixty in 1861 was John Henry Winder, born in 1800, a major of artillery in the old army, who would become notorious as provost marshal of Richmond and commissary general of Federal prisoners. At the other age extreme was William Paul Roberts of North Carolina, who was born on July 11, 1841, and who was in peaceful pursuit of his studies in his native state when war broke out. Seventy of the remaining future brigadiers were between twenty and twenty-nine; 138 were between thirty and thirty-nine; 94 were over forty but less than fifty; and the other 24 were aged fifty to fifty-nine. The average for the entire group was thirty-six years, three months.

Comparative youthfulness was in no sense the sole property of the Confederate higher command. Owing to the maintenance of the old army on a microscopic scale, the trained officer corps available to command the hundreds of thousands of recruits mustered in, north and south, was hugely deficient. Undoubtedly the youngest general officer on either side during the Civil War was Brevet Major General Galusha Pennypacker, U. S. A., who was born on June 1, 1844, and who was not old enough to vote until the war was over. (22)

A word about uniforms: Only one directive was issued on the subject from the Confederate Adjutant and Inspector General's Office, that of June 6, 1861, and known as General Orders, No. 9. (23) At the time the order was drawn up the grade of brigadier general was the highest rank provided for in the Confederate service, and although the grades of major general, lieutenant general, and general were subsequently established, no distinctive uniform for those grades was ever promulgated in orders. Thus the insignia of rank was the same for all four grades of general throughout the war, and was to consist of "a wreath, with three stars enclosed, embroidered in gold" on either side of the front of a stand-up collar. The sleeves were to be embellished with Hungarian loops of four gold braids' width, extending from cuff to elbow, and the gray tunic was to bear "two rows of (bright gilt) buttons on the breast, eight in each row, placed in pairs; the distance between the rows four inches at top and three inches at bottom." Facings and sash were to be of buff, and "trowsers" of "dark blue cloth" with "two stripes of gold lace on the outer seam." Caps (similar to the French *kepi*) were to have "dark blue band, sides and crown" ornamented by "four gold braids."

The foregoing "regulations" were more honored in the breach than in the observance, owing not only to material shortages, but also to the individual predilections of the generals themselves. Virtually the only universal distinguishing mark of rank came to be the "wreath, with three stars enclosed." Many generals wore tunics with collars turned down and stars and wreath embroidered on the lapels; others adopted the Federal button arrangement for major generals, with nine buttons on a side arranged in groups of three. Soft felt hats became the rule rather than the exception. "Confederate gray" (when obtainable) was used in both trousers and coat, and not a few of the "civilian" generals abandoned any pretense of a uniform whatsoever, appearing in everything from linen dusters to beaver hats.

In order to identify rank on the accompanying photographs, many of which were made before the men depicted attained general's rank, the reader should note that the collar insignia prescribed for second lieutenants was one horizontal bar embroidered in gold; for first lieutenants, two bars; for captains, three bars, for majors, one star; for lieutenant colonels, two stars; and for colonels, three stars. It is to be regretted that war-time photographs of all the officers are not available. (24)

In the pages that follow, the author has tried to record at least the main facts about the lives of the Confederate commanders. This work seemed especially worthwhile in the case of those officers whose careers are less celebrated and whose very names, in many instances, have passed almost into oblivion. Here then is the full complement of the GENERALS IN GRAY!

Daniel Weisiger Adams was born in Frankfort, Kentucky, probably in May or June of 1821. After reading law, he was admitted to the Mississippi bar and subsequently practiced in Louisiana. Meantime he had killed in a duel an editor who had criticized in the columns of his paper Adams' father, a Federal judge. In 1861 he was appointed by Governor Moore of Louisiana one of three members of a board to place the state on a war footing. His first army service was as lieutenant colonel of the 1st Louisiana Regulars, of which he was later promoted colonel. Present at Pensacola, his regiment greatly distinguished itself at the battle of Shiloh, where Adams lost his right eye. He was promoted brigadier general on May 23, 1862, and commanded the Louisiana Brigade at Perryville, Murfreesboro (where he was again wounded), and at Chickamauga, where he was a third time wounded and captured. After his recovery and exchange, he was given command of a cavalry brigade in North Alabama. For a time in command of the District of Central Alabama, he was in the last months of the war in charge of the entire state north of the Department of the Gulf, and opposed the Federal General Wilson during the latter's advance, which virtually terminated the war east of the Mississippi. General Adams was paroled at Meridian, Mississippi, on May 9, 1865, and went to England for a time. Upon his return to the United States he resumed the practice of law in New Orleans, where he died on June 13, 1872. He is buried near his brother, General William Wirt Adams, in Jackson, Mississippi, in an unmarked grave. (25)

1

John Adams, the son of Irish parents who emigrated to the United States in 1814, was born on July 1, 1825, in Nashville, Tennessee. Entering West Point in 1841, he was graduated five years later and was commissioned in the 1st Dragoons, with which he served during the Mexican War, receiving a brevet for gallantry at the battle of Santa Cruz de Rosales. Thereafter, and until the outbreak of the Civil War, he did frontier duty in Minnesota, California, and the Southwest; and from 1856 to 1858 was on recruiting service. He resigned his captain's commission on May 31, 1861, and was at once appointed a captain of cavalry in the Regular Confederate Army and placed in command at Memphis. Attaining the grade of colonel in May 1862, he was com-

missioned brigadier general to rank from December 29 of that year and given General Lloyd Tilghman's old brigade of Mississippi regiments. He led this brigade under General Joseph E. Johnston during the Vicksburg campaign, and under Lieutenant General Leonidas Polk in Mississippi. With the latter he joined the Army of Tennessee at Resaca, Georgia, and fought with distinction throughout the Atlanta campaign. Afterwards he accompanied General Hood to Tennessee. On November 30, 1864, in the holocaust at Franklin, Adams was severely wounded in the right arm. Refusing to leave the field, he led his men to the Union breastworks over which he attempted to jump his horse. Here he fell riddled with bullets, in the forefront of the Confederate assault. He is buried at Pulaski, Tennessee.

William Wirt Adams was born in Frankfort, Kentucky, on March 22, 1819, a brother of General Daniel Weisiger Adams. Educated at Bardstown, Kentucky, (26) he saw service in the army of the Republic of Texas in 1839, and then engaged in planting and banking in Mississippi, where he was a member of the legislature in 1858 and 1860. Upon the formation of the Confederate government Adams declined the postmaster-generalship tendered him by President Davis.

Instead, he raised the 1st Mississippi Cavalry regiment of which he was made colonel. During the early part of the war his command operated more or less independently in Mississippi and Tennessee. For services in the Vicksburg campaign Adams was promoted brigadier general to rank from September 25, 1863. Toward the end of 1864 his brigade was attached to Forrest's corps, with which it served until the end. After the war General Adams resided at Vicksburg and subsequently at Jackson. He was state revenue agent in 1880 and postmaster of Jackson in 1885. On May 1, 1888 he was killed in a street encounter with J o h n Martin, a Jackson newspaper editor with whom he had quarreled. General Adams is buried in Jackson.

Edward Porter Alexander, one of three officers who attained the rank of brigadier general of artillery in the Confederate service, (27) was born in Washington, Georgia, on May 26, 1835. He was graduated from West Point in the class of 1857. Resigning from the old army on May 1, 1861, he was at once appointed a Confederate captain of engineers. After serving as signal officer to General Beauregard at First Manassas, he became chief of ordnance of the Army of Northern Virginia, with rank of lieutenant colonel; then chief of artillery of Longstreet's corps; and was appointed brigadier general to rank from February 26, 1864. He participated in all the earlier battles of the army. His seventy-five guns raked the Federal line on Cemetery Ridge in

3

preparation for Pickett's famous assault at Gettysburg. He accompanied Longstreet to Chickamauga and Knoxville, and was in the thick of the fighting at Spotsylvania, Cold Harbor, and Petersburg. Severely wounded at Petersburg, he rejoined his command in time to make the last march to Appomattox. After the war General Alexander had an equally distinguished career as professor of engineering, railroad president, rice planter, and author (see Bibliography #43). Meantime he occupied various governmental posts of honor and responsibility. He died in Savannah, Georgia, April 28, 1910, and is buried in the City Cemetery at Augusta, Georgia.

Henry Watkins Allen was born in Prince Edward County, Virginia, April 29, 1820. He was successively a resident of Missouri, where he received his education at Marion College; Mississippi, where he taught school and became a lawyer and planter; and Louisiana, where he was a member of the legislature for two terms. Meantime he studied law at Harvard, travelled in Europe, and saw service in the Texas War for Independence. He enlisted as a private in the Confederate Army and was immediately elected lieutenant colonel of the 4th Louisiana Infantry, and shortly colonel. He was first wounded at Shiloh in April 1862; and his leg was so shattered at

Baton Rouge in August of that year as to compel him to walk on crutches for the remainder of his life. He was appointed brigadier general on August 19, 1863. General Allen's most distinguished service was as governor of Louisiana during the last year of the war. Faced with enormous difficulties, his accomplishments in shoring up the economy of the Trans-Mississippi Department were unequalled. He was certainly one of the finest administrators produced by the Confederacy. After helping to negotiate the surrender of the forces under Kirby Smith, he went to Mexico City, where he established an English-language newspaper. His death occurred there on April 22, 1866. (28) He is buried in Baton Rouge, on the grounds of the old state capitol.

4

William Wirt Allen was born in New York City on September 11, 1835. He was raised in Montgomery, Alabama, and was graduated from Princeton in the class of 1854. Although he had read law, he took up the life of a planter and was thus engaged at the outbreak of war. Allen was mustered into the Confederate Army as 1st lieutenant in the Montgomery Mounted Rifles; he was soon elected major of the 1st Alabama Cavalry. After fighting at Shiloh, he was promoted colonel of his regiment and commanded it during the Kentucky invasion, being wounded at Perryville and again at Murfreesboro. He was appointed brigadier general to rank from February 26, 1864, and was given command of a brigade in Wheeler's cavalry corps, which he led during the Atlanta campaign;

later he was placed in charge of a division. On March 4, 1865 he was appointed major general with temporary rank, the last such promotion made by the President; however, the Senate failed to act upon the nomination, and he was paroled as a brigadier at Charlotte, North Carolina. (29) After the war General Allen returned to his plantation, and also engaged in the railroad business. For several years he was adjutant general of Alabama; he also served as a United States marshal during Grover Cleveland's first administration. He died at Sheffield, Ala., November 24, 1894, and is buried in Birmingham.

George Burgwyn Anderson was born near Hillsboro, North Carolina, (30) on April 12, 1831. After attending the University of North Carolina, he entered the U. S. Military Academy from which he was graduated in 1852 as a brevet 2nd lieutenant, 2nd Dragoons. Anderson's old army service was entirely on the frontier in the mounted arm. He had advanced to the rank of 1st lieutenant when he resigned his commission, April 25, 1861, to cast his lot with the Confederacy. Immediately commissioned colonel of the 4th North Carolina, he took his regiment to Manassas Junction shortly after the first battle at that place. Here he remained as post commandant until March 1862. Anderson was a furious fighter. His personal bravery at Williamsburg impelled President Davis to appoint him brigadier general to rank from June 9. His brigade was conspicuous during the Seven Days, and Anderson sustained a wound while leading a charge at Malvern Hill. Anderson was under the command of D. H. Hill at South Mountain, and went into his last fight three days later at Sharpsburg on September 17, where, holding a part of the line almost unsupported, he received a ball in his foot. First transported to Shepherdstown and then to Staunton, Virginia, he was subsequently taken to Raleigh, where his foot was amputated. He failed to rally from the operation, and died on October 16, 1862. He is buried in Raleigh, North Carolina.

George Thomas "Tige" Anderson was born in Covington, Georgia, on February 3, 1824. (31) While a student at Emory College, Oxford, Georgia, he left to enter the Mexican War as a lieutenant of Georgia Cavalry in the command of General Stephen W. Kearny; and in 1855 was commissioned into the regular service, from which he resigned in 1858 as a captain of the 1st Cavalry. (32) Elected colonel of the 11th Georgia Infantry in 1861, Anderson acted as brigade commander during the battles of the Seven Days, at Second Manassas, and at Sharpsburg. He was appointed brigadier general November 1, 1862. Anderson was at Fredericksburg, and followed the fortunes of Longstreet's corps in the Suffolk expedition, at Gettysburg (where he was severely wounded), Chickamauga, Knoxville, and through the Virginia campaign of 1864. His brigade was attached to General Charles W. Field's division at Appomattox, and he was there paroled. After the war General Anderson served for a time as freight agent for the Georgia Railroad at Atlanta and was later chief of police of that city. The last years of his life were spent as chief of police and county tax collector at Anniston, Alabama, where he died on April 4, 1901. He is buried in Edgemont Cemetery there.

James Patton Anderson, a native of Tennessee, was born in Franklin County on February 16, 1822. (33) Anderson's antebellum career was one of varied pursuits. He first studied and practiced medicine in Hernando County, Mississippi, from which locality he raised and commanded the 1st Battalion Mississippi Rifles in the Mexican War with rank of lieutenant colonel. After a term in the Mississippi legislature, he was appointed by President Pierce United States marshal for Washington Territory, which he was presently elected to represent as Delegate to Congress. The outbreak of the war found him in Florida, a member of the state secession convention. Appointed colonel of the 1st Florida Infantry, his initial service was with General Bragg at Pensacola. Promoted brigadier general on February 10, 1862, he fought gallantly at Shiloh and commanded a division at Perryville. His brigade especially distinguished itself at Murfreesboro. Again in division command at Chickamauga and Chattanooga, he was promoted major general to rank from February 17, 1864. In command of the District of Florida during the first part of the Atlanta campaign, he was recalled to the Army of Tennessee in time to participate in the battles of Ezra Church and Jonesboro, where he was severely wounded. He rejoined the army in North Carolina and surrendered with it at Greensboro. After the war General Anderson conducted a farm paper in Memphis and was collector of state taxes for Shelby County. He died at Memphis on

September 20, 1872, and is buried there.

Joseph Reid Anderson, "the Krupp of the Confederacy," was born at "Walnut Hill," Botetourt County, Virginia, February 16, 1813, and was graduated from West Point in the class of 1836. Resigning from the army the following year, he turned his talents to engineering, becoming in 1841 superintendent of the Tredegar Iron Works in Richmond, of which he subsequently gained control. Soon after the outbreak of war Anderson entered field service and was commissioned brigadier general, September 3, 1861. First in command at Wilmington, he was called to Virginia in the spring of 1862, and commanded a brigade on the Peninsula and in the battles of the Seven Days, where he was wounded. His services at the Tredegar Works being deemed of inestimably more value than in the field, he resigned his commission on July 19, 1862, and devoted his time thereafter to implementing the Confederate war effort. His company became the mainstay of the Ordnance Department, ceasing operations only upon the evacuation of Richmond. The works, first confiscated by the Federal government, were returned to their owners in 1867 and reorganized with Anderson as president. He operated them until his death on the Isles of Shoals, New Hampshire, September 7, 1892. He also served as president of the Richmond chamber of commerce and as a member of the common council in the postbellum years. General Anderson is buried in Hollywood Cemetery, Richmond.

Richard Heron Anderson was born October 7, 1821 at "Hill Crest," Sumter County, South Carolina. He was graduated in 1842 at West Point, in a class which furnished no less than twenty-two general officers to the Union and Confederate armies from thirty-seven graduates living in 1861. He won the brevet of 1st lieutenant in the Mexican War, and was captain of the 2nd Dragoons when he resigned his commission on March 3, 1861. Commissioned major of infantry

charge of a segment of the Richmond defenses. His troops were shattered and largely dispersed at the battle of Sayler's Creek on April 6, 1865, although he himself escaped and rejoined the main army. As supernumerary—a commander without a command appropriate to his rank—he was relieved and authorized to return home the day before the surrender at Appomattox. (34) His post-bellum career was an unsuccessful struggle against poverty; at the time of his death at Beaufort, South Carolina, June 26, 1879, he was state phosphate agent. He is buried in Beaufort.

in the Regular Confederate service to rank from March 16, he was present at the reduction of Sumter. On July 18 he was promoted brigadier general and succeeded to the command of Charleston when General Beauregard went to Virginia. Early in 1862 he was assigned a brigade in Longstreet's division on the Peninsula and was thereafter connected with the Army of Northern Virginia. Appointed major general July 14, 1862, he commanded his division, first in the 1st Corps, and after Chancellorsville in the 3rd, until Longstreet was wounded and disabled at the battle of the Wilderness. He was then promoted lieutenant general with temporary rank from May 31, 1864, to direct the corps of his old chief. Upon Longstreet's return to the army General Anderson was placed in

Robert H o u s t o u n Anderson (35) was born in Savannah, Georgia, on October 1, 1835. After receiving his early education in the common schools of his native city, he entered West Point and was brevetted a 2nd lieutenant of infantry on July 1,

1857. After service mainly in garrison at Fort Walla Walla, Washington, he resigned from the old army to offer his services to the Confederacy. First appointed a lieutenant of artillery, he was in September 1861 promoted major and assistant adjutant general to General W. H. T. Walker, then in command on the Georgia coast. Transferring to the line, he was made colonel of the 5th Georgia Cavalry in January 1863, which was soon ordered to the Army of Tennessee, where it became a part of W. W. Allen's brigade. After General Allen was given divisional command, Anderson succeeded to the brigade, and on July 26, 1864, was appointed brigadier general. As a part of Wheeler's cavalry corps Anderson's brigade participated in all of the engagements of that command until the surrender in North Carolina. After the close of hostilities General Anderson returned to Savannah and was appointed chief of police in 1867, a position which he occupied until his death, February 8, 1888. In the years 1879 and 1887 he was a member of the Board of Visitors to the United States Military Academy. He is buried in Bonaventure Cemetery, Savannah.

Samuel Read Anderson was born in Bedford County, Virginia, on February 17, 1804. Emigrating at an early age to Kentucky, he later removed to

Tennessee, first residing in Giles and Sumner counties, and later settling permanently in Davidson County. During the war with Mexico he was second in command, as lieutenant colonel, of the 1st Tennessee Infantry. Before the Civil War he was for some time cashier of the old Bank of Tennessee and for eight years postmaster of Nashville. Appointed by Governor Harris as a major general of Tennessee state troops in 1861, he was on July 9 of the same year commissioned brigadier general in the Provisional Army of the Confederate States, and participated in the Western Virginia campaign under General Robert E. Lee and in the Peninsular campaign. Resigning in the spring of 1862 because of ill health, General Anderson was reappointed to the rank of brigadier by President Davis to rank from November 7,

1864. From that time until it was abolished, he was in charge of the bureau of conscription for the state of Tennessee, with headquarters at Selma, Alabama. After the war the general engaged in the mercantile business in Nashville, where he died, January 2, 1883, and where he is buried in the Old City Cemetery. (36)

James Jay Archer, (37) a native of Bel Air, Maryland, was born December 19, 1817. After graduation from Princeton in 1835, he studied law at the University of Maryland and was admitted to the bar. As a captain of infantry and then of voltigeurs in the regular army he received the brevet of major for gallantry at Chapultepec during the war with Mexico, and was honorably mustered out, August 31, 1848. (38) He

followed the legal profession until 1855, when he again entered the regular army as captain of the 9th Infantry. Resigning his commission in 1861, he was mustered into Confederate service as colonel of the 5th Texas, being promoted brigadier general June 3, 1862, to succeed Robert Hatton in command of the Tennessee brigade. As a regimental and brigade commander he took part with great distinction in every battle of the Army of Northern Virginia from the Seven Days until Gettysburg. On July 1, 1863 Archer and a large part of his command, a brigade in Heth's division, were captured. A prisoner for more than a year, he was exchanged in the summer of 1864, his health shattered by his long confinement on Johnson's Island. Posted for duty with the Army of Tennessee on August 9, (39) and ten days later with the Army of Northern Virginia, (40) he commanded for a short time his old brigade and that of General H. H. Walker. He died in Richmond on October 24, 1864, and is buried in Hollywood Cemetery there.

Lewis Addison Armistead was born at New Bern, North Carolina, February 18, 1817. He was a cadet at West Point from 1834 to 1836 and, as the story runs, was dismissed for breaking a mess-hall plate over the head of Jubal Anderson Early. (41) Ap-

handful of men, he scaled the stone wall and drove the Union gunners from their pieces. He fell mortally wounded with his hand on a captured cannon, and as the Confederate tide receded, was taken by the enemy. He died in a Federal field hospital, July 5, 1863. (42) His body was recovered by friends, who took it to Baltimore for burial in St. Paul's Churchyard.

Frank Crawford Armstrong was born on November 22, 1835 at Choctaw Agency, Indian Territory (now the virtually abandoned village of Scullyville, Oklahoma), (43) where his father, an officer of the army, was stationed at the time. The latter died when Armstrong was a boy. His mother took as her second husband General Persifor Frazer Smith, U.S.A., one of the heroes

pointed to the regular army in 1839, he was twice brevetted for gallantry in Mexico, and resigned on May 26, 1861, as captain (and brevet major) of the 6th Infantry. In the Confederate service Armistead was commissioned colonel of the 57th Virginia Infantry, which he commanded for a few months in Western Virginia and North Carolina. He was promoted brigadier general on April 1, 1862. At this time he was given command of a brigade in Pickett's division, which he led with conspicuous bravery from the Peninsular campaign until Gettysburg. On the third day of the latter battle in the final assault on the Union center, Armistead's brigade formed the second rank of the division, supporting Garnett and Kemper. In company with a

of the Mexican War, whom young Armstrong accompanied on a military expedition into New Mexico in 1854. After graduation from Holy Cross Academy in Massachusetts, he was commissioned directly into the regular army the following year. He took part in the battle of First Manassas on the Union side, but resigned on August 13, 1861. (44) His first Confederate service was on the staffs of Generals McIntosh and Ben McCulloch; and he was a few feet away when the latter met his death at Pea Ridge (Elkhorn). Subsequently elected colonel of the 3rd Louisiana Infantry, he was soon after given command of the cavalry in the forces under General Sterling Price. During the balance of the war Armstrong operated under the command of such leaders as Forrest, Wheeler, Stephen D. Lee, and Chalmers. His last battle was that of Selma, Alabama, when the remnant of Forrest's corps surrendered. He had meantime been promoted brigadier general to rank from January 20, 1863. At the close of hostilities he entered the Overland Mail Service in Texas, was United States Indian Inspector from 1885 to 1889, and Assistant Commissioner of Indian Affairs from 1893 to 1895. General Armstrong died at Bar Harbor, Maine, September 8, 1909, and is buried in Rock Creek Cemetery, Georgetown, D. C. (45)

Turner Ashby, a native of Virginia, was born at "Rose Bank," Fauquier County, October 23, 1828, and was educated by his mother, by private tutors, and at Major Ambler's school. Before the war he engaged in business and in the operation of a farm near his birthplace. At the time of John Brown's raid, Ashby, a singularly gifted horseman and natural leader, gathered some mounted men and rode to Charles Town (now in West Virginia), only to find that Brown was already in jail. Upon the secession of Virginia he engaged in helping picket the Potomac, his command later being incorporated into the 7th Virginia Cavalry. He rose from captain to colonel of the regiment in the space of a few months, and was engaged mainly in scouting and outpost duty until the spring of

1862. In command of all of Stonewall Jackson's cavalry, he participated brilliantly in the famous Shenandoah Valley campaign of that year, and was promoted brigadier general on May 23, 1862. After the pursuit of the Federal General Banks to Harpers Ferry and during Jackson's subsequent withdrawal up the Valley, General Ashby was killed on June 6, 1862, while fighting a rear guard action a few miles south of Harrisonburg. A monument marks the spot where he fell. He is buried in Stonewall Cemetery, Winchester, Virginia. (46)

Alpheus Baker was born in Abbeville District, South Carolina, May 28, 1828. (47) He was educated by his scholarly father, and began to teach school himself before he was sixteen. He settled in Eufaula, Alabama, in 1848,

and was admitted to the Alabama bar the year following. A member of the state constitutional convention in 1861, he resigned his seat to enlist as a private in the Eufaula Rifles, a company which subsequently became a part of the 1st Alabama Infantry, and of which Baker was elected captain. After rising to colonel of the 54th Alabama Infantry, he was captured at Island No. 10, but was later exchanged. He served in the Vicksburg campaign under General William W. Loring, and was severely wounded at the battle of Baker's Creek. Promoted brigadier general on March 5, 1864, he participated in the Atlanta campaign, and was again wounded in the attack of S. D. Lee's corps at Ezra Church. After service in the Department of the Gulf, his brigade took part in the closing campaign in the Carolinas, and at Bentonville captured 204 of the enemy. General Baker returned to his law practice after the surrender. In 1878 he moved to Louisville, Kentucky, where he died October 2, 1891, and where he is buried.

Laurence Simmons Baker, whose first name became "Lawrence" through a War Department error, was born in Gates County, North Carolina, May 15, 1830, and was graduated from West Point in 1851. His old army service was principally on the

14

frontier, as a lieutenant in the regiment of Mounted Riflemen. Resigning in May 1861, Baker was immediately appointed lieutenant colonel of the 1st North Carolina Cavalry, a regiment of which he was elected colonel in the spring of 1862. Attached to General Wade Hampton's brigade he and his command participated in all the engagements of the Army of Northern Virginia from the Peninsular campaign until Gettysburg, a few weeks after which he received his commission as brigadier, July 23 1863. Several times wounded, General Baker was assigned departmental command in North Carolina in 1864, and although suffering intensely from injuries, took part in the battle of Bentonville. His command was detached from the main army under General J. E. Johnson at the time of the surrender. He was paroled at Raleigh in May 1865. He first engaged in farming after the war, and later became railroad station agent at Suffolk, Virginia, where he continued until his death, April 10, 1907. He is buried in Cedar Hill Cemetery, Suffolk.

William Edwin Baldwin was born at Statesburg, South Carolina, on July 28, 1827. Removing to Mississippi at an early age, he eventually became engaged in the book and stationery business in Columbus. At the same time he commenced an interest in military affairs by joining a militia company known as the "Columbus Riflemen," of which he served as lieutenant for twelve years. (48) Elected captain of his company in 1861, he took it to Pensacola, and was shortly

elected colonel of the 14th Mississippi Infantry. Soon sent north, Baldwin's regiment was included in the surrender at Fort Donelson, and Baldwin was imprisoned at Fort Warren until August 1862, immediately after which he was commissioned brigadier general to rank from September 19, 1862. His brigade participated in the Vicksburg campaign, during which he was again captured; he was paroled upon the capitulation of the fortress. After his second exchange he served for a short time with the Army of Tennessee, and was then assigned to the District of Mobile with his command. On February 19, 1864, near Dog River Factory, Alabama, a broken stirrup resulted in a fatal fall from his horse. First buried in Mobile, his remains were later taken to Columbus, where they now rest in Friendship Cemetery.

William Barksdale was born in Smyrna, Rutherford County, Tennessee, August 21, 1821. He attended the University of Nashville and then studied law in Columbus, Mississippi, after which he edited the Columbus *Democrat*. He served in the Mexican War as enlisted man and officer; and was in 1852 elected to Congress from Mississippi, where he vehemently upheld the cause of states rights until his resignation upon the secession of his state. Barksdale was at first appointed

quartermaster general of Mississippi; then entered Confederate service as colonel of the 13th Mississippi, which he commanded at First Manassas. First as a regimental commander and subsequently as brigadier, ranking from August 12, 1862, Barksdale distinguished himself on all the early fields of the Army of Northern Virginia, with the exception of Second Manassas, where his brigade was not present. At Fredericksburg "Barksdale's Mississippians" were posted in cellars and behind fences along the river bank. They frustrated for hours the efforts of Burnside's engineers to bridge the Rappahannock. On the second day of the battle of Gettysburg he was mortally wounded during the assault of Hood and McLaws on the Round Tops, and died within the Union lines on the following day, July 3, 1863. His remains were ultimately interred in Greenwood Cemetery, Jackson, Mississippi.

Rufus Barringer was born in Cabarrus County, North Carolina, on December 2, 1821. He was graduated at the University of North Carolina in 1842, studied law, and took up the practice of his profession in Concord, North Carolina. He served in the assembly in 1848 and 1850 and was a Presidential Elector in 1860. He entered Confederate service as a captain of the 1st North Carolina Cavalry at the outbreak of war, and still held this rank as late as the battle of Gettysburg, although he had served gallantly in all the engagements of the Army of Northern Virginia. Thereafter his rise was

rapid. A major in August 1863, by June 1, 1864 he had been appointed brigadier general, in command of a brigade of W. H. F. Lee's division, which he led until its virtual destruction while covering the withdrawal from Richmond in 1865. After the war General Barringer, an oldtime Whig, embraced the policies of Reconstruction, even to the extent of becoming a Republican, and took an active part in politics. The closing years of his life were spent on his estate near Charlotte, where he died, February 3, 1895. By his first marriage to one of the six daughters of the Reverend Doctor R. H. Morrison he was a brother-in-law of Generals D. H. Hill and Stonewall Jackson. He is buried in Charlotte.

John Decatur Barry was born in Wilmington, North Carolina, on June 21, 1839, and was educated at the University of North Carolina. At the outbreak of war he enlisted as a private in Company I of the 18th North Carolina State Troops, originally the 8th North Carolina Volunteers. Upon the reorganization of the regiment in April 1862, he was elected captain of his company. As a part of Branch's (later Lane's) brigade, the 18th fought through the Seven Days, Cedar Mountain, Second Manassas, Chantilly, Harper's Ferry, and Sharpsburg. After the last named battle Barry was pro-

moted major and, after Chancellorsville, colonel of the regiment, which the following month took a gallant part in Pickett's assault at Gettysburg. When General Lane was wounded at Cold Harbor, Barry was appointed brigadier general from August 3, 1864. However, he was himself wounded by a sharpshooter a few days later; and Lane having meanwhile returned to command, Barry's appointment was cancelled. Since he was disabled by his wound, he was assigned to departmental duty in North Carolina. After the war, his health broken, he edited a newspaper in Wilmington, where at the early age of 27, he died on March 24, 1867, and where he is buried in Oakdale Cemetery. (49)

Seth Maxwell Barton was born in Fredericksburg, Vir-

ginia, September 8, 1829. He entered the United States Military Academy at the age of fifteen and was graduated in the class of 1849. Save for a brief tour of duty at Governors Island, his regular army service was entirely in the West. Resigning in June 1861, he was appointed lieutenant colonel of the 3rd Arkansas Infantry, and acted as Stonewall Jackson's engineer officer in the Valley district during the winter of 1861-62. After a prior nomination to the grade of brigadier general had been withdrawn by the President, Barton was appointed to rank from March 11, 1862, and was duly confirmed. He participated in the Vicksburg campaign, where he was captured, paroled, and exchanged. He was soon after given command of Armistead's old brigade of Pickett's division, but was cen-

sured by Pickett for want of co-operation at New Bern. Again criticized and relieved of command by General Robert Ransom at Drewry's Bluff in May 1864, he was unemployed until autumn, when he was assigned a brigade in the Richmond defenses. He was taken prisoner at Sayler's Creek, April 6, 1865. After release from Fort Warren, General Barton made his home in Fredericksburg, and died in Washington, April 11, 1900. None of Barton's superiors questioned his bravery, and after his removal by Ransom, his regimental commanders made repeated application for his reinstatement. (50) He is buried in Fredericksburg. (51)

William Brimage Bate, a native of Bledsoe's Lick (now Castalian Springs), Tennessee, was born October 7, 1826. Possessed of little formal education, he began his career with a position as clerk on a steamboat and ended with a seat in the United States Senate. Before enlisting in the Confederate Army as a private, Bate served in the Mexican War, edited a newspaper, studied law. He was also a member of the Tennessee legislature, and a Breckinridge Elector in 1860. Elected colonel of the 2nd Tennessee Infantry, he led his regiment at Shiloh, where he was severely wounded and incapacitated for some months. He was appointed brigadier general on October 3, 1862. Bate took part in the Tullahoma campaign and fought at Chickamauga, where his brigade artillery is said to have fired the last shot of the battle. After distinguishing himself in the Chattanooga campaign, he was promoted major general to rank from February 23, 1864. He then participated in all the engagements of the Army of Tennessee on the long, bloody trail from Dalton, Georgia, in the spring of 1864, to the final surrender at Greensboro, North Carolina. Bate returned to his law practice in Nashville, and was elected governor of Tennessee in 1882, and United States Senator in 1886, which latter position he held until his death in Washington, March 9, 1905. While a member of the Senate (1893), he was the author of a bill which removed the last vestige of Reconstruction legislation from the statute books. Bate was outstanding as a fighter. He was wounded three times and had six horses killed under him in battle. He is buried in Mount Olivet Cemetery, Nashville.

Cullen Andrews Battle was born at Powelton, Hancock County, Georgia, June 1, 1829. The family moved to Eufaula (then Irwinton), Alabama, when he was seven. He was educated at the state university, studied law, and was admitted to the bar in 1852. An accomplished orator, Battle was a Breckinridge Elector in 1860. Soon after secession he became lieutenant colonel of the 3rd Alabama—with which he served in the Peninsular campaign—and was promoted colonel after Seven Pines. He fought at Sharpsburg and Fred-

ericksburg, and was severely injured by his horse falling with him a few days before Chancellorsville. At Gettysburg on the first day, his regiment fought in Ramseur's brigade, since the other regiments of O'Neal's brigade had been disorganized. He was appointed brigadier general to rank from August 20, 1863. His command lost heavily in the Wilderness and at Spotsylvania. Battle also accompanied Early to the Shenandoah in 1864, and was so badly wounded at Cedar Creek as to be incapacitated for further field service. After the war he resumed his law practice in Tuskegee, Alabama, and was elected to Congress in 1868, but was refused his seat. Removing to New Bern, North Carolina, in 1880, he edited the *New Bern Journal,* and served as mayor of the city for a time. His death occurred in Greensboro, North Carolina, April 8, 1905; he is buried in Petersburg, Virginia. There is no evidence that he was promoted major general, as stated by some sources. (52)

Richard Lee Turberville Beale was born at Hickory Hill, Westmoreland County, Virginia, on May 22, 1819. He was educated at Dickinson College and the University of Virginia, from the latter of which he was graduated in 1837. Admitted to the bar two years later, he commenced the practice of law near his birthplace, and was elected to

Congress in 1846, serving one term. He was a delegate to the state constitutional convention of 1851, and a member of the upper house of the legislature from 1858 to 1860. Beale entered the service of the Confederacy as a 1st lieutenant of a cavalry company known as "Lee's Legion" or "Lee's Light Horse," which later became a part of the 9th Virginia Cavalry. He was successively promoted captain, major, lieutenant colonel, and colonel of this regiment, meantime serving most creditably in all of the campaigns of the Cavalry Division (later Corps) of the Army of Northern Virginia, save for a three-month period in the autumn of 1863, when he was suffering from a wound. For reasons which are not made manifest he tendered his resignation on three separate occasions in 1862 and 1863. None of these was accepted. He took command of a brigade in W. H. F. Lee's division in the fall of 1864, and was commissioned brigadier general to rank from January 6, 1865. After the downfall of the Confederacy General Beale again took up the practice of his profession at Hague, Virginia, and was re-elected to Congress in 1878. He died on April 21, 1893, at Hague, and was buried at Hickory Hill.

William Nelson Rector Beall was born in Bardstown, Kentucky, March 20, 1825. He entered the United States Military Academy in 1844 and was graduated four years later. As with so many of the younger officers of his day, his regular army service was principally on the west-

ern frontier. Having attained the rank of captain in the 1st Cavalry, he resigned his commission, August 20, 1861, and was appointed a captain of cavalry in the Regular Confederate Army to take rank from March 16, 1861. Beall served in Arkansas under General Van Dorn, and was commissioned brigadier general on April 11, 1862. Thereafter he and his mixed brigade of Arkansas, Mississippi, Alabama, and Louisiana troops were stationed at Port Hudson, where they were surrendered on July 9, 1863. General Beall was first imprisoned on Johnson's Island. In 1864, by virtue of an agreement between the authorities at Washington and Richmond, he was released on parole to act as Confederate agent to supply prisoners of war. In this capacity he maintained an office in New York City, and sold cotton, which was permitted to come through the Federal blockade. The proceeds were mainly devoted to the purchase of clothing and blankets for the relief of Confederate soldiers in Northern prison camps. He was finally released on August 2, 1865. He became a general commission merchant at St. Louis, dying in McMinnville, Tennessee, July 25, 1883. He is buried in Mt. Olivet Cemetery, Nashville.

Pierre Gustave Toutant Beauregard was born in Saint Bernard Parish, Louisiana, May 28,

1818, and was graduated second in the class of 1838 at West Point. During the Mexican War he was engineer officer on Winfield Scott's staff, and received two brevets for gallantry. He was assigned in January 1861 as Superintendent of the Military Academy, but was relieved a few days later, probably because of his avowed Southern sympathies. (53) In February he resigned his commission and was appointed brigadier general, Provisional Army, C.S.A., on March 1, 1861. He was then placed in command at Charleston and supervised the reduction of Fort Sumter in April. Two months later at First Manassas he was second in command to Joseph E. Johnston. (For Beauregard's account of this battle, see Bibliography #231.) He was commissioned a full general in the Regular

22

Army, to rank from July 21, 1861, and in 1862 was sent to the West. He was second in command to General Albert Sidney Johnston at Shiloh, and assumed command of the Army of Tennessee when Johnston was killed. Falling back upon Corinth, Mississippi, he had to abandon that place to a larger force under General Halleck. While on sick leave he was superseded in command by Braxton Bragg; and his relations with Jefferson Davis rapidly deteriorated until they were hardly more cordial than those existing between the President and J. E. Johnston. Beauregard was placed in charge of the defense of the South Carolina and Georgia coast and performed ably, especially in defending Charleston in 1863 and 1864. In May 1864 he supported Lee in Virginia, and probably saved Richmond by discerning Grant's intentions against Petersburg before General Lee could be made aware of the situation. (54) He served under General J. E. Johnston in the Carolinas during the closing weeks, returning to New Orleans after the surrender. He was president of two railroads after the war, and with Jubal A. Early, supervised the drawings of the Louisiana Lottery; he was also for many years adjutant general of the state. General Beauregard died in New Orleans on February 20, 1893, and is buried there in Metairie Cemetery.

Barnard Elliott Bee, a native of Charleston, South Carolina, and a brother of General Hamilton P. Bee, was born February 8, 1824. (55) Although his father had expatriated himself by mov-

ing to the then Republic of Texas and becoming its secretary of state, young Bee was appointed to West Point "at large" and was graduated there in 1845. He was twice brevetted for gallantry in Mexico and was presented a sword by the state of South Carolina for his services. He resigned his commission as captain in the 10th Infantry on March 3, 1861. His first Confederate service was as lieutenant colonel of the 1st South Carolina Regulars, an artillery regiment. On June 17, 1861 he was appointed brigadier general and assigned to the command of a bri-

23

gade in the army mobilized at Manassas Junction. His troops sustained the impetus of the initial Federal assault in the memorable battle of July 21, 1861, during which Bee is said to have applied (with an entirely different implication according to at least one source), (56) General T. J. Jackson's sobriquet of "Stonewall." The necessity of holding raw levies to their work required desperate exertions and reckless exposure on the part of the officers. Bee fell mortally wounded just as the tide began to turn in favor of the Confederates, and died the following day (July 22, 1861) in the small cabin near the battlefield, which had been his headquarters. His name was confirmed at the grade of brigadier by the Provisional Congress more than a month later. General Bee is buried in Pendleton, South Carolina.

Hamilton Prioleau Bee, Barnard Elliott Bee's older brother, was also born in Charleston, July 22, 1822, and removed to Texas with his parents when a youth. He was secretary of the commission for establishing the boundary between the United States and the Republic of Texas in 1839, and secretary of the Texas senate in 1846. After service in the Mexican War as a 2nd lieutenant of Texas Rangers, he was a member of the Texas legislature, and speaker of the house for one term. Elected brigadier gen-

eral of militia in 1861, Bee was appointed brigadier general in the Confederate Army to rank from March 4, 1862. He was placed in command at Brownsville, Texas, where he expedited the importation of munitions from Europe through Mexico and the exportation of cotton as payment. He had acquired little military experience in his administrative post, and his handling of troops, when he took the field against Banks in the Red River campaign of 1864, was the subject of some criticism. (57) In February 1865 he was assigned to command a division of cavalry under General John A. Wharton, and was later given a brigade of infantry in General S. B. Maxey's division. (58) At the close of the war he went to Mexico for a time, returning to San Antonio in 1876, where he lived until his death, October 3, 1897, and where he is buried in Confederate Cemetery.

Tyree Harris Bell was born in Covington, Kentucky, September 5, 1815, but moved to Gallatin, Tennessee, in childhood, where he grew up on his father's small plantation. He was educated in the rural schools of the neighborhood, and subsequently became a planter on his own account in Sumner County. At the outbreak of the Civil War he raised one of the first companies of the 12th Tennessee and was elected its captain. He later became lieutenant colonel of the regiment, which he commanded at Belmont and at Shiloh. Promoted colonel in July 1862, Bell participated in the invasion of Kentucky and the battle of Richmond, after which he was given

a cavalry command under Forrest. In January 1864 Forrest placed him in charge of a brigade, which he led until the end of the war. Repeatedly praised in official reports, he was commissioned brigadier general on February 28, 1865. Some ten years after the war he removed with his whole family to California, settling in Fresno County. There he prospered as a farmer and was active in civic affairs. Four days before his eighty-seventh birthday General Bell died September 1, 1902, in New Orleans, while returning from a trip which had included attendance at a Confederate reunion and a visit to his old home in Gallatin. He is buried in Bethel Cemetery, near Sanger, California. (59)

Henry Lewis Benning, "Old Rock," was born in Columbia County, Georgia, April 2, 1814, and was graduated from the University of Georgia (then Franklin College) in 1834. Moving to Columbus, Georgia, he studied law and was admitted to the bar, at which he had a notable antebellum career, including six years as associate justice of the Georgia supreme court. He was prominent in politics as a delegate to the Charleston convention in 1860 and as vice president of the later Baltimore convention which nominated Stephen A. Douglas for the presidency. He was also a delegate to

the Georgia secession convention, and delegate from Georgia to the Virginia convention. Usually regarded as an extreme states rights advocate—to which label his prior utterances, both judicial and political, had given color —he nevertheless exhibited considerable reluctance to encourage secession until the die was absolutely cast, as evidenced by his support of Douglas. Benning's Confederate military career began with appointment to the colonelcy of the 17th Georgia Infantry. At this rank and subsequently as brigadier general, to rank from January 17, 1863, he was attached to Hood's division of the 1st Corps. He took part in many engagements from Second Manassas to Appomattox Court House, where he was paroled April 9, 1865. His nickname adequately testifies to his soldierly qualities. After the war

he returned to Columbus to resume his law practice. He died on his way to court, July 10, 1875, and is buried in Columbus.

Samuel Benton, a nephew of Senator Thomas Hart Benton, was born on October 18, 1820, probably in Williamson County, Tennessee. (60) In early life he taught school, later settling in Holly Springs, Mississippi, where he became a prominent lawyer and politician. Benton represented Marshall County in the state legislature and in the secession convention of 1861, which took Mississippi out of the Union. First a captain in the old 9th Mississippi, a twelve-months regiment, he was, early in 1862, elected colonel of the 37th Infantry, later reorganized as the 34th. His service in 1862 and 1863 was largely in North Mississippi and

Middle Tennessee. He participated in the Atlanta campaign under Joseph E. Johnston in the spring of 1864, and was given command of Walthall's old brigade early in July. On the twenty-second of that month, during the battle of Atlanta, he was struck over the heart by a piece of shell, and also sustained a wound in the foot that necessitated amputation. He died six days later in a hospital in Griffin, Georgia, before receiving his commission as brigadier general, to rank from July 26, 1864. (61) After temporary burial in Griffin, he was re-interred after the war in Holly Springs. The elaborate monument over his grave gives no indication of his connection with the Confederate cause.

Albert Gallatin Blanchard, a native of Charlestown, Massachusetts, was born on September 10, 1810. (62) Graduated from West Point in 1829, he served in the old army until 1840, when he resigned and took up residence in New Orleans, where, except for service in the Mexican and Civil Wars, he remained the rest of his life. He was variously occupied as schoolteacher, merchant, civil engineer, and railroad executive; and from 1866 until his death, as assistant city surveyor. Blanchard entered Confederate service as colonel of the 1st Louisiana Volunteer Infantry, and was promoted brigadier general on September 21, 1861. His war record seems to have been undistinguished, his activities after 1862 being mainly confined to camps of instruction and conscript duty. He was ordered to report to General Kirby Smith at Alexandria, Louisiana, in February 1863, but was again without a command by that August. In May 1864 he was a member of the court of inquiry for General S. M. Barton. General Richard Taylor maintained that he was utterly incompetent, at the same time that General Blanchard, in a letter to Secretary of War Seddon, was deploring his (Blanchard's) condemnation to a state of "disgraceful idleness." (63) The evidence is difficult to evaluate. He died in New Orleans, June 21, 1891, and is buried there in St. Louis Cemetery No. 1.

William Robertson Boggs was born in Augusta, Georgia, March 18, 1829, and after attendance at the Augusta Academy, was graduated from West Point in the class of 1853. Resigning his commission as 1st lieutenant of ordnance in February 1861, he was immediately appointed captain and ordnance officer to General Beauregard at Charleston. He was soon transferred to Pen-

sacola, where he joined the staff of General Bragg as chief of engineers and artillery. During most of the year 1862 he acted as chief engineer of the state of Georgia, and was commissioned brigadier general on November 4. He accompanied General Kirby Smith to the Trans-Mississippi, and was his chief of staff until the last months of the war. General Boggs returned to

Georgia in 1866, but soon after moved to St. Louis, where he engaged in civil engineering. From 1875 until 1881 he taught mechanics at Virginia Polytechnic Institute. After retirement he made his home in Winston-Salem, North Carolina. He died there September 11, 1911. The last years of his life were occupied in writing his military reminiscences(see Bibliography #48)' which represent an especially valuable document on operations in the Confederate Trans-Mississippi Department. (64) The general is buried in Salem Cemetery, Winston-Salem, North Carolina.

Milledge Luke Bonham was born in Edgefield District, South Carolina, December 25, 1813, and was graduated from South Carolina College (now the state university) in 1834. A lawyer by profession, he fought in both the Seminole uprising of 1836 and the Mexican War. His political career began with election to the state house of representatives in 1840. The secession of his state found him a member of the Federal Congress to which he had been elected in 1857 to fill the unexpired term of his cousin, Preston Brooks, who had resigned following his notorious physical assault on Senator Charles Sumner of Massachusetts. Immediately resigning upon the secession of South Carolina, Bonham was appointed major general and commander

28

of the South Carolina army, and on April 23, 1861 a brigadier general in Confederate service. Bonham resigned this commission in January 1862 to take his seat in the First Regular Confederate Congress, a post which he also resigned upon his election as governor of South Carolina in January 1863. At the expiration of his term he was reappointed a brigadier, February 16, 1865, and was present during the closing weeks of General Joseph E. Johnston's campaign in the Carolinas. After the war he again took up his law practice, engaged in planting, was a member of the pre-Reconstruction legislature delegate to the Democratic National Convention of 1868, and served as state railroad commissioner from 1878 until his death at White Sulphur Springs, North Carolina, August 27, 1890. He is buried in Elmwood Cemetery, Columbia, South Carolina.

John Stevens Bowen was born at Savannah, Georgia, October 30, 1830. He received his early education in Milledgeville, and was graduated from West Point in 1853. He resigned three years later to take up the profession of architect in St. Louis, where he was living at the outbreak of war. While a captain of Missouri militia and chief of staff to General D. M. Frost, Bowen was captured at Camp Jackson by the Federal General Lyon. Upon his release he organized and was appointed colonel of the 1st Missouri Infantry. His regiment first saw duty with General Polk at Columbus, Kentucky. After he was promoted brigadier to rank from March 14, 1862, Bowen's command was attached to John C. Breckinridge's divi-

29

sion at Shiloh, where he was wounded. Participating in the Vicksburg campaign, he opposed Grant's advance at Port Gibson. For his distinguished services there he was commissioned major general to rank May 25, 1863. He fought in all the battles preceding the siege of Vicksburg, and was commended numerous times for ability and gallant conduct. His health had been undermined by dysentery contracted during the siege, and General Bowen survived the surrender only a few days. He died, a paroled prisoner of war, near Raymond, Mississippi, on July 13, 1863. Twenty-four years after his death his remains were brought to Vicksburg and reinterred in the Confederate Cemetery. (65)

Braxton Bragg was born in Warrenton, North Carolina, March 22, 1817, and was a graduate of West Point in the class of 1837. He fought against the Seminoles and served gallantly in the Mexican War. After further routine duty, he resigned his lieutenant colonelcy in 1856 to become a planter in Louisiana. On March 7, 1861 he was appointed and confirmed brigadier general in the Provisional Army of the Confederate States and assigned to command the coast from Pensacola to Mobile. He was promoted major general, September 12, 1861, and assumed command of A. S. John-ston's 2nd Corps, which he led at Shiloh. Upon Johnston's death in that battle, he was appointed, and confirmed the same day, a general in the Regular Army to rank from April 6, 1862. In June he replaced P. G. T. Beauregard as commander of the Army of Tennessee, which he led in the abortive invasion of Kentucky, August to October 1862, ending in defeat at Perryville at the hands of D. C. Buell. He was again forced to withdraw before W. S. Rosecrans following the battle of Murfreesboro in early January 1863. After his success at Chickamauga, he besieged Chattanooga, but in November, General U. S. Grant forced him to retire into Georgia, and he yielded command at his own request to J. E. Johnston. An especial favorite of President Davis, Bragg was called to Richmond, where he was charged, under the direction of the President, "with the conduct of the military operations in the armies of the Confederacy." During this period he was, technically at least, superior to his contemporaries in grade, although junior by date of commission. After General Lee's appointment as general in chief, Bragg saw service in North Carolina under Johnston. He became chief engineer of Alabama post bellum, and later moved to Galveston, Texas, where he fell dead, September 27, 1876, while walking down the street with a friend. He is buried in Mobile, Alabama. The argument as to his military capabilities, which began during the war, has not ceased to this day. (66)

Lawrence O'Bryan Branch was born in Enfield, North Carolina, November 28, 1820. In early life he had the unique distinction of having for a tutor Salmon P. Chase, later Lincoln's Secretary of the Treasury and Chief Justice of the United State Supreme Court. After graduation from Princeton in 1838, he edited a newspaper in Tennessee. He also studied law and was admitted to the Florida bar while still under age. Returning to North Carolina, he served in Congress from 1855 until 1861, meantime declining the posts of Secretary of the Treasury and Postmaster General proffered him by President Buchanan. Upon the secession of his state Branch was appointed quartermaster a n d

paymaster-general of North Carolina, a post which he subsequently resigned to accept the colonelcy of the 33rd North Carolina Infantry. He was promoted brigadier general on November 16, 1861, and commanded the troops which disputed Burnside's advance at New Bern. His brigade was then ordered to Virginia and attached to A. P. Hill's "Light" Division, in which command it was distinguished from the Seven Days battles until Sharpsburg. Hurrying to the latter field from Harper's Ferry on the afternoon of September 17, 1862, the three bridgades of Archer, Gregg, and Branch arrived in the nick of time to stem the last Federal onslaught of the day. Soon after, while Hill was consulting with his three brigadiers, Branch was instantly killed by a Federal sharpshooter who fired into the group. He is buried in Raleigh, North Carolina.

William Lindsay Brandon was born near Washington, Adams County, Mississippi, in either 1800 or 1802. Due to destruction of the family records by fire in 1831, the exact date cannot be established. (67) Educated at Washington College and the then College of New Jersey (now Princeton), he became a prominent and typical antebellum planter, much interested in horses and hunting. He served in the legislature in 1826 and became a major general of militia. He had also studied medicine and was often consulted professionally. Despite his advanced age, Brandon entered Confederate service as lieutenant colonel of the 21st Mississippi Infantry. Losing a leg at the battle of Malvern Hill, (68) he was disabled for some months, but returned to duty and was promoted colonel after Gettysburg. After service with General Longstreet at Chickamauga and in the Knoxville campaign, he returned to Virginia with the 1st Corps. He was soon appointed brigadier general, to rank from June 18, 1864, and was placed in command of the bureau of conscription in his state, a post in which he served until the bureau was abolished. He returned to his plantation, "Arcole," in Wilkinson County, Mississippi, after the war. He lived there in comparative retirement until his death, October 8, 1890. He lies in the family burial ground at "Arcole." (69)

William Felix Brantley was born in Greene County, Alabama, March 12, 1830, but was taken to Mississippi while a child. He commenced the practice of law at the now nonexistent town of Greensboro in 1852, and in 1861 represented Choctaw County in the Mississippi secession convention. Elected captain of the Wigfall Rifles, which successively became Company D of the 15th, and later of the 29th, Mississippi, Brantley soon rose to be colonel of the latter regiment. He commanded the 29th with distinction at Murfreesboro, Chickamauga, Chattanooga, and in the Atlanta campaign. His brigade commander, Benton, having been mortally wounded at Atlanta on July 22, 1864, Colonel

Brantley was commissioned brigadier general on July 26. He led the brigade into Tennessee and afterwards, until its surrender with General Joseph E. Johnston in North Carolina. He resumed his law practice, but was assassinated near Winona, Mississippi, November 2, 1870, while riding in his buggy. Although the murderer was never apprehended, Brantley's death apparently resulted from a feud of long standing, of which he was by no means the first victim on either side. General Brantley is buried "behind the church at Old Greensboro, about three miles north of Tomnolen, Webster County, Mississippi." (70)

John Bratton was born at Winnsboro, South Carolina, March 7, 1831. He was educated at Mount Zion Academy and South Carolina College. In 1853 he secured his diploma in medicine, after which he practiced in Winnsboro. Upon the secession of the state he enlisted as a private in the 6th South Carolina Volunteers, and was shortly elected captain of his company, with which he served during the bombardment of Fort Sumter. Upon the translation of the state troops into Confederate service, Bratton again enlisted as a private, and rose rapidly to the grade of colonel. He fought at the battle of Seven Pines, where he was wounded and captured. Almost from the beginning, he was identified with Hood's division of Longstreet's corps of the Army of Northern Virginia, whose fortunes he followed from the Peninsula to the end. He was promoted brigadier general after the death of General Micah Jen-

kins, to rank from May 6, 1864, and surrendered the largest brigade in the army at Appomattox Court House. After the war General Bratton became a farmer and took an active part in Reconstruction politics. He was ·state senator in 1865-66, and a member of Congress in 1884-85. In 1890 he was defeated for the governorship of South Carolina by "Pitchfork Ben" Tillman. General Bratton died in Winnsboro on January 12, 1898, and is buried there.

John Cabell Breckinridge was born near Lexington, Kentucky, January 15, 1821. He was graduated from Centre College in 1839, and after legal studies at Transylvania University, he began practicing law in Lexington in 1845. He enjoyed a meteoric political career and was elected Vice President of the United States at the age of thirty-five. A member of the Kentucky legislature, 1849-51, and of the House of Representatives, 1851-55, he was in 1856 the successful candidate for the vice presidency with Buchanan. In 1859—a year and a half before his term was to expire—he was elected to the U. S. Senate by the Kentucky legislature. He opposed war in the special session of 1861, but when Kentucky declared for the Union in September, he accepted a commission as Confederate brigadier, November 2, 1861, and was

promoted major general to rank from April 14, 1862. He commanded the Reserve Corps at Shiloh, and in the summer of 1862 defended Vicksburg. Failing in an attack on Baton Rouge, he distinguished himself successively at Murfreesboro, in Johnston's campaign to relieve Vicksburg, and at Chickamauga. Having commanded the Department of Southwest Virginia for a time in 1864, he later accompanied General Early in the raid on Washington, and on February 4, 1865 was appointed by President Davis Confederate Secretary of War. Following the surrender he went to England, thence to Canada, returning to Kentucky in 1869, where he was perhaps the most popular man in the state. Because of his political disabilities he disclaimed all ambitions, and quietly resumed his law practice. He died in Lexington, May 17, 1875, from the results of a serious operation, and is buried there.

Theodore Washington Brevard was born in Tuskegee, Alabama, August 26, 1835, and moved with his family to Florida in 1847. After studying law at the University of Virginia, he was admitted to the Florida bar in 1858, and was elected to the state assembly. About this time he married a daughter of General Richard K. Call. He was appointed adjutant and inspector general of the state in 1860, but resigned the post in 1861 to raise a battalion of Partisan Rangers, which he commanded at the battle of Olustee. His battalion went to Virginia as a part of the 11th Florida Infantry of Finegan's brigade, and Brevard was shortly promoted

colonel of the regiment. He was the last general officer appointed by President Davis in the armies of the Confederacy — March 28, 1865 to rank from March 22. According to family tradition, he commanded the Florida Brigade until his capture at Sayler's Creek by Custer. The family also relates that he was subsequently a prisoner on Johnson's Island in Lake Erie. Since the other general officers captured at the battle of Sayler's Creek were confined in Fort Warren (with the exception of G. W. C. Lee, who was paroled), General Brevard may have been taken prisoner prior to the battle, although no official record of his capture and subsequent parole or imprisonment can be found. (71) After the war he resumed his eminently successful law practice in Tallahassee. He died there on June 20, 1882, and is buried in the Episcopal Cemetery. (72)

John Calvin Brown, a native of Giles County, Tennessee, was born on January 6, 1827, and was graduated from Jackson College at Columbia, Tennessee, in 1846. After admission to the bar, he became interested in Whig politics and was a Presidential Elector on the Bell-Everett ticket in 1860. He enlisted in the Confederate Army as a private, but was appointed colonel of the 3rd Tennessee Infantry in May 1861. Captured at Fort Donelson, he was later ex-

changed and promoted brigadier general, to rank from August 30, 1862, and major general from August 4, 1864. Brown followed Bragg into Kentucky and thereafter took a prominent and creditable part in all the campaigns of the Army of Tennessee until the battle of Franklin. There he was severely wounded and incapacitated for several months, having been once before wounded at Perryville. He rejoined the army in North Carolina on April 2, 1865, and was paroled a month later at Greensboro. He then resumed his law practice at Pulaski, Tennessee, and re-entered politics, becoming the first Democrat to be elected governor of the state post bellum (1870). Re-elected in 1872, he was defeated for the United States Senate in 1875 by former President Andrew John-

son. He then engaged in the railroad business, rising to the presidency of the Texas & Pacific. At the time of his death in Red Boiling Springs, Tennessee, August 17, 1889, he was president of the Tennessee Coal, Iron & Railroad Company. General Brown is buried in Pulaski.

William M o n t a g u e Browne, supposedly the nephew of an Irish peer, was born in Dublin, Ireland in 1823, and was educated at the National University. After service in the Crimean War in an English regiment, he emigrated to the United States in 1855 and settled in Washington, where he assisted in editing the *Union* and the *Constitution*, "administration" papers devoted to the policies of James Buchanan. At the outbreak of the Civil War, Browne cast his lot

with the new Confederacy. A prior acquaintance with Howell Cobb enabled him to secure appointment to the personal staff of Jefferson Davis, with rank of colonel of cavalry. From February 17 to March 18, 1862 he served as Secretary of State *ad interim*. In April 1864 he was appointed commandant of conscripts for the state of Georgia, and later that year temporarily commanded a brigade in the defense of Savannah against Sherman. Davis appointed him brigadier general with temporary rank from November 11, 1864; however, the Confederate Senate rejected his nomination to that grade on February 18, 1865. (73) Unsuccessful as a farmer after the war, his friendship with General Cobb obtained for him a chair of history and constitutional law at the University of Georgia, a post which he held until his death. General Browne died in Athens on April 28, 1883, and is buried there in an unmarked grave in Oconee Hill Cemetery. His wife had predeceased him, and they had no children. (74)

Goode Bryan was born in Hancock County, Georgia, August 31, 1811. (75) He was graduated from West Point in the class of 1834 and resigned from the army the following year. From then until the outbreak of the Civil War he was a planter in Georgia and Alabama, and major of the

1st Alabama Volunteers during the Mexican War. In 1861 he was residing in Georgia, and was a member of the Georgia secession convention from Lee County. (76) He entered Confederate service in that year, as captain of the 16th Georgia Infantry, and attained the grade of colonel in February 1862. His

regiment—first attached to General Howell Cobb's brigade of General John B. Magruder's division—participated in the battles of the Seven Days around Richmond; and was later present in the Maryland campaign, and at Fredericksburg, Chancellorsville, and Gettysburg. Bryan was promoted brigadier general to rank from August 29, 1863. His brigade accompanied the 1st Corps to the west, and after the battle of Chickamauga, engaged

37

in the siege of Knoxville. It then returned to Virginia and participated in the battle of the Wilderness and subsequent operations of the army. Failing health compelled Bryan's resignation on September 20, 1864. Semi-retired for many years after the war, General Bryan died in Augusta, Georgia, on August 16, 1885, and is buried in the City Cemetery.

Simon Bolivar Buckner was born in Hart County, Kentucky, April 1, 1823. A West Point graduate of 1844, he resigned from the army in 1855, after earning two brevets in Mexico, and engaged in business in Chicago for several years. At the outbreak of war he was adjutant general of Kentucky in command of the state guard, charged with the impossible task of maintaining neutrality. After declining a commission as brigadier in the Union Army in August, he was appointed brigadier general in the Confederate Army, September 14, 1861. He was left by Generals Floyd and Pillow to consummate the surrender of Fort Donelson. Subsequently exchanged, he led a division in Bragg's invasion of Kentucky and fought at Perryville in October 1862. From December 1862 until April 1863 he was engaged in fortifying Mobile. From May until August he commanded the Department of East Tennessee, and directed a corps at Chickamauga. Thereafter his service

was largely in the Trans-Mississippi, where he was appointed lieutenant general and chief of staff to Kirby Smith, September 20, 1864. He resided in New Orleans for three years after the war; then returned to Kentucky and became editor of the Louisville *Courier*. He was involved in protracted litigation to recover from his brother-in-law's widow some valuable property in Chicago which Buckner's wife had deeded to her brother at the commencement of the war, with the understanding that it would be deeded back at the close of hostilities. With the swing of political opinion in the state back to the old Confederate leaders, he was elected governor in 1887, and in the national campaign of 1896 was vice presidential nominee of the "Gold Democrats." He died on his estate

"Glen Lily" near Munfordville, on January 8, 1914, in his ninety-first year, the last survivor of the three highest grades in the Confederate Army. (77) He is buried in the State Cemetery at Frankfort, Kentucky.

Abraham Buford, two of whose cousins were generals in the Union Army, (78) was born in Woodford, Kentucky, January 18, 1820. After attending Centre College in that state, he was graduated from West Point in 1841, and was brevetted for gallantry in Mexico. He resigned from the old army in 1854 to devote himself to his stock farm near Versailles, Kentucky. Buford appears to have maintained the classic neutrality of his state until the invasion by General Bragg in 1862, when he cast his lot with the South. He was ap-

pointed brigadier general to rank from September 2, 1862. He took part in the Vicksburg campaign, and was later attached to Bedford Forrest's cavalry corps, with which he then largely served until Forrest's surrender at Selma, Alabama, in April 1865. Returning to his farm upon the cessation of hostilities, General Buford became noted as a turfman and owner of several celebrated horses, and was elected to a term in the Kentucky legislature. In later years he suffered severe financial reverses, which culminated in the loss of his home. Weighted down by this and other misfortunes, he took his own life at Danville, Indiana, June 9, 1884. In accordance with a request contained in the note found with his body, he was buried in Lexington, Kentucky, by the side of his wife and son. (79)

Robert Bullock was born in Greenville, North Carolina, December 8, 1828, and attended the common schools of the neighborhood. Moving to Florida at the age of sixteen, he taught school for a time; then became clerk of the circuit court of Marion County. In 1856 he took part in the suppression of the Seminole uprising of that year. Entering the Confederate Army as captain of the 7th Florida Infantry, Bullock was successively promoted through grades to colonel, and was ap-

pointed brigadier general from November 29, 1864. In Finley's brigade (which he subsequently commanded) of Bate's division, he fought gallantly at Chickamauga, in the Atlanta campaign, and in the invasion of Tennessee, where he was badly wounded in the course of the retreat from Nashville. He returned to Florida and was admitted to the bar in 1866; the same year he was elected judge of the probate court. A Democratic Presidential Elector in 1876, he was elected to the Florida legislature in 1879. From 1881 to 1889 he was again clerk of the circuit court of Marion County. He then served two terms in the Federal Congress, not being a candidate for a third term in 1892. At the time of his death at Ocala, Florida, July 27, 1905, he was

judge of the circuit court, an office to which he had been elected in 1903. He is buried in Evergreen Cemetery, Ocala. (80)

Matthew Calbraith Butler was born on March 8, 1836, in Greenville, South Carolina, and was educated at South Carolina College. The secession of his state found him a lawyer, son-in-law of Governor Pickens, and member of the legislature, from which he promptly resigned to accept a captain's commission in the Hampton Legion. Immediately after First Manassas, in which the Legion participated, he was made major, and in August 1862, colonel of the 2nd South Carolina Cavalry. He lost his right foot at the battle of Brandy Station in June 1863; and was commissioned brigadier

general to rank from September 1, 1863, and major general from September 19, 1864. Meantime he had largely distinguished himself as a brigade and division commander under Generals Stuart and Wade Hampton. Financially ruined by the war, Butler became the leading exponent of the "straight-out" Democratic movement in his state, and was elected to the United States Senate in 1876— at the same time Hampton assumed the governor's office — where he served continuously until his defeat by Benjamin F. Tillman in 1894. He donned a blue uniform in 1898 to accept a commission as major general of United States volunteers in the war with Spain. He was honorably discharged on April 15, 1899, after serving as a member of the commission for the Spanish evacuation of Cuba. Later president of a mining company in Mexico, and vice president of the Southern Historical Association, General Butler died in Washington on April 14, 1909, and is buried in Edgefield, South Carolina.

William Lewis Cabell, "Old Tige," (81) was born at Danville, Virginia, January 1, 1827, and was graduated from West Point in 1850. His United States service was principally in the quartermaster's d e p a r t m e n t. Upon his resignation in 1861, he was promptly assigned by the

Confederate War Department as major and chief quartermaster to General Beauregard at Manassas. He later served on the staff of General J. E. Johnston, at which time he assisted these two officers in designing the Confederate battle flag. (82) Transferred to the Trans-Mississippi under General Van Dorn, Cabell was of great service after the battle of Elkhorn, when he ferried the latter's entire command to the eastern bank of the Mississippi River. Later, he was appointed brigadier general to rank from January 20, 1863. While in command of a brigade of cavalry under General Sterling Price, he was captured on a raid into Missouri in October 1864, not being released until August 1865. He then went to Fort Smith, Arkansas, where he studied law and was admitted to the bar. Moving to Dallas, Texas, in 1872, he served four terms as mayor of the city; was United States marshal, 1885-89, and vice president of what is now a part of the Southern Pacific System. From 1893 until 1907 General Cabell was one of the supervisors of the Louisiana State Lottery and of its successor, the Honduras National Lottery. At the time of his death in Dallas, February 22, 1911, he had been for many years commander of the Trans-Mississippi Department, United Confederate Veterans, and honorary commander-in-chief of the organization. He is buried in Greenwood Cemetery in Dallas.

Alexander William Campbell was born in Nashville, Tennessee, June 4, 1828. He was educated at West Tennessee College and Lebanon Law School, later becoming a partner of Howell E. Jackson, a former member of the United States Supreme Court. He enlisted in the Confederate Army as a private, was soon promoted major and assigned to staff duty for a time, and was then appointed colonel of the 33rd Tennessee. While leading his men at Shiloh, he was severely wounded and incapacitated for several months. His next tour of duty was as assistant adjutant and inspector general to Lieutenant General Polk, after which he served with the volunteer and conscript bureau under General Pillow.

Campbell was captured at Lexington, Tennessee, in July 1863, while on a mission for Governor Isham G. Harris to superintend elections and to recruit in the western part of the state. (83) Apparently not exchanged until February 1865, he was, on the eighteenth of that month, announced as acting inspector general in orders from General Forrest's headquarters. A few days later he took command of a brigade in General W. H. Jackson's division of Forrest's corps, with which he served until the surrender. His commission as brigadier general was dated March 1, 1865. Resuming his law practice after the war, he interested himself in politics, and in 1880 unsuccessfully sought the Democratic nomination for governor. He died at Jackson, Tennessee, June 13, 1893, and is buried there.

James Cantey was born at Camden, South Carolina, December 30, 1818. After his graduation from South Carolina College, he studied law, was admitted to practice, and opened an office in his home town. He also served two terms in the state legislature. During the Mexican War he was an officer of the Palmetto Regiment and was wounded. Shortly afterwards he settled in Russell County, Alabama, as a planter. In 1861 he was elected colonel of the 15th Alabama Infantry, which he took to Virginia, serving in the Valley campaign of 1862 under Stonewall Jackson, and in the subsequent battles of that summer around Richmond. Transferred to the western army, Cantey was appointed brigadier general to rank from January 8, 1863, but was not infrequently absent from

his command due to ill health. His brigade took part in the Atlanta campaign and accompanied Hood into Tennessee, finally surrendering with General J. E. Johnston at Greensboro, North Carolina. No record of General Cantey's capture or personal parole has been found. He died on his plantation near Fort Mitchell, Alabama, June 30, 1874, and is buried in the Crowell family cemetery at Fort Mitchell. (84)

Ellison Capers was born in Charleston, South Carolina, October 14, 1837. He was graduated from the South Carolina Military Academy in 1857 and became a teacher. In 1861 he was elected major of a regiment of South Carolina volunteers, which took part in the bombardment of Fort Sumter in April. After helping to recruit a regiment for the war, the 24th South Carolina Infantry, of which he was elected lieutenant colonel, Capers served in North and South Carolina, under General Bragg at Chickamauga, and in the Chattanooga campaign. In the course of the Atlanta campaign he was promoted colonel, and after the death of General S. R. Gist at Franklin, succeeded to brigade command, being formally appointed to rank from March 1, 1865. After the war General Capers entered the Episcopal ministry, in which he had a long and distinguished career.

He became assistant bishop of South Carolina in 1893 and bishop in 1894. For a number of years before his death, which occurred in Columbia, April 22, 1908, he served as chaplain general of the United Confederate Veterans. He contributed the South Carolina volume to *Confederate Military History* (see Bibliography #189). General Capers is buried in Trinity Churchyard, Columbia, under a monument bearing the following inscription: "He rendered unto Caesar the things that are Caesar's and unto God the things that are God's."

William Henry Carroll was born in Nashville, Tennessee, probably in 1810, the eldest son of William Carroll, six - term governor of the state and inti-mate of Andrew Jackson. (85) After operating a plantation in Panola County, Mississippi, the younger Carroll moved to Memphis in 1848, where he was for some years postmaster of the city. Appointed brigadier general in the provisional army of the state of Tennessee, he entered Confederate service as colonel of the 37th Tennessee Infantry, and was promoted to the rank of brigadier on October 26, 1861. He was soon ordered to Knoxville, where he proclaimed martial law in an effort to control the disaffected elements of the eastern section of the state—strongly Unionist in sentiment. Carroll was present at the battle of Fishing Creek, where his brigade sustained comparatively light losses and retired in good order. He was later unsparingly

criticized by General Bragg, who declared him to be "not safe . . . to intrust with command," and was arrested by General Hardee, on Bragg's order, for "drunkenness, incompetency, and neglect." (86) After his appearance before a court of inquiry, General Carroll resigned his commission on February 1, 1863 and went to Canada, where his family had emigrated after the occupation of Memphis by the Federals. He died in Montreal, May 3, 1868. His remains were moved the following year to Elmwood Cemetery, Memphis, where they were re-interred under a headstone which is inaccurate both as to the years of his birth and death. (87)

John Carpenter Carter was born in Waynesboro, Georgia, on December 19, 1837. After attending the University of Virginia from 1854 until 1856, he studied law under Judge Abram Caruthers at Cumberland University in Lebanon, Tennessee. After his graduation and admission to the bar, he was an instructor at the law school. Judge Caruthers had meantime become his father-in-law. Removing to Memphis, he was practicing law there in 1861, when he entered the Confederate Army as a captain of the 38th Tennessee Infantry. Carter won rapid promotion to the grade of colonel, markedly distinguishing himself at the battles of Shiloh, Perry-ville, Murfreesboro, and Chickamauga. The brigade to which his regiment belonged was on detached duty through the Chattanooga campaign which followed; Carter succeeded to command of it (88) during the Atlanta campaign, and was formally promoted brigadier general to rank from July 7, 1864. Carter was temporarily in command of Cheatham's division at the battle of Jonesboro; (89) in the course of Hood's ill-fated invasion of Tennessee that autumn, Carter was mortally wounded in the assault on the Federal works at Franklin on November 30, 1864. He died on December 10, in the Harrison home, three miles south of the battlefield. His remains were interred in Rose Hill Cemetery at Columbia, Tennessee. The burial service was pronounced by his friend, Chaplain (later Bishop) Quintard. (90)

James Ronald Chalmers was born in Halifax County, Virginia, January 11, 1831, and was graduated from South Carolina College at the age of twenty. Taking up the practice of law in Holly Springs, Mississippi, he served as district attorney and was a member of the secession convention which took Mississippi out of the Union in 1861. He was appointed colonel of the 9th Mississippi Infantry and commanded at Pensacola, Florida, for a time. He was promoted brigadier general on February 13, 1862, and fought at Shiloh in the division of General Withers. He led his brigade in the invasion of Kentucky under General Bragg and at the battle of Murfreesboro, after which he

was transferred to the cavalry. Commanding the District of Mississippi and East Louisiana in 1863, he was given a division under General Forrest the following year, which took a brilliant part in the subsequent operations in North Mississippi, Kentucky, and West Tennessee, including Hood's 1864 campaign. After the surrender General Chalmers became prominent in the Reconstruction politics of Mississippi. He represented his adopted state three times in Congress, and was an unsuccessful candidate on three other occasions. Each time the returns were contested either by Chalmers or by his opponent. In 1888 he retired and moved to Memphis, Tennessee, where he practiced law until his death, April 9, 1898. Distinctly an individualist, his relations with Forrest were not always completely harmonious, although his ability and gallantry were unquestioned. General Chalmers is buried in Memphis.

John Randolph Chambliss, Jr. was born in Hicksford (now Emporia), Greensville County, Virginia, January 23, 1833. He was graduated from West Point in the class of 1853. He resigned the following year to become a planter at Hicksford, in which occupation he was engaged until 1861, meantime serving as an officer in the militia and as aide-de-camp to the governor of Vir-

ginia. When the state troops were taken over by the Confederacy, Chambliss was first commissioned colonel of the 41st Virginia Infantry, and in July 1861, colonel of the 13th Virginia Cavalry. After some service south of James River and on the line of the Rappahannock during the Maryland campaign, his regiment was attached to General W. H. F. Lee's brigade in November 1862, with which it served during all of the subsequent operations of the Cavalry Corps. He was promoted brigadier general to rank from December 19, 1863. In the course of an engagement with D. M. Gregg's Federal cavalry on the Charles City Road, north of the James, General Chambliss was killed, August 16, 1864, at the head of his brigade. His death was announced by General Lee with deep regret as one "which will be felt throughout the army." He is buried in Emporia. General Chambliss' father, of the same name, was a member of the Virginia secession convention and of the First Regular Confederate Congress.

Benjamin Franklin Cheatham was born at Nashville, Tennessee, October 20, 1820. After service in Mexico, where he was a colonel of Tennessee Volunteers, he became major general of state militia, while he was also engaged in farming. He was appointed a Confederate brigadier general on July 9, 1861, and major general to rank from March 10, 1862. He distinguished himself as a brigade, division, and corps commander in every engagement of the Army of Tennessee from Shiloh to At-

lanta. Upon General Hood's undertaking the Tennessee campaign in the fall of 1864, Cheatham was placed in command of General Hardee's old corps. In the course of the advance toward Nashville, Hood left two-thirds of S. D. Lee's corps and virtually all the artillery of the army to demonstrate against the Federal General Schofield's forces at Columbia. His plan then called for a flank march which would throw his other two corps under Cheatham and A. P. Stewart across the Columbia-Nashville turnpike, thereby cutting off the Federal withdrawal. The ensuing contretemps at Spring Hill, Tennessee—during which Schofield's troops, unopposed, marched north along the turnpike and occupied a well-nigh impregnable position at Franklin—resulted in severe strictures on Cheatham by Hood for dereliction of duty. It also gave rise to a controversy which was waged unceasingly until the death of both officers (and to this day). The weight of evidence definitely favors Cheatham. (91) After the war he was an unsuccessful candidate for Congress in 1872, superintendent of state prisons, and postmaster of Nashville. He was occupying the last-named office at the time of his death there on September 4, 1886. He is buried in Mount Olivet Cemetery in Nashville.

James Chesnut, Jr., was born at Camden, South Carolina, January 18, 1815. He was graduated from Princeton in 1835, read law, and began practice in the town of his birth. After a number of terms in the South Carolina house and senate, he was elected to the United States Senate in 1858. He resigned before the secession of his state, in order to participate in the convention which took South Carolina out of the Union and initiated the war. He was an aide to General Beauregard at Fort Sumter, a member of the Provisional Confederate Congress, and in 1862 resigned from the South Carolina executive council to serve on the staff of President Davis. On April 23, 1864 he was appointed brigadier general. After the war General Chesnut played a prominent part in the Reconstruction politics of the state, and stood next in importance only to ex-generals Wade Hampton and Matthew C. Butler in the fight to regain control of South Carolina from the carpetbag regime. He died at his home, "Sarsfield," in Camden, February 1, 1885. His wife, Mary (Boykin) Chesnut, wrote the revealing and informative *Diary from Dixie* (see Bibliography #52), which has come to be a virtual primer of wartime life in Richmond and in the plantation South. General Chesnut is buried in a family burial ground near Camden, at Knights Hill. One of his paternal aunts was the mother of General Z. C. Deas.

Robert Hall Chilton, a native of Loudoun County, Virginia, was born on February 25, 1815, (92) and was graduated from West Point in the class of 1837. As a captain of dragoons he won the brevet of major for gallantry in Mexico. Changing over from line to staff in 1854, he resigned as major paymaster, April 29, 1861, and was soon commissioned lieutenant colonel in the Adjutant and Inspector General's Department of the Regular Confederate Army. Chilton served commendably as chief of staff to General Robert E. Lee, an old friend, and as inspector general of the Army of Northern Virginia; however, he experienced great difficulty in securing pro-

motion. His appointment as brigadier (originally to rank from October 20, 1862) was not confirmed by the Senate until February 16, 1864. The following April he was relieved from duty in the field at his own request and assigned to duty in the department in Richmond, in charge of the inspection branch, where he continued until the close of the war. (93) General Chilton was afterwards president of a manufacturing company in Columbus, Georgia. He died there on February 18, 1879. He is buried in Hollywood Cemetery, Richmond.

Thomas James Churchill was born in Jefferson County, Kentucky, on March 10, 1824, and was educated at St. Mary's College and Transylvania University, where he studied law. After the Mexican War, in which he participated as a 1st lieutenant of the 1st Kentucky Rifles, he settled near Little Rock, Arkansas, of which city he was postmaster in 1861. He recruited the 1st Arkansas Mounted Rifles and rendered notable service with this regiment at Wilson's Creek. He was commissioned brigadier general to rank from March 4, 1862. After fighting at Richmond, Kentucky, under Kirby Smith, Churchill in January 1863 made a gallant defense at Arkansas Post, which he was finally forced to surrender in the face of overwhelming odds. He later participated in the Red River campaign against Banks and in the attack on Steele at Jenkins' Ferry, and was promoted major general March 18, 1865, while serving in the Trans-

Mississippi Department. From 1874 until 1880 he was state treasurer of Arkansas, and was elected governor in the latter year by a huge majority. Subsequently a claim for alleged shortages in his accounts while treasurer was pressed by the attorney general of the state; judgment was entered against him for a substantial sum, which he made good. Much of the shortage was apparently due to faulty bookkeeping, and it seems certain that General Churchill did not profit personally. He died in Little Rock on May 14, 1905, and is buried in Mount Holly Cemetery.

James Holt Clanton was born January 8, 1827, in Columbia County, Georgia; the family removed to Alabama in 1835. After service in the Mexican War, he studied law and was admitted to the bar. He served in the Alabama legislature, and was an Elector on the Presidential ticket of Bell and Everett in 1860. An original opponent of secession, he nevertheless promptly went into the Confederate Army when the die was cast, and was elected colonel of the 1st Alabama Cavalry in the fall of 1861. He opened the battle of Shiloh, was present at Farmington and Booneville, and after raising three more regiments, was promoted brigadier general to rank from November 16, 1863. During the balance of

the war he participated in the Atlanta campaign; was active in the Department of Alabama, Mississippi, and East Louisiana; and was badly wounded at Bluff Spring, Florida, in March 1865, being paroled at Mobile on May 25, 1865, presumably while recovering from his wound. Resuming his law practice in 1866, Clanton again became a leader in the Democratic party of Alabama. He was assassinated at Knoxville, Tennessee, September 27, 1871, by a drunken ex-Federal officer (the son of a former Union Congressman from East Tennessee), (94) who provoked a quarrel with him. He is buried in Montgomery, Alabama.

Charles Clark was born in Lebanon, Warren County, Ohio, May 24, 1811. (95) He received his education in Kentucky, and moved to Mississippi about 1831, where he taught school for a time. Later a planter and a Whig adherent of Henry Clay, he served in the Mississippi legislature from 1838 to 1844, and during the Mexican War was colonel of the 2nd Mississippi Infantry. Shortly before the Civil War he became a Democrat and was a delegate to the conventions in Charleston and Baltimore in 1860, where he supported John C. Breckinridge for the presidency. He was early appointed brigadier general of state troops, and later major general. After the acceptance of the Mississippi regiments into Confederate service, Clark was appointed brigadier general, May 22, 1861. First wounded at Shiloh, his hip was so badly shat-

tered at Baton Rouge in August 1862 as to necessitate the use of crutches for the rest of his life. Retiring from army service, he was elected governor of Mississippi in 1863, and served until 1865. At the end of the war he was arrested by the Federal authorities and confined in Fort Pulaski for a time. After his release he took up the practice of law and was appointed chancellor of his district in 1876. General Clark died at his plantation, "Doro," in Bolivar County, December 18, 1877, and is buried there.

John Bullock Clark, Jr. was born in Fayette, Missouri, January 14, 1831. He attended Fayette Academy and the University of Missouri, and after spending two years in California, was graduated from Harvard Law School in 1854. He engaged in the practice of law in Fayette until 1861, when he entered the Confederate Army as a lieutenant. Soon made a captain of one of the companies of the 6th Missouri Infantry, he was a major at the battles of Carthage and Springfield, and with rank of colonel, commanded a brigade at Pea Ridge (Elkhorn). Thereafter he served for some time under General Hindman, until his services in Missouri and Arkansas were at length rewarded by a commission as brigadier general, to rank from March 6, 1864. The remainder of his military career

was with Generals Marmaduke and Shelby in the closing operations of the Trans-Mississippi Department. After the war General Clark resumed his law practice in Fayette, and was elected to Congress in 1873, serving until 1883, when he was elected clerk of the House of Representatives. From 1889 until his death, September 7, 1903, he practiced law in Washington, where he died and is buried. His father, John B. Clark, Sr., served in Congress ante bellum, was a brigadier general of the Missouri State Guard in 1861-62, and subsequently a representative and senator from Missouri in the Confederate Congress. He died in Fayette in 1885.

Henry DeLamar Clayton was born in Pulaski County, Georgia, March 7, 1827. After graduation from Emory and Henry College in Virginia, he read law in Eufaula, Alabama, and afterwards opened an office in nearby Clayton. He was a member of the Alabama legislature, 1857-61. Clayton was at first colonel of the 1st Alabama Infantry, stationed at Pensacola; he then recruited the 39th Alabama, which he led in Bragg's Kentucky invasion, and was later severely wounded at the battle of Murfreesboro. He was promoted brigadier general to rank from April 22, 1863, and major general from July 7, 1864. Meantime he had been conspicuous at Chickamauga and in the opening battles of the Atlanta campaign. Succeeding to the command of General A. P. Stewart's old division, he took part in the battles around Atlanta, Jonesboro, and in the invasion of Tennessee. He was especially commended by General Hood during the first part of the retreat from Nashville, where his division and General E. W. Pettus' brigade acted as rear guard of the army until relieved by General Stevenson. He surrendered with General Joseph E. Johnston in North Carolina. After the return of peace General Clayton engaged in planting and the practice of law, and was for a time a circuit court judge in Alabama. His death occurred in Tuscaloosa on October 13, 1889; he is buried in Eufaula, Alabama.

Patrick R o n a y n e Cleburne, one of two foreign-born officers to attain the rank of major general in the Confederate service, (96) was born March 17, 1828 in Bridgepark Cottage on the River Bride, ten miles west of Cork, Ireland. After a three-year enlistment in Her Majesty's 41st Regiment of Foot, he purchased his discharge and emigrated to the United States in 1849, landing at New Orleans. Educated as an apothecary, he first worked in Cincinnati but soon took up residence in Helena, Arkansas, where he became a partner in a drugstore, and then studied law. By the outbreak of the Civil War he had become successful in the legal profession, and had accumulated considerable property. He was elected colonel of the 15th Arkansas in 1861, and was promoted brigadier general to rank from March 4, 1862. The

first to suggest (in a circular letter) the arming of slaves and their muster into military service, (97) a plan belatedly put forth by the Confederate government at the end of the war. First buried near Franklin, Cleburne's remains were later removed to Helena, Arkansas.

Thomas Lanier Clingman was born at Huntsville, North Carolina, July 27, 1812. (98) He was graduated from the state university in 1832 and was admitted to the bar in 1834. He commenced a political career by election to the state legislature in 1835, and served in the national House of Representatives, 1843-45 and 1847-58, when he was appointed to the Senate, to which he was elected to a full term in 1860. Resigning on March 28, 1861, Clingman was commissioned colonel of the 25th (formerly

month following he led a brigade at Shiloh and later commanded a brigade at Perryville and a division at Richmond. His promotion to major general dated from December 13, 1862. Cleburne rapidly established a reputation as a superb combat officer on every battlefield of the western army. He further distinguished himself at Murfreesboro, and received a vote of thanks from the Confederate Congress for saving the trains of the Army of Tennessee after the Chattanooga campaign. A savage fighter of the Bedford Forrest stamp, his death at the battle of Franklin, on November 30, 1864, in the forefront of his division, was a calamity to the Confederate cause perhaps only exceeded by the demise of Stonewall Jackson. General Cleburne was the

15th) North Carolina Infantry. His principal war service was in North and South Carolina until the spring of 1864, when his brigade was ordered to Virginia. He was present at Cold Harbor, Drewry's Bluff, and Petersburg. In the battle on the Weldon railroad in August he was so badly wounded as to be unable to rejoin his command until a few days before the surrender at Greensboro. His appointment as brigadier general was dated May 17, 1862. After the war General Clingman practiced law and engaged in exploring and measuring the peaks of the Allegheny range. One of the highest mountains in the eastern United States bears his name. He died at Morgantown, North Carolina, November 3, 1897, and is buried in Riverside Cemetery, Asheville, North Carolina.

Howell Cobb, born at "Cherry Hill," Jefferson County, Georgia, September 7, 1815, was graduated from the University of Georgia in 1834, and admitted to the bar two years later. He served in Congress from 1843 to 1851, and was Speaker of the House from 1849 to 1851, when he was overwhelmingly elected governor of Georgia on a Union platform. He returned to Congress in 1855, and was appointed Secretary of the Treasury by President Buchanan in 1857. Upon the election of Lincoln in 1860, he advocated immediate secession. He was a strong candidate for president of the new Confederacy, (99) and was presiding officer of the Montgomery convention which brought it into being. For a time, he served in the Provisional Congress after Jefferson Davis' election; then he took the field as a soldier, being appointed brigadier general to rank from February 12, 1862, and major general from September 9, 1863. Cobb rendered distinguished service in the field, but probably his most important contribution to the Confederate cause was as commander of the District of Georgia. There, as representative of the Richmond administration, he strove to resolve the differences between Davis and Governor Joseph E. Brown. He did not long survive the war, dying in New York City while on a business trip, October

9, 1868. General Cobb is buried in Oconee Hill Cemetery, Athens, Georgia.

Thomas Reade Rootes Cobb, like his brother, Howell, was born at "Cherry Hill," Jefferson County, Georgia, on April 10, 1823. After graduation from the University of Georgia, he took up the law as a profession. Both as advocate and constitutional lawyer he attained great reputa-

tion. He edited twenty volumes of Georgia supreme court reports (1849-57), prepared *A Digest of the Statute Laws of the State of Georgia* (1851), and compiled a new state criminal code (1858-61). Before and during the convention which took Georgia out of the Union, Cobb was recognized as a potent influence for the secession cause, and was elected, along with his brother,

a delegate to the Montgomery convention, which established the Confederacy, and later to the Provisional Congress. Resigning from the latter to enter field service, he recruited Cobb's Legion and was commissioned as colonel. The Legion performed gallant service in the Seven Days battles, at Second Manassas, and in the Maryland campaign; and Cobb was promoted brigadier general on November 1, 1862. On December 13 following, while defending the celebrated "sunken road" at Fredericksburg, his thigh was shattered by a musket ball and he bled to death in a nearby dwelling, which was being used as a field hospital during the battle. He is buried in Oconee Hill Cemetery, Athens, Georgia, near his brother.

Philip St. George Cocke was born at "Bremo Bluff," in Fluvanna County, Virginia, April 17, 1809, and was graduated from West Point in 1832. After less than two years service in the old army he resigned to manage his extensive plantation interests in Virginia and Mississippi. Cocke became renowned for his progressive methods of farming and served as president of the Virginia Agricultural Society, besides contributing numerous articles to agricultural journals north and south. He was also much interested in the Virginia Military Institute, on whose

board of visitors he served for nine years. Upon the secession of Virginia he was appointed a brigadier general in the state service, and upon the transfer of the state troops to the Confederacy, a colonel in the Provisional Army. He was promoted brigadier on October 21, 1861. He commanded the 5th brigade of General Beauregard's forces at First Manassas. After eight months in the field he returned in shattered health to his home, "Belmead," in Powhatan County, where on December 26, 1861, he took his own life. First buried on his estate, his remains were removed in 1904 to Hollywood Cemetery, Richmond, where they now lie.

Francis Marion Cockrell was born near Warrensburg, Missouri, on October 1, 1834. After graduation from Chapel Hill College in Lafayette County, in 1853, he studied law and was admitted to the bar in 1855. In 1861 he allied himself with the cause of the South, and in command of a company of Missouri militia, fought at Carthage, Wilson's Creek, and Elkhorn. He was promoted through grades to colonel. His regiment, in the brigade of General John S. Bowen, was at Grand Gulf, after which he commanded the Missouri brigade at Vicksburg. Captured and paroled there, he was appointed brigadier general to rank from July 18, 1863. In the spring of 1864 General Cockrell led his brigade in the Atlanta campaign and subsequently into Tennessee with General Hood. He was severely wounded at Franklin on November 30, 1864. In the spring of 1865 he was

captured at the capitulation of Mobile, Alabama. Subsequent to the war he resumed his law practice in Missouri, from which state he was elected to the United States Senate in 1874 and served continuously for thirty years. He was later a member of the Interstate Commerce Commission by appointment of President Theodore Roosevelt. General Cockrell died in Washington on December 13, 1915, and is buried in Warrensburg.

Alfred Holt Colquitt was born at Monroe, Georgia, April 20, 1824. Graduated from Princeton in 1844, he afterwards studied law and was admitted to the bar. At the conclusion of the Mexican War, throughout which he had served as a staff major, he commenced the practice of his profession, and in 1852 was

elected to the United States Congress, serving one term. A member of the Georgia legislature in 1859, he became a Breckinridge Elector in 1860 and a member of the state secession convention the following year. Colquitt was elected colonel of the 6th Georgia Infantry in May 1861, with which he was present on the Peninsula, in the Seven Days battles, and at Sharpsburg, Fredericksburg, and Chancellorsville. He was promoted brigadier to rank from September 1, 1862. In 1864 he was in command at the battle of Olustee, Florida, returning thereafter to the Army of Northern Virginia, to which his brigade was attached during the siege of Petersburg. He was paroled at Greensboro, North Carolina, on May 1, 1865. General Colquitt was elected governor of Georgia in 1876 and made a notable record in reorganizing the state finances. At the expiration of his second term as governor in 1882 he was elected to the United States Senate, in which he occupied a seat until his death at Washington, March 26, 1894. He is buried in Rose Hill Cemetery at Macon, Georgia, his home for many years.

Raleigh Edward Colston, by birth a Frenchman, and the adopted son of a Virginia physician sojourning in France, was born in Paris, October 31, 1825. (100) In 1842 he was sent to the United States and entered the

Virginia Military Institute, from which he was graduated four years later. He remained at the Institute as professor of French until 1861, when he was appointed colonel of the 16th Virginia Infantry. Promoted brigadier general on December 24, 1861, Colston commanded a brigade in the Peninsular campaign and in April 1863 was assigned a brigade in Stonewall Jackson's corps. After the battle of Chancellorsville, in which he commanded Trimble's Division, not altogether successfully, he was transferred from the Army of Northern Virginia. He then served under General Beauregard in the defense of Petersburg, and subsequently at Lynchburg. Following the war he conducted a military school in North Carolina; then accepted a colonelcy in the Egyptian army. Returning to the United States in 1879, he was soon reduced to

poverty by the loss of his savings, and, crippled by injuries sustained in the service of the Khedive, he spent the last two years of his life in the Confederate Soldiers' Home in Richmond, where he died, July 29, 1896, and where he lies buried in Hollywood Cemetery.

James Conner was born at Charleston, South Carolina, September 1, 1829, and was graduated from South Carolina College at the age of twenty. He entered the legal profession, in which he soon attained distinction, and was made United States district attorney in 1856. In this office he prosecuted the celebrated case of the slave ship *Echo.* Entering Confederate service as a captain in the Hampton Legion, Conner was present

at First Manassas, becoming colonel of the 22nd North Carolina Infantry immediately after the battle of Seven Pines, a regiment with which he served until his promotion to brigadier general on June 1, 1864. At Gaines's Mill, during the battles of the Seven Days, his leg was broken by a rifle ball, a wound which kept him from duty for two months. After temporarily commanding successively Generals McGowan's and Lane's brigades, he was assigned to General Kershaw's, which he led in the Shenandoah Valley campaign of 1864 until the amputation of his leg, resulting from a wound received in a skirmish at Cedar Creek on October 13. (101) Resuming his law practice after the close of the war, General Conner was elected attorney general of South Carolina in 1876, after which he established the legality of the election of General Wade Hampton as governor of the state. He died in Richmond, Virginia, June 26, 1883, and is buried in Magnolia Cemetery, Charleston.

Philip Cook, a Georgian, was born in Twiggs County, July 31, 1817, and was educated at Oglethorpe University and the University of Virginia Law School. He was graduated from the latter in 1841. On the outbreak of the Civil War he volunteered as a private with the 4th Georgia Infantry. He was soon made regimental adjutant. After the

Seven Days battles he was promoted lieutenant colonel, and after Sharpsburg, colonel. Cook succeeded to the command of General Doles' brigade upon the latter's death at Bethesda Church, and was commissioned brigadier general to rank from August 5, 1864. He sustained the last of several wounds during the Confederate assault on Fort Stedman on the morning of March 25, 1865, while leading his brigade in the last tactical offensive attempted by the Army of Northern Virginia. He was captured in the hospital at Petersburg after the Federal breakthrough on April 2, and was paroled at the end of July. Resuming his law practice in Americus, Georgia, General Cook served in Congress from 1873 to 1883, and was secretary of state of Georgia from 1890 until his death, May 21, 1894, at Atlanta. (102) He had also been a state senator before and during the war and a member of the state constitutional convention of 1865. General Cook is buried in Rose Hill Cemetery, Macon, Georgia.

John Rogers Cooke, son of Brevet Major General Philip St. George Cooke, U.S.A., and brother-in-law of General J. E. B. Stuart, (103) was born at Jefferson Barracks, Missouri, June 9, 1833. He was educated at Harvard and in 1855 was commissioned directly into the United States Army as a 2nd lieutenant, 8th Infantry. When Virginia seceded, he and his brother-in-law promptly resigned their commissions and cast their lot with the Confederacy, while the older Cooke adhered to the Union,

opening a breach which was not to be healed until years after the war. (104) Cooke's promotion was rapid, and in April 1862 he was elected colonel of the 27th North Carolina Infantry. He participated with great gallantry in all the campaigns in Pennsylvania, Virginia, and Maryland. He was promoted brigadier general on November 1, 1862, after being wounded no less than seven times. At the close of hostilities he became a merchant in Richmond. During his later life he was prominently identified with civic affairs there, being one of the founders of the Confederate Soldiers' Home in that city. General Cooke's death occurred at Richmond on April 10, 1891, (105) where he is buried in Hollywood Cemetery. Cooke's outstanding record, attested to by superiors and subordinates alike, makes it apparent that no more capable brigadier served in the Southern armies.

Douglas Hancock Cooper, a native of Mississippi, was born November 1, 1815, probably in Amite County, where his father, a physician and Baptist preacher, was discharging his ecclesiastical duties at the time. After attending the University of Virginia from 1832 to 1834, the son returned to Mississippi and engaged in planting in Wilkinson County. During the Mexican War he served as captain of the 1st Mississippi Rifles, and in

the tribes from their original lands. He died at Old Fort Washita in the Chickasaw Nation (in what is now Bryan County, Oklahoma) April 29, 1879, and is buried in the Fort cemetery in an unmarked grave. (106)

Samuel Cooper, ranking general officer in the Confederate service and Adjutant and Inspector General throughout the war, was born in Dutchess County, N. Y., June 12, 1798. (107) Graduated from West Point in 1815, his long and faithful service in the United States Army was rewarded in 1852 by his appointment as Adjutant General. He had meantime married a sister of Senator James M. Mason of Virginia and had become identified with that state and with

1853 was appointed by President Franklin Pierce U. S. agent to the Choctaw Nation in Indian Territory. In 1861 he was deputed by the Confederate government to secure the allegiance of the Indians, and was commissioned colonel of the 1st Choctaw and Chickasaw Mounted Rifles. He commanded the Indians at Elkhorn and at Newtonia, Missouri, and was subsequently promoted brigadier general to rank from May 2, 1863. His last important military service was rendered as commander of the Indian brigade in General Sterling Price's second invasion of Missouri. After the war General Cooper prosecuted the claims of the Choctaws and Chickasaws against the Federal government, claims arising out of nonperformance by the government in connection with the removal of

the Southern cause. (108) He resigned from the old service on March 7, 1861 and was immediately appointed brigadier general (Regular) in the Confederate Army, and then general on August 31, 1861 to rank from May 16, 1861, being confirmed the day of appointment. Though he was never in field command, his organizational abilities and knowledge of routine procedure made his services invaluable to the Confederacy, particularly in the early days of the war. General Cooper, upon the surrender of the forces of General Johnston in May 1865, turned over the records of his office intact to the United States authorities, thereby making a priceless contribution to the history of the period. (109) Retiring to his farm near Alexandria, Virginia, he died there December 3, 1876. He was buried in Christ Church Cemetery, Alexandria.

Montgomery Dent Corse was born in Alexandria, Virginia, March 14, 1816. After a career which included service in the Mexican War as a captain of Virginia volunteers and several years' residence in California, he returned to Alexandria in 1856 and established himself in the banking business. An officer of militia in 1861, Corse was soon appointed colonel of the 17th Virginia Infantry, which as a part of Longstreet's and later Kemper's brigade, took part in

the battles of First Manassas, Yorktown, Williamsburg, Seven Pines, and the Seven Days. He took a remnant of fifty-six men of his regiment into the fight at Sharpsburg and came out with seven. After this he was promoted brigadier general (November 1, 1862) and given a brigade in Pickett's division. His brigade being on detached duty, was not present at Gettysburg. Thereafter he was in Tennessee, North Carolina, and in the siege of Petersburg and Richmond. During the final retreat after Five Forks, where his brigade had performed magnificently in the face of overwhelming odds, General Corse was one of several general officers captured at the battle of Sayler's Creek on April 6, 1865. Following his release from Fort Warren, he again engaged in the banking business.

During the last years of his life he was totally blind. General Corse died in Alexandria on February 11, 1895 and is buried there in St. Paul's Cemetery.

George Blake Cosby, a native of Louisville, Kentucky, was born on January 19, 1830, and received his early education in private schools. Graduated from the United States Military Academy in 1852, he resigned his commission in the old army one day after his promotion to captain in the 2nd Cavalry, May 10, 1861. As a staff major Cosby bore from General S. B. Buckner to General U. S. Grant the communication which opened negotiations for the surrender of Fort Donelson in February 1862. At the request of General Joseph E. Johnston he was promoted brigadier general to rank from January 20, 1863. He led a cavalry brigade in General Van

Dorn's command, later serving under J. E. Johnston in the campaign around Jackson, Mississippi, designed to relieve Vicksburg. During the last years of the war he was stationed in the Department of West Virginia and East Tennessee. Following the war General Cosby moved to Butte County, California, where he engaged in farming. Subsequently he held a number of state and Federal positions, among which were the secretaryship of the Board of State Engineers and membership on the West Point Board of Visitors. He committed suicide at Oakland, California, June 29, 1909, allegedly because of the effects of old wounds received in Confederate service. (110) His body was cremated and the ashes taken to Sacramento for burial in City Cemetery.

William Ruffin Cox was born at Scotland Neck, Halifax County, North Carolina, March 11, 1832. (111) He was educated and admitted to the bar in Tennessee and returned to North Carolina in 1857. Appointed major of the 2nd North Carolina Infantry in 1861, Cox was continuously with the Army of Northern Virginia during the next four years, being wounded no less than eleven times. His gallant conduct was particularly conspicuous at the battle of Spotsylvania Court House, after which he was promoted briga-

dier with temporary rank from May 31, 1864. Faithful to the bitter end, he was paroled at Appomattox with his brigade in the division of General Bryan Grimes (previously Robert Rodes'). After the close of the war General Cox entered politics in his native state and was elected to a number of offices in the U. S. government, serving in Congress from 1880 until 1886. He was also Secretary of the Senate from 1893 until 1900. Meantime he was prominent in the Masonic Order and in the councils of the Episcopal Church. He died in Richmond, Virginia, December 26, 1919, one of the last survivors among the general officers of the Confederacy, and was buried in Oakwood Cemetery, Raleigh, North Carolina.

George Bibb Crittenden was born at Russellville, Logan County, Kentucky, March 20, 1812. He was graduated from West Point in the class of 1832, and saw service in the Black Hawk War. Resigning from the army the following year, he later went to the Republic of Texas and served in the Texas Army. He was captured by the Mexicans in the Mier expedition of 1843. After his release, he fought in the Mexican War as a captain of U. S. Mounted Rifles, winning the brevet of major for gallant conduct. Remaining in the U. S. Army thereafter, he had attained the rank of lieutenant colonel when he resigned in 1861 to cast his lot with the Confederacy. His brother, Thomas Leonidas Crittenden, adhered to the Union and became a major general of U. S. volunteers. George was commissioned brigadier general in the Confederate Army

on August 15, 1861, and major general on November 9. As the result of disobedience of orders on the part of a subordinate (Zollicoffer), (112) who was killed in the battle, Crittenden was forced to attack the Federal General George H. Thomas at Fishing Creek (Mill Springs) under unfavorable circumstances and was badly defeated, losing his artillery and trains. (113) He resigned his commission of major general in October 1862 and served out the balance of the war in various subordinate capacities. He was subsequently librarian of the state of Kentucky, and died in Danville, November 27, 1880. He is buried in the State Cemetery at Frankfort.

Alfred Cumming was born at Augusta, Georgia, January 30, 1829, and was graduated from West Point in 1849. His old army service was principally in the West, where he was for two years aide-de-camp to General David E. Twiggs, and later accompanied the Mormon expedition of 1857-60 under General Albert Sidney Johnston. Cumming's uncle (of the same name) had been appointed governor of Utah to succeed Brigham Young. Resigning in January 1861, Cumming was first engaged in drilling Georgia volunteers, and was appointed lieutenant colonel of the 10th Georgia Infantry in June of that year, and colonel in

October. He was wounded at Malvern Hill and again at Sharpsburg, and promoted brigadier general, October 29, 1862. Transferred to General Pemberton's army, he fought throughout the Vicksburg campaign, and was captured upon the capitulation of the city in July 1863. After his exchange General Cumming was assigned a brigade in General Carter L. Stevenson's division of the Army of Tennessee, which he led until he was disabled by wounds at the battle of Jonesboro on August 31, 1864. After the war he farmed near Rome, Georgia, and was a member of the American Military Commission to Korea in 1888. He died at Rome, December 5, 1910, in his eighty-second year, and is buried in Augusta.

Junius Daniel was born at Halifax, North Carolina, on June 27,

1828. He was graduated from West Point in 1851 and served seven years in the army before he resigned to take charge of his father's plantation in Louisiana. Upon the secession of his native state in 1861 he was elected colonel of the 14th North Carolina Infantry, which he led in the Seven Days battles in Virginia. He was promoted brigadier general to rank from September 1, 1862. After service in North Carolina in the winter of that year, his brigade was assigned to General Robert E. Rodes' division of the 2nd Corps, Army of Northern Virginia. At Gettysburg the command suffered the greatest losses of any brigade in the corps on the first day of the battle, in which Daniel greatly distinguished himself. He was then continuously with General R. E. Lee's

army until May 12, 1864. On this date at the "Bloody Angle" of Spotsylvania Court House, he was mortally wounded while heroically striving to recapture the Confederate works "at the tip of the mule-shoe," which had been overrun by a Federal assault at dawn. He died the following day and was buried in the old churchyard at Halifax. (114)

Henry Brevard (115) **Davidson** was born in Shelbyville, Tennessee, January 28, 1831, (116) and when but fifteen years of age, enlisted as a private in the 1st Tennessee Volunteers for service in the Mexican War. For gallantry in action he was promoted sergeant, and received an appointment to West Point in 1848, where he was graduated in the class of 1853. After service on the frontier as an officer of dragoons, he resigned in 1861 and went into the Confederate Army with appointment as major in the Adjutant and Inspector General's Department. He was attached successively to the staffs of Generals Floyd, Buckner, A. S. Johnston, and Mackall, and was promoted to colonel. With Mackall he was captured at Island No. 10 by the Federal General John Pope in April 1862. (117) Commissioned brigadier general on August 18, 1863 and assigned to a command in Wheeler's cavalry corps, he was subsequently transferred to Vir-

ginia, where he operated under General Lomax in the Valley campaign of 1864. The close of the war found him in North Carolina, where he surrendered with General Joseph E. Johnston at Greensboro. General Davidson took up residence in California post bellum, engaged in civil engineering, was deputy secretary of state for some years. Toward the end of his life he became agent of the Southern Pacific Railroad at Danville. He died near Livermore, California, March 4, 1899, and is buried in Oakland. (118)

Joseph Robert Davis, a nephew of the President of the Confederacy, was born in Woodville, Mississippi, January 12, 1825, and was educated in Nashville and at Miami University in Oxford, Ohio. Trained in the law, he practiced his profession in Madison County, Mississippi, and was elected to the Mississippi senate in 1860. Entering Confederate service as captain of a company from Madison County, he was soon made lieutenant colonel of the 10th Mississippi Infantry, after which he served on his uncle's staff in Richmond with the rank of colonel. Commissioned brigadier general to rank from September 15, 1862, and confirmed by the Senate only after charges of nepotism were freely aired and his nomination once rejected, (119) Davis was assigned a brigade in the Army of Northern Virginia, which he led through some of the bitterest battles of the war. He fought at Gettysburg (where his command formed a support to Pickett in the celebrated charge of the third day),

in the Wilderness campaign, and at the siege of Petersburg. Paroled at Appomattox Court House in April 1865, he returned to Mississippi and resumed his law practice, spending most of the remainder of his life at Biloxi, where he died, September 15, 1896, and where he is buried in Biloxi Cemetery.

William George Mackey Davis, a native of Virginia, was born at Portsmouth, May 9, 1812. He ran away to sea at the age of seventeen. Later he engaged in various occupations, and ultimately settled in Apalachicola, Florida, where he soon gained prominence as a lawyer and cotton speculator. In 1861 he donated $50,000 to the Confederate cause, and recruited and equipped the 1st Florida Cavalry of which he was elected colonel. Promoted brigadier general on November 4, 1862, he served for a time in command of the Department of East Tennessee, resigning his commission on May 6, 1863. He subsequently and until the end of the war lived in Richmond, Virginia, and Wilmington, North Carolina. His principal wartime occupation thereafter seems to have been the operation of a fleet of blockade runners to Nassau. Settling in Jacksonville, Florida, after the close of hostilities, he later removed to Washington and resumed his law practice. General Davis died at Alex-

andria, Virginia, March 11, 1898, and is buried in Remington, Virginia. (120)

James Dearing was born at "Otterburne," Campbell County, Virginia, April 25, 1840. He was graduated at Hanover Academy and appointed to West Point in 1858. He resigned from the Military Academy on April 22, 1861, and entered Confederate service as a lieutenant of the Washington Artillery. He served in that arm until after the battle of Gettysburg, where he commanded a battalion of guns with rank of major. Dearing was then transferred to the cavalry and promoted colonel, and on April 29, 1864 was commissioned brigadier general. His brigade distinguished itself during the Petersburg campaign and until the evacuation of

Richmond, serving in General W. H. F. Lee's division. On the retreat to Appomattox on April 6, 1865, during an action at High Bridge, General Dearing was mortally wounded, while engaged in a pistol duel with the Federal General Theodore Read, who was killed. (121) The desperately wounded officer was taken to Lynchburg and lingered for some time in the Ladies' Aid Hospital, dying on April 23, 1865, two weeks after the surrender of the Army of Northern Virginia. Shortly before his death he was visited and paroled by his old West Point classmate, Brigadier General Ranald S. Mackenzie, U.S.A., then commanding in Lynchburg. The last Confederate general officer to die of wounds received in action, (122) he is now buried in Spring Hill Cemetery, Lynchburg.

Zachariah Cantey Deas, a cousin (123) of General James Chesnut, was born in Camden, South Carolina, October 25, 1819, but removed to Mobile, Alabama, as a youth. He saw military service in Mexico, and by 1861 had amassed a considerable fortune as a cotton broker. Soon after the secession of Alabama he recruited and equipped at his own expense the 22nd Alabama Infantry, which he commanded at Shiloh, where he was badly wounded. For a time during this battle he was in brigade command after the mortal wounding of General Gladden. Recovering in time to take part in General Bragg's invasion of Kentucky, he was promoted brigadier to rank from December 13, 1862. He led his brigade of five Alabama regiments at Murfreesboro, at Chickamauga

(where the command captured seventeen pieces of Federal artillery), at Chattanooga, and in all the subsequent engagements of the Army of Tennessee, serving with marked distinction untill he fell ill during the Carolinas campaign in the spring of 1865. At the close of hostilities General Deas moved to New York City, took up his former occupation of broker, and became a prominent member of the stock exchange. He died there on March 6, 1882, and is buried in Woodlawn Cemetery.

Julius Adolph de Lagnel, a native of New Jersey, was born near Newark, (124) July 24, 1827, (125) and was commissioned directly into the army as a 2nd lieutenant of artillery in 1847. Promoted 1st lieutenant in 1849, he resigned in 1861 to associate himself with the Confederate cause and was assigned to the staff of General Robert Selden Garnett as chief of artillery. De Lagnel made a gallant defense of the crest of Rich Mountain in July 1861 against a largely superior force of Federals, with a few companies of infantry and a single piece of artillery. Finally overwhelmed by Rosecrans' attack, while fighting his gun alone, he fell badly wounded, but managed to hide himself in a nearby thicket. After recovering in the home of a friendly mountaineer, he was ultimately captured while attempting to make his way to the Confederate lines disguised as a herder. Upon his exchange he was appointed and confirmed as brigadier general to rank from April 15, 1862, but declined the commission. Thereafter he served in the ordnance bureau in Richmond with the rank of lieutenant colonel, and was for a time inspector of arsenals. For many years after the war he engaged in the Pacific steamship service, dying in Washington, D. C., June 3, 1912, a few weeks before his eighty-fifth birthday. He is buried in Alexandria.

James Deshler was born at Tuscumbia, Alabama, February 18, 1833, the son of Pennsylvania parents, and was graduated from West Point in the class of 1854. He served in California; at Carlisle Barracks, Pennsylvania; against the Sioux; in the Utah

expedition; and in 1861 was stationed at Fort Wise, Colorado. He appears not to have formally resigned from the old army in 1861, but was dropped on July 15 for overstaying leave. Appointed a captain of artillery in the Regular Confederate service, Deshler went to Western Virginia in the command of General Henry R. Jackson, acting as brigade adjutant during the Cheat Mountain campaign. At t h e skirmish of Alleghany Summit, December 13, 1861, he was shot through both thighs. Having recovered, he was promoted colonel of artillery and assigned to the staff of General T. H. Holmes in North Carolina. He was Holmes' chief of artillery in the Seven Days battles, and later accompanied him to the Trans-Mississippi. Captured while in command of a brigade at Arkansas Post in January

1863, upon his exchange Deshler was appointed brigadier general on July 28 and assigned a brigade in General P. R. Cleburne's division of the Army of Tennessee. At the battle of Chickamauga, on September 20, 1863, he was instantly killed by a shell while examining the cartridge boxes of his men preparatory to an assault. He is buried in Oakwood Cemetery, Tuscumbia.

George Gibbs Dibrell was born at Sparta, Tennessee, April 12, 1822. Notwithstanding a scanty education, he became a successful merchant and farmer in his home town. In 1861 he was elected to the state convention as a Union delegate, but after the majority of the voters decided in favor of secession, he enlisted as a private in the Confederate Army. The following year he recruited the 8th Ten-

nessee Cavalry, which was attached to Bedford Forrest's command, with himself as colonel. Rising to brigade command in 1863, he served with Forrest until detached to join General Joseph E. Johnston at Dalton, after which time he served in the corps of General Joseph Wheeler. He was appointed brigadier general on January 28, 1865 to rank from July 26, 1864. After the fall of Richmond and during the flight of the Confederate government southward, he was in charge of the archives. He was finally paroled at Washington, Georgia, on May 9, 1865. After the war General Dibrell had a notable career as merchant, financier, and member of Congress (1874-84); he was also president of the Southwestern Railroad and principal developer of the Bon Air coal mines. The last years of his life were spent in Sparta, Tennessee, where he died, May 9, 1888, (126) and where he is buried.

Thomas Pleasant Dockery was born in North Carolina, probably in Montgomery County, on December 18, 1833. (127) His father, Colonel John Dockery, soon moved to Tennessee, and subsequently to Arkansas, where he established a large plantation in Columbia County, and where he was instrumental in constructing the first railroad in the state. The younger Dockery went into the Confederate Army

as colonel of the 5th Arkansas State Troops, later becoming colonel of the 19th Arkansas Infantry, which he commanded at the battle of Wilson's Creek. He participated in the battle of Corinth, and recrossing the Mississippi River with General Sterling Price, was for a time in command of a subdistrict in Arkansas. He commanded the 2nd brigade of General John S. Bowen's division at Vicksburg, where he was captured and paroled; and was commissioned brigadier general on August 10, 1863. In 1864, directing a brigade of Arkansas regiments, he took part in the battles of Jenkins' Ferry and Marks' Mills, during the campaign which arrested the advance of the Federal General William Steele. His property swept away by the war, General Dockery afterwards took up the profession of civil engi-

73

neering, and lived for some years in Houston, Texas. His death occurred in New York City on February 27, 1898. His body was taken to Natchez, the residence of his two daughters, for burial.

George Pierce Doles was born at Milledgeville, Georgia, May 14, 1830. He was educated in his home town and engaged in business there before the war. In 1861 he was captain of a militia company called the "Baldwin Blues." The company entered Confederate service as part of the 4th Georgia Infantry and was stationed near Norfolk during the first year of the war. Elected colonel of the regiment in May 1862, and joining the Army of Northern Virginia after the Seven Days battles, Doles was conspicuous at South Mountain and Sharpsburg, and was promoted brigadier on No-

vember 1, 1862. Continuing his gallant service at Fredericksburg, Chancellorsville, Gettysburg, the Wilderness, and Spotsylvania, he came to be esteemed one of the best brigadiers in the army. On June 2, 1864, near Bethesda Church, while supervising the entrenchment of his line, General Doles was instantly killed by the bullet of a Federal sharpshooter. His death was a prime example of the attrition at command level which overtook Lee's army during the fateful days of 1864, and which ultimately resulted in an impoverishment of officers qualified for their positions. He is buried in Milledgeville. (See Bibliography #224.)

Daniel Smith Donelson was born in Sumner County, Tennessee, on June 23, 1801, and was graduated from the Military Academy in the class of 1825, resigning the following year. Subsequently a planter in Sumner County, he was active in the militia, and served in the Tennessee house of representatives, being speaker of that body at the beginning of the Civil War. First commissioned brigadier general of state troops, he received the same appointment in the Confederate Army on July 9, 1861 and was assigned to command in Western Virginia under General W. W. Loring. After service in Charleston, South Carolina, he was ordered to join General Bragg at Tupelo,

Thomas Fenwick Drayton, a brother of Captain Percival Drayton of the Union Navy, was born in South Carolina, probably at Charleston, on August 24, 1808. He was graduated from West Point in the same class (1828) with Jefferson Davis, who was his lifelong friend. Drayton resigned from the army in 1836 to engage in planting and railroad construction. He also served in the South Carolina legislature. Early in the Civil War he was appointed a brigadier general in the Confederate Army (September 25, 1861) and commanded the unsuccessful defense of Port Royal. He was later attached to Longstreet's corps of the Army of Northern Virginia. He took part in the battles of Second Manassas, South Mountain, and Sharpsburg, but seems to have been

Mississippi, and commanded a brigade of Cheatham's division at Murfreesboro. In January 1863 he was given command of the Department of East Tennessee. Promoted major general on April 22, 1863, and confirmed the same day, to rank from January 17, 1863, General Donelson had meantime died on April 17 at Montvale Springs, Tennessee —a fact apparently unknown to the War Department at the time. In announcing his death, General Bragg referred to him as "Brigadier General." He was a nephew of Andrew Jackson, and a brother of the latter's private secretary and namesake, Andrew Jackson Donelson, who adhered to the Union cause during the war. (128) General Donelson is buried in the Presbyterian Cemetery at Hendersonville, Tennessee.

inefficient as a field commander, and was subjected to considerable criticism by his superior officers. (129) During the last two years of the war he was employed in minor departmental command and on boards of inquiry in the Trans-Mississippi Department. H i s post-bellum career was spent as a farmer in Dooly County, Georgia, until 1871, after which he became an insurance agent in Charlotte, North Carolina. He also acted as president of the South Carolina Immigrant Society until shortly before his death, which occurred in Florence, South Carolina, on February 18, 1891. He is buried in Charlotte.

Dudley McIver DuBose was born in Shelby County, Tennessee, October 28, 1834. After attending the University of Mississippi, he was graduated from the Lebanon (Tennessee) Law School, and was admitted to the bar in 1857. Having removed to Augusta, Georgia, in 1860, he entered Confederate service as a lieutenant, and was commissioned colonel of the 15th Georgia Infantry in January 1863. The regiment was present at Gettysburg in General John B. Hood's division, where it lost heavily, and in the subsequent movements of the 1st Corps of the Army of Northern Virginia. DuBose was promoted brigadier from November 16, 1864. Attached to General

Ewell's forces during the retreat from Richmond, he was captured along with that officer and a number of other generals at Sayler's Creek on April 6, 1865, and was not released from Fort Warren until July. He subsequently made his residence in Washington, Georgia, and resumed the practice of law. General DuBose was a Representative in Congress, 1871 to 1873, after which he resided in Georgia until his death, which occurred on March 2, 1883, in the town of his adoption. His wife was a daughter of General Robert Toombs. He is buried in Rest Haven Cemetery at Washington, Georgia.

Basil Wilson Duke was born in Scott County, Kentucky, May 28, 1838, and was educated at Centre College and Transylvania University Law School. The outbreak of war found him a member of the legal profession in St. Louis, where he warmly espoused the Southern cause and took a prominent part in the secession movement of the state. Duke then enlisted as a private in the Lexington Rifles, the company of his brother-in-law, John Hunt Morgan; and he was soon elected 2nd lieutenant. When this unit became a part of the 2nd Kentucky Cavalry he was appointed lieutenant colonel and later colonel. Taking a conspicuous part in all the operations of Morgan's command, Duke was captured during the celebrated raid into Ohio and Indiana and was a prisoner of war for more than a year. After his exchange he commanded in Eastern Kentucky and Western Virginia, and was promoted

brigadier general to rank from September 15, 1864. In the closing days his brigade acted as escort to Jefferson Davis and the fugitive Confederate government. After the war General Duke had a distinguished career as lawyer, legislator, a u t h o r , and editor. His own *Reminiscences* and his *Morgan's Cavalry* (see Bibliography ## 57, 207) rank high as charming and reliable accounts of the period. He was also a commissioner of Shiloh National Military Park from 1895 until his death in New York City, September 16, 1916. He is buried in Lexington, Kentucky. Mrs. Duke's sister was the wife of General A. P. Hill; her brother was John Hunt Morgan.

Johnson Kelly Duncan was born at York, Pennsylvania, March 19, 1827, and was graduated from West Point in the class of 1849. After service in Florida against the Seminoles and in the Northwest, where he helped to explore a route for the Northern Pacific Railroad, he resigned his army commission in 1855 to become superintendent of government construction in New Orleans. In 1861 he was chief engineer of the Board of Public Works of Louisiana. His residence and associations prompted him to cast his lot with the South, and he was soon commissioned colonel of artillery and placed in command of the coast defenses in and around

New Orleans, including Forts Jackson and St. Philip. He was promoted to brigadier general on January 7, 1862. After a stubborn defense, Duncan was forced to capitulate in April to the invading Federal fleet; he was captured and later exchanged. Upon his release he was appointed chief of staff to General Bragg, with whom he served but a few months before his death from fever at Knoxville, Tennessee, December 18, 1862. Perhaps because Knoxville was a Union stronghold, his remains were interred in the McGavock Cemetery at Franklin, Tennessee.

John Dunovant, (130) a native of South Carolina, was born at Chester, March 5, 1825. After service in the Mexican War as a sergeant of the Palmetto Regiment, he was commissioned directly into the regular U. S. Army in 1855 as a captain of the 10th Infantry. Resigning a few days after the secession of his state, he was commissioned major of militia, and shortly thereafter colonel of the 1st South Carolina Regulars in Confederate service. In June 1862, while in command of this regiment on John's Island, Dunovant was cashiered for drunkenness, and dismissal from the service was resoundingly endorsed by the President. (131) However, he was soon after appointed colonel of the 5th South Carolina Cavalry by Governor Pickens—a regiment which was ordered to Virginia in March 1864. Colonel Dunovant seemingly redeemed himself in the eyes of the President by gallant conduct in the brigade of General M. C. Butler, for on

August 22, 1864 Davis appointed him brigadier general with temporary rank. In the fighting following the capture of Fort Harrison, he was killed in action on the Vaughan Road south of James River on October 1, 1864. He is buried in the family ground three miles southeast of Chester.

Jubal Anderson Early was born in Franklin County, Virginia, November 3, 1816, and was graduated from West Point in 1837. After service against the Seminoles, he resigned the following year to study law and afterwards began practice in Rocky Mount, Virginia. He became a member of the house of delegates, commonwealth's attorney, and in the Mexican War was a major of Virginia volunteers. He voted against secession in the Virginia convention in April 1861, but promptly entered the Confederate Army as colonel of the 24th Virginia Infantry, which he led at the battle of First Manassas. He was promoted brigadier general to rank from July 21, 1861. He took part in all the engagements of the Army of Northern Virginia from 1862 till 1864. Promoted major general from January 17, 1863, he was prominent at Salem Church and in the Gettysburg campaign. At the Wilderness he commanded A. P. Hill's corps for a time, and was promoted lieutenant g e n e r a l from May 31, 1864. After the temporary retirement of General

Ewell from field duty, Early was given c o m m a n d of the 2nd Corps, and following Cold Harbor, Lee ordered him to the Shenandoah Valley against the Federal General Hunter. He drove Hunter westward into the mountains, defeated Wallace at Monocacy (Maryland), and was before Washington on July 11, 1864. The arrival of the 6th Corps of the Army of the Potomac from Petersburg forced Early to retreat into Virginia; but he struck back across the Potomac later the same month. His cavalry conducted wide-ranging and destructive raids and burned the town of Chambersburg, Pennsylvania. But in September, Early was defeated by Sheridan at Winchester and Fisher's Hill. A last surprise attack on Sheridan at Cedar Creek was repelled, and the remnant of Early's command was dispersed by General Custer at Waynesboro, Virginia, in March 1865. After the surrender he made his way to Mexico in disguise, and later returned to Lynchburg to resume his law practice. He b e c a m e the first president of the Southern Historical Society, and wrote his memoirs (see Bibliography ## 58, 59). The later years of his life were mainly occupied in supervising the drawings of the Louisiana Lottery and in an acrimonious effort to destroy the military reputation of General Longstreet. (132) He died and was buried at Lynchburg on March 2, 1894, "unreconstructed" to the end.

John Echols was born at Lynchburg, Virginia, March 20, 1823, and was graduated from Washington College (now Washington and Lee University. He studied law at Harvard and was admitted to practice in 1843. Prior to the Civil War he was commonwealth's attorney, member of the general assembly, and a delegate to the secession convention. After recruiting service in the western counties, Echols commanded the 27th Virginia Infantry at First Manassas with rank of lieutenant colonel, and was shortly afterwards promoted colonel. He was severely wounded at Kernstown during the Valley campaign of 1862, and was commissioned brigadier general to rank from April 16, 1862.

His later service was almost entirely in Western Virginia (save for a brief period at Cold Harbor), during which he participated in numerous engagements including the battle of New Market. After the war General Echols became a prominent businessman in Staunton, Virginia, and Louisville, Kentucky, helping to organize the Chesapeake & Ohio Railway out of the old Virginia Central, and serving on the board of visitors of the Virginia Military Institute and Washington and Lee University. A huge man, six feet four inches tall and weighing two hundred and sixty pounds, he was said to have rarely made an enemy and never lost a friend. He died in Staunton, May 24, 1896, and is buried there.

Matthew Duncan Ector was born in Putnam County, Georgia, on February 28, 1822, and was educated at Centre College, Kentucky. After admission to the Georgia bar in 1844, he served one term in the legislature and then removed to Henderson, Texas, where he was elected to the legislature of that state in 1855. Enlisting as a private in 1861, he was soon appointed adjutant of General J. L. Hogg's brigade, which he accompanied to Corinth, Mississippi. He was shortly thereafter elected colonel of the 14th Texas Cavalry. This regiment, dismounted, he led through General Bragg's invasion of Kentucky, and distinguished himself by hard fighting at the battles of Richmond and Murfreesboro. He had mean-time been commissioned brigadier general to rank from August 23, 1862. He was present at

Chickamauga, and returned from Mississippi to take part in the Atlanta campaign, during which he had a leg amputated because of wounds. This injury put an end to his active field service, although he participated in the defense of Mobile in the last days of the war. Returning to Texas, he resumed his law practice and was later elevated to the bench. At the time of his death in Tyler, Texas, October 29, 1879, General Ector was presiding justice of the Texas court of appeals. He was buried in Marshall, Texas. (133)

Stephen Elliott, Jr. was born at Beaufort, South Carolina, October 26, 1830. He attended Harvard for a time, and was graduated from South Carolina College in 1850. He then became a planter on Parris Island, South Carolina. Elliott was well-known as a yachtsman and fisherman, served in the South Carolina legislature, and captained a militia company—the Beaufort Volunteer Artillery. His service from 1861 until 1864 was entirely in his native state. He took part in the defense of Port Royal in November 1861, and was promoted from captain to colonel over the next three years. He was ordered to Petersburg in command of Holcombe's Legion, and after promotion to brigadier from May 24, 1864, he was assigned to command General N. G. Evans' old brigade. This com-

mand occupied the salient which was blown up by a Federal mine in the famed battle of the Crater, and Elliott was badly wounded, while making dispositions to resist the assault which followed. After being incapacitated for field service for several months, he joined General Joseph E. Johnston's army, near Bentonville, and was again badly injured. General Elliott was reelected to the legislature at the war's end, but exhausted by wounds and exposure, survived only a few months. He died at Aiken, February 21, 1866. He is buried at Beaufort in the Episcopal Churchyard. (134)

Arnold Elzey (Jones) was born at "Elmwood," Somerset County, Maryland, on December 18, 1816. He was graduated from West Point in 1837, at that time

dropping his patronymic for his more distinctive middle name. (135) He served first in one of the periodic Seminole uprisings, won a brevet for gallantry in Mexico, and was in command of the United States arsenal at Augusta, Georgia, at the outbreak of the Civil War. Resigning his commission of captain, 2nd Artillery, on April 25, 1861, he entered the Confederate Army as colonel of the 1st Maryland Infantry. He was promoted brigadier general for his services at the battle of First Manassas. He also distinguished himself during the Shenandoah Valley campaign of 1862 and in the beginning of the Seven Days' fighting around Richmond, where he was desperately wounded and incapacitated for many months. Upon his partial recovery, he was commis-

sioned major general on December 4, 1862, and was given command of the Department of Richmond, where he organized the Local Defense Brigade of government clerks. Towards the end of the war he acted as chief of artillery for the Army of Tennessee for a time, (136) but apparently did not take part in the invasion of Tennessee under General Hood. He was paroled at Washington, Georgia, on May 9, 1865. He spent the remaining five years of his life on a small farm in Anne Arundel County, dying in Baltimore, February 21, 1871, where he is buried in Green Mount Cemetery.

Clement Anselm Evans, a native of Stewart County, Georgia, was born February 25, 1833, and was educated in the schools of Lumpkin, Georgia, and at an Atlanta law school. He was licensed to practice before he was nineteen. A judge at twenty-two, he was state senator in 1859 and a Presidential Elector the following year. Enlisting in the 31st Georgia Infantry, he was commissioned major in November 1861, and colonel in April 1862. Virtually all of his service was with the Army of Northern Virginia in the division successively commanded by Generals Stonewall Jackson, Early, and John B. Gordon. Evans was present in every engagement from the Peninsular campaign onward, and while in divisional command at Appomattox, made the last captures of the army. His appointment as brigadier general was dated May 19, 1864. He was wounded five times during the war. Afterwards he engaged in a number of business ventures, and entered the Methodist Episcopal ministry. In 1892 he retired and devoted the remainder of his life to writing and to the affairs of the United Confederate Veterans, of which he had lately been commander-in-chief at the time of his death in Atlanta, July 2, 1911. His most notable historical contribution was made as editor of the twelve-volume *Confederate Military History,* published in 1899. (See Bibliography # 189). General Evans is buried in Atlanta.

Nathan George "Shanks" Evans was born at Marion, South Caro-

lina, February 3, 1824, and educated at Randolph-Macon College and at West Point, from which he was graduated in 1848. Following duty on the frontier as an officer of dragoons and cavalry, he resigned in 1861 to enter the service of the Confederacy. At First Manassas, Evans was in command of a small brigade on the extreme left of the line. He detected McDowell's turning movement in time to redeploy his troops and present a front to the enemy, which went far towards saving the day for the South. After Ball's Bluff (137) he was promoted brigadier general as of October 21, 1861. He was assigned a command which, because of its ubiquity, was known as the "Tramp Brigade." Evans was present at Second Manassas, South Mountain, and Sharpsburg; with Joseph E. Johnston's army during the Vicksburg campaign, and also at the battle of Kinston, N o r t h Carolina. From early in 1863 he was in constant difficulties because of his deportment. Tried for intoxication and acquitted, he was subsequently tried for disobedience of orders and again acquitted. General Beauregard removed him from command for a long period, considering him incompetent, and his brigade inspection reports reflected unfavorably on him as well. His career in the last part of the war was obscure. Subsequently he became principal of a high school at Midway, Alabama, where he died on November 23, 1868. General Evans is buried in Cokesbury, South Carolina. General M. W. Gary was his brother-in-law.

Richard Stoddert Ewell was born in Georgetown, D.C., February 8, 1817, and was graduated from West Point in 1840. He spent his entire ante-bellum career in the Southwest, winning a brevet for gallantry in the Mexican War prior to his resignation on May 7, 1861. He was commissioned brigadier general in the Provisional Army on June 17, 1861; major general on January 24, 1862; and lieutenant general, to succeed Stonewall Jackson in command of the 2nd Corps, on May 23, 1863. He fought with distinction at First Manassas, in the Valley campaign of 1862, the

Seven Days, and the Second Manassas campaign, where he lost a leg at the battle of Groveton. Equipped with a wooden replacement (concerning which he was not in the least sensitive), he commanded the 2nd Corps from Gettysburg to Spotsylvania, after which his health compelled his temporary retirement from active field duty. He subsequently was in charge of the Richmond defenses, and was captured at Sayler's Creek on April 6, 1865. After his release from Fort Warren, General Ewell resided on a farm near Spring Hill, Tennessee, where he died January 25, 1872. He was a bold and canny fighter as brigade and division commander, but the responsibility of directing a corps seemed to weigh too heavily on him. His performance at the grade of lieutenant general left something to be desired, particularly at Gettysburg, where his hesitation to exceed orders on the first day cost the Confederates Cemetery Hill, possession of which might have turned the Union withdrawal toward that position into a rout. He is buried in the Old City Cemetery, Nashville.

James Fleming Fagan was born in Clark County, Kentucky, March 1, 1828, and the family moved to Arkansas when he was ten. He served as a lieutenant in Colonel Archibald Yell's regiment in the Mexican War, and one term in the Arkansas legislature thereafter. Among the first in his state to recruit men for the Confederate cause in 1861, he became colonel of the 1st Arkansas Infantry, which he led at the battle of Shiloh. Commissioned

brigadier general to rank from September 12, 1862, Fagan was transferred to the Trans-Mississippi Department and took part in the battle of Prairie Grove, the repulse of Steele's Camden expedition, and the last invasion of Missouri by General Sterling Price. He was promoted major general to rank from April 25, 1864. Not paroled until June 20, 1865, his post-bellum career was devoted to planting and politics. His acceptance of the office of United States marshal from President Grant in 1875, and that of receiver for the Land Office two years later, possibly caused his defeat in 1890, when he was a candidate for state railroad commissioner. General Fagan's death occurred at Little Rock, September 1, 1893, and he is buried there in Mount Holly Cemetery. His first wife was a sister of General W. N. R. Beall.

Winfield Scott Featherston, "Old Swet," was born near Murfreesboro, Tennessee, August 8, 1820. (138) He fought in the Creek War at the age of seventeen, and was admitted to the bar in Mississippi, from which state he was elected to Congress, in 1847, and served four years. A resident of Holly Springs, Mississippi, in 1861, Featherston was elected colonel of the 17th Mississippi Infantry, which served with the Army of Northern Virginia during the year 1862. Featherston was commissioned brigadier to rank from March 4. Transferred to the Vicksburg area the following year, his brigade (a part of Loring's division) became separated from the main army under General Pemberton and thus escaped capture when the city capitulated. Continuing in General Loring's division in General Leonidas Polk's corps, he thereafter took part in all of the operations of the western army, and was paroled at Greensboro, North Carolina, in May 1865. Returning to his law practice in Mississippi, General Featherston became an important factor in the fight to overthrow the carpetbag regime of Governor Adelbert Ames, and served several terms in the state legislature. He was elevated to the bench in 1882, and was a member of the constitutional convention of 1890. He died at Holly Springs, May 28, 1891, and is buried there.

Samuel Wragg Ferguson, a member of the class of 1857 at West Point, was born in Charleston, South Carolina, November 3, 1834. (139) After participating in the Mormon expedition of 1857-58, he resigned in March 1861, and was attached to the staff of General Beauregard, with whom he served until after the battle of Shiloh. He saw a good deal of cavalry duty in the Vicksburg campaign, and was appointed brigadier general from July 23, 1863. From then until the end of the war his brigade was a part of General W. H. Jackson's division; and after a tour of duty in Mississippi, was mainly employed on the flanks of Sher-

man's army in Georgia and the Carolinas. When, in A u g u s t 1864, his name was suggested for promotion to major general, his superior, General Joseph Wheeler, strenuously objected, stating that he was a trouble maker and that his command was notorious for desertion. (140) General Ferguson lived for more than a half century after the close of hostilities, making his home for the most part in Greenville, Mississippi, where he studied law and was admitted to the bar. He was president of the board of Mississippi levee commissioners for several years, and in 1885 was appointed by President Arthur to the Mississippi River Commission. His death occurred at Jackson, Mississippi, February 3, 1917, and he is buried there.

Charles William Field was born at "Airy Mount," Woodford County, Kentucky, April 6, 1828, and was graduated from West Point in the class of 1849. After resigning his United States commission in May 1861, he was first appointed colonel of the 6th Virginia Cavalry. He was later commissioned brigadier general to rank from March 9, 1862 and transferred to the infantry. His brigade was in the Seven Days battles, at Cedar Mountain, and in the engagement of Second Manassas, where Field received a desperate w o u n d . During his long convalescence, he served for a time as superintendent of the

Bureau of Conscription in Richmond. On February 12, 1864 he was promoted major general and assigned to the command of General Hood's old division of the 1st Corps. This he led with marked distinction through the remaining campaigns of the Army of Northern Virginia, and was finally paroled at Appomattox Court House. General Field had a varied post-bellum career. He engaged in business for a time, was in the service of the Khedive of Egypt, was doorkeeper of the national House of Representatives, was a civil engineer in government employ, and was superintendent of the Hot Springs, Arkansas, reservation. He died in Washington, D.C., on April 9, 1892, and is buried in Loudon Park Cemetery, Baltimore. (141)

Joseph Finegan, a native of Clones, Ireland, was born November 17, 1814. He migrated in his early twenties to Florida, where he first established himself as a planter and subsequently built a lumber mill in Jacksonville. He later moved to Fernandina and was associated with United States Senator David L. Yulee in railroad construction. A member of the secession convention in 1861, he was placed in charge of military affairs for the state by Governor Milton, and on April 5, 1862 was commissioned brigadier general in the Confederate Army. He was commander of the District of Middle and East Florida until after the battle of Olustee, in which he was in nominal command of the troops engaged. Transferred with a bri-

gade of Florida regiments to Virginia in May 1864, Finegan took part in the battle of Cold Harbor, continuing to serve with the Army of Northern Virginia until March 20, 1865, when he was again ordered to duty in Florida. After the war he was a member of the Florida state senate (1865-66) and a cotton broker in Savannah, Georgia. The last years of his life were spent in Rutledge, Florida, where he died on October 29, 1885. General Finegan is buried in the Old City Cemetery, Jacksonville, Florida. (142)

Jesse Johnson Finley was born in Wilson County, Tennessee, November 18, 1812, and educated at Lebanon. After service as captain in the Seminole outbreak of 1836, he pursued the study of law and was admitted to the bar. Finley changed his residence several times ante bellum, and in the space of ten years, served in the legislatures of Arkansas and Florida and as mayor of Memphis, Tennessee. Meanwhile he continued his law practice. Elevated to the Florida bench in 1852, he was appointed Confederate district judge for the state in 1861, but resigned to enter the army as a private in April 1862. Soon promoted to colonel of the 6th Florida Infantry, he took part in the Kentucky campaign under General Kirby Smith and was present at Chickamauga the following year. Commis-

sioned brigadier general from November 16, 1863, and assigned to the command of the Florida infantry regiments in the Army of Tennessee, Finley led his brigade with great credit at Chattanooga and in the Atlanta campaign. He was twice severely wounded, and was incapacitated for further field duty after the battle of Jonesboro. After the war General Finley served a part of three contested terms in the national House of Representatives, and in 1887, was refused a seat in the United States Senate because of a technicality. He died in Lake City, Florida, November 6, 1904, and is buried in Gainesville.

John Buchanan Floyd was born at "Smithfield," Montgomery County, Virginia, June 1, 1806,

89

and was graduated from South Carolina College in 1829. He had a most remarkable, if controversial, career. A lawyer by profession, he lost a large fortune and his health in a cotton-planting venture in Arkansas. He was elected to the Virginia house of delegates in 1847, and governor of the state in 1848, serving until 1852. As a reward for Floyd's political activities in the state election of 1855, President Buchanan appointed him his Secretary of War in 1857, a post which he occupied until his resignation on December 29, 1860. This was precipitated by the refusal of Buchanan to order Major Anderson back from Fort Sumter to Fort Moultrie. Floyd was subsequently bitterly criticized in the North for alleged transfer of unwarranted numbers of arms from Northern to Southern arsenals,

and for the substitution of his own acceptances to War Department contractors for a large sum of Indian Trust bonds in the Interior Department. Commissioned a Confederate brigadier on May 23, 1861, he served in the West Virginia campaign under General R. E. Lee, and was then ordered to Fort Donelson. His transfer of the command to General Pillow, and his escape with his own troops prior to the surrender of the work, caused his removal by Jefferson Davis, without a court of inquiry, on March 11, 1862. He was commissioned a major general of Virginia state troops, but his health soon broke and he died near Abingdon, Virginia, August 26, 1863, and was buried there. (143)

John Horace Forney, a younger brother of William Henry For-

ney, was born at Lincolnton, North Carolina, August 12, 1829, and was educated at West Point, where he was graduated in 1852. His parents had meantime moved to Alabama, and upon his resignation from the old army at the outbreak of war, he entered Confederate service as colonel of the 10th Alabama Infantry. He was promoted brigadier to rank from March 10, 1862, and major general on October 27. There appears to be no valid reason for his rapid promotion, inasmuch as his war record was neither particularly impressive, nor was he accorded special approbation by his superiors. He saw action at First Manassas in Kirby Smith's brigade and was wounded at Dranesville in December 1861. He held departmental command in Alabama and Florida and directed a division of General John C. Pemberton's army at Vicksburg, where he was captured. His subsequent service was in the Trans-Mississippi Department, where he succeeded to the command of John G. Walker's division. For a time he was supernumerary and without a command. After the war General Forney was a farmer and civil engineer in Alabama. He died in Jacksonville, September 13, 1902, and is buried there. (144)

William Henry Forney, a brother of John Horace Forney, was also born at Lincolnton, North Carolina, on November 9, 1823, and

accompanied his parents to Alabama in 1835. He was graduated from the state university in 1844. His law school studies were interrupted by a year's military service in Mexico, after which he was admitted to the bar and began practice. He was a member of the Alabama legislature in 1859. Forney entered the Confederate Army as captain of the 10th Alabama Infantry, quickly earning a reputation as a fearless and efficient officer. He was left on the field at Gettysburg covered with wounds, was captured, and remained in prison for more than a year. He had meantime been promoted through grades to colonel. After his exchange he was assigned to command a brigade in General Mahone's division of the 3rd Corps, which he led until the surrender at Appomattox. His commission as brigadier general dated from February 15, 1865. After the war he resumed his law practice in Jacksonville, Alabama and served in Congress continuously from 1875 to 1893. He died at Jacksonville, January 16, 1894, and is buried there.

Nathan Bedford Forrest was born in Bedford County, Tennessee, on July 13, 1821. A self-made man with little formal education, he had acquired by the time of the war a substantial fortune as a planter and slave dealer. He enlisted as a private in the 7th Tennessee Cavalry and raised and equipped at his own expense a battalion of mounted troops, of which he was elected lieutenant colonel in October 1861. Taking part in the defense of Fort Donelson, he asked and received permission to lead out his men before the surrender. He was

elected colonel of the 3rd Tennessee just before Shiloh, and two months later, in June, assumed command of a cavalry brigade in the Army of Tennessee. The next month he captured the Union garrison with its stores at Murfreesboro, and on July 21, 1862 he was promoted brigadier. With a fresh command he succeeded in severing Grant's communications in West Tennessee in December, and in May 1863 saved the railroad between Chattanooga and Atlanta. He took part in the Chattanooga campaign, until a quarrel with General Bragg led him to ask for and receive from President Davis an independent command in North Mississippi and West Tennessee. He was promoted major general, December 4, 1863. By this time his fame as a leader of cavalry had become almost legendary, and his exploits went unabated till the end of the war. In April 1864 he captured Fort Pillow; in June he brilliantly routed a superior force at Brices Cross Roads; and the following month he stood off General A. J. Smith at Tupelo. These lightning blows of Forrest's caused Sherman some alarm for the safety of his communications. In November and December 1864 he served under Hood in the Tennessee campaign and was in command of all cavalry. He was promoted lieutenant general to rank from February 28, 1865. General Forrest was finally overwhelmed by greatly superior forces at Selma, Alabama, in April 1865. After the close of hostilities he was again a planter and was for some years president of the Selma, Marion & Memphis Railroad, which he helped to promote. He died, probably of diabetes, at Memphis on October 29, 1877, and is buried there. (145) Many military critics pronounce him the foremost cavalry officer produced in America.

John Wesley Frazer was born in Hardin County, Tennessee, January 6, 1827. After graduation from West Point in 1849, Frazer did routine garrison duty at various points, resigning his United States commission in March 1861. Appointed lieutenant colonel of the 8th Alabama Infantry, he soon resigned to assume the colonelcy of the 28th, which he led

in the Kentucky campaign. He was appointed brigadier general on May 19, 1863, and was sent with three regiments of Georgia and North Carolina troops and a battery to oppose the Federal occupation of East Tennessee. After fortifying Cumberland Gap, Frazer learned that Knoxville had already been occupied by the Federal General Burnside and that General Buckner had been forced to retreat toward Chattanooga. He forthwith surrendered unconditionally to Burnside, an action which was severely criticized and which probably caused the rejection of his nomination as brigadier by the Senate. (146) Apparently never paroled or exchanged, he was still a prisoner at Fort Warren on April 16, 1865, when he and fourteen other Confederate generals imprisoned there, wrote a letter to General Grant expressing their regret for the assassination of President Lincoln. For some years after the war General Frazer operated a plantation in Arkansas, later moving to New York City, where he prospered in business. He died there as the result of an accident, March 31, 1906, and is buried in Clifton Springs, New York. (147)

Samuel Gibbs French, born in Gloucester County, New Jersey, November 22, 1818, was graduated at West Point in 1843, and won two brevets in Mexico as an artillery officer, being severely

wounded at Buena Vista. He acquired by his marriage a plantation in Mississippi and resigned from the army in 1856 to supervise it. At the outbreak of war he was chief of ordnance of his adopted state, and was appointed brigadier general on October 23, 1861, and major general to rank from August 31, 1862. After intermittent service in the neighborhood of Richmond, Petersburg, and Suffolk, and in North Carolina, French was attached to J. E. Johnston's forces at Jackson, Mississippi, and on May 18, 1864, joined the Army of Tennessee. He led his division until the battle of Nashville, but was relieved from duty before that battle because of an eye infection that had rendered him temporarily almost blind. After his recovery he served at Mobile until its surrender in April 1865. His

post-war career spanned forty-five years, during which he was again a planter, later retiring to Florida where he died at Florala, April 20, 1910, in his ninety-second year. His autobiographical *Two Wars* (see Bibliography # 62), published in 1901, is especially interesting for references to his Northern birth and upbringing a n d t h e consequent reaction, North and South, to his Confederate adherence. General French is buried in Pensacola.

Daniel Marsh Frost was born in Schenectady County, New York, August 9, 1823, and was graduated from West Point in the class of 1844. After winning a brevet for gallantry at Cerro Gordo during the war with Mexico, he resigned from the army in 1853 and engaged in manufacturing in St. Louis. He also served in the state senate, on the Board of Visitors

94

to the U. S. Military Academy, and was active in the Missouri militia, being a brigadier general in that body in 1861. As such, he surrendered Camp Jackson at St. Louis to the Federal General Lyon and was paroled. After his exchange he was appointed brigadier in the Confederate Army from March 3, 1862, and was offered command of a brigade of Missouri state troops at the battle of Elkhorn, but "declined so small a command, and watched the battle from a convenient height." (148) Frost served for a few weeks as General Bragg's inspector general and subsequently under General Hindman in Arkansas, being present at the battle of Prairie Grove. In the fall of 1863 his wife's banishment from their home near St. Louis and the resultant suffering to his family caused him to leave the army and go to Canada, apparently without going through the formality of submitting his resignation to the War Department. He was, in any event, dropped from the army rolls on December 9, 1863. (149) After the war he returned to his home in St. Louis County, where he engaged in agricultural pursuits until his death, October 29, 1900. He is buried in Calvary Cemetery, St. Louis.

Birkett Davenport Fry, born in Kanawha County, (West) Virginia, June 24, 1822, was educated at the Virginia Military

Institute and subsequently attended West Point with the class of 1846, although he did not graduate, but chose instead to study law. After service in the Mexican War as a 1st lieutenant of voltigeurs, he emigrated to California, where he remained until 1859, meantime accompanying the filibuster, William Walker, to Nicaragua. The outbreak of the Civil War found him in Alabama engaged in cotton manufacturing. Appointed colonel of the 13th Alabama Infantry, he took his regiment to Virginia and was severely wounded at Seven Pines, again at Sharpsburg, and a third time at Chancellorsville. He performed notable service at Gettysburg, where he commanded Archer's brigade after the latter's capture. He participated in Pickett's historic charge, was again wounded near the Federal battle line, and fell into the hands of the enemy. By a special exchange he returned to the army in time to take a part in the preliminary stages of the siege of Petersburg, and was promoted to brigadier general on May 24, 1864. During the last months of the war, he commanded a district in South Carolina and Georgia. Emigrating to Cuba at the close of hostilities, General Fry returned to the United States in 1868 to embark on a successful business career in Alabama and Florida. In 1881 he removed to Richmond, where he was for ten years president of a cotton mill and where he died, January 21, 1891. He was buried in Montgomery, Alabama.

Richard Montgomery Gano, born in Bourbon County, Kentucky, June 17, 1830, was educated at Bacon College, Harrodsburg, Kentucky; Bethany College, Virginia; and Louisville University Medical School. Thereafter he practiced medicine in Bourbon County for eight years. Removing to Tarrant County, Texas, in 1859, he saw service against the Indians, and was a member of the legislature. He entered the Confederate Army as commander of a squadron in John Hunt Morgan's command, and participated in the Kentucky invasion of 1862 and in the Tullahoma campaign as colonel of the 7th Kentucky Cavalry. He was also for a time in command of Morgan's division. Later transferred to the Trans-Mississippi Department with rank of colonel, Gano was assigned to Indian Territory in command of a brigade of cavalry and artillery. After distinguishing himself in the Camden campaign against Steele, in which he was wounded, he was first assigned to duty as brigadier general by General Kirby Smith, later receiving official appointment from President Davis to rank from March 17, 1865. After the war General Gano returned to Texas and entered the ministry of the Christian Church, which he served faithfully for more than forty-five years. Active in the affairs of the United Confederate Veterans until the last, he died in Dallas, March 27, 1913, and is buried there. (150)

96

Franklin Gardner, born in New York City, January 29, 1823, (151) and appointed to the Military Academy from Iowa, was graduated four numbers above U. S. Grant in the class of 1843. He subsequently won two brevets for gallantry in Mexico. Appointed lieutenant colonel of infantry in the Regular Confederate States Army on March 16, 1861, Gardner apparently did not go through the formality of resigning from the old army; he was dropped from the rolls on May 7. His early services were in Tennessee and Mississippi. He was present at Shiloh in command of a brigade of cavalry, after which he was promoted brigadier general to rank from April 11, 1862. He engaged in General Bragg's invasion of Kentucky where he was in command of a brigade in General Withers'

division of General Leonidas Polk's corps. He was appointed major general to rank from December 13, 1862, and was confirmed on June 10, 1864. Meantime Gardner was placed in command at Port Hudson early in 1863, a post which capitulated after a stubborn defense following the fall of Vicksburg. After being exchanged in August 1864, he was assigned to duty in Mississippi, serving toward the end of the war under General Richard Taylor. The few remaining years of his life were spent as a planter near Vermillionville (now Lafayette), Louisiana, where he died on April 29, 1873, and where he is buried. General Gardner had married into the Mouton family of Louisiana (152) as had his sister. His brother, however, took an active part in the war on the Union side, and his father, Colonel Charles K. Gardner, who had been adjutant general of the army during the War of 1812, although retired since 1818, also supported the Union, and was a clerk in the Treasury Department in Washington until his retirement in 1867. (153)

William Montgomery Gardner, a graduate of West Point in the class of 1846, was born at Augusta, Georgia, June 8, 1824. (154) Wounded and brevetted for gallantry in Mexico, he resigned from the old army in January 1861 and went to Virginia with the first troops from his

state as lieutenant colonel of the 8th Georgia. His leg was so badly shattered by a ball at First Manassas that he did not recover for a year and was incapacitated for active field service for the balance of the war. He was appointed a brigadier general during his convalescence, to rank from November 14, 1861, and although maimed for life, he subsequently commanded the District of Middle Florida, participated in the battle of Olustee, and in 1864 was assigned to the command of military prisons east of the Mississippi. During the closing weeks of the war he was commandant of the post at Richmond, Virginia. When peace was declared General Gardner returned to Georgia, living first near Augusta and later at Rome. The last years of his life were spent at the home of a son in Memphis, Tennessee,

where he died, June 16, 1901, and where he is buried in Elmwood Cemetery. (155)

Samuel Garland, Jr., a collateral descendant of President James Madison, was born at Lynchburg, Virginia, December 16, 1830, and was graduated from the Virginia Military Institute in 1849 and from the University of Virginia Law School in 1851. He then practiced his profession in Lynchburg until the secession of the state, meantime organizing the Lynchburg Home Guard, a militia company of which he was elected the first captain. This unit was mustered into Confederate service as Company G of the 11th Virginia Infantry, and Garland was commissioned colonel of the regiment. He was present at First Manassas, Dranesville, and at Williamsburg, where he

was wounded. Promoted brigadier general on May 23, 1862, he
was assigned to a brigade in D. H.
Hill's division, which he commanded with distinction at Seven
Pines, in the battles of the Seven
Days, and in the Second Manassas campaign. Garland's brigade,
scarcely one thousand men, was
posted in Fox's Gap at South
Mountain to resist McClellan's
advance during the Maryland
campaign. During the fight of
September 14, 1862, he sustained
a mortal wound, from which he
died on the field. He is buried
in Lynchburg. (156)

Richard Brooke Garnett, a cousin of General Robert Selden Garnett, was born at "Rose Hill,"
Essex County, Virginia, November 21, 1817. (157) The cousins
graduated together at West Point
two numbers apart in the class of
1841. Richard then went to the
Florida War of 1841-42. His service thereafter was in the South
and West, although he saw no
active service in the war with
Mexico. Resigning in May 1861,
Garnett was commissioned a major in the Regular Confederate
Army and, on November 14,
brigadier general in the Provisional Army. He commanded the
Stonewall Brigade at Kernstown,
and was court-martialled thereafter by Stonewall Jackson, but
was never tried. In all probability Jackson's action was not justi-
fied. He was then assigned to
Pickett's division of Longstreet's
corps, with which he served at
South Mountain and Sharpsburg.
On the third day at Gettysburg
his brigade of five Virginia regiments was in the front rank of
Pickett's assault. Some twenty
yards from the Federal battle line
Garnett disappeared in the holocaust of flame and smoke, and a
few moments later his riderless
horse, streaming blood, came gal-
loping to the rear. It is supposed
that his sidearms and insignia of
rank were removed by a Federal
soldier, and that as a result, his
body was interred in a burial
trench with the unidentified Confederate dead. Since these soldiers were re-interred at various
points in the South some years
after the war, the location of Garnett's grave is unknown. Years
later his sword was found in a
Baltimore pawnshop. (158)

Robert Selden Garnett was the first general officer on either side to fall on the field of battle in the Civil War. A cousin of General Richard Brooke Garnett, he was born in Essex County, Virginia, December 16, 1819, and was graduated from West Point in 1841. Twice brevetted for gallantry in Mexico, he was one of the most accomplished of the younger officers of the old army when he resigned his commission of major in the 9th Infantry, April 30, 1861, to enter the service of the Confederacy. Garnett was almost at once appointed brigadier general in the Provisional Army (June 6, 1861), and ordered to Staunton to assume command in Northwestern Virginia. Entrenching on Rich Mountain, he was soon compelled by superior numbers to evacuate his position there and on Laurel Hill. Being closely pursued by the Federals under Generals McClellan and Rosecrans, he deployed his rear guard near Corrick's (159) Ford on Cheat River, July 13, 1861, and while directing the dispositions of a skirmish line and awaiting the arrival of other troops which had been sent for, he was mortally wounded. His body fell into the hands of the enemy, but was returned to his family and ultimately buried in the Green-Wood Cemetery, Brooklyn, New York. (160)

Isham Warren Garrott, a native of North Carolina, was born in either Wake or Anson County in 1816. (161) After graduation from the state university he studied law, and in 1840 moved to Marion, Alabama. He soon became prominent in local affairs and was elected to the legislature in 1845 and re-elected in 1847. A Breckinridge Elector in 1860, he was sent by Governor Moore the following year as commissioner to North Carolina, to enlist its aid in the secession movement. He later aided in recruiting the 20th Alabama Infantry, of which he was made colonel. With this regiment he was stationed at Mobile during 1861 and 1862. In the spring of 1863 his command was transferred to Mississippi as a part of General Edward D. Tracy's brigade, and helped in resisting Grant's advance at Port Gibson, and in the battle of Baker's Creek. Soon after Pem-

berton's retirement to the Vicksburg defenses, and four days before the investment of the city was made complete, Garrott was killed on the skirmish line, June 17, 1863, while he was firing a borrowed rifle at the enemy. His commission as brigadier general, to rank from May 28, 1863, was received at army headquarters after his death. He was buried in Vicksburg. (162)

Lucius Jeremiah Gartrell was born in Wilkes County, Georgia, January 7, 1821, and obtained his education at Randolph-Macon College, Virginia, and Franklin College, Georgia; after which he studied law and was admitted to the bar. He was successively solicitor general of the northern judicial district, member of the legislature, Presidential Elector in 1856, and from 1857 to 1861 a member of the United States Congress. Resigning his Congressional seat in January 1861, he organized the 7th Georgia Infantry, of which he was elected colonel, and led it at First Manassas. Having been elected to the Confederate Congress, he resigned his army commission in January 1862, and served until 1864 in the House of Representatives. In that year Gartrell was appointed brigadier general to rank from August 22. He proceeded to recruit four regiments of Georgia reserves, with which he did good service in opposing Sherman's advance into South Carolina. He was wounded near Coosawhatchie. After the surrender General Gartrell returned to his law practice in Atlanta, and in 1877 was a member of the state constitutional convention. Five years later he ran against Alexander H.

Stephens for the Democratic gubernatorial nomination, but was unsuccessful. He died at Atlanta, April 7, 1891, and is buried in Oakland Cemetery.

Martin Witherspoon Gary, a brother-in-law of General N. G. Evans, was born in Cokesbury, South Carolina, on March 25, 1831. Expelled from South Carolina College as the result of a rather humorous incident known as the "biscuit rebellion," he entered Harvard and was graduated in 1854. He then studied law and soon became a markedly successful criminal lawyer and a member of the South Carolina legislature. Entering the service of the Confederacy as a captain in the Hampton Legion, he commanded it at First Manassas after the wounding of Hampton and the death of Lieutenant Colonel

Johnson. First dismounted and later as cavalry, the legion was led by Gary, with the rank of colonel, throughout most of the war. He was promoted brigadier general from May 19, 1864, and had his brigade enlarged by three additional regiments. Commanding the last Confederate troops to leave Richmond, General Gary cut his way out after Lee's surrender at Appomattox and helped escort Jefferson Davis and his cabinet south. The last meeting of the cabinet took place in the home of Gary's mother at Cokesbury. A most effective stump speaker, he championed the cause of white supremacy after the war, along with Generals Hampton and Butler, and served four years in the state senate. Twice defeated for the United States Senate by his onetime associates, with whom he had broken politically, he died in Edgefield County, South Carolina, April 9, 1881, and is buried in Cokesbury.

Richard Caswell Gatlin was born in Lenoir County, North Carolina, January 18, 1809. He attended the University of North Carolina, and was graduated at West Point in the class of 1832. His extended ante-bellum career in the old army was marked by a brevet for gallant and meritorious service at the battle of Monterey in the Mexican War. Resigning his commission as major, 5th Infantry, in May 1861, he was appointed adjutant general of

North Carolina and colonel of infantry in the Regular Confederate Army. Promoted brigadier general in the Provisional Army to rank from July 8, 1861, he was assigned to command of the Department of North Carolina, and was thus charged with responsibility for the coast defenses of the state. Whether rightly or wrongly, he was accordingly made to bear the onus of the loss of Fort Hatteras and the subsequent surrender of New Bern, and was relieved on March 19, 1862. He resigned his Confederate commission the following September, but continued to serve as state adjutant general until the end of the war. After the close of hostilities General Gatlin engaged in farming in Sebastian County, Arkansas, dying at Mount Nebo (Yell County, on September 8, 1896, in his eighty-eighth year. He is buried in the National Cemetery at Fort Smith, Arkansas.

Samuel Jameson Gholson was born in Madison County, Kentucky, May 19, 1808. He moved to Alabama with his parents as a small boy; later he studied law and was admitted to the bar in 1829, and then moved to Mississippi. He was a member of the Mississippi state legislature on three different occasions in the 1830's; he also served parts of two consecutive terms in Congress; and, from 1839 until 1861, was United States district judge. When Mississippi seceded, Gholson enlisted as a private in the state forces and rose to brigadier general. His commission in the Provisional Army dated from May 6, 1864. Meanwhile, he was at Fort Donelson, at Iuka, and at

Corinth. During the balance of the war he operated in Alabama, Mississippi, and East Louisiana, where he was in command of a brigade of cavalry attached to Chalmers' division of Forrest's corps. He was severely wounded and lost an arm during an engagement at Egypt, Mississippi, in December 1864. Again elected to the state legislature in 1865, he served until passage of the Reconstruction Act of 1867, and was once more elected in 1878. General Gholson died at his home in Aberdeen, Mississippi, October 16, 1883, and is there buried in Odd Fellows Cemetery.

Randall Lee Gibson was born at the residence of his grandfather near Versailles, Kentucky, September 10, 1832, while his parents were there on a visit. He received his early education from a private tutor on his father's plantation, "Live Oaks," in Terrebonne Parish, Louisiana, and at Yale University, from which he was graduated in 1853. After completing his law studies, he spent several years abroad, and was for six months attaché of the American embassy in Madrid. At the outbreak of war he served for a time as aide-de-camp to Governor Moore of Louisiana and, in August 1861, was commissioned colonel of the 13th Louisiana Infantry, which he led at Shiloh, in the Kentucky campaign, and at Chickamauga. Promoted brigadier general from January 11,

1864, he was distinguished during the Atlanta campaign and in Hood's later invasion of Tennessee. His last military service was in the defense of Spanish Fort near Mobile, Alabama. General Gibson's post-bellum career was no less noteworthy. While practicing law in New Orleans, he was elected to the lower house of Congress in 1872, but was refused his seat. Again elected in 1874, he served until 1882, at which time he won a seat in the United States Senate, and was re-elected to that body in 1888, but died at Hot Springs, Arkansas, on December 15, 1892, before the expiration of his term. Besides his Congressional activities he served on the boards of numerous educational and scientific institutions, and was president of the board of administration of Tulane University from

1884 until his death. He is buried in Lexington, Kentucky.

Jeremy Francis Gilmer, born in Guilford County, North Carolina, February 23, 1818, was graduated in the class of 1839 at West Point, one number below Major General Henry Wager Halleck, who was for a time Commander-in-Chief of the armies of the United States during the Civil War. As an engineer officer in the old army, Gilmer saw service in almost all parts of the country from the time of his graduation until he submitted his resignation, which was accepted June 29, 1861. Gilmer's first Confederate duties were as chief engineer to General Albert Sidney Johnston; and he was wounded at Shiloh, where his commanding officer was killed. Promoted directly from colonel of engineers to

major general on August 25, 1863, he had meantime been chief engineer of the Department of Northern Virginia and chief of the engineer bureau of the Confederate War Department. He later assisted in laying out the defenses of Charleston and Atlanta. General Gilmer was perhaps the outstanding military engineer in the service of the South. From 1867 until his death in Savannah, December 1, 1883, he was president of the Savannah Gas Light Company. He is buried in Laurel Grove Cemetery, Savannah.

Victor Jean Baptiste Girardey, a native of France, was born on June 26, 1837, in Lauw, Department of Haut-Rhin. (163) When the boy was five years of age the family emigrated to the United States and settled in Augusta, Georgia. His father died soon after, and upon the death of his mother, he was left an orphan at the age of sixteen. He spent the next few years in New Orleans completing his education. He married there in 1858 a Louisianian of French descent and was presumably living in Augusta in 1861, although the records exhibit that he enlisted in Louisiana. His first appointment was that of 1st lieutenant and aide-de-camp from the state of Louisiana October 12, 1861. However, he was captain and assistant adjutant general on the staff of General A. R. Wright in the Seven Days

battles, and was nominated to the Senate at that grade as being from the state of Georgia. Girardey continued to serve on Wright's staff until May 21, 1864, and was repeatedly commended for his skill, bravery, and efficiency. He was transferred to the divisional staff of General Mahone in the same capacity. So outstanding was his performance at the battle of the Crater, in organizing and timing Mahone's counterattack after the explosion of the Federal mine, that four days later he was jumped to the grade of brigadier general with temporary rank from July 30. This was the only instance in the Confederate Army of such a promotion. On August 16, 1864, only thirteen days after he had received his commission, while commanding the brigade of which he had formerly been adjutant, General Girardey was killed near Fussell's Mill on the Darbytown Road, while resisting a Federal assault on the east end of the Richmond defenses. (164) He is buried in Augusta.

States Rights Gist was born in Union District, South Carolina, on September 3, 1831. After obtaining his early education at neighborhood schools and at a preparatory school in Winnsboro, he graduated from South Carolina College in 1852, and from Harvard University law school two years later. Returning to Union, he commenced the practice of law and served in the South Carolina militia, of which he became a brigadier in 1859, and adjutant and inspector general of the state after secession. He was present at First Manassas as volunteer aide to General Barnard E. Bee, and succeeded to

the command after the latter's death. On March 20, 1862 he was appointed brigadier general in the Provisional Confederate Army, and ordered to report to General Pemberton in South Carolina. Later he was sent to the Vicksburg area, where he served with Joseph E. Johnston in the campaign intended for the relief of the Mississippi fortress. He was then assigned to the Army of Tennessee. With his brigade, a part of W H. T. Walker's division, he fought gallantly at Chickamauga, Chattanooga, and in the Atlanta campaign. While attached to John C. Brown's division of Cheatham's corps at the battle of Franklin, during Hood's invasion of Tennessee, he was instantly killed while leading his men against the Federal breast-works, November 30, 1864. First buried in a private cemetery in Franklin, General Gist's remains now lie in Trinity Episcopal Churchyard, Columbia, South Carolina. (165)

Adley Hogan Gladden was born in Fairfield District, South Carolina, October 28, 1810. Moving to Columbia in 1830, he engaged in business as a cotton broker, served in one of the Seminole uprisings in Florida, and was appointed postmaster of Columbia by President Tyler. As major and lieutenant colonel of the Palmetto Regiment he rendered distinguished service in Mexico, and

was severely wounded in the assault on Belen Gate. Settling in New Orleans after the war, he first accepted the lieutenant colonelcy of the 1st South Carolina regiment in 1861; later, however, he resigned to become a member of the Louisiana secession convention. Appointed colonel of the 1st Louisiana Regulars, he took his regiment to Pensacola, where he was appointed brigadier general on September 30, 1861. The following spring, at the request of Braxton Bragg, Gladden was ordered to Corinth, Mississippi, where he led a brigade of mixed Alabama and Louisiana troops into the battle of Shiloh. Early on the first day he was struck by a fragment of shell, and his arm was amputated on the field. Taken to Beauregard's headquarters near

Corinth, he survived only a few days, dying on April 12, 1862. He is buried in Magnolia Cemetery, Mobile, Alabama. (166)

Archibald Campbell Godwin, born in Nansemond County, Virginia, in 1831, (167) and brought up in his grandmother's house in Portsmouth, left home at the age of nineteen to seek his fortune in California. He was successful as a miner and rancher in that state, and failed by but one vote to secure the Democratic nomination for governor in 1860. Returning to Virginia at the outbreak of war, he offered his services to President Davis and was commissioned major and assistant provost marshal in charge of Libby Prison in Richmond. Subsequently assigned to construct and organize the prison stockade at Salisbury, North

Carolina, Godwin recruited the 57th North Carolina Infantry, which he led at the battle of Fredericksburg in December 1862. He was present at the second battle of that name during the campaign of Chancellorsville, and also rendered distinguished service at Gettysburg. He was captured with most of his command in the action of Rappahannock Bridge in November 1863. Exchanged and promoted brigadier general to rank from August 5, 1864, he took part with his brigade in the subsequent Shenandoah Valley campaign as a part of Ramseur's division. At Winchester, September 19, 1864, he was instantly killed by a shell fragment. He is buried there in Stonewall Cemetery.

James Monroe Goggin was born in Bedford County, Virginia, October 23, 1820, and attended West Point in the class of 1842, although he did not graduate. Emigrating to the then Republic of Texas, he served in its army as a lieutenant, meantime acquiring landholdings in Waller County. He went to California in 1848, where he was employed in establishing mail routes. Later he moved to Memphis and was engaged there in the cotton brokerage business at the outbreak of the Civil War. In 1861 Goggin entered Confederate service as major of the 32nd Virginia Infantry and served on the Penin-

sula under General Magruder. Transferring to staff in the spring of 1862, he was assigned to Mc-Laws' division as assistant adjutant general. He served under the latter and his successor, J. B. Kershaw, through all the campaigns of the 1st Corps, and was on numerous occasions commended for gallantry and fidelity. In the temporary absence, due to wounds, of General James Conner, Goggin commanded the latter's brigade at the battle of Cedar Creek, and was appointed brigadier general to rank from December 4, 1864. The records exhibit that the appointment was subsequently cancelled, however, (168) and it would appear that he returned to staff duty with General Kershaw, (169) with whom he was captured at Sayler's Creek on April 6, 1865. (170)

Following the war he returned to Texas. He resided for a time in Waller County, and later at Austin, where he died, October 10, 1889, and where he is buried in Oakwood Cemetery. (171)

George Washington Gordon was born in Giles County, Tennessee, October 5, 1836, and was graduated from Western Military Institute in Nashville in 1859. He then took up the work of surveying. Entering Confederate service as drillmaster of the 11th Tennessee Infantry, he was successively promoted through grades until he became colonel of the regiment in December 1862. After service in East Tennessee, he took part in the battles of Murfreesboro, Chickamauga, Chattanooga, the Atlanta campaign, and Hood's invasion of

Tennessee. He was wounded and captured at Franklin. He had meantime been appointed brigadier general to rank from August 15, 1864. Returning home after his release from Fort Warren in July 1865, he took up the study of law and began practice at Memphis. In 1883 General Gordon entered public life, and held a number of administrative offices under city, state, and national government. In 1906 he was elected to Congress, and was twice re-elected. He was the last Confederate general to sit in that body. At the time of his death in Memphis, August 9, 1911, he was commander-in-chief of the United Confederate Veterans. He is buried in Elmwood Cemetery.

James Byron Gordon, a distant relation of Major General John Brown Gordon, was born at Wilkesboro, North Carolina, November 2, 1822, and educated at Emory and Henry College, Virginia. Before the Civil War he operated a mercantile business, engaged in farming, and was a member of the North Carolina legislature in 1850. In 1861 Gordon enlisted as a private in the Wilkes Valley Guards, of which he was elected 1st lieutenant and later captain. Subsequently, he was appointed major of the 1st North Carolina Cavalry, which went to the front in Virginia. His regiment was assigned

to Hampton's brigade of Stuart's Cavalry Corps in 1862, and fought in all the engagements of the latter command. Gordon was promoted colonel in the spring of 1863. Commissioned brigadier general on September 28, 1863, and assigned to the command of the North Carolina brigade, he took a gallant part in the engagements at Bethesda Church, Dumfries, and Buckland Mills. In the campaign of May 1864 Gordon's outposts were the first to confront Grant crossing the Rapidan. The day after the fight at Yellow Tavern, which resulted in the death of Stuart, General Gordon was mortally wounded near Meadow Bridge, while under attack by Sheridan's force, during the latter's raid upon Richmond. General Gordon died in the Confederate capital, May 18, 1864,

110

and his body was taken to Wilkesboro for burial. (172)

John Brown Gordon, born in Upson County, Georgia, February 6, 1832, had one of the most spectacular wartime and post-bellum careers of any civilian who fought for the Confederacy. He attended the University of Georgia, but did not graduate, and was trained in the law. In 1861 he was engaged in developing coal mines in the northwest corner of his native state, and at the time had had no previous military training. His army service began with election as captain of a mountaineer company known as the "Raccoon Roughs" and ended as a corps commander at Appomattox. In the interval he fought superlatively on every field in which the Army of

Northern Virginia participated, except when he was absent because of wounds. During the battle of Sharpsburg he was so severely wounded in the head that only a bullet hole in his hat prevented his drowning in his own blood as he lay on the ground unconscious. Shortly afterwards, on November 1, 1862, he was promoted brigadier general. He compiled a brilliant record in the Wilderness campaign, May to June 1864, and in the Shenandoah Valley under Jubal A. Early. His promotion to major general dated from May 14, 1864. (173) On the retreat from Petersburg he was in command of one-half of Lee's organized infantry. Returning to Georgia after the surrender, he took up residence in Atlanta and threw himself into the thick of the fight to secure the restoration of home rule to the state. For forty years he was the idol of the people of Georgia. He was three times elected to the United States Senate (1873-80 and 1891-97) and was once governor (1886-90). He wrote *Reminiscenses of the Civil War* (see Bibliography # 64). General Gordon was a prime mover in the organization of the United Confederate Veterans and became its first commander-in-chief, serving from 1890 until his death, January 9, 1904, at Miami, Florida. He is buried in Oakland Cemetery, Atlanta.

Josiah Gorgas, a native of Pennsylvania, was born at Running Pumps, Dauphin County, on July 1, 1818, and was graduated from West Point in 1841. In 1853 he was married to the daughter of ex-Governor Gayle of Alabama. Since he had served in the Ordnance Department during his entire old army career, it was natural that President Davis should appoint him Chief of Ordnance of the Confederate States in 1861, with rank of major. Gorgas rendered notable service throughout the war, and was finally promoted brigadier general to rank from November 10, 1864. He was largely responsible for keeping the armies supplied with powder, caps, bullets, and arms from a country in which the manufacture of these things was almost unknown be-

fore 1861. Gorgas is also due great credit for the Confederate attempt to break the stranglehold of the blockade. Foreign materiel was absolutely essential to the war effort in the South, and thus Gorgas early took a strong interest in blockade-running. With no real co-operation from the Secretary of War he bought five blockade-runners, that managed a large number of successful trips through the Federal squadrons. In the words of General Joseph E. Johnston: "He created the ordnance department out of nothing." After the war he went to Alabama, and for a time served as superintendent of the Brierfield Iron Works there. In 1868 he was elected vice-chancellor of the University of the South at Sewanee, Tennessee, and in 1878 president of the University of Alabama. General Gorgas died at Tuscaloosa, Alabama, May 15, 1883, and is buried there. See Bibliography # 65 for Gorgas' *Civil War Diary.*

Daniel Chevilette Govan was born in Northampton County, North Carolina, July 4, 1829, but was brought up in Mississippi, and attended the University of South Carolina. Joining in the gold rush to California in 1849 with his kinsman, Ben McCulloch, who was also to become a Confederate general officer, Govan returned to Mississippi in

1852, and then moved to Arkansas, in 1861, where he engaged in planting. Raising a company, which became part of the 2nd Arkansas Infantry, he became its lieutenant colonel and participated in all the campaigns of the western army, rising to the rank of brigadier general, from February 29, 1863. He was captured at the battle of Jonesboro during the Atlanta campaign. Surrendering with General Joseph E. Johnston in 1865, General Govan returned to his plantation in Arkansas, where he continued to live until 1894, when he accepted from President Cleveland a post as Indian agent in the state of Washington. The last years of his life were spent in the homes of one or another of his fourteen children in Tennessee and Mississippi. He died in Memphis on March 12, 1911, and is buried in Holly Springs, Mississippi.

Archibald Gracie, Jr., a native of New York City, was born December 1, 1832, and was educated in Heidelberg, Germany, and at West Point, from which he was graduated in 1854. He resigned from the army in 1856 to enter business with his father, then a merchant in Mobile. The same year he married Josephine Mayo of Richmond. As captain of the Washington Light Infantry, a Mobile militia company, Gracie entered Confederate service in the 3rd Alabama Infantry. After being promoted major of the 11th Alabama, he recruited the 43rd Alabama in the spring of 1862 and was elected its colonel. He was promoted brigadier

from November 4, 1862, and served in East Tennessee, in the Kentucky campaign, and at Chickamauga, where his brigade sustained some seven hundred casualties in two hours. He was subsequently severely wounded at Bean's Station, but recovered in time to serve under General Beauregard in Virginia in the campaign of May 1864. From then until his death his brigade was on duty in the Petersburg trenches. On December 2, 1864, while observing the enemy through a telescope, General Gracie was instantly killed by an exploding shell. The other members of his family, including his father, adhered to the Union and resided in New York during the war. The cordial relations which existed between father and son until General Gracie's d e a t h , furnish one of the striking examples of the divided allegiance which rent families of the period. The general is buried in Woodlawn Cemetery, New York City. (174)

Hiram Bronson Granbury was born in Copiah County, Mississippi, March 1, 1831, and was educated at Oakland College, Rodney, Mississippi. Removing to Texas in the early 1850's, he established himself in Waco, studied law, was admitted to the bar, and served as chief justice of McLennan County from 1856 to 1858, an office roughly com-

parable to that of chairman of a county board of supervisors. He recruited the Waco Guards in 1861, took it east, and was elected major of the 7th Texas Infantry in October of that year. After being captured and exchanged at Fort Donelson, he became colonel of the 7th Texas, serving in the Vicksburg campaign, at Chickamauga, and at Chattanooga. Granbury, who was in brigade command during the retreat from Chattanooga, was especially commended by his division commander, General Pat. R. Cleburne. Commissioned brigadier general to rank from February 29, 1864, he led the Texas brigade through the Atlanta campaign and into Tennessee with Hood. At the battle of Franklin, November 30, 1864, Granbury was one of six Confederate general officers killed or mortally wounded. He died along with Cleburne within a few rods of the Federal works. First buried near Franklin, his remains were removed twenty-nine years later to the town of Granbury, Texas, named in his honor. (175)

Henry Gray was born in Laurens District, South Carolina, January 19, 1816, and was graduated from South Carolina College (now the University of South Carolina) in 1834. Admitted to the bar, he shortly settled in Mississippi, where he was for some years district attorney of Winston County. After serving a term in the legislature, he ran unsuccessfully for Congress on the Whig ticket. He moved to Louisiana in 1851, and was a

Buchanan Elector in 1856. While a member of the Louisiana legislature in 1860, he was defeated for a seat in the United States Senate by but one vote; his opponent was Judah P. Benjamin. Upon the secession of Mississippi, Gray enlisted as a private in a regiment from that state; however, President Davis (an intimate friend) recalled him from this duty, and he was elected colonel of the 28th Louisiana Infantry, which he had organized at Davis' request. Gray led his regiment at Mansfield and Pleasant Hill during the Red River campaign, and was at times in brigade command. He was promoted brigadier general, March 17, 1865, while he was representing North Louisiana in the Confederate Congress, an office to which he had been elected in his absence and without his knowledge. After serving a post-bellum term in the Louisiana state senate, General Gray retired from public life, thereafter remaining in virtual seclusion until his death at Coushatta, Louisiana, December 11, 1892. (176) He is buried there in Springville Cemetery.

John Breckinridge Grayson, born at "Cabell's Dale," Fayette County, Kentucky, October 18, 1806, (177) was graduated from West Point in the class of 1826. His long service in the old army embraced action against the

Seminoles in Florida, and duty as Winfield Scott's chief of commissariat in the Mexico City campaign of 1847. He received the brevets of major for gallant and meritorious conduct at the battles of Contreras and Churubusco, and lieutenant colonel at Chapultepec. He resigned his commission of major-commissary of subsistence, July 1, 1861 (date of acceptance), while serving in New Mexico Territory. President Davis soon after commissioned him brigadier general in the Provisional Army, from August 15, 1861, and assigned him to command of the Department of Middle and Eastern Florida, with headquarters at Fernandina. However, he contracted a "disease of the lungs," to which he succumbed at Tallahassee on October 21, 1861. General Gray-

son's remains were brought to New Orleans for burial by his son, a captain in the Washington artillery, in St. Louis Cemetery No. 1. (178)

Martin Edwin Green, a native of Fauquier County, Virginia, was born June 3, 1815. In 1836, with his young bride, he went by wagon to Wheeling, (West) Virginia; then by boat down the Ohio and up the Mississippi to St. Louis; and then, again by wagon, to Lewis County, Missouri, where he established with his brothers a steam sawmill. At the outbreak of war in 1861 he organized a cavalry command in Northeastern Missouri, with which he joined General Sterling Price's army. This became a part of what was later known as "Green's Missouri Cavalry Regi-

ment," of which he was elected colonel. He was present at the capture of Lexington, at Elkhorn, and at Iuka and Corinth, east of the river. He was commissioned brigadier from July 21, 1862. In command of a brigade of General John S. Bowen's division, he opposed Grant's advance at Port Gibson, and subsequently took part in the campaign which culminated in the siege of Vicksburg. He was slightly wounded on June 25, 1863. Two days later, while looking over the parapet at a sap being run by the enemy some sixty yards away, he was struck in the head by a ball from the rifle of a Federal sharpshooter and almost instantly killed. He was first buried in a private lot in the city cemetery of Vicksburg; the exact present location of his remains seems to be unknown. He was a brother of U. S. Senator James Stephen Green of Missouri. (179)

Thomas Green was born in Amelia County, Virginia, January 8, 1814, and was graduated from the University of Nashville. He studied law under the tutelage of his father, a justice of the Tennessee supreme court. Removing to Texas in 1835, he fought at San Jacinto in the War for Texas Independence, and served with General Zachary Taylor's command in the Mexican War as captain of the 1st

Texas Rifles. In the interim he held the office of clerk of the Texas supreme court from 1841 to 1861. Green entered the Confederate Army as colonel of the 5th Texas Cavalry, which he led at the engagement of Valverde in New Mexico Territory. He subsequently distinguished himself at Galveston in January 1863, and under General Richard Taylor in Louisiana. He was promoted brigadier general from May 20, 1863. Since he had been in command of a cavalry division for some time, his further promotion to major general was requested by Taylor, but does not seem to have been forthcoming from Richmond. While he was participating in the battles of Mansfield and Pleasant Hill, during the Red

117

River campaign, General Green was killed in action at Blair's Landing, Louisiana, April 12, 1864, by a shell from one of the Federal gunboats which had accompanied Banks' expedition. General Green was a brother-in-law of General James P. Major by the latter's first wife. He is buried in Oakwood Cemetery at Austin, Texas. (180)

Elkanah Brackin Greer was born at Paris, Tennessee, October 11, 1825. (181) He moved to Mississippi as a young man and took part in the Mexican War as a member of the 1st Mississippi Rifles, whose colonel was Jefferson Davis. In 1848 he moved to Marshall, Texas, where he established himself as a planter and merchant, and became grand commander of the Knights of the Golden Circle in 1859. Commissioned colonel of the 3rd Texas Cavalry in July 1861, his first engagement was that of Wilson's Creek, Missouri, the following month. He was present at Elkhorn Tavern, where he was slightly wounded. Promoted brigadier general on October 8, 1862, he was soon after appointed chief of the bureau of conscription in the Trans-Mississippi Department. His time in this office was mainly spent in a courageous, but not altogether successful, endeavor to reconcile the laws of the Richmond government with those of the state of Texas. During the operations of 1864 General Greer also commanded the reserve forces of the Department. After the war he continued to live in Marshall, and died while on a visit to his sister in DeVall's Bluff, Arkansas, March 25, 1877. He is buried in Elmwood Cemetery, Memphis, Tennessee. (182)

John Gregg, a native of Lawrence County, Alabama, was born September 28, 1828, and moved to La Grange, Alabama, in boyhood. He received his early education at La Grange College, after which he studied law in Tuscumbia. Emigrating to Fairfield, Texas, in 1852, he was elected district judge in 1856, a member of the secession convention in 1861, and to the Provisional Confederate Congress the same year. Resigning his seat in

the latter body after the battle of First Manassas, he returned to Texas and recruited the 7th Texas Infantry, of which he was elected colonel. He and his regiment were surrendered at Fort Donelson the following February, and after exchange he was promoted brigadier general to rank from August 29, 1862. He was assigned to John B. Hood's division of Longstreet's corps, and his brigade was part of the "wedge" driven into the Federal line at Chickamauga. Gregg himself was severely wounded in the battle. After his recovery he was assigned to command of the Texas brigade, which he led with conspicuous bravery at the Wilderness and during the ensuing Overland campaign of 1864. He was killed in action on the Charles City Road below Richmond, on the morning of Octo-

ber 7, 1864. General Gregg is buried in Aberdeen, Mississippi. (183)

Maxcy Gregg was born at Columbia, South Carolina, August 1, 1814. (184) After attendance at South Carolina College, he studied law with his father and was admitted to the bar in 1839. He served for a time as major of the 12th U. S. Infantry in the Mexican War; he was honorably mustered out at the close of hostilities and resumed his law practice. A longtime leading exponent of the principle of states rights, Gregg was commissioned colonel of the 1st South Carolina Infantry (a six-months regiment) soon after the secession of the state, and served in Charleston Harbor until after the fall of Fort Sumter. He was commis-

sioned a brigadier general from December 14, 1861, and took a distinguished part in the Peninsular campaign of 1862 and the battles of Cedar Mountain, Second Manassas, Harpers Ferry, and Sharpsburg in General A. P. Hill's division. At Fredericksburg his command was in bivouac on the right of the Confederate line, and in the rear of a "gap" between the brigades of Archer and Lane. A melee resulted from the Federal penetration of the unprotected sector. While rallying his men—who, fearing no attack, had stacked arms—General Gregg was mortally wounded. He died in a nearby residence on December 15, 1862, and is buried in Columbia, South Carolina.

Richard Griffith was born near Philadelphia, Pennsylvania, January 11, 1814, and was graduated from Ohio University at Athens, Ohio, in 1837. Twenty years later he received an honorary master's degree from his alma mater. Removing to Vicksburg, Mississippi, soon after his graduation, he engaged in teaching until the outbreak of the Mexican War, when he enlisted in the 1st Mississippi Rifles. He was elected 1st lieutenant and regimental adjutant and formed a warm and lasting friendship with his commanding officer, Jefferson Davis. After returning from Mexico, Griffith was for some years a banker in Jackson, Mississippi, a United States marshal, and also served two terms as state treasurer. Shortly after the secession of the state he was elected colonel of the 12th Mississippi, and on November 12, 1861 became brigadier general in the Provisional Confederate States Army, assigned to command of a brigade of four Mississippi regiments in Virginia. His troops were in reserve at Seven Pines, but in the subsequent battles of the Seven Days were heavily engaged as a part of Magruder's division. At the battle of Savage's Station, June 29, 1862, he was mortally wounded, dying the same day in Richmond. (185) He is buried in Greenwood Cemetery, Jackson, Mississippi.

Bryan Grimes was born at "Grimesland," Pitt County,

North Carolina, November 2, 1828. Upon graduation from the University of North Carolina in 1848, he engaged in planting, travelled in Europe, and was a member of the state secession convention in 1861. Entering Confederate service as major of the 4th North Carolina, Grimes had a notable career in the Army of Northern Virginia, and was distinguished for his leadership under the most trying conditions. Except when disabled by wounds or illness, he took part in all the battles of the army. After his election as colonel in 1862, he was promoted brigadier general to rank from May 19, 1864, and major general from February 15, 1865—the last such appointment made in Lee's army. A furious fighter, his escapes from death were legendary, and he com-

manded one of the last attacks at Appomattox on the morning of the surrender. General Grimes then returned to his North Carolina plantation, where he resided for fifteen years. On the evening of August 14, 1880, he was almost instantly killed from ambush by one William Parker, a hired assassin, whose employers Grimes had been endeavoring to expel from the country as undesirable citizens. He is buried at "Grimesland." (186) See Bibliography # 67.

Johnson Hagood was born on February 21, 1829 at Barnwell, South Carolina After graduation from South Carolina Military Academy in 1847, he studied law and was admitted to the bar in 1850. He was active in the state militia in ante-bellum days and held in it rank of brigadier general. He was elected colonel of the 1st South Carolina Volunteers in 1861, participated in the reduction of Sumter, and took part in the battle of First Manassas, after which he returned to South Carolina with his regiment, and was promoted brigadier general on July 21, 1862. Part of Hagood's brigade arrived at Petersburg on May 6, 1864, and went into battle against Butler at Walthall's Junction, later fighting at Drewry's Bluff and Cold Harbor, and in the entrenchments until December, when it was ordered

121

Wade Hampton was born in Charleston, South Carolina, March 28, 1818, and was graduated from South Carolina College in 1836. He later served in both houses of the South Carolina legislature (1852-61). In 1861 he was reputed to be the largest landowner in the South. Organizing the Hampton Legion, of which he became colonel, and equipping it at his own expense, he took it to Virginia in time to participate in the battle of First Manassas, where he was wounded. He commanded an infantry brigade in the Peninsular campaign, and was appointed brigadier general on May 23, 1862. In July he assumed command of a brigade of J. E. B. Stuart's Cavalry Corps of the Army of Northern Virginia and participated in most

to the relief of Fort Fisher. General Hagood's last months in the war were spent attached to the forces under General Joseph E. Johnston, with which Hagood's brigade surrendered at Durham Station, North Carolina. Although he was included in the Sherman-Johnston convention of April 26, 1865, no record of his personal parole has been found. (187) During the reconstruction period he took a prominent part in the restoration of home rule. He was elected comptroller general of South Carolina in 1876 on the Hampton ticket, re-elected in 1878, and elected governor of the state in 1880. He died January 4, 1898, and is buried in the Episcopal Churchyard at Barnwell. See Bibliography #68.

of Stuart's operations from 1862 to 1864. He was again severely wounded at Gettysburg, and was promoted major general to rank from August 3, 1863. After the death of Stuart at Yellow Tavern, Hampton succeeded to command of the Corps. Though his resources were steadily diminishing, he performed brilliantly in keeping the Federal cavalry around Richmond and Petersburg at bay until winter. In January 1865 he was ordered, with part of his force, to J. E. Johnston in the Carolinas, where he remained until the surrender to Sherman. Hampton was promoted to lieutenant general on February 15, 1865 to rank from February 14. After the war he was instrumental in reclaiming his state from the Reconstruction regime. He was elected governor in 1876 over the carpetbagger D. H. Chamberlain, then in office. He was re-elected in 1878, and served as United States Senator from 1879 to 1891, in which year he finally yielded his domination of South Carolina politics to "Pitchfork Ben" Tillman. Subsequently he was for five years commissioner of Pacific Railways (1893-99). He died at Columbia, South Carolina, April 11, 1902, and is buried there. General Hampton was one of three civilians without formal military training to attain the rank of lieutenant general in Confederate service; the other two were

Richard Taylor and Bedford Forrest.

Roger Weightman Hanson, "Old Flintlock," (188) was born in Clark County, Kentucky, August 27, 1827. He served as a 1st lieutenant of Kentucky volunteers in the Mexican War, after which he studied law and commenced practice in his native state. In 1853 and 1855 a member of the Kentucky legislature, he was a Fillmore Elector in 1856, was defeated for Congress the following year, and stumped the state for the Presidential ticket of Bell and Everett in 1860. Though strongly conservative and first opposed to secession, Hanson in 1861 was enrolled in the Kentucky State Guard as colonel, and on September 3 of that year was com-

missioned colonel of the 2nd Kentucky Infantry in the Confederate service. Captured at Fort Donelson, while serving in General S. B. Buckner's command, and not exchanged until late in 1862, he was promoted brigadier general, to rank from December 13. He was assigned to the command of the Kentucky brigade of John C. Breckinridge's division, which he led at the battle of Murfreesboro. In a charge which cost his brigade four hundred casualties and the division as a whole seventeen hundred, Hanson was mortally wounded on January 2, 1863, and died two days later in a house near the battlefield. He is buried in Lexington, Kentucky. (189)

William Joseph Hardee, "Old Reliable," was born in Camden

County, Georgia, October 12, 1815, and was graduated from West Point in 1838. He was twice brevetted for gallantry in Mexico. Afterwards he served as commandant of cadets at the Military Academy and wrote the standard textbook, *Rifle and Light Infantry Tactics* (1853-55; published Philadelphia, 1861). When Georgia seceded from the Union he resigned his lieutenant colonelcy, January 31, 1861, and was appointed brigadier general on June 17, and major general on October 7, 1861. Early in the war he organized a brigade of Arkansas regiments and operated in that state until he was summoned to join General A. S. Johnston just before the battle of Shiloh. Subsequently he commanded a wing of the Army of Tennessee in Bragg's Kentucky campaign and at Murfreesboro, and was promoted lieutenant general to rank from October 10, 1862. He commanded a corps at Chattanooga and served under J. E. Johnston in the Atlanta campaign. In the last months he opposed Sherman in Georgia and South Carolina, and in the closing weeks was again under Johnston, his old friend and commander. After yielding Savannah and Charleston to Sherman's army, he finally surrendered in North Carolina in April 1865. Hardee had declined command of the Army of Tenneessee after the Chattanooga campaign, but his lack of confidence in John Bell Hood caused him to request transfer after the battle of Jonesboro, with the remark that his first refusal of command was not for all time. Along with Stonewall Jackson and Longstreet, General Hardee was recognized as one of the outstanding corps commanders in Confederate service. After the war he was a planter at Selma, Alabama. He died, while on a trip, at Wytheville, Virginia, on November 6, 1873, and is buried at Selma. General Hardee's niece was the wife of General William W. Kirkland.

William Polk "Gotch" (190) Hardeman was born in Williamson County, Tennessee, November 4, 1816, and moved to Texas in 1835. (191) He took part in the War for Texas Indepen-

dence, and later in the Mexican War under Ben McCulloch. As a captain of the 4th Texas Cavalry, his first Confederate service was in General H. H. Sibley's expedition into New Mexico, where he was present at Valverde and was commended by his superior. He was subsequently promoted lieutenant colonel and, in the latter part of 1862, colonel of his regiment. In the Red River campaign of 1864 Hardeman led his command at Mansfield and Pleasant Hill, and during the subsequent pursuit of Banks. Upon the recommendation of Kirby Smith, he was promoted brigadier general to rank from March 17, 1865. After the close of hostilities General Hardeman was until 1874 a planter; he then served as assistant sergeant-at-arms of the Texas house of representatives; as inspector of railroads; and, during the last years of his life, as superintendent of public buildings and grounds, a post that included supervision of the Texas Confederate Soldiers' Home. He died in Austin, April 8, 1898, and is buried in the State Cemetery there.

Nathaniel Harrison Harris was born at Natchez, Mississippi, August 22, 1834. He was a law graduate of the University of Louisiana (now Tulane), and settled thereafter in Vicksburg to practice his profession. In 1861

125

he organized the Warren Rifles, which was mustered into Confederate service as Company C, 19th Mississippi Infantry. Harris rose from captain to colonel of this regiment, meantime taking part in the various campaigns of the Army of Northern Virginia, including Chancellorsville and Gettysburg. Commissioned brigadier general from January 20, 1864, he was assigned to a brigade in Mahone's division of the 3rd Corps. He fought with great gallantry at Spotsyvlania, in the siege of Petersburg, and with particular distinction during the Federal assaults on Batteries Gregg and Whitworth. He was finally paroled at Appomattox Court House. Following the war General Harris resumed his law practice in Vicksburg, and later became president of the reor-

ganized Mississippi Valley & Ship Island Railroad, also serving for a time as register of the U. S. Land Office in Aberdeen, South Dakota. After 1890 he made his home in California, where he engaged in business with John Hays Hammond. He died at Malvern, England, August 23, 1900, while on a business trip. He never married. At his own request his remains were cremated, and the ashes conveyed to the Green-Wood Cemetery, Brooklyn, New York, for burial.

James Edward Harrison, a brother of General Thomas Harrison, was born in Greenville District, South Carolina, April 24, 1815. His family soon after moved to Alabama and then to Mississippi, where Harrison eventually served two terms in the

state senate. Moving to Texas in 1857, he settled near Waco, and in 1861, was commissioner to treat with the Indians on behalf of the state of Texas. He also became a member of the Texas secession convention. Harrison entered Confederate service in the 15th Texas Infantry, with which almost his entire army career was connected in comparatively minor operations west of the Mississippi River. He participated under the command of General Thomas Green in the Louisiana campaigns of 1863 and 1864. In both campaigns he received favorable mention by Green and General Richard Taylor. He was appointed brigadier general to rank from December 22, 1864. After the war he returned to Waco, where he was prominent in local affairs and served as a trustee of Baylor University until his death, February 23, 1875. He is buried in Waco. (192)

Thomas Harrison was born in Jefferson County, Alabama, on May 1, 1823, but was brought up in Monroe County, Mississippi. He moved to Texas in 1843 and studied law in Brazoria County. Later he returned to Mississippi, from which state he went to the Mexican War as a member of the 1st Mississippi Rifles. Living first in Houston after that war, he served a term in the Texas legislature from Harris County, and

then settled permanently in Waco. As captain of a volunteer militia company, he served for a time in West Texas, later entering the Confederate Army with his company in the 8th Texas Cavalry, better known as "Terry's Texas Rangers." He was promoted colonel just prior to the battle of Murfreesboro. His regiment served with Wheeler's command at Chickamauga and during the subsequent campaigns in Georgia and the Carolinas. He was appointed brigadier general in the last months of the war, to rank from January 14, 1865. Returning to Waco after the close of hostilities, General Harrison was elected district judge and was a Democratic Presidential Elector in 1872. His death occurred on July 14, 1891 at Waco, where he is buried. He was a brother

127

of General James E. Harrison.
(193)

Robert Hopkins Hatton, a native of Ohio, was born at either Steubenville or Youngstown, (194) November 2, 1826, and was graduated from Cumberland University at Lebanon, Tennessee, in 1847. While a tutor at the latter institution and later, while principal of a local school, he studied law, and was admitted to the bar in 1850. He served as a member of the state house of representatives from 1855 to 1857, was an unsuccessful candidate for governor in the latter year, and in 1859 was elected to Congress by the American (Know-Nothing) party, where he sat until 1861. Commissioned colonel of the 7th Tennessee Infantry on May 26, 1861, he served in the Cheat Mountain campaign under General W. W.

Loring that summer and fall, and under Stonewall Jackson the following winter. Hatton was promoted brigadier general on May 23, 1862, and eight days afterwards with his command (later Archer's) took part in the battle of Seven Pines under General Joseph E. Johnston. On the afternoon of May 31, 1862, while attacking in the tangled woods around Fair Oaks Station, he was instantly killed at the head of his brigade. He is buried in Cedar Grove Cemetery, Lebanon.

James Morrison Hawes was born in Lexington, Kentucky, January 7, 1824, (195) and was graduated from West Point in the class of 1845. He won the brevet of 1st lieutenant in Mexico. His later service in the old army was marked by a two-year tour of duty at the cavalry school in Saumur, France. For a time at the beginning of the Civil War, he was colonel of the 2nd Kentucky Cavalry, but resigned to accept a commission as major in the Regular Confederate Army. At the request of General Albert Sidney Johnston, he was promoted brigadier general in the Provisional Army, to rank from March 5, 1862, and assumed command of the cavalry in the Western Department of the Confederacy. Relieved at his own request after the battle of Shiloh, Hawes subsequently commanded a brigade in John C. Breckinridge's divi-

sion, served in Arkansas under General T. H. Holmes, led an infantry brigade at Milliken's Bend during the Vicksburg campaign, and in 1864 was in charge of the troops and fortifications on Galveston Island, Texas. When the war ended, General Hawes settled in Covington, Kentucky, where he engaged in the hardware business until his death, November 22, 1889. (196) He is buried in Highland Cemetery, Covington.

Alexander Travis Hawthorn was born near Evergreen, in Conecuh County, Alabama, January 10, 1825, and was educated at Evergreen Academy and Mercer University. He then studied law at Yale University for two years, from 1846 to 1847, and located in Camden, Arkansas, where he commenced his practice. When

the 6th Arkansas Infantry was organized in 1861, he was elected first its lieutenant colonel and then, the following spring, was appointed its colonel. He was present at the battle of Shiloh and took a gallant part in the assault on Fort Hindman, in 1863, during the attack on Helena, Arkansas. In 1864 he led a brigade in General Churchill's division, during the joint campaign of the Federal Generals Banks and Steele; and was a participant in the battle of Jenkins' Ferry. Meanwhile he had been promoted brigadier from February 18, 1864. He continued in Churchill's division until the close of the war. He emigrated to Brazil at that time, but returned to the United States in 1874 and engaged in business in Atlanta. Six years later General Hawthorn entered the Baptist ministry and was ordained, after which he

lived in Texas until his death, May 31, 1899, at Dallas. (197) He is buried in Marshall, Texas.

Harry Thompson Hays was born in Wilson County, Tennessee, April 14, 1820. He was brought up by an uncle in Wilkinson County, Mississippi, because of the early death of both of his parents. He was graduated from St. Mary's College in Baltimore and studied law in that city. He began the practice of his profession in New Orleans, where he soon became prominent as an advocate and politician. After distinguished service in the Mexican War, he was active in the Whig party during the 1850's and was a Presidential Elector on the Scott ticket in 1852. Entering the Confederate Army as colonel of the 7th Louisiana Infantry, he fought at First Manassas and in Jackson's Valley campaign of 1862. He was severely wounded at Port Republic. Returning to duty, he was commissioned brigadier general on July 25, 1862. Hays rendered outstanding service at Sharpsburg, Fredericksburg, Chancellorsville, Gettysburg, and in the beginning of the Wilderness campaign. Again badly wounded at Spotsylvania, he was transferred upon his recovery to the Trans-Mississippi, where in May 1865, after the Confederacy had virtually ceased to exist, he was "assigned to duty" as a major general by General Kirby Smith, and was paroled as such. Returning to New Orleans, he was appointed sheriff of Orleans Parish in 1866, but was removed from office by General Sheridan. Thereafter he practiced law until his death, from Bright's disease, August 21, 1876. General Hays is buried in Washington Avenue Cemetery, New Orleans.

Louis Hébert, a first cousin of General Paul O. Hébert, and a brother-in-law of General Walter H. Stevens, was born in Iberville Parish, Louisiana, March 13, 1820. His early education came from private tutors on the family plantation. Later he attended Jefferson College in Louisiana and was graduated third in the class of 1845 at West Point. He resigned two years later to take

engineer of the Confederate War Department in that state. He returned to Louisiana upon the cessation of hostilities and spent the remaining years of his life editing a newspaper and teaching in private schools in Iberville and St. Martin Parishes, in the latter of which his death occurred on January 7, 1901. He is buried in Breaux Bridge, Louisiana. (198)

Paul Octave Hébert, like his cousin Louis Hébert a native of Iberville Parish, Louisiana, was born December 12, 1818. A brilliant scholastic career was capped by his graduation first in his class at Jefferson College in 1836. He enjoyed the same distinction at West Point four years later, where William T. Sherman and George H. Thomas were his classmates. Resigning from the army in 1845, he had a notable career

charge of his father's sugar interests. During the years before the outbreak of the Civil War, he was an officer of militia, a member of the state senate, and chief engineer of Louisiana. Hébert entered the Confederate Army as colonel of the 3rd Louisiana Infantry. He fought with credit at Wilson's Creek, and was captured with a large part of his command at the battle of Elkhorn. After being exchanged, he was promoted brigadier general on May 26, 1862. He commanded the 2nd Brigade of General Henry Little's division of Price's army in North Mississippi, taking a gallant part in the battles of Iuka, Corinth, and in the siege of Vicksburg. He was subsequently and until the end of the war in charge of the heavy artillery in and around Fort Fisher, North Carolina; and also acted as chief

ante bellum, which included distinguished service in the war with Mexico (during which he received the brevet rank of colonel for gallantry at Molino del Rey), and election as governor of Louisiana in 1852. At the time he was said to be the youngest man ever elected to that office. Commissioned colonel of the 1st Louisiana Artillery early in 1861, he was soon appointed brigadier general, on August 17, and commanded in Louisiana for a time. Soon after he was transferred to what later became the Trans-Mississippi Department. He commanded successively the Department of Texas, the Galveston defenses, and the Subdistrict of North Louisiana; meantime he engaged in only one action of consequence, that of Milliken's Bend. During the post-bellum period he led the wing of the Louisiana Democrats which supported Horace Greeley for the Presidency of the United States in 1872. Suffering from cancer, he died in New Orleans on August 29, 1880, (199) and is buried near Bayou Goula, Louisiana.

Benjamin Hardin Helm was born at Bardstown, Kentucky, June 2, 1831, (200) and was graduated from West Point in the class of 1851. He resigned the following year to take up the study and practice of law. In 1856 he married Emily Todd, half sister of Mrs. Abraham Lin-

coln. He served in the Kentucky legislature in 1855-56, and was commonwealth attorney from 1856 to 1858. In April 1861 he was offered a commission as major-paymaster in the United States Army by Lincoln. However, Helm declined the President's proffer, in order to recruit the 1st Kentucky (Confederate) Cavalry, of which he was commissioned colonel on October 19, 1861. He was a brigadier general in the Provisional Confederate Army from March 14, 1862. He served in the Vicksburg area and in Louisiana until, in January 1863, he was assigned to the command of General R. W. Hanson's old brigade in General John C. Breckinridge's division of the Army of Tennessee. This he led in the operations around Tullahoma, and was at times in command of the division. At the battle of Chickamauga, on September 20, 1863, in the first assault of Lieutenant General Leonidas Polk's wing on the Federal breastworks, General Helm was mortally wounded. He died the day following and was first buried in Atlanta; his remains were moved to Elizabethtown, Kentucky, twenty-one years later.

Henry Heth, said to have been the only officer in the Army of Northern Virginia whom General Robert E. Lee addressed by his given name, (201) was born in Chesterfield County, Virginia, December 16, 1825. He was graduated from West Point in 1847 at the bottom of his class. He achieved his captaincy on routine frontier duty with the old army, from which he resigned in 1861.

He shortly afterwards became colonel of the 45th Virginia Infantry. After service in Western Virginia under General Floyd, where he was promoted brigadier from January 6, 1862, he took part in the Kentucky campaign in Kirby Smith's column. He joined the Virginia Army in February 1863 and was assigned a brigade in A. P. Hill's division, which he led at Chancellorsville. Heth had previously been named to the Senate as major general to rank from October 10, 1862. This nomination was rejected, and he was renominated to rank from May 24, 1863, and was confirmed on February 17, 1864. It was General Heth who touched off the Battle of Gettysburg. The evening before the conflict a reconnaissance by Pettigrew's brigade had developed the presence of Federal troops in the town. On the following morning Heth, against orders, but with the abetment of A. P. Hill, advanced his four brigades against General John Buford's Federal cavalry. Heth was severely wounded in the battle, but managed to participate in all the subsequent engagements of the army. He was finally paroled at Appomattox. After the war he engaged in the insurance business at Richmond. He died in Washington, D. C., September 27, 1899, and is buried in Hollywood Cemetery, Richmond.

Edward Higgins, a native of Norfolk, Virginia, (202) was born in 1821. (203) While living with an uncle in Iberville Parish, Louisiana, he received an appointment as midshipman in the Navy from that state at the age of fourteen. (204) For the next eighteen years he was almost continuously at sea, resigning as a lieutenant in 1854 in order to remain in the mail steamship service betwen New York and New Orleans. (205) At the outbreak of the Civil War, Higgins went into the Confederate Army as a captain of the 1st Louisiana Artillery, (206) serving as aide-de-camp to General Twiggs, while the latter was post commander at New Orleans. (207) Having been commissioned lieutenant colonel of the 21st Louisiana Infantry, (208) he made a gallant defense of Forts Jackson and St. Philip during the Federal invasion of Louisiana in 1862; later, with rank of colonel, he commanded the river batteries at Vicksburg. Captured and exchanged for the second time upon the capitulation of the city, (209) he was promoted brigadier general to rank from October 29, 1863, (210) and at the express request of General Dabney H. Maury, was detailed to the command of the bay and harbor defenses of Mobile. (211) From the last post he was apparently relieved, since in February 1865 he was residing in Macon, Georgia, "awaiting orders." (212) No record of his final capture or parole appears. (213) Following the war he engaged in the insurance and import business in Norfolk, and was prominent in local affairs. After a flood which occurred in Norfolk in 1872, General Higgins removed to San Francisco, there becoming agent for the Pacific Mail Steamship Company. He died in San Francisco on January 31, 1875, (214) and is buried in Holy Cross Cemetery.

Ambrose Powell Hill was born in Culpeper, Virginia, November 9, 1825, and was graduated from West Point in 1847. After service in Mexico and against the Seminoles, he resigned from the U. S. Army on March 1, 1861, entering Confederate service as colonel of the 13th Virginia In-

fantry. He was appointed brigadier general on February 26, 1862. After a distinguished performance at Williamsburg and in the Peninsular campaign, he was promoted major general, May 26, 1862. During the Seven Days battles Hill and his command were a tower of strength. Afterwards he fought under Stonewall Jackson until the latter's death. Hill's fast-marching "Light" Division was invaluable to Jackson at Cedar Mountain; and at Sharpsburg it was Hill who reinforced Lee in the nick of time to repell Burnside's assault. After Jackson was mortally wounded at Chancellorsville, he turned over command to Hill, who after being wounded himself, was replaced by J. E. B. Stuart. Hill was promoted lieutenant general from May 24, 1863, and afterwards led the newly-constituted 3rd Corps. This corps began the fighting at Gettysburg, where Hill directed the battle on the first day. He fought through most of the Wilderness campaign in 1864 and in the defense of Petersburg in 1864-65. He was killed by a Federal straggler on the Petersburg lines on April 2, 1865, soon after Grant's final assult, while attempting with a lone orderly to reach his troops. After advancement to corps command, Hill—the victim of what now seems to have been a psychosomatic ailment—performed somewhat unevenly and was often incapacitated. It is recorded that while Heth was inaugurating the battle of Gettysburg a few miles away, Hill, his corps commander, was found by General Lee in an ambulance at Cashtown. (215) Subsequently, at Bristoe Station, Hill's impetuous assault on the Federal position without proper reconnaissance cost the 3rd Corps more than thirteen hundred casualties. (216) Withal he was a magnificent combat officer, and when a major general was pronounced by Lee to be the best at that grade in the army. (217) He is buried in Richmond, under a monument to his memory. Hill married a sister of General John H. Morgan, and was thus also a brother-in-law of General Basil Duke.

Benjamin Jefferson Hill, a native of Tennessee, was born near

McMinnville on June 13, 1825. After receiving his education in the common schools of the neighborhood, he entered the mercantile business, and in 1855 was elected to the state senate. At the outbreak of war he was appointed colonel of the 5th Regiment, Provisional Army of Tennessee, which later became the 35th Tennessee Volunteer Infantry. The command was assigned to Cleburne's brigade, and Hill led it with marked gallantry at Shiloh, in Bragg's Kentucky campaign, and in the battles of Chickamauga and Chattanooga. In late 1863 he was appointed provost marshal of the Army of Tennessee and served in that capacity during the Atlanta campaign, being relieved August 24, 1864. He was promoted brigadier general on November 30, 1864, as a reward for distinguished services during Hood's Tennessee campaign. In this campaign he led a cavalry command and co-operated with Bate's division in the attempted destruction of the railroad and blockhouses between Murfreesboro and Nashville. In the last months of the war he commanded a brigade under Forrest, and participated in the latter's campaign against the Federal General Wilson. General Hill returned to McMinnville at the close of hostilities and re-entered the mercantile business. He subsequently engaged in the practice of law until his death in McMinnville, January 5, 1880, (218) where he is buried.

Daniel Harvey Hill, a West Pointer of the celebrated class of 1842, was born in York District, South Carolina, on July 12, 1821. He served in the Mexican War, in which he earned two brevets for gallantry, before resigning from the army in 1849 to become an educator. He was professor of mathematics at Washington College (afterwards Washington and Lee University) from 1849 to 1854, and at Davidson College from 1854 to 1859. From that time until the war he was superintendent of the North Carolina Military Institute. He entered Confederate service as colonel of the 1st North Carolina Infantry. Appointed brigadier general on July 10, 1861, he had on June 8

won the first "battle" of the war at Big Bethel Church on the Virginia Peninsula. (219) As major general, appointed March 26, 1862, he fought at Yorktown, Williamsburg, and Seven Pines under General J. E. Johnston. During the Seven Days, under General R. E. Lee, his division again distinguished itself; as it did later at Second Manassas, South Mountain, and Sharpsburg. In 1863 he assumed command of the Department of North Carolina. While Lee was at Gettysburg, Hill defended Richmond, and was promoted lieutenant general on July 11, 1863. He was then ordered to the Army of Tennessee under Bragg, and commanded a corps at Chickamauga in the Chattanooga campaign. His outspoken criticism of Braxton Bragg as a field commander caused not only his relief shortly thereafter, but also the President's refusal to nominate Hill to the Confederate Senate at the grade to which he had earlier appointed him. Except for an interval at Petersburg in 1864, he saw no further active service until the closing scenes in the Carolinas, where, as a major general, he commanded a division of Johnston's forces at Bentonville. After the war General Hill edited *The Land We Love,* a magazine (see Bibliography # 28). He was president of the University of Arkansas, 1877-1884, and of the Middle Georgia Military and Agricultural College, 1886–1889. He died at Charlotte, North Carolina, September 24, 1889, and was buried in Davidson College Cemetery, Davidson, North Carolina. General Hill was a brother-in-law of Stonewall Jackson and of Rufus Barringer.

Thomas Carmichael Hindman was born in Knoxville, Tennessee, January 28, 1828, and served with conspicuous heroism in Mexico as a 2nd lieutenant in the 2nd Mississippi Infantry. Upon his return from the war he was admitted to the state bar. After serving a term in the Mississippi legislature, he was elected and re-elected to Congress from Arkansas in 1858 and 1860, although he did not take his seat after his second election. He was instrumental in securing the secession

of his adopted state. He entered the Confederate Army as colonel of the 2nd Arkansas Infantry, and was promoted brigadier general from September 28, 1861, and major general from April 14, 1862. After commanding the Trans-Mississippi Department for a time, he was relieved by General Holmes. He fought the drawn battle of Prairie Grove, and subsequently commanded a division at Chickamauga, at Chattanooga, and in the Atlanta campaign, in which he was so severely wounded as to incapacitate him for further field duty. (220) He moved to Mexico upon the downfall of the Confederacy, but returned to Arkansas in 1868 and resumed his law practice. On September 28, 1868 he was assassinated in his home at Helena, Arkansas, by an unknown assail-

ant. This act was probably inspired by Hindman's determined and outspoken stand in opposition to the existing carpetbag regime. He is buried in Maple Hill Cemetery, Helena.

George Baird Hodge was born in Fleming County, Kentucky, April 8, 1828, and was graduated from the U. S. Naval Academy at Annapolis in 1845. Resigning his commission of passed midshipman (acting lieutenant) in 1850, he studied law, was admitted to the Kentucky bar, and attained some prominence in politics. He served in the legislature and was an unsuccessful candidate for Congress in 1852. Enlisting in the Confederate Army as a private in 1861, he was soon after elected to the Provisional Congress of the Confeder-

acy from his native state, and later to the First Regular Congress. Hodge seems to have divided his time betwen the legislative halls and the tented field. He served on the staff of General John C. Breckinridge with successive promotions to captain, major, and colonel. He later commanded a cavalry brigade under Wheeler, and in the closing months of the war was in command of the District of Southwest Mississippi and East Louisiana. He was twice appointed brigadier general by President Davis, first to rank from November 20, 1863, and on the second occasion from August 2, 1864. Both nominations were rejected by the Senate, the last on February 8, 1865. (221) He was, however, paroled as a brigadier at Meridian, Mississippi, May 10, 1865, (222) after which he returned to his home in Newport, Kentucky, and resumed his law practice. He was Presidential Elector for Greeley in 1872 and a member of the Kentucky senate from 1873 to 1877. He moved to Florida in the latter year, and died in Longwood, Orange County, August 1, 1892. (223) His body was taken to Newport for burial.

Joseph Lewis Hogg was born in Morgan County, Georgia, on September 13, 1806. At the age of twelve he moved with his parents to Tuscaloosa County, Alabama.

There he lived the life of a well-to-do planter until 1839, when he moved to Texas. He had meantime studied law, taken an interest in politics, and served in the militia. Soon elected to the eighth congress of the Texas Republic, Hogg served in the Mexican War as a private, after which he was elected to the state senate from Cherokee County, Texas, where he had settled and was practicing law. During the 1850's he actively sponsored railroad building in his adopted state, and by 1860 had attained a position of substantial prominence. Elected to the seccession convention the following year, he cast his ballot to take Texas out of the Union, and was shortly occupied in organizing troops with commission of colonel from the governor. Appointed a brigadier

general in the Provisional Army of the Confederate States on February 14, 1862, Hogg and his command were ordered to Corinth soon after the battle of Shiloh. Arriving there early in May 1862, he soon fell a victim to the dysentery then raging in Beauregard's camp; he died on May 16. It is stated that he never had opportunity to don a Confederate uniform, so rapidly was he stricken. First buried near Mount Holly School House, his remains were moved in 1918 to the Confederate Cemetery at Corinth. His son, James Stephen Hogg, was governor of Texas from 1892 to 1896. (224)

Robert Frederick Hoke was born at Lincolnton, North Carolina, May 27, 1837, and was educated in the local schools and at Kentucky Military Institute. The outbreak of war in 1861 found him managing his family's various manufacturing enterprises, which included a cotton mill and an iron-works. He entered the Confederate Army as a 2nd lieutenant of the 1st North Carolina Volunteers, with which he took part in the battle of Big Bethel. He was subsequently promoted major and lieutenant colonel of the 33rd North Carolina and colonel of the 21st. Hoke made a distinguished record on all the battlefields of the Army of Northern Virginia from the Seven Days to the campaign of Chancellors-

ville. He was severely wounded during Early's defense of Marye's Heights during the latter campaign. Meantime, he had been appointed brigadier general to rank from January 17, 1863. After his recovery he was stationed in North Carolina. For his brilliant exploit in capturing Plymouth and its garrison of three thousand Federals, he was promoted major general from April 20, 1864. He aided Beauregard in bottling up Butler at Drewry's Bluff and in the repulse of Grant at Cold Harbor; and his division was again ordered to North Carolina in December 1864. After participating in the defense of Fort Fisher, he served gallantly under Joseph E. Johnston at Bentonville and until the final surrender. His farewell message to his command bade them teach their children that "the proudest day in all your proud careers was that on which you enlisted as Southern soldiers." After the war General Hoke returned to private pursuits and lived nearly a half century. He died at Raleigh, July 3, 1912, and is buried there.

Theophilus Hunter Holmes was born in Sampson County, North Carolina, November 13, 1804, and was graduated from West Point in 1829. He had attained the regular rank of major in the 8th Infantry and a brevet for gallant service in Mexico when he resigned, April 22, 1861. He was one of the fifteen field-grade officers of the line of the old army to cast their lot with the Confederacy. He was successively appointed brigadier general on June 5, 1861, major general on

October 7, 1861, and lieutenant general to rank from October 10, 1862, in the Provisional Army of the Confederate States. He commanded a brigade at First Manassas and a division during the Seven Days. He was subsequently assigned to the command of the Trans-Mississippi Department, from which he was ultimately relieved by General Kirby Smith. General Holmes then commanded the District of Arkansas for a time; and later organized the reserves of his native state. After the war he cultivated a small farm near Fayetteville, in Cumberland County, North Carolina, where he died June 21, 1880. Although undoubtedly the possessor of many soldierly qualities, it is apparent that he was unequal to his high rank. He was unsparingly criticized by D. H. Hill for apathy at Malvern Hill; and numerous complaints of Holmes' inefficiency and jealousy of Sterling Price were received in Richmond during his service in the Trans-Mississippi. He was described personally as being "simple in his tastes, brave, true, and just in his deportment . . . a splendid example of an unpretentious North Carolina patriot and gentleman." (225) He is buried in Fayetteville, North Carolina.

James Thadeus Holtzclaw was born at McDonough, Henry County, Georgia, December 17,

1833. His parents were residents of Chambers County, Alabama; and he grew up in the latter community, obtaining his primary education at the Presbyterian high school. He received an appointment to West Point in 1853, but did not enter; instead, he took up the study of law in Montgomery, Alabama, where, after admission to the bar in 1855, he practiced his profession with the exception of the war years until his death. Entering Confederate service as a lieutenant of the Montgomery True Blues, he was in August 1861 appointed major of the 18th Alabama. He was shot through the lung at Shiloh, supposedly a mortal wound; however, he returned to duty in ninety days. He was promoted colonel and served for a time at Mobile. He subsequently took a

gallant part in the battles of Chickamauga and Chattanooga, commanding Clayton's brigade for a time in the latter campaign. During the Atlanta campaign Holtzclaw was promoted brigadier general from July 7, 1864, assigned to the permanent command of Clayton's brigade, and with it took part in Hood's campaign into Tennessee. In the course of the retreat from Nashville, his brigade acted for a time as rear guard of the army. Early in 1865 he was sent to Mobile where he assisted in the defense of the city, and was paroled at Meridian, Mississippi, in May. After the war General Holtzclaw was prominent in Democratic politics and, a few months before his death, was appointed to the Alabama railroad commission. He is buried in Montgomery, where he died on July 19, 1893.

John Bell Hood, born in Owingsville, (226) Kentucky, June 1, 1831, and graduated from West Point in the class of 1853, had by all odds the most spectacular advance in rank of any officer in Confederate service. After serving in California and Texas, he resigned his commission as 1st lieutenant in the old army on April 17, 1861. Thereafter he distinguished himself on a dozen fields as a regimental, brigade, and division commander in the Army of Northern Virginia. Promoted brigadier general to rank

from March 3, 1862, he fought in the Peninsular campaign and at Second Manassas. He was appointed major general to rank from October 10, 1862, and as a division commander under General Longstreet, distinguished himself at Sharpsburg and Fredericksburg. After being severely wounded in the arm at Gettysburg and after losing a leg at Chickamauga, he was appointed lieutenant general on February 1, 1864, to rank from September 20, 1863, and assigned to a corps under J. E. Johnston, whom he ultimately superseded (July 1864). Hood was promoted full general with temporary rank on July 18, 1864. Repulsed by Sherman in the several battles of Peachtree Creek, Atlanta, Ezra Church, and Jonesboro, Hood marched his army into Tennes-

see. The Federal General J. M. Schofield withdrew before Hood, but finally crippled him in a bloody engagement at Franklin. Hood pressed on to Nashville, where his army was shattered by General Thomas. He was then relieved at his own request (January 1865) and reverted to his permanent rank of lieutenant general. In May he surrendered himself at Natchez, Mississippi. He later made his residence in New Orleans, where he died of yellow fever, together with his wife and one of their children, (227) on August 30, 1879. He is buried in Metairie Cemetery in New Orleans. General Hood wrote a volume of memoirs, *Advance and Retreat* (see Bibliography # 73).

Benjamin Huger was born at Charleston, South Carolina, November 22, 1805, and was graduated from the U. S. Military Academy in the class of 1825. His career in the old army was most distinguished and included command of a number of United States arsenals, membership on the Ordnance Board, and the post of chief of ordnance under General Winfield Scott in Mexico, for which service he received the brevets of major, lieutenant colonel, and colonel. After the fall of Fort Sumter he resigned his commission to enter the service of the Confederacy, and was appointed brigadier gen-

eral on June 17, 1861, and major general on October 7. General Huger soon demonstrated that his talents lay more in the staff than in the line. Placed in command of the department embracing Norfolk in May 1861, he believed himself too weak to withstand attack. Accordingly, he dismantled his fortifications, set fire to the Navy Yard, blew up the *Merrimac,* and evacuated the city in May 1862. Later he was in command of a division at Seven Pines and during t h e Seven Days battles, but his record of accomplishment left much to be desired; he was harshly censured, leading to an investigation in Congress. Relieved of field command on July 12, 1862, he was assigned as inspector of artillery and ordnance, his proper sphere. These duties he energet-

ically and faithfully discharged until the close of the war, most of the time in the Trans-Mississippi Department. After the war he lived on a farm in Fauquier County, Virginia, and returned to Charleston shortly before his death, December 7, 1877. He is buried in Green Mount Cemetery, Baltimore.

William Young Conn Humes was born at Abingdon, Virginia, May 1, 1830, and was graduated second in the class of 1851 at the Virginia Military Institute. Removing to Tennessee, he settled in Memphis, studied law, and was admitted to the bar. He was engaged in law practice in 1861, when he entered Confederate service as a lieutenant of artillery. He was soon promoted captain, and served under General John P. McCown at New

Madrid, Missouri, and was captured at Island No. 10. Subsequently exchanged, he became chief of artillery to General Joseph Wheeler in March 1863, after which his wartime career was entirely with the latter's cavalry corps. Commissioned a brigadier general to rank from November 16, 1863, Humes was assigned a brigade of cavalry and participated in all the engagements incident to the Atlanta campaign. He accompanied Wheeler on the raid into North Georgia, Tennessee, and North Alabama in the fall of 1864, and then harassed Sherman in his march to the sea and through the Carolinas. During the last months of the war he was nominally in division command, but the records do not disclose that he was ever officially advanced to the grade of major general. Following the cessation of hostilities General Humes returned to Memphis and resumed his law practice. He died at Huntsville, Alabama, September 11, 1882, (228) and is buried in Memphis.

Benjamin Grubb Humphreys was born in Claiborne County, Mississippi (then Mississippi Territory), on either August 24 or 26, 1808. He was one of sixteen children. After attending school at Russellville, Kentucky, and Morristown, New Jersey, he entered West Point in 1825, but was dismissed from the academy

following a cadet riot on Christmas Eve, 1826. Returning to Mississippi, he studied law, engaged in planting, and served in both houses of the legislature. A Whig opponent of secession, Humphreys nevertheless raised a company for Confederate service and was commissioned captain in the 21st Mississippi Infantry in May 1861; he was promoted colonel in November. He led his regiment through the battles of the Army of Northern Virginia until Gettysburg, when, after the death of his brigade commander, General William Barksdale, he was promoted brigadier general to rank from August 12, 1863. His brigade accompanied Longstreet to Georgia and Tennessee, and was under Early in the Shenandoah Valley in 1864, where he was wounded at Berry-

ville in September. General
Humphreys was the first elected
governor of Mississippi after the
war. He was inaugurated on
October 16, 1865, after receiving
a pardon from President Johnson. He was ejected from office
on June 15, 1868, when the
President's Reconstruction plan
collapsed under fire from the
Radicals in Congress. Thereafter
he was for a time an insurance
agent at Jackson and Vicksburg.
He died on his plantation in Le-
flore County, Mississippi, December 20, 1882, and is buried in
Port Gibson.

Eppa Hunton was born in Fauquier County, Virginia, September 22, 1822. (229) He received
his education at New Baltimore
Academy. He taught school for
three years; then studied law and
was admitted to the bar in 1843.
After settling in Prince William
County, he became prominent
as colonel and brigadier general
of Virginia militia, and as commonwealth's attorney of his
county. Hunton was also a member of the secession convention
in 1861, and soon took the field
as colonel of the 8th Virginia
Infantry. Warmly commended
for his performance at the battle
of First Manassas, he led his
regiment in most of the important campaigns of the Army of
Northern Virginia. His promotion to brigadier, to rank from
August 9, 1863, had been de-

layed, largely because of his ill
health. He was also wounded at
Gettysburg. In March 1865 he
attempted gallantly to stave off
disaster at Five Forks, and was
finally taken prisoner at Sayler's
Creek. After his release from
Fort Warren, General Hunton
resumed his law practice at Warrenton, Virginia. He served in
the national House of Representatives from 1873 to 1881, and
in the Senate from 1892 to 1895.
He was the only Southern member of the famed electoral commission of 1877, which decided
the disputed Hayes-Tilden Presidential election. Following his
retirement from the Senate, he
again resided in Warrenton until his death at Richmond, October 11, 1908. He is buried in
Hollywood Cemetery, Rich-
mond.

John Daniel Imboden was born near Staunton, Virginia, February 16, 1823. He attended a country school until his sixteenth year, after which he had two terms at Washington College. Thereafter he taught school for a time, studied law, and opened an office in Staunton. He was twice the representative of his district in the legislature and an unsuccessful candidate for the Virginia secession convention. He entered Confederate service at the very beginning of war as captain of the Staunton Artillery, a light battery which he commanded at the initial capture of Harper's Ferry. After service at First Manassas he organized the 1st Virginia Partisan Rangers (later called the 62nd Virginia Mounted Infantry) and took part in the battles of Cross Keys and Port Republic under Stonewall

Jackson. Promoted brigadier general to rank from January 28, 1863, Imboden conducted a famous raid into Northwestern Virginia, where he severed the Baltimore & Ohio Railroad and captured several thousand cattle and horses. On the retreat from Gettysburg he was instrumental at Williamsport in saving the trains of the army. He later captured the garrison at Charlestown, West Virginia, and fought gallantly during Early's Valley campaign of 1864. Incapacitated by typhoid in the autumn of 1864, General Imboden served during the balance of the war on prison duty at Aiken, South Carolina, following which he settled in Richmond and resumed his law practice. During the later years of his life he resided in Washington County, Virginia, where he pioneered in developing the mining resources of the area. His death occurred at Damascus, a small town which he had founded, on August 15, 1895; he is buried in Richmond.

Alfred Iverson (Jr.), the son of Senator Alfred Iverson, with whom he is sometimes confused, was born at Clinton, Jones County, Georgia, February 14, 1829. (230) His career as a soldier began in his seventeenth year as a 2nd lieutenant of Georgia volunteers in the war with Mexico. He was commissioned directly into the regular

army, on March 3, 1855, as 1st lieutenant of the 1st Cavalry. Tendering his resignation six years later, he was soon elected colonel of the 20th North Carolina Infantry, a regiment which he had largely recruited and which he led with considerable distinction during the battles of the Seven Days, where he was wounded. After his recovery he fought at South Mountain and Sharpsburg in D. H. Hill's division. When General Samuel Garland was killed at South Mountain, Iverson was promoted brigadier on November 1, 1862. He commanded his brigade at Chancellorsville and Gettysburg, and was subsequently ordered to relieve General H. R. Jackson in command of the state forces at Rome, Georgia. (231) During the 1864 campaign he led a bri-

gade of cavalry in Martin's division of Wheeler's corps, capturing the Federal General Stoneman and five hundred of his men at Sunshine Church. After the war General Iverson engaged in business at Macon until 1877, when he moved to Florida and became an orange grower near Kissimee. He died in Atlanta, March 31, 1911, and is buried there in Oakland Cemetery.

Alfred Eugene Jackson was born in Davidson County, Tennessee, January 11, 1807. He received his education at Washington and Greeneville Colleges, and early began farming on the Nolichucky River in East Tennessee. He afterwards became a dealer in produce and manufactured goods. A man of indomitable energy, he was soon trading all over the South, using wagons

148

and boats equally as means of transportation for his merchandise. His various enterprises, which included stores, mills, manufactories, and farms, ranged at one time from North Carolina to the Mississippi River. In 1861 Jackson entered Confederate service as a quartermaster with rank of major on the staff of General Zollicoffer, with whom he served until the latter's death at Mill Springs; and was subsequently a paymaster in Knoxville. He was appointed brigadier general to rank from February 9, 1863 and assigned to the command of an infantry brigade in the Department of East Tennessee. With these troops he participated in a number of minor engagements, including the capture of the 100th Ohio Infantry at Telford's Station, Tennessee, in September 1863. In this action he commanded 1,500-1,800 men. Virtually impoverished by the war, General Jackson rented land in Washington County, Virginia, in 1866, and undertook its cultivation with his own hands. He was subsequently issued a special pardon by President Johnson for kindnesses shown the latter's family during the war. His estates were gradually restored to him, and he was able to take up residence at Jonesboro, Tennessee, where he died, October 30, 1889, in his eighty-third year, (233) and where he is buried.

Henry Rootes Jackson, a native of Georgia, was born at Athens on June 24, 1820, and was graduated from Yale in the class of 1839. Taking up the practice of law in Savannah, he was appointed a United States district attorney before he was twenty-four. He served as colonel of a Georgia volunteer regiment in Mexico, was a newspaper editor, a superior court judge, and U. S. minister resident to Austria. In 1859 he assisted in the government prosecution of the captain and owners of the slave-ship *Wanderer.* He was a delegate to both the Charleston and Baltimore conventions of 1860, an Elector on the Breckinridge ticket, and a member of the Georgia secession convention. He was appointed brigadier general in the Provisional Confeder-

149

ate Army on June 4, 1861, after resigning a Confederate judgeship. Following service under General Robert E. Lee in Western Virginia, Jackson resigned on December 2, 1861 to accept command of a division of Georgia state troops, with rank of major general. He was left without a command upon the passage of the Conscript Act, which resulted in turning his division over to the Confederacy. He served for a time as aide on the staff of General W. H. T. Walker, and was recommissioned brigadier in the Confederate service on September 23, 1863. (234) After duty in various capacities during the Atlanta campaign, he accompanied John B. Hood into Tennessee and was captured in action at Nashville, while in command of a brigade of Cheatham's corps. Released from Fort Warren in July 1865, General Jackson resumed his law practice in Georgia, and in 1885 was appointed minister to Mexico by President Cleveland. For nearly twenty-five years before his death at Savannah, May 23, 1898, he was president of the Georgia Historical Society. He is buried in Bonaventure Cemetery, Savannah.

John King Jackson was born at Augusta, Georgia, on February 8, 1828, and was educated at Richmond Academy (Georgia) and the University of South Carolina, where he was graduated with honors in 1846. After studying law and being admitted to the bar in 1848, he practiced his profession in his native city until the outbreak of war, meantime serving in the Oglethorpe Infantry as lieutenant and captain. Elected colonel of the 5th Georgia Infantry in May 1861, Jackson was on duty at Pensacola until January 1862, when he was promoted brigadier general, to rank from January 14, and ordered to Grand Junction, Tennessee. There he was placed in charge of organizing the troops that were arriving and being forwarded to Corinth preparatory to the campaign of Shiloh. He commanded a brigade at the latter battle and in the subsequent invasion of Kentucky. He later fought at Chickamauga, Chatta-

nooga, and in the Atlanta campaign. After July 1, 1864 he commanded the District of Florida for a time, participated in the defense of Savannah under General Hardee, and in the last months of the war, was in charge of supply depots in the Carolinas. After the surrender General Jackson resumed his law practice in Augusta, and while on a trip to Milledgeville, contracted pneumonia and died on February 27, 1866. His remains lie in an unmarked grave in the City Cemetery of Augusta.

Thomas Jonathan "Stonewall" Jackson, "Old Jack," "Old Blue-Light," was born in Clarksburg, (West) Virginia, on January 21, 1824. He was graduated from West Point in 1846, in a class which was to furnish twenty-four general officers to the United States and Confederate armies between 1861 and 1865. Having received the brevets of captain and major during the war with Mexico, he resigned his commission in 1852 to become an instructor at Virginia Military Institute. At the beginning of the war Jackson became a colonel of Virginia militia and was ordered to command at Harpers Ferry. In May J. E. Johnston superseded him there (relinquishing the post to the Union the next month), and Jackson was promoted brigadier general on June 17, 1861. After distinguished service at First Manassas—where General Barnard E. Bee gave the sobriquet "Stonewall" to him and his brigade — Jackson was promoted major general on October 7, 1861. He rapidly became a military celebrity. In November he was dispatched to the Shenandoah Valley, where he waged a magnificent campaign the following year against the three Federal armies that were threatening Richmond. In April 1862 Lee suggested that Jackson move against General Banks, with the idea of preventing McDowell's army from joining McClellan at Richmond. Jackson first defeated part of Frémont's army near Staunton, Virginia, on May 8. He then returned to the Valley to strike Banks' army, which was advancing from the north, at Front Royal and Win-

151

chester on May 23-25, and drove him across the Potomac. Fearing that Jackson would attack Washington, the Administration detached Shields from McDowell's army and sent him to cut off Jackson from the east, while Frémont attacked from the west. At this juncture, Jackson executed a remarkable tactical maneuver, defeating Frémont at Cross Keys on June 8 and Shields at Port Republic on June 9. He subsequently joined Lee against McClellan in the Seven Days battles around Richmond. His performance in the first of these battles was not outstanding. Jackson seems not to have been at his best unless he was in independent command. (235) At any rate, he won new laurels at every succeeding engagement. His lightning-like turning movement against General Pope in August 1862 was a crucial factor in the victory that followed at Second Manassas. Again, after capturing Harpers Ferry with its garrison of some twelve thousand men, Jackson saved Lee at Sharpsburg, when he learned that his chief had been surprised by a large Union force. Thereafter Lee reorganized the Army of Northern Virginia, and Jackson was promoted lieutenant general from October 10, 1862 and made commander of the 2nd Corps. In December 1862 he commanded the right wing in the victory at Fredericksburg. His career

reached its high point in the justly famous flank march at Chancellorsville, where his savage assault on the Federal right threatened at one time to roll up Hooker's entire line against the fords of the Rapidan. Later the same night, May 2, 1863, he was wounded by elements of his own command, while making a reconnaissance with members of his staff. He died on May 10 from pneumonia, which developed after the amputation of his left arm. General Lee wrote of him with deep feeling: "He has lost his left arm; but I have lost my right arm." (236) General Jackson is buried in Lexington, Virginia.

William Hicks "Red" Jackson was born at Paris, Tennessee, October 1, 1835. (237) He attended West Tennessee College and was graduated from West Point in the class of 1856. In May 1861 he resigned his commission as a lieutenant of mounted riflemen to enter Confederate service as a captain of artillery. He was soon severely wounded at the battle of Belmont. Upon his recovery he was appointed colonel of the 1st (later 7th) Tennessee Cavalry, and for gallantry at the capture of Holly Springs, was promoted brigadier general to rank from December 29, 1862. He served throughout the Vicksburg campaign, was in command of Polk's cavalry during the

Meridian expedition, and had charge of the cavalry corps of the Army of Mississippi (238) in the Atlanta campaign. He was attached to Hood's army during the invasion of Tennessee in the autumn of 1864; and in February 1865, was placed in command of all the Tennessee cavalry in General N. B. Forrest's Department. Although he was never formally advanced to the grade of major general, he led one of Forrest's two divisions at the close of the war. In 1868 Jackson married the daughter of General William G. Harding of "Belle Meade" near Nashville. He occupied himself for the rest of his life in the breeding and development of thoroughbred horses, and brought the farm to first rank in the South. For many years also he was president of the National Agricultural Congress and the Tennessee Bureau of Agriculture, among others. He died at "Belle Meade" on March 30, 1903, (239) and is buried in Mount Olivet Cemetery, Nashville.

William Lowther "Mudwall" Jackson, second cousin of "Stonewall," (240) was also born at Clarksburg, (West) Virginia, February 3, 1825. After his admission to the bar in 1847 he had a distinguished ante-bellum career, which included the offices of commonwealth attorney, jurist, membership in the Virginia house of delegates, and election as lieutenant governor of the state. Resigning as judge of the nineteenth judicial circuit in 1861, he enlisted in the Confederate Army as a private and

rapidly rose to the colonelcy of the 31st Virginia Infantry. After the close of General R. S. Garnett's disastrous campaign in Western Virginia in which he participated, he served on Stonewall Jackson's staff until April 1863, when he recruited the 19th Virginia Cavalry within the Federal lines and was elected its colonel. With this command, a part of the brigade of General A. G. Jenkins, he was active in West Virginia and in the Shenandoah Valley campaign of 1864. He was promoted brigadier general to rank from December 19, 1864. Finally paroled at Brownsville, Texas, July 26, 1865, General Jackson went to Mexico for a time. He returned to his home to find that a provision of West Virginia law aimed at ex-Confederates prohibited his practicing law in that state. He removed to Louisville, Kentucky, and a few years later he was appointed to the Kentucky bench, where he remained by successive elections until his death at Louisville, March 24, 1890. He is buried there in Cave Hill Cemetery.

Albert Gallatin Jenkins, a native of what is now West Virginia, was born in Cabell County, November 10, 1830. After graduation from Jefferson College in Canonsburg, Pennsylvania, in 1848, and from Harvard Law School two years later, (241) he practiced law at Charleston,

(West) Virginia, until his election to the Federal Congress in 1856. He resigned his seat in April 1861, in order to recruit a company of cavalry in the mountain counties of his native state. Soon he rose to be colonel of the 8th Virginia Cavalry, with which he participated in a number of demoralizing raids. As a result, he won considerable renown as a leader of independent horse. Jenkins was elected to the First Regular Confederate Congress, and was shortly promoted brigadier general on August 5, 1862. He led his command on a five hundred mile raid into Western Virginia and Ohio. Severely wounded at Gettysburg, he returned to his mountain command in the autumn of 1863, and on May 9, 1864 opposed the greatly superior force of the Federal General George Crook on Cloyd's Mountain near Dublin, in Pulaski County. In an attempt to rally a regiment which had broken, General Jenkins was wounded and captured. His arm was amputated at the shoulder by a Federal surgeon, but, failing to rally from the operation, he died on May 21. Twice previously interred, he is now buried in Spring Hill Cemetery, Huntington, West Virginia.

Micah Jenkins was born on Edisto Island, South Carolina, December 1, 1835, in a plantation house which has been continuously in the possession of the family since 1791. After being graduated from the South Carolina Military Academy at the head of his class in 1854, he helped to organize King's Mountain Military School at Yorkville,

South Carolina, with which he was connected until 1861. He was elected colonel of the 5th South Carolina in that year and fought conspicuously at First Manassas. He subsequently formed the Palmetto Sharpshooters, a regiment made up of transfers from the 2nd, 5th, and 9th South Carolina Infantry, which he led during the Seven Days. He was promoted brigadier general on July 22, 1862. After being severely wounded at Second Manassas, Jenkins accompanied the 1st Corps of the Army of Northern Virginia to Chickamauga, where he commanded Hood's division during that battle. Later he participated in the Knoxville campaign, and returned to Virginia in time to command his old brigade on the second day of the battle of the Wilderness. Soon after the 1st Corps' successful assault on Hancock's lines, he rode forward at the side of General Longstreet on a reconnaissance of the Federal position. In an almost exact parallel to the wounding of Jackson the previous year at Chancellorsville, and near the same spot, Longstreet and Jenkins were struck down by the fire of their own men, the latter mortally. With a ball lodged in his brain, he continued in his delirium to urge his men to press forward. He died a few hours later on May 6, 1864. He is buried in Charleston, South Carolina.

Adam Rankin "Stovepipe" Johnson, a native of Henderson, Kentucky, was born on February 8, 1834. At the age of twenty he emigrated to Burnet County, Texas, then the far frontier, where he became noted as surveyor, Indian fighter, and Overland Mail station contractor. Returning to the east in 1861, he served as a scout for Bedford Forrest, and later escaped from Fort Donelson with General John B. Floyd. His subsequent exploits as a partisan ranger within the Federal lines in Kentucky earned him the commission of colonel in August 1862, and brigadier general to rank from June 1, 1864. One of Johnson's most amazing exploits was his capture of the town of Newburgh, Indiana, from a large Union detachment, with the help of twelve men and two joints of stovepipe mounted on the running-gear of a decrepit wagon. This adventure won him the nickname by which he became known throughout the South. When John H. Morgan's forces were surrounded and cut off at Buffington's Island during the raid into Indiana and Ohio, Johnson and a number of his command escaped by swimming the Ohio River. On August 21, 1864, while attacking at daylight a Federal encampment at Grubbs Crossroads, in Caldwell County, Kentucky, he was accidentally shot by his own men; both of his eyes were destroyed. Totally blind, he located again in Texas after the war and lived nearly sixty years, founding the town of Marble Falls, and becoming one of the most prominent figures in Central Texas. His death occurred at Burnet, Texas, October 20, 1922, in his eighty-ninth year. He is buried in Austin. (242) See Bibliography # 213.

Bradley Tyler Johnson was born at Frederick, Maryland, September 29, 1829. He was graduated at Princeton in 1849, studied law, and was admitted to the Maryland bar in 1851. During the next ten years he gained some prominence as state's attorney, chairman of the state Democratic committee, and delegate to the conventions of 1860 at Charleston and Baltimore,

where he staunchly supported John C. Breckinridge. He aided in the recruitment of the 1st Maryland (Confederate) Infantry, and served with it as major and colonel at First Manassas, in Jackson's Valley campaign, and during the Seven Days. An able officer, recognition of his services was long in coming from Richmond. This was mainly due, it can be presumed, to the non-existence of Maryland units. Nonetheless, he was assigned to various important field duties by his superior officers. After the death of General William E. Jones he was promoted brigadier general on June 28, 1864. While serving under General McCausland he executed General Early's orders to McCausland to burn the town of Chambersburg, Pennsylvania. This act was in re-taliation for excesses committed by General David Hunter in the Shenandoah. Because of heavy losses in the cavalry of Early's command and resultant consolidation, Johnson, in effect a "foreigner," spent the last months of the war at Salisbury, North Carolina, in charge of the prison stockade. Thereafter he practiced law in Richmond and served four years in the Virginia senate until 1879, when he removed to Baltimore. The last years of his life were occupied in writing a number of historical and legal works. He died at Amelia, Virginia, October 5, 1903, and is buried in Loudon Park Cemetery, Baltimore.

Bushrod Rust Johnson was born in Belmont County, Ohio, October 7, 1817. Following his graduation from West Point in the class of 1840, he saw service in the Seminole War in Florida and in the war with Mexico. He resigned from the army in 1847 to become a teacher. Successively associated with Western Military Institute at Georgetown, Kentucky, and the Military College of the University of Nashville, Johnson was active in the militia of both states, with rank of colonel. Entering Confederate service as a colonel of engineers, he was appointed brigadier general on January 24, 1862. He was captured at Fort Donelson but escaped. Later he was

157

severely wounded at Shiloh.
After his recovery he led his
brigade in the Kentucky campaign of 1862, at Murfreesboro
and Chickamauga, and in the
Knoxville campaign under
Longstreet. He was then transferred to the East, where he took
part in the defense of Petersburg
against Butler's army. He was
commissioned major general to
rank from May 21, 1864. Thereafter his service was with the
Army of Northern Virginia. His
men bore much of the bitter
fighting in the trenches during
the protracted siege which followed. His division was shattered
at Sayler's Creek, although he
himself escaped; and he was
without a command at Appomattox, where he was paroled.
In 1866 General Johnson returned to Tennessee and in 1870

became chancellor of the University of Nashville. Subsequently a preparatory school
with which he was connected
was forced to close its doors.
Broken in health, he retired to
a farm near Brighton, Illinois,
where he died on September 12,
1880. (243) Originally interred in
an obscure cemetery at Miles Station,
near Brighton, he is now buried in
City Cemetery, Nashville, Tennessee.

Edward Johnson, "Old Allegheny," was born at Salisbury,
Chesterfield County, Virginia,
April 16, 1816. He moved to
Kentucky with his parents in
childhood and obtained his early
education there. A graduate of
West Point in the class of 1838,
he saw service in the Seminole
War and in Mexico, where he
was brevetted captain and major

for gallant and meritorious service and was voted a sword by the state of Virginia. Resigning from the old army on June 10, 1861, he went into Confederate service as colonel of the 12th Georgia Infantry. He was promoted brigadier general on December 13, 1861, and major general to rank from February 28, 1863. Johnson participated with distinction in the Valley campaign of 1862, where he was severely wounded, and led Stonewall Jackson's old division at Gettysburg, the Wilderness, and Spotsylvania. At the latter place he, along with most of his command, was captured while defending the "Bloody Angle." Subsequently exchanged, he led a division of General S. D. Lee's Corps in the Tennessee campaign, and was again captured at the battle of Nashville, not being released from the Old Capitol Prison in Washington until July 1865. He afterwards engaged in farming at his old home in Chesterfield County, and died at Richmond on March 2, 1873. (244) General Johnson is buried in Hollywood Cemetery, Richmond.

Albert Sidney Johnston was born in Washington, Kentucky, on February 2, 1803. He was educated at Transylvania University and at West Point, from which he was graduated in 1826. He served in the army for a number of years and saw action in the

Black Hawk War before resigning in 1834. In 1836 he went to Texas and enlisted as a private in the revolutionary army. Within a year he rose to be senior brigadier general and chief commander. He was secretary of war of the Republic of Texas from 1838 to 1840. After Texas was admitted to the Union, he became colonel of a regiment of Texas volunteers in the Mexican War and fought at Monterrey. He was reappointed to the U. S. Army in 1849 and served on the Texas frontier, becoming colonel of the 2nd Cavalry in 1855, and was in command of the Department of Texas from 1856 to 1858. He led the Utah expedition against the Mormons in 1857 and was made brevet brigadier general for his services. From 1858 to 1860 he commanded the Department of

159

Utah. When Texas seceded from the Union Johnston was commanding the Department of the Pacific; he resigned his commission on May 3, 1861, and was appointed a full general in the Regular Army of the Confederacy on August 31, 1861 to rank from May 30, 1861. Placed in command of all Confederate troops west of the Alleghenies, he strove to implement the current Richmond strategy of holding all points of the invaded states with isolated detachments. After concentrating an army at Corinth, Mississippi, he successfully attacked Grant at Shiloh; but he was mortally wounded in the engagement and died on the battlefield, April 6, 1862. Johnston's military capabilities constitute one of the more controversial issues of the Civil War. President Davis, who had implicit confidence in him, remarked in the face of entreaties for his removal after the loss of Forts Henry and Donelson that, "if Sidney Johnston is not a general . . . we have no general." (245) On the other hand, Grant in retrospect felt him to be distinctly overrated, and though bold in design, "vacillating and undecided in his actions." (246) Strictly on the basis of performance it cannot be said that he made any monumental contribution to the Confederate cause; and his death occurred after many of the initial advantages enjoyed by the

South in the area west of the mountains had been yielded. He is buried in the State Cemetery, Austin, Texas.

George Doherty Johnston was born at Hillsboro, North Carolina, on May 30, 1832. When he was two years old he was taken by his father to Alabama, where he was educated in private schools and at Howard College. He was graduated in law at Cumberland University, Lebanon, Tennessee, and began practice in Marion, Alabama. He served as mayor of the town in 1856, and in the state legislature in 1857-58. Enlisting in the Confederate Army as 2nd lieutenant of Company G, 4th Alabama Infantry, he fought at the battle of First Manassas. He was commissioned major of the 25th Alabama in January 1862, rising to colonel in September

1863. Johnston and his regiment were present at every engagement of the Army of Tennessee from Shiloh to Bentonville. Two days after his promotion to brigadier general, on July 26, 1864, he was severely wounded in the leg at Ezra Church and was on crutches much of the time during Hood's Tennessee campaign. When the army was surrendered at Durham Station, North Carolina, Johnston was on his way to join General Richard Taylor; no record of his personal parole has been found. After the war he was commandant of cadets at the University of Alabama, superintendent of the South Carolina Military Academy, and United States Civil Service Commissioner during President Cleveland's second term. (247) After returning to Tuscaloosa, Alabama, to live, he was elected to the state senate. His death occurred at Tuscaloosa on December 8, 1910, in his seventy-ninth year, and he is buried there.

Joseph Eggleston Johnston was born at "Cherry Grove," Farmville, Virginia, on February 3, 1807. A classmate of General R. E. Lee at West Point, he served with great distinction in the Seminole and Mexican Wars, in which he was wounded and brevetted repeatedly. Appointed quartermaster general with the staff rank of brigadier general on June 28, 1860, he resigned April 22, 1861 to enter the Confederate service. He was commissioned a brigadier in the Regular Army of the Confederacy in May 1861 and placed in command at Harpers Ferry. Eluding the Union force under General Patterson, he marched to P. G. T. Beauregard's assistance at the battle of First Manassas. His performance there won him a full generalcy on August 31, 1861 to rank from July 4, and the command of the Army of Northern Virginia. His being ranked below Samuel Cooper, Sidney Johnston, and R. E. Lee gave rise to an acrimonious debate with President Davis, (248) which rendered great disservice to the Confederate cause. He opposed McClellan in the Peninsular campaign until he was severely wounded at Seven Pines, May 1862, when the army

161

command passed to R. E. Lee. The following November he was made commander of the Department of the West. In 1863 Johnston was in the anomalous position of attempting to retrieve the situation at Vicksburg, while the city's commander, General Pemberton, was receiving contrary orders from Richmond. He was assigned to the command of the Army of Tennessee after Bragg's debacle at Chattanooga in November 1863. However, his plan of strategic withdrawal before Sherman displeased Davis, who ordered John Bell Hood to replace Johnston in front of Atlanta, July 17, 1864. He saw no more active service until reassigned by Lee in February 1865 to oppose Sherman's march north. After Lee's surrender to Grant, he capitulated to Sherman on April 26, 1865. From 1879 to 1881 Johnston served in the U. S. House of Representatives from Virginia, and was U. S. commissioner of railroads by appointment of President Cleveland from 1885 to 1891. He also wrote *Narrative of Military Operations* (see Bibliography #74). He died in Washington on March 21, 1891, supposedly as the result of a cold contracted while marching bareheaded in the funeral procession of his old adversary, Sherman. (249) During the retreat of the army from Dalton to Atlanta Johnston demonstrated himself to be at least the equal

of Lee as a defensive tactician; whether he possessed other qualifications requisite in an army commander has long been disputed. He is buried in Green Mount Cemetery, Baltimore.

Robert Daniel Johnston was born in Lincoln County, North Carolina, on March 19, 1837. After he was graduated from the University of North Carolina, he studied law at the University of Virginia and was admitted to the bar of his native state. At the time of the secession of North Carolina he was a lieutenant in the Beattie's Ford Rifles, a militia company. He entered the service of the Confederacy as captain of Company K, 23rd North Carolina Infantry. He took part in the Peninsular campaign in the spring of 1862, and was promoted lieutenant colonel in May. He was wounded at Seven Pines and fought with conspicuous bravery at South Mountain and Sharpsburg. Distinguished service at Chancellorsville and Gettysburg won him the commission of brigadier at the age of twenty-four, to rank September I, 1863. Again wounded at Spotsylvania, he returned to his brigade to lead it in Early's Valley campaign of 1864, rendering a particularly gallant account of himself at the battle of Winchester in September of that year. After fighting in the trenches during the siege of Petersburg he was sent in March 1865 to guard the line of the Roanoke River and to collect deserters. He was paroled at Charlotte, North Carolina, in May. For twenty years thereafter he practiced law in Charlotte. (250) He removed in 1887 to Birmingham, Alabama, where he became president of the Birmingham National Bank, and was also at one time register of the U. S. Land Office. One of the last surviving generals of the Confederacy, General Johnston died at Winchester, Virginia, on February 1, 1919, and is buried there.

David Rumph "Neighbor" Jones was born in Orangeburg District, South Carolina, April 5, 1825. He attended the common schools of the neighborhood and was graduated from the United States Military Academy in 1846. By

marriage to a niece of President Zachary Taylor he was connected to both Jefferson Davis and to Lieutenant General Richard Taylor, C.S.A. Both were cousins of his wife, the former by marriage and the latter by blood. After being brevetted 1st lieutenant for gallantry in Mexico, he resigned his commission in the old army to enter Confederate service as chief of staff to General Beauregard at Charleston, where he is said to have hauled down the United States flag on Fort Sumter after the surrender of the place. (251) Appointed brigadier general in the Provisional Army on June 17, 1861, he led his command at First Manassas, and was promoted major general from March 10, 1862. He participated in the Peninsular campaign and in the battles of the Seven Days. The high point of his Confederate career was reached by his timely seizure of Thoroughfare Gap in the campaign of Second Manassas, which enabled Longstreet to come to Jackson's rescue on August 30, 1862. Jones subsequently played a most important part in defending one of the passes of South Mountain in the Maryland campaign. He was in command of the Confederate right at Sharpsburg, where his advanced troops were forced from the lower Antietam bridge by Burnside's assault. (252) A. P. Hill's arrival from Harpers Ferry with his division at the critical moment enabled the two commanders to organize a counterattack which saved the day. Shortly thereafter General Jones developed serious heart trouble, from which he died at Richmond, Virginia, January 15, 1863. He is buried in Hollywood Cemetery there.

John Marshall Jones was born at Charlottesville, Virginia, July 26, 1820, and was graduated from West Point in the class of 1841. Since he was an instructor at the Military Academy at the time, he did not actively participate in the Mexican War. Resigning from the United States Army as a captain of the 7th Infantry, he entered the Confederate Army at the same grade. Subsequently serving as assistant adjutant general and adjutant and inspector general to Generals Magruder, Ewell, and Early, he was repeatedly commended for bravery and efficiency during the various battles of the Army of Northern Virginia. After Chancellorsville he was promoted from a staff lieutenant colonel to brigadier general, to rank from May 15, 1863, and assigned to the command of a brigade in Edward Johnson's division of the 2nd Corps. He was seriously wounded at Gettysburg in the attack on Culp's Hill; he returned to duty in September 1863 and was again wounded on the Rapidan in November, in an action known as the battle of Payne's Farm. On May 5, 1864 Jones' brigade opened the battle of the Wilderness against the Federal skirmish line and was supported by the brigades of

164

Battle and Doles. Shortly thereafter a furious assault was made on the Confederate front. General Jones is variously reported as having been killed "while sitting on his horse gazing at the approaching enemy," and while engaging "in a desperate effort to rally [his] brigade." (253) He is buried in Charlottesville.

John Robert Jones, a native of Harrisonburg, Virginia, was born March 12, 1827 and educated at Virginia Military Institute, from which he graduated in 1848. After teaching school in Florida, where he was active in the state militia, he became principal of a military school in Urbana, Maryland. Returning to Harrisonburg at the outbreak of the Civil War, he recruited a company of the 33rd Virginia Infantry, which was attached to the Stonewall Brigade. He fought

with the 33rd Virginia at First Manassas and in the Valley campaign of 1862, rising to the rank of lieutenant colonel. Upon the recommendation of General T. J. Jackson, Jones was appointed brigadier general, to rank from June 23, 1862, and assigned to the command of a brigade in Trimble's division of the 2nd Corps. During the battle of Chancellorsville he left the field "owing to the ulcerated condition of one of his legs." By this action he virtually removed himself from the army roster. (254) He was immediately relieved (255) and his brigade assigned to General John Marshall Jones. It is recorded that J. R. Jones was captured at Smithburg, Tennessee, July 4, 1863. (256). He spent the balance of the war as a prisoner on Johnson's Island and at Fort Warren, (257) from which he was released on July 24, 1865. (258) No effort seems to have been made by the Confederate government to effect his exchange, nor was he confirmed at the grade of brigadier by the Senate. (259) After the war General Jones engaged in the farm implement business in his native city and later was appointed commissioner in chancery of the circuit court, an office which he held until his death at Harrisonburg, April 1, 1901. He is buried there in Woodbine Cemetery.

Samuel Jones was born in Powhatan County, Virginia, December 17, 1819, and was a graduate of the Military Academy in the class of 1841. He served as an instructor there during the Mexican War and for five years thereafter. In 1858, while he was a captain of the 1st Artillery, he was detailed as assistant to the judge advocate of the army. Resigning on April 27, 1861, Jones was immediately commissioned a major of artillery in the Regular Army and acted as chief of artillery to General Beauregard at the battle of First Manassas. He was promoted brigadier general in the Provisional Army to rank from July 21, 1861, and major general from March 19, 1862. He relieved General Bragg at Pensacola, and later was assigned a division under Van Dorn at Corinth. Afterwards he exercised

departmental and district command at various points in Tennessee until December 1862, when he took command of the Department of Western Virginia. His direction of the Department rightly or wrongly caused his relief in March 1864. He was then assigned to the Department of South Carolina, Georgia, and Florida, where he served until superseded by General Hardee in October. He had charge until the end of the war of the Department of South Georgia and Florida. He was paroled at Tallahassee in May 1865. From 1866 to 1880 General Jones engaged in farming near Mattoax, Virginia, after which he secured a clerkship in the War Department. His death occurred at Bedford Springs, Virginia, July 31, 1887, and he was buried in Richmond. (260)

William Edmondson "Grumble" Jones was born on the Middle Fork of Holston River, Washington County, Virginia, May 9, 1824. He was educated at Emory and Henry College and at West Point, from which he was graduated in 1848. Jones then served on the frontier until 1857, when he resigned his commission, and after a visit to Europe, settled on his estate near Glade Spring Depot, Virginia. Upon the secession of his state he organized a company known as the "Washington Mounted Rifles," of which

Longstreet's Knoxville expedition and fighting at Cloyd's Mountain, General Jones was ordered to intercept Hunter in the latter's raid up the Shenandoah Valley. At the battle of Piedmont, June 5, 1864, he was struck by a ball and instantly killed while encouraging his men in the front line. In the subsequent confusion and retreat his body fell into the hands of the Federals, by whom it was returned to his friends, and buried in the yard of Old Glade Spring Presbyterian Church. (261)

he was elected captain and with which he took part under J. E. B. Stuart in the campaign of First Manassas. He became colonel of the 1st, and then the 7th, Virginia Cavalry. He continued under Stuart and was promoted brigadier general to rank from September 19, 1862. Particularly distinguishing himself at the battle of Brandy Station (Fleetwood) in June 1863, Jones, who had been pronounced the "best outpost officer" in the cavalry by his superior, protected the flank and rear of the army en route to Pennsylvania. However, a disagreement with Stuart caused his relief; he was then assigned to command the Department of Southwest Virginia and East Tennessee, where he organized a brigade and rendered excellent service. After participating in

Thomas Jordan was born at Luray, Virginia, September 30, 1819. After a common-school education, he was graduated in 1840 from West Point, where he was the roommate of William T. Sherman. He saw service both in the Seminole War and in the war with Mexico, and resigned his commission of captain and assistant quartermaster on May 21, 1861. His entire Confederate service was as a staff officer. He was adjutant general of the army at First Manassas under Beauregard; assistant adjutant general under A. S. Johnston at Shiloh, and under Beauregard after Johnston's death; and was made chief of staff to Bragg in July 1862. He served again under Beauregard during the siege of Charleston. He had been promoted to brigadier for gallantry on the field at Shiloh to rank

ver. Among his other writings were numerous contributions to *Battles and Leaders of the Civil War*. He died at New York City, November 27, 1895, and is buried in Mount Hope Cemetery, near Hastings-on-Hudson.

John Herbert Kelly, the youngest general officer in the Confederate Army at the time of his appointment, was born at Carrollton, Pickens County, Alabama, March 31, 1840. He was orphaned at the age of six and was brought up in the home of his maternal grandmother at Pineapple, Alabama. He entered West Point in 1857, but resigned from the Academy on December 29, 1860, and was shortly commissioned a 2nd lieutenant of artillery in the Regular Army of the Confederate States. Kelly had an all-too-brief but most distin-

from April 14, 1862. During the last months of the war he commanded the 3rd military district of South Carolina. Jordan wielded a facile pen and had written a treatise on the South in 1860. At the close of hostilities he returned to his writing, and in 1866 became editor of the Memphis *Appeal.* In 1869 he espoused the insurrectionary cause in Cuba, and became chief of staff and later commander of the Cuban revolutionaries. In 1870 Spain is said to have placed a price of $100,000 on his head. The movement subsequently collapsed and General Jordan returned to the United States and resumed his literary pursuits. At the same time he became founder and editor of the *Financial and Mining Record* of New York, a publication devoted to free sil-

guished record. First on the staff of General Hardee with rank of captain, he was on September 23, 1861 commissioned major of the 14th Arkansas. At Shiloh he commanded the 9th Arkansas Battalion, and for gallantry on the field was promoted colonel of the 8th Arkansas a month later. He commanded his regiment at Perryville and Murfreesboro, and led a brigade of Buckner's corps at Chickamauga, after which he was endorsed for appointment to the grade of brigadier general. Commissioned brigadier to rank from November 16, 1863, General Kelly was assigned a division of cavalry in Wheeler's corps and made a handsome reputation during the Atlanta campaign. In the course of Wheeler's raid on Sherman's communications in the late summer of 1864, Kelly was mortally wounded in an engagement at Franklin, Tennessee, on September 2. (262) Left in the care of the family of William H. Harrison, five miles south of the town, he died a few days later, probably on the fourth. (263) He was first buried in the yard of the Harrison home; his remains were re-interred in Mobile in 1866.

James Lawson Kemper was born in Madison County, Virginia, June 11, 1823. He was graduated from Washington College in 1842, served as captain of Virginia volunteers in the Mexican War, and later practiced law. He served five terms in the Virginia house of delegates, during which time he was speaker of the house, chairman of the committee on military affairs, and president of the board of visitors of Virginia Military Institute. He was commissioned colonel of the 7th Virginia Infantry, and led his regiment from First Manassas to Williamsburg. He was then given a brigade and promoted to brigadier general on June 3, 1862. With this command in Pickett's division he rendered most efficient service until the battle of Gettysburg, where he fell desperately wounded on the third day, within a few rods of the historic stone wall. Captured by the Federals, he was subsequently exchanged, but was unfitted by his wounds for further field service.

169

Promoted to major general on September 19, 1864, he commanded the reserve forces of Virginia until the close of the war, and was paroled at Danville on May 2, 1865. Returning to his law practice in Madison, General Kemper, who was an orator of renown, was soon back in politics. After canvassing the state for Greeley in 1872, he won the Democratic nomination for governor the following year and was elected, serving from 1874 to 1877. His administration was marked by strife between the "Debt-payers" and "Readjusters" over the question of the state debt incurred during the war. Again returning to private life, he died in Orange County, Virginia, April 7, 1895, where he is buried.

John Doby Kennedy was born at Camden, South Carolina, January 5, 1840. He attended South Carolina College from 1855 to 1857. He then studied law and was admitted to the bar a few weeks before the outbreak of the Civil War. Enlisting in the 2nd South Carolina Infantry in April 1861, he was elected captain of Company E, and became colonel of the regiment in January 1862, after the promotion of Joseph B. Kershaw to brigadier. Kennedy was wounded at First Manassas, and incapacitated by fever after the battle of Savage's Station during the Seven Days. He subse-quently took part in all the engagements of Kershaw's brigade (and division) from Jackson's capture of Harpers Ferry in 1862 to the battle of Cedar Creek in 1864. After the fall of Atlanta, Governor Magrath of South Carolina requested that the brigade (which Kennedy had been commanding since Kershaw's promotion to major general) be detached to oppose Sherman's march northward. Thus in the last months of the war he fought under Joseph E. Johnston, and was promoted to brigadier general from December 22, 1864. Paroled at Greensboro in May 1865, he re-entered the legal profession at Camden, and was elected to Congress in December of that year, but was denied his seat because of his refusal to take the "iron-clad oath." He became prominent in the councils of the

Democratic party after the re-establishment of white supremacy in South Carolina. He served in the legislature and as lieutenant governor, and was named consul general at Shanghai by President Cleveland in 1885. His death occurred suddenly at Camden from a stroke on April 14, 1896, and he is buried there.

Joseph Brevard Kershaw was born at Camden, South Carolina, January 5, 1822. He studied law and was admitted to the bar in 1843. After serving one year in the Mexican War as a lieutenant of the Palmetto Regiment, he resumed his law practice, and was twice elected to the legislature, and to the secession convention in 1860. Entering the Civil War as colonel of the 2nd South Carolina, he was present on Morris

Island during the bombardment of Fort Sumter, and at First Manassas. He was promoted brigadier general to rank from February 13, 1862, and major general from May 18, 1864. Kershaw played a gallant and distinguished part in all the operations of the 1st Corps—almost literally from Manassas to Appomattox. While temporarily attached to General Ewell's command in the retreat from Richmond he was captured at Sayler's Creek on April 6, 1865, and was not released from Fort Warren until July. After the war he returned to the practice of law, and was elected to the state senate in 1865. In 1870, as a member of the Union Reform party convention, he prepared resolutions recognizing the Reconstruction acts. He was elected judge of the fifth circuit court of the state in 1877 and held the office until failing health compelled him to resign in 1893. He was thereafter postmaster of Camden, where he died on April 13, 1894, and where he is buried in the Quaker cemetery. Kershaw is a striking example of the citizen-soldier, who with little military background, developed into a wholly dependable, although not spectacular, brigade and division commander.

William Whedbee (264) **Kirkland** was born at "Ayrmont," Hillsboro, North Carolina, February 13, 1833. He was appointed

to West Point in 1852, but did not graduate. He was commissioned a 2nd lieutenant in the U. S. Marine Corps in 1855 and resigned in August 1860. His name was sent to the Provisional Confederate Congress for appointment as captain of infantry in the Regular Army on March 16, 1861. Early in June he was elected colonel of the 21st North Carolina Infantry. This regiment he led at First Manassas and in Jackson's Valley campaign of 1862. At the first battle of Winchester in May of that year he was badly wounded and incapacitated for months; however, while still recuperating he acted as chief of staff to General Cleburne at the battle of Murfreesboro. (265) Rejoining his regiment during the invasion of Pennsylvania, he fought gallantly at Gettysburg, and was again wounded at Bristoe Station in October, having been promoted brigadier general from August 29, 1863. During the Overland campaign of 1864 he was a third time badly wounded near Gaines's Mill on June 2. After his return to the army in August he was assigned to the command of James G. Martin's old brigade of Hoke's division, and served under Longstreet north of the James until ordered to North Carolina in December. He was present during both assaults on Fort Fisher, and took part in the battle of Bentonville, finally surrendering with Joseph E. Johnston. At the close of the war General Kirkland settled in Savannah, where he was engaged in the commission business for a number of years. His daughter, Bess, became famous on the Broadway stage under the name of Odette Tyler, and he subsequently moved to New York, where he held a position in the post office. He was invalided near the turn of the century and spent the last years of his life in a soldiers' home in Washington, D. C. He died on May 12, 1915, and is buried in an unmarked grave on the outskirts of Shepherdstown, West Virginia.

James Henry Lane was born at Mathews Court House, Virginia, July 28, 1833. He was graduated from Virginia Military Institute

172

in 1854, and from the University of Virginia three years later. He then returned to the Institute to become assistant professor in mathematics and tactics. At the outbreak of the Civil War he was professor of natural philosophy and instructor in military tactics at North Carolina Military Institute. He was elected major of the 1st North Carolina Volunteers, whose participation in the battle of Bethel on June 10, 1861 earned it the title of the "Bethel Regiment." When the volunteers had been reorganized into regiments for the war, Lane was made colonel of the 28th North Carolina. He served throughout with the Army of Northern Virginia and was three times wounded. His promotion to brigadier dates from November 1, 1862. Lane's

28th North Carolina formed the rear guard of the army in the retreat from Sharpsburg. At Gettysburg his brigade took part both in the first day's fighting and—as a part of Trimble's division—in Pickett's charge on the third day. Its casualties were almost fifty per cent in killed and wounded. After the surrender at Appomattox General Lane returned to civil life to find his parents in want and the family plantation desolated. After seven years as a teacher in private schools in Virginia and North Carolina, he was associated with Virginia Polytechnic Institute, the Missouri School of Mines, and for the last twenty-six years of his life with Alabama Polytechnic Institute, as professor of civil engineering. He died at Auburn, Alabama, on September 21, 1907, and is buried there.

Walter Paye Lane, a native of Ireland, was born in County Cork, February 18, 1817, and emigrated to the United States with his parents in 1821. The family first settled in Guernsey County, Ohio. At the age of eighteen Lane went to Louisville and then to Texas, where he fought in the battle of San Jacinto. His subsequent antebellum occupations ranged from cruising the Gulf of Mexico as a member of the crew of a Texas privateer to fighting Indians and teaching school, and included

service in the Mexican War as captain of a company of rangers. From 1849 to 1858 he spent much of his time in mining in California, Nevada, Arizona, and Peru, making and losing several small fortunes. He was elected lieutenant colonel of the 3rd Texas Cavalry in 1861, with which he fought at Wilson's Creek and Elkhorn Tavern (Pea Ridge). Lane was later active in Louisiana in 1863, and in the Red River campaign the following year. He was severely wounded at the battle of Mansfield. He was recommended for promotion by General Kirby Smith and was commissioned brigadier general to rank from March 17, 1865, being confirmed the last day on which the Confederate Senate met. After the war he returned to his home

at Marshall, Texas, and became a merchant, and also wrote his memoirs (see Bibliography # 76a). As the years passed he became symbolic of the heroic age in Texas history, and was for long an idol of the Daughters of the Republic of Texas and the United Daughters of the Confederacy. Never married, General Lane died at Marshall, January 28, 1892, and is buried there.

Evander McIvor (266) **Law** was born at Darlington, South Carolina, August 7, 1836. He was graduated from the South Carolina Military Academy in 1856, where he had acted as instructor of belles lettres during his senior year. After spending the next several years teaching and aiding in the founding of the Military

High School at Tuskegee, Alabama, he recruited in 1861 a company of state troops, which he took to Pensacola. Subsequently elected lieutenant colonel of the 4th Alabama, he was severely wounded at First Manassas, and was elected colonel of the regiment in November. He led his command at Seven Pines and during the battles of the Seven Days; he was also present at Second Manassas and Sharpsburg. His promotion to brigadier general dates from October 2, 1862. Law's 4th Alabama, a part of Hood's division of Longstreet's corps, distinguished itself both at Gettysburg and at Chickamauga, where after the wounding of Hood, Law succeeded to command. Law fought gallantly at the Wilderness, Spotsylvania, and Cold Harbor, and was again wounded. After his recovery he was relieved at his own request from duty with the Army of Northern Virginia, and commanded a force of cavalry under Joseph E. Johnston in the Carolinas campaign of 1865. General Law lived for fifty-five years after the close of hostilities, and was an alert observer of the changing aspects of American life until his death at Bartow, Florida, October 31, 1920. During this period he played a large part in establishing the foundation of the educational system of Florida, and was an active newspaperman until his eightieth

year. He also served as commander of the Florida division of the United Confederate Veterans, and wrote a number of articles on the Civil War campaigns in which he participated. He is buried in Bartow.

Alexander Robert Lawton, a brother-in-law of General E. P. Alexander, was born in Beaufort District, South Carolina, November 4, 1818. He was graduated from West Point in 1839 and resigned in 1841 to enter Harvard Law School, from which he was in turn graduated the following year. Settling in Savannah, Georgia, which was to be his home until his death, he practiced law, was president of the Augusta & Savannah Railroad, and served in both houses of the Georgia legislature. He struck the first blow for independence in Georgia by seizing Fort Pulaski. He was appointed brigadier general in the Provisional Army of the Confederacy on April 13, 1861, and was duly confirmed by the Provisional Congress on August 28. Following a most creditable record with the Virginia Army in the Seven Days battles, and at Sharpsburg, where he was badly wounded, he was placed in command of the quartermaster general's department in the fall of 1863. He remained there and rendered distinguished service until the end of the war. General Lawton then resumed the practice of his profession in Savannah, and soon became an important figure in politics. After being a member of the legislature from 1870 to 1875, he was chairman of the state electoral commission in 1876, president *pro tem.* of the state constitutional convention of 1877, and leader of the Georgia delegation at the Democratic National Conventions of 1880 and 1884. Defeated by Joseph E. Brown (a sometime Republican who espoused the policies of Reconstruction) for the United States Senate in 1880, he was in 1887 appointed minister to Austria by President Cleveland. His death occurred at Clifton Springs, New York, July 2, 1896, whence his body was taken to Savannah for burial.

Danville Leadbetter, a native of the state of Maine, was born at Leeds, August 26, 1811. (267) He was graduated from West Point in 1836, standing third in his class. As an officer of engigeers he served in all parts of the country in the construction of fortifications. He resigned his commission on December 31, 1857 at Mobile, where he had been occupied for the preceding four years in the construction and repair of the harbor forts, and was then appointed chief engineer of the state of Alabama. Leadbetter served mainly as an engineer officer during the Civil War, with rank of brigadier general from February 27, 1862. (268) He superintended the erection of the defenses at Mobile, laid out Bragg's lines at Chattanooga, and accompanied Longstreet to

Knoxville in the latter's campaign against that place. Later chief engineer for a time on the staff of General Joseph E. Johnston, he was again at Mobile toward the close of the war. No record of his final capture or parole has been found; he is recorded as having first gone to Mexico and then to Canada, where he died at Clifton, (269) September 26, 1866. His remains were subsequently interred in Magnolia Cemetery, Mobile. It is difficult to adequately appraise Leadbetter's services to the Confederacy. Although apparently highly esteemed by such officers as Generals Bragg, Beauregard, Maury, and Joseph E. Johnston, yet General E. P. Alexander felt that the adoption of Leadbetter's views by Longstreet at Knoxville "robbed (Longstreet) of most of his few remaining chances of victory." (270)

Edwin Gray Lee, a son-in-law of General William N. Pendleton, (271) was born at "Leeland," Virginia, on May 27, 1836. (272) He received his early education at Hallowell's school at Alexandria, was graduated from the College of William and Mary, and then took up the legal profession. Entering Confederate service as a 2nd lieutenant of the 2nd Virginia, he subsequently became major, lieutenant colonel, and colonel of the 33rd. He served as an aide to Stonewall

Jackson at Harpers Ferry during June and July 1861, and took part in the Valley campaign of 1862, the Seven Days battles, Second Manassas, Sharpsburg, and Fredericksburg. He resigned in December 1862 because of ill health, and was recommissioned colonel in 1863, and given duty in Richmond. On May 17, 1864 he was assigned to command the post at Staunton, with orders to recruit local troops for the defense of the Shenandoah. Appointed brigadier general on September 23, 1864 to rank from September 20, Lee was on November 28, 1864 given a six-months' leave of absence for his health. (273) His nomination to the grade of brigadier was rejected by the Senate on February 24, 1865, although he apparently was continued on the

177

army rolls until the end of the war. Shortly before, he and his wife ran the blockade and went to Montreal, where they remained until the spring of 1866. He was suffering from a "disease of the lungs," and only five years of life remained to him. He died at Yellow Sulphur Springs, Virginia, August 24, 1870, at the early age of thirty-four. He is buried in Lexington, Virginia.

Fitzhugh Lee, a nephew of General Robert E. Lee and, on his mother's side, of General Samuel Cooper, (274) was born at "Clermont," Fairfax County, Virginia, November 19, 1835. He was graduated forty-fifth in a class of forty-nine at West Point in 1856. He was wounded on frontier duty in an Indian fight, and was in 1861 at the Military Academy as an assistant instructor of tactics. He resigned his 1st lieutenant's commission in May 1861 to enter Confederate service with the same rank. He was on the staff of Joseph E. Johnston at First Manassas, and became lieutenant colonel of the 1st Virginia Cavalry in August 1861; brigadier general for services during the Peninsular campaign on July 24, 1862; and major general to rank from August 3, 1863, following the Pennsylvania invasion. An especial favorite of General J. E. B. Stuart, Lee played a gallant part in all of the operations of the Cavalry Corps, particularly distinguishing himself at Spotsylvania Court House, where the stand of his division made it possible for the 1st Corps to secure the strategic crossroads in advance of Grant's arrival with the main Federal column. After Wade Hampton was ordered to North Carolina in January 1865, Lee commanded the remnant of the Cavalry Corps until Appomattox. After the war he engaged in farming in Stafford County, Virginia; was elected governor of the state in 1885; and after his defeat for the United States Senate in 1893, was appointed consul-general at Havana by Cleveland. At the outbreak of the war with Spain he was commissioned major general of United States Volunteers, and once again donned the blue uniform which he had put off in 1861. After serving creditably he was retired with rank of brigadier general, U.S.A., in 1901. General Lee died at Washington, April 28, 1905, and is buried in Hollywood Cemetery, Richmond.

George Washington Custis Lee, eldest son of Robert E. Lee, was born at Fortress Monroe, Virginia, September 16, 1832. Upon his graduation from the Military Academy at the head of the class of 1854, he served as an engineer officer in various parts of the country. He resigned his 1st lieutenant's commission on May 2, 1861. As a captain of engineers in the Confederate Army the younger Lee was first engaged in the construction of the fortifications around Richmond, later serving on the staff of Presi-

dent Davis with rank of colonel. Davis recognized his military ability by advancing him to brigadier general from June 25, 1863, and major general on October 20, 1864. The latter appointment was to permanent rank and was confirmed on February 3, 1865. Lee was entrusted with numerous important missions by the President and was sometimes consulted by his father. He saw no active field service until the last months of the war, when he organized a force of clerks and mechanics for emergency defense of the capital. Attached to Ewell's corps on the retreat from Richmond, he was captured along with that officer and several other generals at Sayler's Creek, April 6, 1865. Because of the illness of his mother he was almost at once paroled and thus did not join his contemporaries at Fort Warren. For more than thirty years thereafter General Lee was connected with Washington College (now Washington and Lee University), succeeding his father as president upon the latter's death. Resigning in 1897, he took up residence at "Ravensworth," an ancestral home, where he died, February 18, 1913. He is buried in Lexington.

Robert Edward Lee, perhaps the most universally revered of American soldiers, was born at "Stratford" in Westmoreland

County, Virginia, on January 19, 1807. He was the fifth child of Henry "Light-Horse Harry" Lee of Revolutionary War fame and the latter's second wife, Ann Hill (Carter) Lee. Harry Lee destroyed his brilliant prospects by a mania for land speculation, and "Stratford" passed to a son by his first marriage. The family was compelled to remove to a small house in Alexandria, where it existed on the income from a trust fund established for Mrs. Lee by her father. When Robert was eleven, Harry Lee died while en route home from a trip to the West Indies. After receiving his early education in the Alexandria schools, young Lee obtained in 1825 an appointment to West Point, from which he was graduated second in the class of 1829, without a demerit standing against his name for the

four years of his course. (In Lee's time, cadets at West Point could "work off" demerits by standing extra guard, and so on.) He was commissioned a brevet 2nd lieutenant of engineers. The seventeen years between his graduation and the outbreak of the Mexican War were passed in discharging with energy and distinction the duties of his profession at Forts Pulaski, Monroe, and Hamilton, and as superintending engineer for St. Louis harbor. The interval was particularly marked by his marriage on June 30, 1831 to Mary Ann Randolph Custis, the only child of George Washington Parke Custis, a grandson of Martha Washington by her first marriage. The Custis estate of "Arlington" on the Virginia shore of the Potomac opposite Washington thus became Lee's home after the death of his father-in-law in 1857. From this union seven children were born; all of the three boys later served in the Confederate Army. George Washington Custis and William Henry Fitzhugh attained the grade of major general, and Robert E., Jr., that of captain. In 1846 Lee, then a captain of engineers, was sent to San Antonio, Texas, as assistant engineer to General John E. Wool, but soon joined General Winfield Scott in the Vera Cruz expedition. On the march to Mexico City his extraordinary industry and capacity won him the lasting confidence and esteem of Scott. During the various engagements leading up to the capture of the Mexican capital, in one of which he was slightly wounded, Lee's regular rank was augmented by three brevets for gallantry and distinguished conduct to that of colonel. He returned to the United States in 1848 and supervised the construction of Fort Carroll in Baltimore Harbor, until his appointment as superintendent of the Military Academy in 1852. Three years later, with the approval of the then Secretary of War, Jefferson Davis, Lee transferred from staff to line and was commissioned lieutenant colonel of the 2nd Cavalry and sent to West Texas, where he served from 1857 to 1861. He was at Arlington House on extended leave at the time of John Brown's raid on Harpers Ferry, and was placed in command of the detachment of Marines that stormed the engine-house, capturing Brown and his "garrison" in October 1859. In February 1861, when the lower South seceded, General Scott recalled Lee from Texas. Politically a Whig, Lee was strongly attached to the Union and the Constitution; and the fact that he later manumitted the slaves who came to him through the will of his father-in-law showed that he entertained no special sympathy for the insti-

tution of slavery. However, when it became manifest that his native state would withdraw from the Union and that he would be expected to aid in "suppressing insurrection," he promptly resigned his commission in the United States Army on April 20, 1861. He had already refused, on April 18, the offer of the chief command of the U. S. forces made by General Scott at the instance of President Lincoln. Proceeding immediately to Richmond he was designated commander in chief of the military and naval forces of Virginia by Governor Letcher. Upon the transfer of the Virginia troops to Confederate service, he was appointed and confirmed brigadier general in the Regular Confederate States Army on May 14, 1861 (then the highest provided for by law), and subsequently general to rank from June 14, 1861. Lee ably discharged the duties of arming and equipping the Virginia contingents and then passed into a wider field of endeavor. He was first assigned to resist the Federal columns advancing through t h e trans-Allegheny counties of the state; but his campaign was unsuccessful, principally because of the adherence of the populace to the Union cause. After a short tour of duty examining the defenses of the South Atlantic seaboard, he returned to Richmond in March 1862 to act as military adviser to President Davis. At this time Lee devised a plan—which was magnificently executed by Stonewall Jackson —to prevent reinforcements from reaching McClellan at Richmond. The wounding of General Joseph E. Johnston at the battle of Seven Pines, on May 31, 1862, precipitated Lee into the command of the Army of Northern Virginia. This fortuitous association continued uninterrupted until the end of the war. Lee took the initiative at once and foiled McClellan's threat against Richmond in the Seven Days battles, June 26-July 2, 1861. At Second Manassas, August 29-30, he decisively defeated General Pope, but was checked by McClellan the following month in his Northern thrust in the Maryland campaign. Lee repulsed General Burnside at Fredericksburg on December 13, 1862, and General Hooker at Chancellorsville on May 2-4, 1863. Since the South had to contend against a large superiority in men and materiel, it soon became apparent that even Confederate successes could not be so exploited as to achieve positive results. After the Pennsylvania campaign of 1863, culminating in the repulse at Gettysburg, Lee was forced to turn more and more to defensive measures, both strategically and tactically, always in the hope that some miraculous recogni-

tion of the Confederacy by European powers might take place. Utilizing to the fullest extent the newly-developed art of field fortification, he fought what was in essence a rear-guard action from the Wilderness (May to June 1864) to Petersburg (July 1864 to April 1865), always on the alert for an opportunity to "strike a blow." Casualties of almost three to one in his favor, and the advantage of fighting behind entrenched lines, however, could not compensate for the undiminished resources and determination of the Federals, nor for the steadily waning resources at his own command. Lee was ultimately compelled to stretch out too thinly to oppose the masses of Grant, and the inevitable breakthrough occurred at Petersburg on April 2, 1865. Seven days later, at Appomattox Court House, Lee surrendered the remnant of what had been the Army of Northern Virginia. Two months and a week before, under the act of January 23, 1865, he had been confirmed General in Chief of the Armies of the Confederate States. By signing this act into law President Davis had virtually abdicated his prerogatives as Commander in Chief. Under the provisions of the act Lee manifestly attained the highest rank of any officer in the Confederate military service.

General Lee returned to Richmond as a paroled prisoner of war, and submitted with the utmost composure to an altered destiny. He devoted the remainder of his life to setting an example of conduct for other thousands of ex-Confederates. He refused a number of offers which would have secured substantial means for his family. Instead, he assumed the presidency of Washington College at Lexington, Virginia (now Washington and Lee University). As a result of the war, the college was at that period rather a landmark than a going concern. Lee's enormous wartime prestige, both in the North and South, and the devotion inspired by his unconscious symbolism of the "Lost Cause" made him a legendary figure even before his death. He died at Lexington on October 12, 1870, and is buried there.

Stephen Dill Lee, the youngest lieutenant general of the Confederacy, was born in Charleston, South Carolina, September 22, 1833. He was graduated from West Point in 1854. Resigning his commission on February 20, 1861, he entered Confederate service as captain and aide-de-camp to General Beauregard. By profession an artillerist, he served in the artillery through all the Virginia campaigns until Sharpsburg, and was meantime promoted through grades to colo-

nel. On November 6, 1862, he was appointed brigadier general and was assigned to the command of General Pemberton's artillery at Vicksburg. He was exchanged after the capitulation of the place in July 1863, and was promoted major general on August 3. He was then placed in command of the cavalry in the Department of Mississippi, Alabama, West Tennessee, and East Louisiana. Appointed lieutenant general to rank from June 23, 1864, he assumed command of Hood's old corps of the Army of Tennessee, which he led during the Tennessee campaign and in the closing days, until the surrender of General Joseph E. Johnston in North Carolina. After the war General Lee resided in Mississippi, where he was farmer, state senator,

183

and the first president of Mississippi State College. He was also a leading figure in the United Confederate Veterans, whose organization he headed as commander-in-chief from 1904 until his death at Vicksburg, May 28, 1908. Despite his youth and comparative lack of experience, Lee's prior close acquaintanceship with all three branches of the service—artillery, cavalry, and infantry—rendered him one of the most capable corps commanders in the army. He is buried in Columbus, Mississippi.

William Henry Fitzhugh Lee, the second son of Robert E. Lee, and called "Rooney" to distinguish him from his first cousin, General Fitzhugh Lee, was born in the Custis home, "Arlington," May 31, 1837. He was educated at Harvard, where he was noted as an oarsman, and was commissioned directly into the United States Army in 1857. Two years later he resigned to engage in farming at "White House" plantation on the Pamunkey River, an estate he had inherited from his Grandfather Custis. Upon the secession of Virginia Lee promptly entered Confederate service, and soon rose to the colonelcy of the 9th Virginia Cavalry. With this regiment he followed General J. E. B. Stuart through virtually all the campaigns of the Cavalry Corps of the Army of Northern Virginia. He was promoted brigadier general to rank from September 15, 1862. He was severely wounded at Brandy Station the following June, and while recuperating, was captured by the Federals and imprisoned. Not exchanged until March 1864, he was promoted major general on April 23 (the youngest in Confederate service), (275) after which he continued to play a most important part in the closing operations of the cavalry, and was second in command thereof at Appomattox. Following the war he returned to farming, served as president of the Virginia Agricultural Society, and was for four years a state senator. In 1887 General Lee was elected to Congress, and occupied his seat until his death at "Ravensworth," near Alexandria, on October 15, 1891. First buried in the family ground there, his remains were re-interred in the Lee mausoleum at Lexington in 1922.

Collett Leventhorpe, an Englishman, was born at Exmouth, Devonshire, May 15, 1815. He received an appointment to Her Majesty's 14th Regiment of Foot and put in a number of years of colonial duty with this regiment. Later he emigrated to the United States and married into a prominent North Carolina family. At the outbreak of the Civil War he offered his services to his adopted state and was elected colonel of the 34th North Carolina, and in 1862, of the 11th, which prior to its reorganization had been the Bethel Regiment of D. H. Hill. Leventhorpe was mainly on duty in North Carolina, where he par-

ticipated with great credit in a number of local engagements. In 1863 his regiment joined the Army of Northern Virginia and took part in the battle of Gettysburg in Pettigrew's brigade of Heth's division. On the first day he was badly wounded and during the retreat from Pennsylvania fell into the hands of the enemy; he was not exchanged for some nine months. He then was appointed by Governor Zebulon Vance a brigadier general of state troops, and operated on the Roanoke River and the Weldon railroad until the close of the war. President Davis appointed him a brigadier in the Confederate service on February 18, 1865, and he was duly confirmed by the Senate; however, for reasons not apparent, he declined the appointment on March 6, 1865. Some years after the war he made his home with his wife's sister and her husband at "The Fountain" in the valley of the Yadkin (Wilkes County, N. C.), where he died December 1, 1889. (276) He is buried in the Episcopal Cemetery in Happy Valley, near Lenoir, North Carolina.

Joseph Horace Lewis was born near Glasgow, Barren County, Kentucky, October 29, 1824. He was graduated from Centre College in 1843; then studied law and was admitted to the bar in 1845. Elected three times to the Kentucky legislature, and twice

defeated for Congress, Lewis discarded his original Whig principles to throw in his lot with the Confederacy. He was commissioned colonel of the 6th Kentucky Infantry in September 1861. He took part in the battles of Shiloh, Murfreesboro, and Chickamauga, and was commended repeatedly by General John C. Breckinridge. Upon the death of Ben Hardin Helm, he succeeded to the command of the Orphan Brigade, and was promoted brigadier general from September 30, 1863. After the capture of Atlanta the brigade was mounted and attached to Wheeler's cavalry corps, with which it served against Sherman in the march to the sea and in the Carolinas. General Lewis finally surrendered as a part of Jefferson Davis' escort, and was paroled at Washington, Georgia, on May 9, 1865. Again taking up the practice of law at Glasgow, he was elected to the state legislature in 1868, and in 1870 to Congress, and was twice reelected. In 1880 he commenced eighteen years of service on the Kentucky bench, the last four as chief justice of the court of appeals. Retiring at the expiration of his third elected term, he took no further part in public life. He resided on his farm in Scott County, and died there on July 6, 1904. He is buried in Glasgow.

William Gaston Lewis was born at Rocky Mount, North Carolina, September 3, 1835. After receiving his early education at Lovejoy's Military School at Raleigh, he was graduated from the University of North Carolina at

the age of nineteen. Subsequently a school teacher in North Carolina and Florida, and a government surveyor in Minnesota, he assisted in the construction of the Wilmington & Weldon Railroad from 1858 to 1861. He served at the outbreak of war in the Bethel Regiment, and was elected major of the 33rd North Carolina. He was present at New Bern, and was promoted lieutenant colonel of the 43rd North Carolina in April 1862. He was at Gettysburg in 1863, and after the capture of Plymouth, North Carolina, in April 1864, he took part in the initial stages of the siege of Petersburg under General Beauregard. His promotion to brigadier general dates from May 31, 1864. Assigned to Ramseur's division, Lewis' brigade took part in Early's Valley campaign of that year, and was in the trenches at Petersburg the following winter. On the retreat toward Appomattox he was wounded and captured at Farmville, Virginia, April 7, 1865. (277) After his parole he resumed the practice of civil engineering, which he carried on with considerable success for more than thirty years; for some thirteen years he was state engineer of North Carolina. He died at Goldsboro, North Carolina, January 7, 1901, and is buried there.

St. John Richardson Liddell was born at "Elmsley" plantation,

near Woodville, Mississippi, September 6, 1815. He received an appointment to West Point in 1833, but remained for only one year, presumably resigning because of his relatively low class standing. (278) His father then purchased him a plantation in Catahoula Parish, Louisiana, which became his home for the rest of his life. He was volunteer aide-de-camp with rank of colonel on the staff of General Hardee, and acted as confidential courier to General Sidney Johnston. Later he commanded a brigade at Corinth, and was promoted to brigadier general to rank from July 17, 1862. Liddell fought at Perryville, Murfreesboro, and Chickamauga, after which he was assigned to the Trans-Mississippi Department. He was active in the Red River campaign under General Richard Taylor, and toward the end of the war, took part in the defense of Mobile, where he was captured at Fort Blakely on April 9, 1865. Some years later, on February 14, 1870, differences between himself and a neighboring planter, Charles Jones, late lieutenant colonel of the 17th Louisiana Infantry, resulted in Liddell's death on board a Black River steamboat at the hands of Jones and his two sons. General Liddell is buried on his plantation in Catahoula Parish. (279)

Robert Doak Lilley was born near Greenville, Augusta County, Virginia, on January 28, 1836. He was educated at Washington College (now Washington and Lee University). Prior to the Civil War he was engaged in selling surveying instruments invented by his father. He was in Charleston at the time of the bombardment of Fort Sumter; returning to Virginia, he recruited the Augusta Lee Guards, which saw service in the Western Virginia campaign of 1861 as one of the companies of the 25th Virginia. This regiment was a part of Early's brigade of Ewell's division in 1862, and with it Lilley was present at Cedar Mountain, Second Manassas, and Sharpsburg. He was promoted major in January 1863, and lieutenant colonel after Gettysburg. Following the opening battles of the 1864 campaign he was commissioned brigadier general from May 31, 1864, and assigned to the command of Early's old brigade of the 2nd Corps. He was wounded three times and captured in a reconnaissance near Winchester in July 1864; his arm was amputated, and he was left in Winchester by the Federals. Subsequently he recovered sufficiently to command the reserve forces in the Shenandoah during the closing days of the war. The greater part of his post-bellum career was spent as financial agent for his alma mater, for whose endowment he raised substantial sums; he was also a member of the Presbyterian Synod of Virginia. He died in Richmond on November 12, 1886, while attending a meeting of the Synod, and was buried in Staunton. (280)

Lewis Henry Little, a native of Baltimore, was born March 19,

sion by General Bragg after the evacuation of Corinth. Little's troops fought the battle of Iuka against the forces of Rosecrans, although Price was in chief command. During the engagement, and while he was seated on his horse conversing with Generals Price, Louis Hébert, and Whitfield, a ball from the Federal lines passed under the arm of Price and struck Little in the forehead, killing him instantly. He was buried by torchlight that night, September 19, 1862, in the garden behind his headquarters in Iuka. His remains were later removed to Green Mount Cemetery, Baltimore. (281)

1817, son of a long-time Maryland Congressman and veteran of the War of 1812. He was commissioned directly into the army in 1839. He was brevetted for gallant and meritorious conduct at the battle of Monterey in the Mexican War, resigning May 7, 1861 to cast his lot with the Confederacy. First commissioned a major of artillery in the regular service, he was soon attached to the staff of General Sterling Price as colonel and assistant adjutant general, and became one of Price's especial favorites. Little distinguished himself at the battle of Elkhorn in command of a brigade, and upon the recommendations of Price and General Earl Van Dorn, was promoted brigadier general on April 16, 1862. Subsequently he was assigned to the command of a divi-

Thomas Muldrup Logan was born in Charleston, South Carolina, November 3, 1840. After

189

being graduated at the head of the class of 1860 at South Carolina College, he first served as a volunteer during the bombardment of Fort Sumter; later he was elected 1st lieutenant of Company A of the Hampton Legion. He was promoted captain after First Manassas, was wounded during the Seven Days battles, and was advanced to major for "great bravery" at Sharpsburg. He then served in Micah Jenkins' brigade during the Suffolk campaign and at Chickamauga and Knoxville with rank of lieutenant colonel. Logan accompanied Wade Hampton to South Carolina in February 1865, and was promoted brigadier general to rank from the fifteenth of that month. He commanded M. C. Butler's old cavalry brigade in the closing operations against Sherman. A month after the surrender at Durham Station he borrowed five dollars from a friend and was married to the daughter of Judge James H. Cox of Chesterfield County, Virginia. Afterwards he studied law and embarked on a highly successful career in railroad development and management. At times associated with John D. Rockefeller, Logan was a principal organizer of what is now the Southern Railway. In addition to his various business ventures, he also served as chairman of the Virginia Democratic Executive Committee in 1879, and of the Virginia

"Gold Democrat" party in 1896. General Logan won and lost several fortunes in the course of a notable career. He died in New York City on August 11, 1914, and is buried in Hollywood Cemetery, Richmond, Virginia.

Lunsford Lindsay Lomax, of an old Virginia family, was born at Newport, Rhode Island, November 4, 1835. At the time his father was stationed there as a captain of the 3rd U. S. Artillery. Lomax was educated in the schools of Richmond and Norfolk, Virginia, and was graduated from West Point in the class of 1856. After routine frontier duty in the cavalry, he tendered his resignation on April 25, 1861, and soon received a captain's commission in the state forces of Virginia. Until 1863 he served on the staffs of Generals Ben Mc-Culloch, J. E. Johnston, and Van Dorn, and was promoted to lieutenant colonel. After acting as inspector general of the Army of West Tennessee, he was transferred to the eastern theatre and commissioned colonel of the 11th Virginia Cavalry. He served in the Gettysburg campaign, and was promoted brigadier general to rank from July 23, 1863. He participated in the Overland campaign of 1864, in which his brigade was part of the division of Fitzhugh Lee. Appointed major general on August 10, 1864, he commanded Early's cavalry in the Shenandoah, participating in the battles of Winchester and Cedar Creek, and on March 29, 1865, was placed in command of the Valley District. Lomax surrendered his division at Greensboro, North Carolina, and became a farmer near Warrenton, Virginia, where he remained until elected to the presidency of Virginia Polytechnic Institute in 1885. He resigned this position in 1899, and spent the next six years aiding in the compilation of the *Official Records*. Afterwards he was appointed a commissioner of the Gettysburg National Military Park. General Lomax died at Washington, May 28, 1913—the last but one of the surviving major generals of the Confederacy—and was buried in Warrenton, Virginia.

Armistead Lindsay Long was born in Campbell County, Virginia, September 3, 1825. (282) He was graduated from West Point in the class of 1850, and served in the artillery until May 20, 1861. At this time he was made aide-de-camp to his father-in-law, Brigadier General Edwin V. Sumner, U.S.A., whose daughter Long had married the previous year. (282-A) He nevertheless resigned his commission on June 10, and was appointed major of artillery in the Confederate service. First attached to the staff of General Loring in Western Virginia, he was soon ordered to report to General R. E. Lee in Charleston. When Lee assumed command of the Army of Northern Virginia, Long became his military secretary with rank of colonel. Their intimate association resulted in Long's writing after the war one of the ablest contemporary biographies of Lee. (See Bibliography #152.) Although nominally a staff officer, and indispensable at headquarters, Long's superior judgment in the posting and effective use of batteries, finally caused Lee to assign him to command of the artillery of the 2nd Corps. He was commissioned brigadier general of artillery on September 21, 1863. From that time he served with the 2nd Corps until the end, and was paroled at Appomattox. General Long was appointed chief engineer of a Virginia canal company, but became totally blind in 1870. Using a slate he wrote his Lee biography as well as a number of articles for various historical publications. He died at Charlottesville, Virginia, April 29, 1891, where his wife had been appointed postmistress by President Grant. He is buried in Charlottesville.

James Longstreet, "Old Pete," senior lieutenant general of the Confederate Army, was born in Edgefield District, South Carolina, January 8, 1821, and was graduated from West Point in 1842. He served in various Indian campaigns and won two brevets for gallantry in Mexico. At the time of his resignation from the old army on June 1, 1861, he was a major (paymaster). Appointed brigadier general in

the Confederate service on June 17, 1861, he fought at First Manassas the following month. He was promoted major general on October 7, 1861 and rendered distinguished service in the Peninsular campaign, from April to July 1862, and at Second Manassas and Sharpsburg in the two months succeeding. He was made lieutenant general from October 9, 1862. In December his 1st Corps occupied an impregnable position on Marye's Heights at Fredericksburg and inflicted terrible losses on the attacking Federals. Longstreet in 1862-63 was on detached service south of the James River and thus arrived too late to participate at Chancellorsville. He commanded the right wing at Gettysburg and was charged post bellum with losing the battle by his failure to attack at daylight on the second day, in accordance with Lee's orders. This unwarranted charge plagued him to the end of his life. At Chickamauga in September 1863, he was largely responsible for the Confederate victory, but was unsuccessful in an attempt to take Knoxville. He arrived at the Wilderness on May 6, 1864, with the leading division of his corps, in time to repulse the Federal assault of that morning and to organize a brilliant counterattack. A few hours later he sustained a critical wound, which incapacitated him until late fall, but he was again at the head of his corps in the closing months. With Lee he surrendered to Grant at Appomattox Court House. After the war Longstreet settled in New Orleans. He became a Republican and was a personal friend of Grant, who made him U. S. minister to Turkey in 1880. He was also the commissioner of Pacific railroads under McKinley and Roosevelt, from 1897 to 1904. Lee affectionately called Longstreet "my old War Horse." He unquestionably had no superior in either army as a battlefield tactician; his record in independent command, however, was not distinguished. For his war memoirs, *From Manassas to Appomattox*, see Bibliography #80. He died at Gainesville, Georgia, on January 2, 1904, the last of the high command of the Confeder-

acy. He is buried in Gainesville. (283)

William Wing Loring, "Old Blizzards," was born in Wilmington, North Carolina, December 4, 1818. His parents shortly afterwards took him to Florida. His diverse career began as a mere youth with operations against the Seminoles. Later he studied law, and was elected to the Florida legislature. Commissioned directly into the regular army in 1846 as a captain of the newly-established Regiment of Mounted Riflemen, he won the brevets of major and lieutenant colonel in Mexico, losing an arm at the battle of Chapultepec. Promoted colonel of his regiment on December 30, 1856, he was both then and at the time of his resignation, on May 13, 1861, the youngest line colonel in the old army. (284) He was appointed brigadier general in the Confederate Army on May 20. 1861, and major general on February 15, 1862. Loring was the senior major general on active field duty in Confederate service when he surrendered with General Joseph E. Johnston in April 1865. He clashed violently with Stonewall Jackson over the conduct of operations in the Romney Expedition during the winter of 1861-62. He was relieved from duty with Jackson, and then commanded in Southwestern Virginia. Assigned to the Army of Mississippi in December 1862, his division was cut off from the main body of Pemberton's forces at the battle of Baker's Creek, and thus escaped capture at Vicksburg. From then until the end of the war he commanded a division under General Leonidas Polk and in the Army of Tennessee under Generals Johnston and Hood. He went abroad after the termination of hostilities, and entered the service of the Khedive of Egypt in 1869. He rose to the rank of general of division and was twice decorated. (285) He returned to the United States in 1879, where he died in New York City on December 30, 1886. He is buried in St. Augustine, Florida. (For his memoirs, see Bibliography #81.)

Mansfield Lovell was born in Washington, D. C., (286) October 20, 1822. He was graduated from West Point in the class of 1842. During the Mexican War, he received a severe wound at Belen Gate and the brevet of captain for gallantry at Chapultepec. He resigned from the army in 1854 and engaged in business. Later he became deputy street commissioner of New York City under Gustavus W. Smith. Almost immediately after his resignation from this post he was appointed major general in the Confederate Army, October 7, 1861, and assigned to the command of New Orleans. Hampered by an insufficiency of men and materiel, he could not successfully dispute the Federal land and sea invasion, and was at length compelled to evacuate the

194

place. Even though his dispositions were commended by Robert E. Lee, he held no further responsible command after the battle of Corinth in October 1862, where he directed a corps and subsequently a most skillful retreat. He was eventually relieved of responsibility for the loss of New Orleans by a court of inquiry; and both Generals Joseph E. Johnston (in January 1864) and John B. Hood (in July) requested his services as a corps commander during the Atlanta campaign, but to no avail. Apparently in response to a further request by Johnston, made on March 23, 1865, General Lovell was ordered by the Secretary of War to report to General Robert E. Lee for assignment. He was presumably en route to Johnston's army when hostilities terminated. (287) After the war he returned to New York and served as assistant engineer to General John Newton in the removal of the East River obstructions. He died there on June 1, 1884, and was buried in Woodlawn Cemetery.

Mark Perrin Lowrey, born in McNairy County, Tennessee, December 30, 1828, was the son of parents who had immigrated to the United States from Ireland and England, and was virtually without a formal education. Following the death of his father, the family moved to Tishomingo

County, Mississippi, in 1845; and the year after, Lowrey enlisted in the 2nd Mississippi Volunteers for service in Mexico. Subsequently he was a brick mason, and boarded the village schoolteacher in order to learn from him at night. In 1853 he entered the Baptist ministry and continued in it until 1861. After commanding the 4th Regiment of Mississippi State Troops (a sixty-day regiment), he was appointed colonel of the 32nd Mississippi Infantry in 1862, and fought with notable distinction in the Kentucky campaign and at Chickamauga. He was promoted brigadier general from October 4, 1863. During the Atlanta campaign Lowrey's brigade was attached to the corps of General Hardee, in Pat Cleburne's division. He then accompanied

195

Hood into Tennessee, and participated in the battles of Franklin and Nashville. General Lowrey resigned his commission on March 14, 1865. In 1873 he founded the Blue Mountain Female Institute, at Blue Mountain, Mississippi, with which he was connected as president and professor of history and moral science until his death. Prominent to the last in the councils of the Baptist denomination, he fell dead in the railway station at Middleton, Tennessee, February 27, 1885; he is buried in Blue Mountain.

Robert Lowry, a native of South Carolina, was born in Chesterfield District on March 10, 1830. His parents removed first to Tennessee and then to Tishomingo County, Mississippi, where they settled in 1840. For a time engaged in the mercantile business, he later studied law and was practicing his profession in 1861. He enlisted as a private in the Rankin Grays, and was soon elected major of the 6th Mississippi Infantry. After being twice wounded at Shiloh, he was promoted colonel, and served in the Vicksburg campaign with the forces of General Joseph E. Johnston. He led his regiment in the Atlanta and Tennessee campaigns, and succeeded to brigade command after the death of General John Adams at Franklin; he was appointed brigadier general to rank from February 4, 1865. The following month he joined Johnston in South Carolina, and after participating in the battle of Bentonville, was paroled at Greensboro, North Carolina, in May. A state senator in 1865-66, General Lowry was defeated for the office of attorney general of Mississippi in 1869, but after taking an active part in the overthrow of the carpet bag regime, was elected governor as a compromise candidate in 1881, and was re-elected without opposition four years later. In 1898 he was defeated for a seat in the United States Senate to succeed General Walthall. For seven years before his death, which occurred at Jackson, January 19, 1910, he was state commander of the United Confederate Veterans. Some years before he had been co-author of a history of Mississippi. He is buried in Brandon, Mississippi.

Hylan Benton Lyon was born at "River View," Caldwell (now Lyon) County, Kentucky, February 22, 1836. Orphaned at the age of eight, he attended a number of Kentucky schools before receiving an appointment to West Point in 1852. He was graduated four years later as a brevet 2nd lieutenant of artillery, and resigned on April 30, 1861 to enter Confederate service. First a battery captain, he was elected lieutenant colonel of the 8th Kentucky Infantry on February 3, 1862, was taken prisoner at Fort Donelson, and was exchanged after seven months' imprisonment on Johnson's Island. His regiment was assigned to General Lloyd Tilghman's division of the army of West Tennessee and served at Holly Springs and Vicksburg. Lyon made his escape from the latter place during the siege, together with his command. His rank of brigadier general dates from June 14, 1864. He commanded a brigade of four Kentucky cavalry regiments in Forrest's corps until, toward the end of the war, he succeeded General Adam R. Johnson in command of the District of Western Kentucky. During the battle of Chattanooga he had temporary charge of all of Bragg's artillery, the greater part of which he brought off the field after the Confederate defeat. General Lyon went to Mexico upon the close of hostilities, returned to Kentucky in 1866, and farmed near Eddyville for a time. He was later one of the lessees of the state penitentiary, and also served as a commissioner to build a branch penitentiary at Eddyville. He died on his farm there, April 25, 1907. (288) He is buried in Eddyville.

John McCausland was born at St. Louis, Missouri, the son of a native of Ireland, on September 13, 1836. (289) He received his early education at Point Pleasant, (West) Virginia, and was graduated first in his class at the Virginia Military Institute in 1857. He also became an assistant professor of mathematics at the Institute after his graduation from

the University of Virginia in 1858. In 1859 he was present with a cadet detachment at the execution of John Brown at Charles Town. Recruiting the 36th Virginia in 1861, he was commissioned its colonel, and after service in the brigade of John B. Floyd in Western Virginia, was transferred with his regiment to Albert Sidney Johnston's army at Bowling Green, Kentucky. He escaped with his command from Fort Donelson, and in 1862 and 1863, he fought in Virginia under Generals Loring, Echols, and Sam Jones. After the death of General A. G. Jenkins at Cloyd's Mountain, McCausland assumed command of the shattered Confederate forces, and was promoted brigadier general from May 18, 1864. From then until the end of the war he was conspicuous for his operations in the Shenandoah Valley, and for his raids into Maryland and Pennsylvania. On July 30, 1864, under orders from General Early, he burned the town of Chambersburg, Pennsylvania, in retaliation for the wanton destruction of private property by the Federal General Hunter in the Shenandoah. Subsequently attached to Rosser's division, he fought at Petersburg, Five Forks, and on the retreat to Appomattox, cutting his way through the Federal lines before the surrender. Ultimately paroled at Charleston, West Virginia, General McCausland spent two years in Europe and Mexico before returning home. He then acquired a tract of 6,000 acres in Mason County, West Virginia, where he resided for more than sixty years. When he died on his farm, "McCausland," January 22, 1927, in his ninety-first year, there remained but one other survivor of the generals of the Confederacy. He is buried at Henderson, West Virginia.

William McComb, a native of Pennsylvania, was born in Mercer County, November 21, 1828. This date accords with his death certificate, (290) although a sketch of his life written in 1885 records his birth four years later. (291) He went to Tennessee in 1854 and took up residence at Clarksville, where he engaged in various manufacturing interests,

including the erection of a flour mill on the Cumberland River. Enlisting as a private in the 14th Tennessee Infantry, he was elected 2nd lieutenant in May 1861, and major the following year; rising to lieutenant colonel after Cedar Mountain, and colonel after Second Manassas. Meantime he had served gallantly in all the battles of the Army of Northern Virginia from the Seven Days onward, as well as in the Cheat Mountain campaign of 1861. Severely wounded at Sharpsburg and Chancellorsville, he was not present at Gettysburg, but took part in the Overland campaign of 1864 and in the subsequent siege of Petersburg. He was promoted brigadier general to rank from January 20, 1865. Paroled at Appomattox Court House, General McComb resided in Alabama and Mississippi for a time, and in 1869 moved to

Louisa County, Virginia, where he was engaged in farming for nearly fifty years; but toward the latter part of his life, he spent his winters in Richmond. (292) He died on his plantation near Gordonsville, July 21, 1918, presumably in his ninetieth year, and is buried in Louisa County.

John Porter McCown was born near Sevierville, Tennessee, August 19, 1815, (293) and was graduated from West Point in 1840. He won a brevet at the battle of Cerro Gordo in the Mexican War, and resigned his captain's commission in the 4th Artillery on May 17, 1861 to enter Confederate service as colonel of the Tennessee Artillery Corps. Promoted brigadier general on October 12, 1861, and major general from March 10, 1862, he was present at Belmont,

New Madrid (before Pope's investment of that place), (294) and Fort Pillow; he also temporarily commanded the Army of the West in June 1862. Later he was in command in East Tennessee, and his division launched the attack of Bragg's army at the battle of Murfreesboro on December 31, 1862. Bragg preferred charges against him, in February 1863, for disobedience of orders; (295) he had previously reported to the War Department that McCown was unfit for responsible command. (296) The greater part of his division was ordered to Mississippi in May 1863, and General McCown served out the balance of the war in relative obscurity. In April 1865 he defended a crossing of the Catawba River near Morganton, North Carolina, with a single piece of artillery and 300 men against a division of cavalry under Brigadier General Alvan C. Gillem, U.S.A. (297) After the war he taught school in Tennessee for a time, later removing to a farm near Magnolia, Arkansas. He died in Little Rock, January 22, 1879, while attending a meeting of the Masonic Lodge. (298) He is buried in Magnolia.

Ben McCulloch, elder brother of General Henry E. McCulloch, was born in Rutherford County, Tennessee, November 11, 1811. After an early life typical of the frontier of the day, he followed

his neighbor, "Davy" Crockett, to Texas in time to see action at the battle of San Jacinto. He was subsequently a surveyor and Indian fighter, and rendered brilliant service in the Mexican War under Zachary Taylor. A "forty-niner," he returned to Texas to serve as United States marshal for the coast district for six years. In February 1861, while he was a colonel in the state troops, he received the surrender of General Twiggs at San Antonio. He was commissioned brigadier general in the Provisional Confederate Army on May 11, 1861, and was assigned to the command of troops in Arkansas. In August he won the battle of Wilson's Creek with these men, together with Price's Missouri troops. This victory—in which the Confederates were at first taken by surprise by the forces under the

Federal General Lyon—went unexploited. Under the command of General Earl Van Dorn at Elkhorn Tavern on March 7, 1862, and while directing the right wing of the army, McCulloch was fatally wounded in the breast by a Federal sharpshooter. He died almost immediately. Invariably refusing to wear a uniform, he was attired in a suit of black velvet at the time of his death; (299) he was then second ranking brigadier in the Confederate service. (300) General McCulloch's body was subsequently removed to the State Cemetery in Austin, Texas.

Henry Eustace McCulloch was born in Rutherford County, Tennessee, December 6, 1816. His elder brother was General Ben McCulloch. He moved to

Texas in 1837 and settled in Guadalupe County, where he was elected sheriff in 1843. He served in the war with Mexico as captain of a company of Texas Rangers, and was elected to the legislature in 1853 and to the state senate in 1855. Four years later President Buchanan appointed him U. S. marshal for the eastern district of Texas, an office he was occupying at the outbreak of war. He was commissioned colonel of the 1st Texas Mounted Riflemen on April 15, 1861, and brigadier general to rank from March 14, 1862. McCulloch's service was almost entirely within the boundaries of Texas, and he was in command of various districts and subdistricts. However, he participated in the campaign for the relief of Vicksburg and unsuccessfully stormed the Federal fortifications at Milliken's Bend in June 1863. Toward the end of the war he commanded a brigade in John G. Walker's division. General McCulloch's life after the war was uneventful. Described as gentle and unassuming, he lived for thirty years on his farm in Guadalupe County, and died in Rockport, Texas, on March 12, 1895. Survived by seven of his children, he was buried in Seguin, Texas. (301)

Samuel McGowan, the son of Irish Presbyterian immigrants, was born in Laurens District, South Carolina, October 9, 1819.

201

He was graduated from South Carolina College in 1841; he then studied law at Abbeville and was admitted to the bar the following year. He served for thirteen years in the state house of representatives, and was commended for gallantry in the Mexican War, during which he rose to the rank of staff captain. McGowan was a major general of militia in 1861 and commanded a brigade at the reduction of Fort Sumter in April of that year. In 1862 he was made colonel of the 14th South Carolina Infantry, and after the death of General Maxcy Gregg at Fredericksburg, was promoted brigadier general to rank from January 17, 1863. McGowan's career and reputation were not excelled by those of any other brigade commander in the Army of Northern Vir-

ginia. When not disabled by one or another of the four wounds which he sustained during the war, he participated with great gallantry in every engagement of the army from the Seven Days to Appomattox, where he was paroled. He returned to Abbeville at the close of hostilities, and was immediately elected to Congress, but was refused his seat. A leader in the fight against carpet bag rule, he was again elected to the legislature in 1878, and the year following an associate justice of the South Carolina supreme court, a position which he continued to occupy until 1893, when he was defeated for re-election by the efforts of "Pitchfork Ben" Tillman. General Mc-Gowan died at his home in Abbeville on August 9, 1897, and is buried in Long Cane Cemetery.

James McQueen McIntosh was born at Fort Brooke (now Tampa), Florida, in 1828. (302) He was the son of Colonel James S. McIntosh, U.S.A., who was mortally wounded at the battle of Molino del Rey in the Mexican War. Appointed to West Point from the state of Florida, young McIntosh was graduated last in the class of 1849. Thereafter he served on the frontier and was promoted captain of the 1st Cavalry in 1857. He resigned his commission on May 7, 1861, and was first appointed captain of cavalry in the Regular Confeder-

ate Army; shortly afterwards he became colonel of the 2nd Arkansas Mounted Rifles. On January 24, 1862 he was promoted brigadier general in the Provisional Army of the Confederacy. Commanding the cavalry of General Ben McCulloch's wing of General Earl Van Dorn's army at Elkhorn on March 7, 1862, McIntosh met his death within a few minutes of General McCulloch. After leading a brilliant charge of cavalry, McIntosh rushed into the thickest of the fight, again at the head of his old regiment, and was shot through the heart. His body, with that of General McCulloch, was conveyed by wagon to Fort Smith, Arkansas, where he now lies buried in the National Cemetery. McCulloch's remains were subsequently removed to the state cemetery in Austin, Texas. General McIntosh's brother, John Baillie McIntosh, a graduate of Annapolis, served with distinction in the Union Army during the war, attaining the brevet rank of major general in both the regular and volunteer forces.

William Whann Mackall was born in Cecil County, Maryland, January 18, 1817, (303) and was graduated from West Point at the age of twenty in the class of 1837 —also that of Braxton Bragg. He was severely wounded in the Seminole War, and was twice brevetted for gallant and meritorious conduct in Mexico. On May 11, 1861 he was appointed lieutenant colonel and assistant adjutant general, U.S.A., but declined the promotion. He resigned his commission on July 3.

Appointed lieutenant colonel in the Confederate adjutant general's department, he served on the staff of General Albert Sidney Johnston, and was promoted brigadier general to rank from February 27, 1862. He was captured at Island No. 10 in April, and was later exchanged. After holding various district commands, he became chief of staff to his old classmate, Bragg, in April 1863. Relieved at his own request after the battle of Chickamauga, he was effusively commended by Bragg for his services. He again joined the Army of Tennessee, as chief of staff to General Joseph E. Johnston in January 1864. He served most efficiently until the relief of Johnston by Hood in front of Atlanta, when he declined to serve under the new army commander and once more was relieved at his own request. He saw no further active service. After the war General Mackall resided in Fairfax County, Virginia, where he owned several farms. On one of them, "Langley," his death occurred on August 12, 1891, and on another, "Lewinsville," near McLean, Virginia, he is buried.

Lafayette McLaws, a nephew by marriage of Zachary Taylor, (304) was born at Augusta, Georgia, January 15, 1821. He was graduated from West Point in the class of 1842 with his future corps commander, James Long-

street. McLaws' Mexican War record was not so distinguished as to win him brevet promotions. He resigned from the United States Army on March 23, 1861, and entered the Confederate Army as colonel of the 10th Georgia Infantry. Promoted brigadier general on September 25, 1861, and major general on May 23, 1862, for his services during the early part of the Peninsular campaign, he performed capably as a division commander in the 1st Corps of the Army of Northern Virginia. During the Knoxville campaign, however, he was relieved by Longstreet for alleged failure to make proper preparation for and "for lack of confidence in" the unsuccessful assault on Fort Sanders. Exonerated by President Davis, who refused to order a court, McLaws was restored to his command; but after an acrimonious controversy, during which Longstreet threatened to resign, McLaws was assigned to command in Georgia. (305) He subsequently served under Joseph E. Johnston and then surrendered with him at Greensboro, North Carolina. General McLaws then engaged in the insurance business in Augusta, and was collector of internal revenue and postmaster at Savannah in 1875 and 1876. He died in Savannah, July 24, 1897, and is buried there. In justice to General McLaws it should be said that his tactical dispositions were usually sound and not infrequently the object of commendation by his superiors, including Longstreet himself.

Evander McNair was born near Laurel Hill, Richmond County,

North Carolina, April 15, 1820. His parents removed the following year to Mississippi, and eventually settled in Simpson County. At the age of twenty-two McNair set up as a merchant in Jackson. During the Mexican War he was a member of Company E, 1st Mississippi Rifles, of which regiment Jefferson Davis was colonel. Removing to Washington, Arkansas, in 1856, McNair continued in the mercantile business, and in 1861 raised a battalion of seven companies of infantry. This was later r e c r u i t e d to the full strength of a regiment, was denominated the 4th Arkansas Infantry, and McNair was elected its colonel. With General Ben McCulloch he fought at Wilson's Creek and Elkhorn. Under the command of General Kirby Smith he took part in the battle of Richmond, Kentucky, where he is said to have been promoted brigadier general on the field (his commission, however, bears a later date—from November 4, 1862). He was at Murfreesboro, was later attached to Joseph E. Johnston's army in the effort to relieve Vicksburg, and was subsequently wounded at Chickamauga. Thereafter McNair's brigade was assigned to the Trans-Mississippi Department, where he took part in Price's "Missouri Raid." After the war the General moved from Arkansas to New Orleans; then to Magnolia, Mississippi; and ultimately to Hattiesburg, Mississippi, where he died, November 13, 1902, in the home of a son-in-law. (306) He is buried in Magnolia.

Dandridge McRae was born in Baldwin County, Alabama, October 10, 1829. He was graduated from South Carolina College in 1849; he took up residence in Searcy, Arkansas, where he was admitted to the bar, and was for six years clerk of the county and circuit courts. In 1861 he was inspector general of the state on the staff of Governor Rector, and was one of the first to enter Confederate service as major of the 3rd Battalion of Arkansas Infantry. As colonel of the 21st Arkansas he took part in the battles of Wilson's Creek and Elkhorn, and was promoted brigadier general on November 5, 1862. He participated in the attempt to cap-

ture Helena, Arkansas, in 1863, in order to make a diversion in favor of beleaguered Vicksburg. McRae's brigade was later in the command of Sterling Price, during the Red River campaign, in which it fought at Marks' Mills and Jenkins' Ferry. Resigning his commission in 1864, General McRae returned to his home in Searcy and resumed his law practice. Elected deputy secretary of state in 1881, he subsequently became a one-man state chamber of commerce, serving as commissioner to various expositions, and as president of the state bureau of information. He died at Searcy, April 23, 1899, (307) and is buried there.

William MacRae was born at Wilmington, North Carolina, September 9, 1834. He was educated as a civil engineer and was

so engaged at Monroe, North Carolina, in 1861. Enlisting as a private in the Monroe Light Infantry, he was elected captain when the company became a part of the 15th North Carolina; he was promoted lieutenant colonel of the regiment in April 1862, and colonel in February 1863. The 15th was in Virginia during the Seven Days battles, Second Manassas, Sharpsburg, and Fredericksburg; afterwards it served in North Carolina for a time in the brigade of John R. Cooke. Rejoining the Army of Northern Virginia, MacRae distinguished himself during the campaign of 1864; and after the wounding of General Kirkland at Cold Harbor, he was appointed brigadier general from June 22. This temporary rank was made permanent, under the act of October 13, 1862, to rank from November 4, 1864. Small in stature, and an iron disciplinarian, MacRae was said to have the ability of instilling more "fight" into his troops than any other officer in the army, John B. Gordon excepted. Paroled at Appomattox, he returned to his home, penniless. Subsequently he became general superintendent of a number of southern railroads, but his intense application to his duties destroyed his health, and he died, February 11, 1882, at Augusta, Georgia, at the early age of forty-seven. He was buried in Wilmington, North Carolina. (308)

John Bankhead Magruder, "Prince John," was born at Port Royal, Virginia, May 1, 1807, and was graduated from West Point in the class of 1830. He was three times brevetted for gallant and meritorious conduct in Mexico as an artillery officer. At the time of his resignation from the old army, April 20, 1861, he was exercising command at his brevet rank of lieutenant colonel, rather than at his regular rank of captain. Appointed brigadier general in the Provisional Confederate Army on June 17, 1861, and major general on October 7, he distinguished himself in the early part of the Peninsular campaign, completely deceiving General McClellan as to the size of his forces at Yorktown. He was less successful during the Seven Days battles, where it was alleged he failed to take advantage of several golden opportunities. He was later assigned to command the District of Texas, New Mexico, and Arizona. Here he was signally successful for a time in the recapture of Galveston and the dispersal of the Federal blockading fleet. After the war General Magruder went to Mexico without being formally paroled and joined the Imperial forces with the rank of major general. Following the downfall of the Emperor Maximilian he made his home in Houston, Texas, where he died in comparative poverty on February 18, 1871. First buried there in the lot of a friend, his remains were later re-interred in Galveston. Contrary to numerous published sources which state that he never married, he was, in fact, married at Baltimore in 1831 to Henrietta Von Kapff, by whom he had at least three children. (309)

William Mahone, the son of a tavern-keeper, was born in Southhampton County, Virginia, December 1, 1826, and was graduated from the Virginia Military Institute in 1847. Studying engineering while a teacher at Rappahannock Military Academy, he was successively engineer of several Virginia railroads, and in 1861 was president and superintendent of the Norfolk & Petersburg. He was early appointed colonel of the 6th Virginia Infan-

try. He took part in the capture of the Norfolk Navy Yard and commanded the Norfolk District until its evacuation. After aiding in the erection of the defenses at Drewry's Bluff, Mahone was continuously with the Army of Northern Virginia from Seven Pines to Appomattox Court House, except while recuperating from a severe wound received at Second Manassas. He was promoted brigadier general on November 16, 1861, and major general for his part in the battle of the Crater, to rank from July 30, 1864. He had declined a previous temporary appointment to major general, (310) and seems to have grown with his responsibilities. After the war General Lee is said to have remarked that of the surviving younger men in the army Mahone made the largest contribution to organization and command. (311) Returning to his railroad after the surrender, General Mahone soon created what is now the Norfolk & Western system. At the same time he built for himself a strong political machine, and although several times defeated in his aspirations, was elected to the United States Senate in 1880 on the "Readjuster" ticket, which was in effect the Republican party of Virginia, and which he dominated absolutely. He died at Washington on October 8, 1895, and is buried in Blandford Cemetery, Petersburg, Virginia.

James Patrick Major, a native of Fayette, Missouri, was born May 14, 1836. (312) He won an appointment to West Point in 1852, and was graduated four

years later. After a year at Carlisle Barracks, Pennsylvania, he served with the famous 2nd Cavalry on the Texas Frontier, where in one engagement with Indians he personally accounted for three "hostiles." At this time he married a sister-in-law of General Thomas Green, (313) then clerk of the Texas supreme court. He resigned from the U. S. Army on March 21, 1861, and his first Confederate service was on the staffs of Generals Van Dorn and Twiggs. In August 1861 he took part in the battle of Wilson's Creek, Missouri, as lieutenant colonel of a Missouri State Guard regiment. As acting chief of artillery to Van Dorn he aided in repulsing the Federal fleet at Vicksburg in 1862. Thereafter, in common with many of the capable officers in the Trans-Mississippi Department, his service was mainly distinguished by participation in the Red River campaign, during which he fought commendably at Mansfield and Pleasant Hill. Upon the recommendation of General Richard Taylor he had meantime been appointed brigadier general to rank from July 21, 1863. The end of the war found him directing a brigade of cavalry in John A. Wharton's command. After his parole at New Iberia, Louisiana, June 11, 1865, General Major lived in France for a time and then engaged in planting both in Louisiana and

Texas. He died at Austin, Texas, May 7, 1877. By his second marriage he became a brother-in-law of General Paul O. Hébert of Louisiana, (314) and is buried in the tomb of his father-in-law, John Andrews, in Donaldsonville, Louisiana.

George Earl Maney was born at Franklin, Tennessee, August 24, 1826. He was educated at the Nashville Seminary and the University of Nashville, where he was graduated in 1845. After participating in the war with Mexico, both as a volunteer and in the regulars, he was admitted to the bar in 1850, practicing law in Nashville until 1861. First a captain in the 11th Tennessee, he was elected colonel of the 1st Tennessee in May, and took part in the Cheat

Mountain campaign under General R. E. Lee, and served under Stonewall Jackson at Bath and Romney. Thereafter his service was with the Army of Tennessee. For gallantry at Shiloh he was promoted brigadier general to rank from April 16, 1862; and then fought in the battles of Perryville, Murfreesboro, Chickamauga, Chattanooga, and in the Atlanta campaign. While he was in temporary command of Cheatham's division at Jonesboro, he seems to have been relieved on the night of August 31, 1864, (315) and makes no further appearance in the records, although he is stated to have been paroled at Greensboro, North Carolina, May 1, 1865. (316) General Maney became president of the Tennessee & Pacific Railroad in 1868, and was the Republican nominee for governor of Tennessee in 1876, but withdrew his candidacy before the general election. From 1881 until 1894 he occupied successive diplomatic posts in Colombia, Bolivia, Paraguay, and Uruguay. His death occurred suddenly in Washington, D. C., February 9, 1901. He is buried in Mount Olivet Cemetery, Nashville.

Arthur Middleton Manigault was born at Charleston, South Carolina, October 26, 1824. After finishing elementary school, he entered the commission business

210

with which he was identified until the secession of his state in 1860. During the Mexican War he was a lieutenant in the Palmetto Regiment and saw service under General Winfield Scott. First elected captain of the North Santee Mounted Rifles, a local militia company, Manigault superintended the construction of batteries in Charleston harbor and was aide on the staff of General Beauregard during the attack on Fort Sumter, with rank of lieutenant colonel. As colonel of the 10th South Carolina Infantry he commanded the first military district of the state; after the battle of Shiloh he was ordered west with his regiment. From then on his services were with the Army of Tennessee. He took a gallant part in the campaigns of that army, from the oc-

cupation of Corinth to the battle of Franklin in November 1864, where he was wounded in the head and incapacitated for further duty. His commission of brigadier general dated from April 26, 1863. At the close of the war he became a rice planter, and in 1880 was elected adjutant and inspector general of South Carolina, an office which he held until his death. From the long-continued effects of his old wound General Manigault died at South Island, Georgetown County, South Carolina, on August 17, 1886. He is buried in Magnolia Cemetery, Charleston.

John Sappington Marmaduke was born near Arrow Rock, Missouri, March 14, 1833. He studied both at Yale and at Harvard before being graduated from West Point in 1857. Re-

signing his United States commission in 1861, he was first a colonel in the Missouri militia, then lieutenant colonel of the 1st Arkansas Battalion, and colonel of the 3rd Confederate Infantry. Highly commended for his conduct at Shiloh and Prairie Grove, he was promoted brigadier general to rank from November 15, 1862. Marmaduke twice raided into Missouri in 1863, and took part in the attack on Helena, Arkansas, in July of that year. During General Sterling Price's defense of Little Rock in September, Marmaduke was in command of the cavalry of Price's command. He here fought a duel with General L. M. Walker which resulted in the latter's death. Active in the Red River campaign of 1864, he later in the year accompanied Price into Missouri; and on the retreat, while in command of the rear guard, was captured at Mine Creek, a tributary of the Marais des Cygnes in Kansas, on October 25, 1864. While yet in prison he was the last major general appointed in the armies of the Confederacy—on March 18, 1865 to rank from March 17. (317) Upon his release from Fort Warren in July he returned to Missouri and engaged in the insurance business in St. Louis. He was later editor of an agricultural journal, and was defeated for the governorship of the state in 1880, but served

four years as a member of the Missouri Railway Commission. In 1884 General Marmaduke was elected governor with little opposition, but died at Jefferson City before the expiration of his term, December 28, 1887. He is buried there.

Humphrey Marshall, a nephew of the anti-slavery leader, James G. Birney, was born at Frankfort, Kentucky, January 13, 1812. A year after his graduation from West Point in 1832 he resigned his army commission to become a lawyer. He was colonel of the 1st Kentucky Cavalry in the Mexican War. He was elected to Congress in 1848 on the Whig ticket, and was re-elected in 1850. After serving for a year as U. S. minister to China, he re-entered Congress in 1855 and

remained until 1859, having declined to run for re-election the preceding year. A Breckinridge supporter in 1860, Marshall endeavored to maintain the border states in a posture of neutrality. When this attempt failed he accepted a commission as brigadier general in the Confederate Army on October 30, 1861. Marshall's military record was not remarkable; his most outstanding success was a minor affair at Princeton, (West) Virginia. Resigning from the army on June 16, 1862, he was reappointed four days later to rank from the date of his first appointment; (318) however, the records of the Confederate Senate do not reveal that the second appointment was submitted for confirmation. (319) After participating in Bragg's Kentucky invasion in the fall of 1862, he saw no further active service. He resigned a second time on June 17, 1863, after which he practiced law in Richmond, and was elected a member of the Second Confederate Congress (from Kentucky), serving until the end of the war. General Marshall fled to Texas after the collapse of the Confederacy. He returned to Louisville in 1866, and practiced law there until his death, March 28, 1872. He is buried in the State Cemetery at Frankfort.

James Green Martin was born at Elizabeth City, North Carolina, February 14, 1819, and was graduated from the U. S. Military Academy in 1840. He rendered most distinguished service in the Mexican War, and his right arm was amputated as the result of a wound received at Churubusco, where he was brevetted major for gallantry. At the outbreak of the Civil War, Martin resigned his commission and was appointed adjutant general of the ten regiments of North Carolina state troops then being raised. In September 1861 he became major general of militia in charge of the defense of the entire state. His administrative service in this capacity was brilliantly successful, and allegedly resulted not only in North Carolina in the first year of war supplying more troops to the

Confederate armies than any other state, but also in their being the best equipped. (320) Requesting field duty, he was appointed brigadier general to rank from May 15, 1862, but for a reason not apparent in the records, he resigned on July 25. He was reappointed on August 11 to rank from the date of his first appointment, and was confirmed by the Senate on September 30, 1862. (321) He was in command of the District of North Carolina, and was ordered to Petersburg in the summer of 1864. His bravery there was so conspicuous that at one time his soldiers carried him about on their shoulders giving cheers for "Old One Wing." His health broke down under the strain of the siege, and he finished out the war in command of the District of Western North Carolina. General Martin then took up the study of law and practiced in Asheville, North Carolina, until his death, October 4, 1878. He is buried there.

William Thompson Martin, a native of Glasgow, Kentucky, was born on March 25, 1823. He was graduated from Centre College in 1840. Two years later he removed to Natchez, Mississippi. He was admitted to the bar in 1844, and served several terms as district attorney. By conviction a strong Unionist Whig, he nevertheless recruited

a company of cavalry in 1861, which he led to Richmond after the fall of Fort Sumter. Successively promoted major, lieutenant colonel, and colonel of the Jeff Davis Legion, he commanded the rear third of J. E. B. Stuart's column in the celebrated "ride around McClellan" in 1862, and was present during the battles of the Seven Days and at Sharpsburg. He was commissioned brigadier general on December 2, 1862, and ordered to the West. Martin commanded a division in the Tullahoma campaign and at Chickamauga, and accompanied Longstreet to Knoxville. He was promoted major general to rank from November 10, 1863. In the Atlanta campaign he led a division of Wheeler's corps, and toward the close of the war, commanded the

District of Northwest Mississippi. General Martin's career after the war was distinguished by active participation in the fields of politics, education, and railroad building. A delegate to all the Democratic national conventions between 1868 and 1880, he served twelve years in the Mississippi senate. He was also a trustee both of the state university and of Jefferson College at Washington, Mississippi. In 1884 he completed the construction of the Natchez, Jackson, & Columbus Railroad, of which he was president. He died near Natchez, March 16, 1910, and is buried in City Cemetery. (322)

Dabney Herndon Maury was born in Fredericksburg, Virginia, May 21, 1822. He was graduated from the University of

Virginia in 1842. He commenced the study of law, but soon obtained an appointment to West Point, from which he was graduated in 1846. His antebellum record in the old army was distinguished and included the brevet of 1st lieutenant for gallant and meritorious service at Cerro Gordo in the Mexican War. He was dismissed on June 25, 1861, "it having been ascertained to the satisfaction of the War Department that he entertained and had expressed treasonable designs . . . ." Maury's first post of importance in the Confederacy was as colonel and chief of staff to General Van Dorn, then commanding in the Trans-Mississippi. He was promoted brigadier general for his conduct at Pea Ridge on March 18, 1862 to rank from March 12. He fought gallantly at Iuka and Corinth and was appointed major general November 4, 1862. After brief service at Vicksburg and in East Tennessee, he assumed command at Mobile, which he most ably defended until its capture at the close of the war. In 1868 he was the founder of the Southern Historical Society. He also served as a member of the executive committee of the National Guard Association, and was for four years United States minister to Colombia. When old and financially much straitened, General Maury declined to lend his name as one of the supervisors of the Louisiana Lottery. He died at the home of a son in Peoria, Illinois, January 11, 1900, and was buried in the town of his birth. Maury wrote the charming *Recollections of a Virginian*. (See Bibliography # 84.)

Samuel Bell Maxey was born at Tompkinsville, Kentucky, March 30, 1825. He was graduated from West Point in the class of 1846, and was brevetted for gallantry in the war with Mexico. In 1849 he resigned his commission to study law. In 1857

he and his father, who was also an attorney, moved to Texas, where they practiced in partnership until the outbreak of the Civil War. Resigning a seat in the Texas senate, the younger

Maxey organized the 9th Texas Infantry, and with rank of colonel joined the forces of General Albert Sidney Johnston in Kentucky. He was promoted brigadier general to rank from March 4, 1862. He served in East Tennessee, at Port Hudson, and in the Vicksburg campaign, under General J. E. Johnston. In December 1863 Maxey was placed in command of Indian Territory, and for his effective reorganization of the troops there, with which he participated in the Red River campaign, he was assigned to duty as a major general by General Kirby Smith on April 18, 1864. (323) He was not, however, subsequently appointed to that rank by the President. (324) After the war General Maxey resumed the practice of law in Paris, Texas, and in 1873 declined appointment to the state bench. Two years later he was elected to the United States Senate, where he served two terms, being defeated for re-election in 1887. He died at Eureka Springs, Arkansas, August 16, 1895, and is buried in Paris, Texas.

Hugh Weedon Mercer, a grandson of the Revolutionary General Hugh Mercer, was born at "The Sentry Box," Fredericksburg, Virginia, on November 27, 1808. He was graduated third in the class of 1828 at West Point, and was stationed for

field duty. Paroled at Macon, Georgia, May 13, 1865, General Mercer returned to banking in Savannah the following year. He moved to Baltimore in 1869, where he spent three years as a commission merchant. His health further declined, and he spent the last five years of his life in Baden-Baden, Germany, where he died on June 9, 1877. (325) His remains are buried there in an unknown grave.

some time in Savannah, Georgia, where he married into a local family. He resigned his commission on April 30, 1835 and settled in Savannah. From 1841 until the outbreak of the Civil War he was cashier of the Planters' Bank there. Upon the secession of Georgia, Mercer entered Confederate service as colonel of the 1st Georgia Volunteers. He was promoted brigadier general on October 29, 1861. During the greater part of the war, with a brigade of three Georgia regiments, General Mercer commanded at Savannah, but he and his brigade took part in the Atlanta campaign of 1864, first in W. H. T. Walker's division and then in Cleburne's. On account of poor health he accompanied General Hardee to Savannah after the battle of Jonesboro, and saw no further

William Miller, a native of Ithaca, New York, was born on August 3, 1820. His parents moved to Louisiana while he was in his infancy. He was educated at Louisiana College, and afterwards studied law. He fought in the Mexican War in General Zachary Taylor's army,

217

and soon after, settled near Pensacola, Florida. At the beginning of the Civil War he had been operating for some years a saw mill in Santa Rosa County. He first commanded a battalion with rank of major. His six companies were consolidated into the 1st Florida Infantry after the battle of Shiloh, and he led this regiment in General Bragg's invasion of Kentucky. He was later seriously wounded at Murfreesboro. After recuperating, he served as commandant of conscripts for the state of Florida, and on August 2, 1864 was commissioned brigadier general and placed in command of the reserve forces of the state. He later commanded the District of Florida. At the conclusion of the war General Miller moved to Washington County, where he again engaged in the lumber business and in the operation of large farming interests. He served one term in the lower house of the legislature in 1885, and the following year was elected to the state senate, and was again elected in 1903. He died at Point Washington, Florida, August 8, 1909, five days after his eighty-ninth birthday, and was first buried in the yard of his home. Some years later his remains were re-interred in St. John's Cemetery, Pensacola. (326)

Young Marshall Moody was born in Chesterfield County, Virginia, June 23, 1822. Going to

Alabama at the age of twenty, he settled in Marengo County, and was successively school teacher, merchant, and clerk of the circuit court from 1856 until 1861. He entered Confederate service as a captain in the 11th Alabama Infantry. He assisted in raising the 43rd Alabama, of which he was elected lieutenant colonel, and Archibald Gracie, colonel. Upon the latter's pro-

motion to brigadier in November 1862, Moody was appointed colonel of the regiment. He participated in t h e Kentucky campaign, and fought with great distinction at Chickamauga; later he accompanied General Longstreet on the Knoxville expedition. Early in 1864 he was at Petersburg, Virginia, under General Beauregard; he was severely wounded at Drewry's Bluff in May. During the siege he commanded his regiment until General Gracie was killed in December, after which he was placed in charge of the brigade, with formal promotion to brigadier general from March 4, 1865. General Moody was paroled at Appomattox Court House, and then went to Mobile to engage in business. While in New Orleans on business in the late summer of 1866, he contracted yellow fever and died on September 18. He was buried in New Orleans. (327)

John Creed Moore was born in Hawkins County, Tennessee, February 28, 1824. He obtained his preparatory education at Emory and Henry College, (328) and was graduated from the U. S. Military Academy in 1849. After seeing action in Florida against the Seminoles and garrison duty in Santa Fe and Baton Rouge, he resigned his commission in 1855. In 1861 he was a professor at Shelby College, Kentucky. He went to Galveston, Texas, in that year, and organized the 2nd Texas Infantry, of which he was elected colonel. At the head of this regiment he participated in the battle of Shiloh, and was commended for outstanding gallantry by his superior, General Withers. He was promoted brigadier general on May 26, 1862. He took part in the attack on Corinth, and in the Vicksburg campaign. After his capture and subsequent ex-

change at Vicksburg, he fought at Chattanooga under General Bragg. He was then sent to assist in the defense of Mobile, at the special request of General Maury, who assigned him to command the Eastern and Western Districts of the Department of the Gulf on December 10, 1863. (329) For reasons not made apparent by the records General Moore resigned his commission in the Confederate service on February 3, 1864. (330) For many years after the war he taught school in Texas, residing variously at Mexia and Dallas, and was a prolific contributor to magazines and journals. His death occurred at Osage, Coryell County, Texas, in his eighty-seventh year on December 31, 1910. He is buried in Osage.

Patrick Theodore Moore, a native of Ireland, was born at Gal-

way on September 22, 1821. The family came to Canada in 1835. Soon after, his father was appointed British consul at Boston. The younger Moore removed to Richmond in 1850, and became a merchant there, and was for some time a captain of militia. He offered his services to the Confederacy at the outbreak of war, and was commissioned colonel of the 1st Virginia Infantry, which he led at First Manassas in the brigade of Longstreet. He here sustained a severe wound in the head, which incapacitated him for further duty at the head of his regiment. However, he acted as volunteer aide on J. E. Johnston's staff until the latter was wounded at Seven Pines, and on Longstreet's staff during the Seven Days battles. Thereafter he performed court martial duty, and in 1864 was temporarily assigned to organize, under General Kemper, the reserve forces of Virginia. He was promoted brigadier general to rank from September 20, 1864. At the close of the war he commanded a brigade in General Ewell's Richmond local defense troops, but he apparently did not accompany them on the retreat from the capital, since no record exists of his capture at Sayler's Creek. He was paroled at Manchester, Virginia, April 30, 1865. (331) General Moore's former business had been swept away by the war, and he opened an insurance agency in Richmond. He died there on February 19, 1883, and was buried in Shockoe Cemetery. (332)

John Hunt Morgan, whose two sisters married Generals A. P. Hill and Basil W. Duke, was born at Huntsville, Alabama, June 1, 1825. Educated at Transylvania College in Lexington, Kentucky (his mother's home), he enlisted in the Mexican War and saw service at Buena Vista. He was mustered out in 1847, and commenced the manufacture of hemp in Lexington, and engaged in the general merchandising business left him by his grandfather Hunt. He organized the Lexington Rifles in 1857, but when the Civil War came, Morgan led his command to Bowling Green and joined the forces of General Buckner. From

he was placed in command of the Department of Southwestern Virginia in April 1864. He bivouacked in Greeneville, Tennessee, on the night of September 3, 1864, while en route to attack Federal forces near Knoxville. Early the next morning he was surprised by a detachment of Union cavalry and was killed in the garden of the house where he had been sleeping. He is buried in Lexington, Kentucky. (333)

John Tyler Morgan was born in Athens, Tennessee, June 20, 1824. He was educated by his mother and in the country schools of Calhoun County, Alabama, where the family moved in his ninth year. He studied law in Tuskegee, Alabama, and was admitted to the bar in 1845; in 1855 he moved to Selma. A Breckinridge Elector in 1860 and a member of the Alabama secession convention, he enlisted as a private in the Cahaba Rifles in 1861, at the age of thirty-seven. He soon rose to major and lieutenant colonel of the 5th Alabama Infantry, of which Robert E. Rodes was colonel. He resigned in 1862, and recruited the 51st Alabama Partisan Rangers, of which he became colonel. He declined a promotion to command Rodes' old brigade of the Army of Northern Virginia after the latter's elevation to major general, but he was later appointed its brigadier to rank

then until his death three years later his exploits made him one of the legendary figures of the Confederacy, ranking then and to this day with Jeb Stuart in the hearts of Kentuckians as a symbol of the "Lost Cause." He was promoted colonel of the 2nd Kentucky Cavalry on April 4, 1862, and brigadier general on December 11. His series of raids into Tennessee, Kentucky, Indiana, and Ohio earned him a vote of thanks from the Confederate Congress and the undying animosity of a large segment of the frightened North. On his most famous raid north of the Ohio in 1863 he was captured near New Lisbon and imprisoned in the Ohio State Penitentiary, together with a number of his officers. Contriving to escape and make his way south,

from November 16, 1863. Morgan led his two different regiments and his brigade at such widely separated fields as First Manassas, Murfreesboro, and Chickamauga; and served under Generals Beauregard, Longstreet, Forrest, and Wheeler. His last field service was the harassment of Sherman's column en route from Atlanta to Savannah. At the close of the war he was attempting to recruit Negro troops in Mississippi. In 1876, after resuming the practice of law, and becoming a standard-bearer in the fight for white supremacy, General Morgan was elected to the United States Senate from Alabama, where he served until his death at Washington, June 11, 1907. His long tenure in the Senate was particularly marked by an uninter-

rupted effort to secure a canal route from the Atlantic to the Pacific through Central America. He felt that such a canal would enable Southern trade to compete in Pacific markets. He is buried in Selma, Alabama.

Jean Jacques Alfred Alexander Mouton was born at Opelousas, Louisiana, February 18, 1829, the son of the ex-Governor and United States Senator, Alexander Mouton. Jean was brought up in the French tongue and learned to speak English only as a young man. He received his early education in the schools of Lafayette (then Vermillionville), Louisiana, and was graduated from West Point in the class of 1850. Almost immediately, he resigned to become a railroad construction engineer and brigadier gen-

eral of Louisiana militia. At the beginning of the Civil War he recruited a company in Lafayette Parish, and was elected colonel of the 18th Louisiana Infantry in October 1861. At the head of this regiment he rendered outstanding service at the battle of Shiloh, where he sustained a nearly fatal wound. He was promoted brigadier general to rank from April 16, 1862. After his recovery General Mouton led a brigade of Louisiana regiments in General Richard Taylor's Department, and was frequently commended by Taylor for his ability and skill. On April 8, 1864, while in command of his own brigade and that of General Prince de Polignac, he opened the battle of Mansfield in the Red River campaign against the Federal General Banks, and was killed while leading a charge. He is buried in Lafayette, Louisiana. His stepmother was a sister of General Franklin Gardner.

Allison Nelson was born in Fulton County, Georgia, March 11, 1822. He was trained as a lawyer, and was a member of the Georgia legislature in 1848-49; and was also mayor of Atlanta in 1855. However, his primary interest was in military affairs. During the Mexican War he recruited a company of volunteers of which he was elected captain. Later he espoused the cause of Cuban independence and attached himself to the forces of General Narcisco Lopez, by whom he was appointed a brigadier. He was in Kansas during the "border troubles," and removed to Bosque County, Texas, in 1856, where he rendered gallant service in the Indian campaigns of the period before the Civil War. He was elected to the Texas legislature in 1859, and to the secession convention in 1861. Nelson was instrumental in raising the 10th Texas Infantry for Confederate service, and was elected colonel of this regiment. The command reported to General Hindman in Arkansas, and took part in a minor engagement at DeVall's Bluff on White River. Nelson was promoted brigadier general to rank from September 12, 1862 upon the recommendation of

General Holmes. He was assigned to command the 2nd Division of Holmes' infantry, consisting of his own and Colonel Flournoy's brigades on September 28, 1862, the day after he fell ill of fever. General Nelson died in camp near Austin, Arkansas, on October 7, 1862, and was buried in Little Rock, then headquarters of the Trans-Mississippi Department. (334)

Francis Redding Tillou Nicholls was born at Donaldsonville, Louisiana, August 20, 1834. He was graduated from West Point in 1855, and resigned his commission the following year to study law at the University of Louisiana, now Tulane University. He was practicing at Napoleonville at the beginning of

the war. He entered the Confederate Army as captain of the Phoenix Guards, but was soon elected lieutenant colonel of the 8th Louisiana. With this regiment he fought at First Manassas and in Jackson's Valley campaign, and was wounded and taken prisoner at Winchester. He lost his left arm as a result of this wound; and at Chancellorsville, his left foot was torn off by a shell. In the latter battle he was in command of one of the Louisiana brigades, having been promoted brigadier general on October 14, 1862. Unfit for further field duty, General Nicholls commanded the post at Lynchburg, Virginia, for a time, and was then in charge of the volunteer and conscript bureau of the Trans-Mississippi Department until the termination of hostilities. In 1876 his friends nominated "all that is left of General Nicholls" for Democratic governor of Louisiana. He refused to accept defeat at the hands of his Republican opponent, and was ultimately recognized by the Federal authorities after a period of dual administration in the state. He was in semi-retirement for eight years after the expiration of his first term, and was again elected governor in 1888 and served until 1892. During this term he aided in suppressing the notorious Louisiana Lottery. From then until a year before his death on his plantation near Thibodeaux, General Nicholls was either associate or chief justice of the Louisiana supreme court. He retired in 1911, and died on January 4, 1912. He is buried in Thibodeaux.

Lucius Bellinger Northrop (335) was born at Charleston, South Carolina, September 8, 1811, and was graduated from West Point in 1831. During the 1839 Seminole War he was so severely wounded as to be retired from the army on permanent sick furlough, after which he studied medicine in Philadelphia. He returned to Charleston, and was dropped from the army in 1848 for practicing medicine, but was soon reinstated. This grace was supposedly due to Jefferson

Davis, with whom he had been intimate since West Point days. Still on sick furlough Northrop engaged in his new profession until 1861, when he resigned on January 8. He was soon appointed colonel and commissary general of the Confederacy by Davis, and assumed the enormous responsibility of providing food not only for the Southern armies, but for the tens of thousands of Union prisoners as well. Though bitterly criticized by many of his contemporaries, and deemed to be a "pet" of the President's, it seems apparent now that no one could have discharged Northrop's duties to the satisfaction of all concerned. This was especially true in view of the shortages of food and transportation, the latter being under the control of the quartermaster's department. Davis had appointed him brigadier general, to rank from November 26, 1864, but does not appear to have risked forwarding his nomination to the Senate, where it doubtless would have been rejected. (336) Finally relieved on February 15, 1865, when the end was already in sight, he was arrested by the Federal authorities on June 30, 1865, on suspicion of having deliberately starved prisoners of war. The charges were manifestly absurd, and he was released in October. He spent the next twenty-five years of his life on a farm near Charlottesville, Virginia. Stricken with paralysis in 1890, he died in the Confederate Home at Pikesville, Maryland, on February 9, 1894. He is buried in New Cathedral Cemetery, Baltimore.

Edward Asbury O'Neal, a life-long resident of Alabama, was born in Madison County, Sep-

tember 20, 1818. After graduating from LaGrange College in 1836, he was admitted to the bar and commenced practice in Florence. He was soon chosen by the legislature as solicitor of the fourth circuit. Defeated for Congress in 1848, he became one of North Alabama's leading advocates of secession, and in 1861 enlisted in the 9th Alabama Infantry, of which he was elected major and subsequently lieutenant colonel. In 1862, as colonel of the 26th Alabama, he led his regiment in the Peninsular campaign, and was wounded at Seven Pines. He was again wounded at Boonsboro in the Maryland campaign, and commanded Rodes' brigade with unquestioned courage at Chancellorsville and was at Gettysburg. Immediately before the latter battle General Lee had recommended O'Neal for promotion to brigadier and permanent command of the brigade. A commission at that grade was evidently issued and forwarded to Lee's headquarters, bearing the date of June 6, 1863. The document, however, was not delivered to O'Neal, and Lee subsequently recalled his recommendation, which was returned to Richmond and cancelled by order of the President. (337) In 1864 the 26th Alabama was sent home to recruit. It later served in Cantey's brigade (which O'Neal commanded for a time) in the Atlanta campaign. O'Neal was relieved before the Tennessee expedition, and was at the end of the war arresting deserters in North Alabama. Resuming his law practice in Florence, he became the Democratic leader of his section of the state, and was elected governor in 1882 and 1884. He died at Florence, November 7, 1890, and is buried there.

Richard Lucian Page, nicknamed "Ramrod" and "Bombast

Page" in the old navy, was born in Clarke County, Virginia, December 20, 1807. He became a midshipman in the United States Navy in 1824, and the following year was aboard the *Brandywine* when it conveyed General Lafayette back to France. He rose to the rank of commander in 1855, and did sea duty in virtually every portion of the globe, as well as three tours of ordnance duty and one as executive officer of the Norfolk Navy Yard. Upon the secession of Virginia he resigned his commission, and supervised the construction of works on the James and Nansemond rivers. In June 1861, with rank of Commander, C.S.N., he was assigned as ordnance officer at Norfolk. He was promoted captain, and later established an ordnance and naval construction bureau at Charlotte, North Carolina, which he operated for two years. Meantime he took part in the naval battle off Port Royal. On March 1, 1864 Captain Page became a brigadier general in the Provisional Army, and was assigned to duty in command of the outer defenses of Mobile Bay, with headquarters at Fort Morgan. He gallantly defended the latter work against the combined Federal sea and land attack of August 1864. He was compelled to surrender on the twenty-third, and was held as a prisoner of war at Fort Delaware until July 24, 1865. He then settled in Norfolk, Virginia, and from 1875 to 1883 served as the city's superintendent of schools. He died at Blue Ridge Summit, Pennsylvania, August 9, 1901, in his ninety-fourth year, and is buried in Cedar Hill Cemetery, Norfolk. General Page was a first cousin of Robert E. Lee; his mother was a sister of Lee's father.

Joseph Benjamin Palmer was born in Rutherford County, Tennessee, November 1, 1825. Left an orphan in infancy, he was reared by his grandparents. He was educated at Union University in Murfreesboro and admitted to the bar in 1848. The following year he was elected to the state legislature, and was re-elected in 1851; from 1855 to 1859 he was mayor of Murfreesboro. By political conviction

paign, and fought at Bentonville. He was paroled at Greensboro, North Carolina, May 1, 1865. Following the surrender General Palmer marched the Tennessee troops home and quietly resumed his law practice. Although several times asked to run for governor on the Democratic ticket, he refrained from active politics. He died at his home in Murfreesboro, November 4, 1890. and is buried there in Evergreen Cemetery. (338)

Mosby Monroe Parsons was born at Charlottesville, Virginia, May 21, 1822. He moved as a young man to Cole County, Missouri, where he studied law, and was admitted to the bar. During the war with Mexico he commanded a company of mounted volunteers. From 1853 to 1857 he was attorney general of Missouri, and subsequently was elected to the state senate. Parsons was actively allied with Governor Claiborne Jackson in an effort to hold Missouri to the Confederate cause. He commanded the 6th Division of the Missouri State Guard from the outbreak of war until he was commissioned brigadier in the Confederate service on November 5, 1862. (339) He fought at Carthage, Springfield, and Elkhorn, and in the Arkansas campaigns of 1862 and 1863. The following year he was sent to reinforce Richard Taylor during the Red River campaign, where

a staunch Unionist Whig, he followed his state into the Confederacy and raised a company which became part of the 18th Tennessee, of which he was elected colonel. He was captured at Fort Donelson and later exchanged. He took a gallant part in the battle of Murfreesboro, where he was three times wounded. At Chickamauga he was again dangerously wounded, and did not rejoin his command until just before the battles around Atlanta; he was again wounded at Jonesboro. Promoted brigadier general from November 15, 1864, he led John C. Brown's old brigade at Franklin during Hood's Tennessee campaign. In the retreat from Nashville his brigade was a part of the rear guard of the army. He was in command of the consolidated Tennessee regiments in the Carolinas cam-

he was present at Pleasant Hill, and later participated in the engagements at Marks' Mills and Jenkins' Ferry against Steele. As of April 30, 1864 he was assigned to duty as a major general by Kirby Smith and was so paroled, although he was never officially appointed by the President. (340) He accompanied Sterling Price on the 1864 raid into Missouri, and went to Mexico after the close of the war. Accounts of his death vary. It seems reasonably certain that he attached himself to the Imperialist forces, and was killed by Republican irregulars, probably on August 15, 1865, in the vicinity of China, on the San Juan River, in the state of Nuevo Leon. (341) So far as is known, the bodies of Parsons and his five companions — including his brother-in-law

and ex-adjutant, Captain A. M. Standish, and A. H. Conrow, late a member of the Confederate Congress—were buried in the neighborhood. (342)

Elisha Franklin "Bull" Paxton was born in Rockbridge County, Virginia, March 4, 1828. He was graduated from Washington College in 1845, and from Yale two years later; he then studied law at the University of Virginia. After being admitted to the bar, he practiced for some years in Ohio before opening an office in Lexington, Virginia, in 1854. He abandoned his profession in 1859 because of failing eyesight. He was living on his estate near Lexington at the outbreak of war, and went into the army as a lieutenant of the Rockbridge Rifles, which later became part of the

27th Virginia Infantry. Paxton took part in the battle of First Manassas, and during the campaigns of 1862, was a member of the staff of Stonewall Jackson with rank of major and assistant adjutant general. On Jackson's recommendation he was, on November 1, 1862, promoted over the heads of all the regimental commanders to brigadier general, and assigned to the command of the Stonewall Brigade. This selection met with a mixed reception and resulted in at least one resignation. General Paxton led his brigade in but two battles, Fredericksburg and Chancellorsville. His command was not in the fight on the first day of Chancellorsville, having been left to guard a road junction. Deployed in line that night, the brigade was advancing shortly after daylight the following morning, May 3, 1863, when he was almost instantly killed by a Minié ball while he was in the front line. General Paxton was temporarily buried in the yard of the house in which Jackson later died; his remains now lie in Lexington within a few feet of his old commander. (343)

William Henry Fitzhugh Payne was born in Fauquier County, Virginia, January 27, 1830. He was graduated from the Virginia Military Institute in 1849, and the following year from the University of Virginia, where he

studied law. In 1856 he was elected commonwealth attorney, and was living at Warrenton in 1861. He enlisted as a private, and was present at the occupation of Harpers Ferry in the first days of the war. He had a notable career as a cavalryman in the Army of Northern Virginia, and rose to the rank of brigadier general from November 1, 1864. He was wounded and captured at Williamsburg in May 1862; was again wounded and captured during the Pennsylvania campaign; and being once more wounded at Five Forks in April 1865, was unable to rejoin his command. He was captured a third time near Warrenton on the night of Lincoln's assassination. He spent more than fourteen months on Johnson's Island in the course of his two imprisonments there, and was finally released on May 29, 1865. Resuming his law practice, he was elected to the Virginia house of delegates for one term in 1879. He later moved to Washington, where he became general counsel for the Southern Railway, and where he died, March 29, 1904. General Payne is buried in Warrenton. (344)

William Raine Peck, a native of Jefferson County, Tennessee, was born January 31, 1818. (345) In the early 1840's he moved to Louisiana and purchased a plantation near the now extinct village of Milliken's Bend, in Madison Parish opposite Vicksburg. He prospered there and acquired other lands in the vicinity. On July 7, 1861 he enlisted at Camp Moore in the 9th Louisiana In-

fantry as a private. (346) The first colonel of this regiment was Richard Taylor, later lieutenant general; the second was Leroy A. Stafford, subsequently brigadier general; and the third was Peck. Arriving at the battlefield of First Manassas just after the Federal retreat, the 9th fought in every engagement of the Army of Northern Virginia thereafter. It surrendered sixty-four men and four officers at Appomattox Court House. Peck was meantime promoted through grades to colonel, from October 8, 1863, and with this rank commanded the brigade in several actions, including that of the Monocacy, in which he was highly commended by his division commander, John B. Gordon. His appointment as brigadier general dated from February 18, 1865. Peck himself was not at Appomattox; he was paroled at Vicksburg, June 6, 1865. (347) Nearly six and a half feet tall, and proportionately built, he never received so much as a flesh wound throughout the war, though he exposed himself repeatedly. After his parole he returned to his plantation, "The Mountain," where he died, January 22, 1871. (348) He is buried in the family cemetery at Jefferson City, Tennessee.

John Pegram was born at Petersburg, Virginia, January 24, 1832, and was graduated from West Point in the class of 1854. His

routine frontier service was followed by two years spent in Europe on leave of absence. He resigned his commission on May 10, 1861. As a lieutenant colonel he took part in the Rich Mountain campaign of that summer under General R. S. Garnett, and was captured. After his return to the army Pegram was promoted colonel, and in 1862, served on the staffs of Generals Beauregard and Bragg as chief engineer. He was chief of staff to Kirby Smith during the invasion of Kentucky. Appointed brigadier general to rank from November 7, 1862, he was assigned a cavalry brigade, and fought at Murfreesboro. At Chickamauga he led a division of Forrest's corps. He was subsequently transferred to the Army of Northern Virginia, and was given an infantry brigade in Early's division of the 2nd Corps, which he led with notable skill and gallantry at the battle of the Wilderness, where he was wounded, and in the Shenandoah. After the death of Rodes at Winchester, General Pegram succeeded to the command of the division, although he was never formally promoted to major general. (349) In the fight at Hatcher's Run, February 6, 1865, he was struck near the heart by a musket ball, and died almost immediately. (350) His funeral was conducted from St. Paul's Church, Richmond, where only three weeks before he had been married. His remains were interred in Hollywood Cemetery.

John Clifford Pemberton was born in Philadelphia, Pennsylvania, August 10, 1814, and was graduated in the class of 1837 at West Point. He won two brevets for gallantry in Mexico. In 1848 he married Martha Thompson of Norfolk, Virginia, a connection which no doubt contributed largely to his decision to resign from the old army on April 24, 1861. (351) His early Confederate service as commander of the Department of South Carolina, Georgia, and Florida was hardly such as to warrant his rapid promotion from brigadier general (June 17, 1861) to major general ranking from January 14, 1862, and to lieutenant general ranking from October 10, 1862. At this juncture he was assigned to the command of the Department of Mississippi and Eastern Louisiana, an area which embraced the all-important stronghold of Vicksburg. He was hampered by conflicting orders at the outset, and was finally compelled after a stubborn defense to capitulate on July 4, 1863. No further duty was found for him commensurate with his rank. He resigned his commission of lieutenant general in 1864, and was appointed by President Davis a lieutenant colonel of artillery, in which capacity he served faithfully until the end of the war. He subsequently lived on a farm near Warrenton, Virginia. Later he returned to Pennsylvania, where he died on July 13, 1881, at Penllyn. He was buried in Philadelphia. Despite much contemporary vilification of him because of his Northern birth, General Pemberton's complete loyalty to the Confederate cause cannot be questioned.

William Dorsey Pender was born in Edgecomb County, North Carolina, on February 6, 1834. He received his early education in the common schools of the county, and worked as a clerk in his brother's store before receiving an appointment to West Point at the age of sixteen. Graduated in the class of 1854, his old army service was mainly on the Pacific coast, during which he was involved in a number of Indian skirmishes. Pender resigned his 1st lieutenant's commission on March 21, 1861, and entered the Confederate Army as colonel of the 3rd (later 13th) North Carolina. His regiment was first attached to Whiting's brigade of G. W. Smith's division. He was promoted brigadier general for gallant service at Seven Pines, to rank from June 3, 1862, and given command of a brigade in A. P. Hill's division. This he ably led from the Seven Days to Chancellorsville, and was three times wounded. Promoted major general on May 27, 1863, he led his division to Gettysburg, where on the second day he was wounded in the leg by a fragment of shell. On the long road back to Staunton, Virginia, infection set in, which necessitated amputation on his arrival there.

came rector of Grace Church, Lexington, Virginia, a post he occupied until his death. Upon the outbreak of the Civil War the Reverend Pendleton unhesitatingly offered his services to Virginia. He was elected captain of the Rockbridge Artillery, and was rapidly promoted to colonel and chief of artillery on the staff of General Joseph E. Johnston. He became brigadier general on March 26, 1862. He served uninterruptedly with the Army of Northern Virginia from First Manassas to Appomattox, and was for a large part of the war the nominal chief of artillery of the army. However, during the last two years his duties were largely administrative and confined to active command of the reserve ordnance. He never lost sight of his calling, and frequently

From this operation he failed to rally, dying in Staunton on July 18. At the time he was perhaps the most outstanding of the younger general officers of the army. His body was taken to North Carolina and buried in the yard of Calvary Church at Tarboro.

William Nelson Pendleton was born in Richmond, Virginia, December 26, 1809. He was instructed by tutors and went to a private school in Richmond. He later attended West Point and was graduated fifth in the class of 1830. Resigning three years later to engage in teaching, he determined to enter the Episcopal ministry, and was ordained in 1838. In 1847 he ceased teaching to devote all his time to ecclesiastical pursuits. In 1853 he be-

preached to the soldiers. Returning to Lexington after the war, General Pendleton resumed his rectorship and carried on a noble struggle against poverty in his desolated parish, and against the hostility of the Federal authorities. He was an intimate of General Robert E. Lee, who was a member of his vestry, and was the father-in-law of General Edwin G. Lee. He died at Lexington on January 15, 1883, and is buried there. (352)

Abner Monroe Perrin, a native of South Carolina, was born in Edgefield District, February 2, 1827. (353) He took part in the Mexican War as a 2nd, and later 1st, lieutenant of infantry in the regular army. He afterwards studied law and was admitted to the bar in Columbia in 1854. En-

tering Confederate service as captain of the 14th South Carolina, he went to Virginia in the spring of 1862, and participated in the Seven Days battles, Cedar Mountain, Second Manassas, Harpers Ferry, Sharpsburg, and Fredericksburg. He was promoted colonel on February 20, 1863, and led the regiment at Chancellorsville and, after the wounding of McGowan, Perrin led the brigade there and at Gettysburg. He was commissioned brigadier general to rank from September 10, 1863, and was given command of Wilcox's old brigade of Anderson's division of the 3rd Corps. He was conspicuous for his bravery at the Wilderness, and is said to have declared before the battle of Spotsylvania Court House that, "I shall come out of this fight a live major general or a dead brigadier." During the early morning hours of May 12, 1864—after Hancock's men had overrun the "Mule Shoe" and captured the greater part of Edward Johnson's division—A. P. Hill was called upon for reinforcements. As Perrin was leading his men up to the works sword in hand through a veritable hail of fire, he fell dead from his horse, pierced with seven balls. He was buried in the City Cemetery in Fredericksburg, Virginia. (354)

Edward Aylesworth Perry was a native of Massachusetts, born at

Richmond on March 15, 1831. He received his elementary education at Richmond Academy, and entered Yale in 1850, but withdrew the following year to teach school and study law in Alabama. He removed to Pensacola, Florida, in 1857, and engaged in the practice of law there. In 1861 he went into the Confederate Army as captain of Company A, 2nd Florida Infantry, of which he became colonel in May 1862. He was severely wounded at Frayser's Farm during the Seven Days battles. Promoted brigadier general to rank from August 28, 1862, he led the Florida Brigade at Chancellorsville. Soon after, he came down with typhoid fever. He was again on active duty during the Overland campaign of 1864, and was a second time severely wounded at the Wilderness. After his re-

covery he was assigned to duty with the reserve forces of Alabama, where he served until the close of the war. General Perry soon thereafter attained great prominence at the Florida bar. As an outspoken opponent of carpetbag rule, he was elected governor of the state in 1884 on the Democratic ticket. He retired to private life at the end of his term, and died suddenly from a stroke while visiting in Kerrville, Texas, on October 15, 1889. He is buried in Pensacola.

William Flank Perry was born in Jackson County, Georgia, March 12, 1823. (355) His parents moved to Chambers County, Alabama, when he was ten. With little or no formal schooling, he taught himself, and then proceeded to teach others. He studied law, and was admitted to the bar in 1854, but never prac-

ticed. The same year he was elected Alabama's first superintendent of public instruction, and was twice re-elected. In this office he laid the foundations for the state's public school system. From 1858 to 1862 Perry was president of the East Alabama Female College, a position from which he resigned to enlist in the Confederate Army as a private in the 44th Alabama; a few weeks later he was elected its major. The 44th fought at Second Manassas and Sharpsburg, after which Perry became colonel of the regiment. As a part of Law's brigade in the 1st Corps the regiment was present at Gettysburg, Chickamauga, the Wilderness, and Spotsylvania. After Cold Harbor, Perry led Law's brigade until the final surrender at Appomattox, and was repeatedly recommended for promotion by Longstreet and others. He was finally commissioned brigadier general to rank from February 21, 1865. Returning to Alabama after the war, General Perry spent two years as a planter, and then moved to Kentucky to engage in his old occupation of teaching. At the time of his death, December 18, 1901, he had been for many years professor of English and philosophy at Ogden College, Bowling Green, Kentucky. He is buried there in Fairview Cemetery.

James Johnston Pettigrew was born at "Bonarva," the family

home in Tyrrell County, North Carolina, on July 4, 1828. He entered the University of North Carolina at the age of fifteen. His scholastic career was so brilliant, that upon his graduation in 1847, President Polk tendered him an appointment as assistant professor at the Naval Observatory in Washington. After two years there he commenced the study of law. He travelled abroad, and later practiced in Charleston. He was elected to the South Carolina legislature in 1856. As a colonel of militia in 1861, he saw service in Charleston harbor during the fateful days of April, and subsequently enlisted in the Hampton Legion. Soon elected colonel of the 12th South Carolina, Pettigrew went to Virginia and after some protest on his own part, accepted a commission as brigadier general to rank from February 26, 1862. He served under Joseph E. Johnston in the Peninsular campaign, and was severely wounded and captured at Seven Pines. Upon his exchange two months later, he served for a time in command of the defenses of Petersburg and in North Carolina. His brigade was in Heth's division of A. P. Hill's corps during the Gettysburg campaign. After the wounding of his immediate superior, he commanded the division, and was conspicuous in the attack of the third day against the Federal center. General Pettigrew was in command of a portion of the rear guard during the retreat to the Potomac; he was fatally wounded shortly before noon on July 14, 1863 at Falling Waters, Maryland, by a sudden dash of Federal cavalry. (356) He died three days later near Bunker Hill, Virginia, and was buried at "Bonarva."

Edmund Winston Pettus, a native of Alabama, was born in Limestone County, July 6, 1821. He was educated at Clinton College, Smith County, Tennessee. He read law at Tuscumbia, and was admitted to practice in 1842, following which he settled in Gainesville. He served as solicitor of his district, and later as judge of the seventh circuit. He removed to Cahaba in 1858, and was living there in 1861. At this

time he was sent as a commissioner of the state to Mississippi, of which his brother, John J. Pettus, was governor. He aided in the recruitment of the 20th Alabama, and was elected its major, and in October 1861, lieutenant colonel. Pettus was a fearless and dogged fighter and distinguished himself on many fields in the western theatre of war. Captured at Vicksburg and exchanged, he became colonel of the 20th after the concurrent promotion and death of General Garrott. On September 18, 1863, he was himself promoted brigadier general. Thereafter, he followed with conspicuous bravery every forlorn hope which the Confederacy offered, from Chattanooga to Bentonville, including the invasion of Tennessee by

Hood. He was wounded in the Carolinas campaign. At the close of the war General Pettus returned to Alabama and took up residence at Selma. He resumed his law practice, and became prominent in the Democratic affairs of the state. He nevertheless did not offer for public office until 1896, when he was elected to the United States Senate, and was re-elected in 1902. He served until his death, July 27, 1907, at Hot Springs, North Carolina—the last of the Confederate brigadiers to sit in the upper house of the national Congress. He is buried in Selma.

George Edward Pickett was born in Richmond, Virginia, on January 28, 1825. He was graduated from West Point in 1846, last in his class. (357) Brevetted twice for gallantry in Mexico, he later served on the Texas frontier from 1849 to 1855, and in Washington Territory from 1856 to 1861. He gained much favorable notice for his defiance of the British in the San Juan Island Affair (358) in 1859, when he occupied the island with a small force of United States troops. His first Confederate service was as colonel in command of the defenses of the Lower Rappahannock. He was appointed brigadier general to rank from January 14, 1862, and led his brigade with great dash through the Peninsular campaign. He was subsequently severely wounded at Gaines's Mill, but rejoined his command after the first Maryland invasion. Promoted major general on October 10, 1862, he was present at Fredericksburg and with Longstreet at Suffolk. The highwater mark of his career, and that of the Army of Northern Virginia, was reached on July 3, 1863 at Gettysburg, when he advanced his small division (two of the brigades of which were on detached duty), together with large support from the 3rd Corps, against the all but impregnable Federal center on Cemetery Ridge. The casualties in the assault were frightful, and numbered every field and general officer save one in Pickett's own division. (359) Picket later commanded the Department of Virginia and North Carolina, and in 1864 was one of the defenders

of Petersburg. His defeat at the hands of Philip Sheridan in the battle of Five Forks on April 1, 1865, though in no way demonstrably discreditable, seemingly earned him Lee's censure; and after Sayler's Creek he was relieved from command, though he continued with the army until its surrender at Appomattox. (360) He was afterwards an insurance agent in Norfolk, Virginia, where he died on July 30, 1875. He is buried in Richmond.

Albert Pike was born in Boston, Massachusetts, December 29, 1809. He was a many-sided character who is best remembered for his accomplishments as a brilliant teacher, poet, author, lawyer, editor, and exponent of Freemasonry, rather than as a brigadier general of the Confederacy, which he incidentally became. An avowed Whig and anti-secessionist, he was a prominent lawyer and large land owner in Arkansas in 1861, and cast his lot with the South rather than desert his friends and his property. He had meantime taken a creditable part in the Mexican War. His Civil War career was unfortunate, to say the least, and resulted in his arrest by General Hindman and the remark by General Douglas Cooper that he was "either insane or untrue to the South." He had been commissioned brigadier general on August 15, 1861 to negotiate treaties with the Indians west of the Arkansas River and ally them to the Confederate cause. With these Indian troops he fought at Elkhorn Tavern, and their dubious conduct reflected, perhaps unjustly, on Pike. He later alleged they had been recruited only for service in defense of their own territory. After much acrimony Pike resigned on July 12, 1862; his resignation was accepted on November 5, 1862. He lived in semi-retirement during the balance of the war, and after it ended, he was regarded with suspicion by both parties to the conflict. He was indicted for treason by the United States authorities, but was subsequently restored to his civil rights, and after some years in Memphis moved to Washington. During the remainder of his life he devoted his attention to writing legal treatises and expounding the morals and dogma of the

Masonic order. He died in the house of the Scottish Rite Temple, Washington, on April 2, 1891, and is buried in Oak Hill Cemetery. (361)

Gideon Johnson Pillow was born in Williamson County, Tennessee, June 8, 1806. After his graduation from the University of Nashville in 1827, he practiced law for some time in Columbia, Tennessee, with James Knox Polk (later President of the United States) as a partner. An unsuccessful aspirant for the office of vice president in 1852 and 1856, Pillow had been appointed in 1846 a brigadier general of volunteers by his former associate. Subsequently he was advanced by Polk to the grade of major general. Twice wounded in the Mexico City campaign, he fell out with General Winfield Scott, but was sustained by the President on all occasions, who declared that he had been "greatly persecuted." He was named senior major general of Tennessee's provisional army upon the secession of the state in 1861, and was appointed brigadier general in the Provisional Army of the Confederacy on July 9 of that year. Pillow was at the battle of Belmont, Missouri, in November 1861, and was second in command to General John B. Floyd at Fort Donelson the following February. During Grant's siege of Fort Donelson, Floyd passed

the command to Pillow, who in turn passed it to General Simon B. Buckner. The first two made their escape before the surrender of the work. Subsequently relieved from duty, he held no important command thereafter. He was assigned to the volunteer and conscript bureau in Tennessee during the latter part of the war, and was commissary general of prisoners after the death of General J. H. Winder in February 1865. (362) He was forced into bankruptcy after the war; but practiced law in Memphis, with former Governor Isham G. Harris as his partner. General Pillow died near Helena, Arkansas, October 8, 1878, (363) and is buried in Memphis.

Camille Armand Jules Marie, Prince de Polignac, was born at Millemont, Seine-et-Oise, France, February 16, 1832. He was the

241

son of the president of King Charles X's council of ministers and an English mother. Educated at the College of Stanislaus in Paris, he entered the 3rd Regiment of Chasseurs in 1853, served with the 4th Hussars in the Crimea, and then with rank of lieutenant transferred to the 4th Chasseurs. He secured his discharge in 1859, and was in Central America at the outbreak of the Civil War. He immediately offered himself to the Confederate cause. On July 16, 1861 he was commissioned lieutenant colonel and served on the staffs of Generals Beauregard and Bragg in the spring and summer of 1862. He was promoted brigadier general on January 10, 1863, and major general from April 8, 1864. Polignac's later service was principally in Louisiana in the army of General Richard Taylor, where he largely distinguished

himself in the battles of Mansfield, Pleasant Hill, and the other engagements of the Red River campaign. Toward the end of the war he was sent to France by the Confederate government to secure the intervention of Napoleon III. He ran the blockade on March 17, 1865, and the war ended shortly after his arrival in Spain. He devoted himself thereafter to the study of mathematics and political economy, but led the 1st (French) Division in the Franco-Prussian War, and was awarded the Legion of Honor. During the remainder of a long life he was engaged in the study of mathematics, in which field he achieved considerable reputation. His death in Paris, November 15, 1913, marked the passing of the last survivor of the major generals of the Confederacy. (364) He was buried in Frankfort-on-Main, Germany.

Leonidas Polk, the "Bishop-Militant," was born in Raleigh, North Carolina, April 10, 1806. He was graduated from West Point in a class (1827) which immediately preceded that of Jefferson Davis, with whom Polk thereafter enjoyed the closest personal relations. He resigned almost immediately after graduation and entered the Episcopal ministry, and later became Missionary Bishop of the Southwest. Exchanging his clerical vestments for a uniform upon the outbreak of the Civil

at Pine Mountain, near Marietta, Georgia, June 14, 1864. At the time he was in command of a corps of the Army of Tennessee. His performance upon some occasion was judged to be hardly commensurate with his rank, and he was particularly censured by General Bragg for dilatory tactics at Chickamauga. (365) First buried in Augusta, Georgia, General Polk's remains and those of his wife were re-interred in Christ Church Cathedral in New Orleans in 1945. (366) He was an uncle of General Lucius E. Polk.

Lucius Eugene Polk, a nephew of General Leonidas Polk, was born at Salisbury, North Carolina, July 10, 1833. The family removed to a plantation near Columbia, Tennessee, when he was two. After attending the Uni-

War, he was appointed major general in the Provisional Army of the Confederacy on June 25, 1861, and lieutenant general to rank October 10, 1862. In the early months of the conflict he commanded the vast territory of Department No. 2, including the Mississippi River defenses from the Red River to Paducah, Kentucky. He also organized the Army of Mississippi, later a part of the Army of Tennessee. Superseded in command by General Albert Sidney Johnston, he subsequently served as a corps commander at Shiloh, Perryville, Murfreesboro, Chickamauga, and in the opening operations of the Atlanta campaign. While examining the Federal position in company with Generals Johnston and Hardee, General Polk was instantly killed by a cannon shot

versity of Virginia in 1850-51, he settled near Helena, Arkansas, and engaged in planting on his own account. He enlisted in 1861 as a private in the Yell Rifles, whose captain was Pat Cleburne; and he served under Cleburne during most of the war. He was promoted from junior 2nd lieutenant to colonel of the 15th Arkansas Infantry after Shiloh, where he was wounded in the face. He was made brigadier general to rank from December 13, 1862, and succeeded Cleburne in brigade command. Polk fought gallantly at Murfreesboro, Chickamauga, Chattanooga, and in the Atlanta campaign. At Kennesaw Mountain in June 1864, he was so severely wounded (for the fourth time during the war) that he never fully recovered, and was compelled to retire from the army. Returning on crutches to his old home near Columbia, he lived quietly until his death, which occurred on December 1, 1892. General Polk was a delegate to the Democratic National Convention at Chicago in 1884, and in 1887 was elected to the Tennessee state senate. Two of his sons served in the Spanish-American War, and one of them was subsequently a member of Congress from Pennsylvania. The general is buried in St. John's Churchyard at Ashwood, near Columbia, Tennessee.

Carnot Posey was born in Wilkinson County, Mississippi, on August 5, 1818. He obtained his college education in Jackson, Louisiana, after which he studied law at the University of Virginia. Returning home, he occupied himself as a planter for some years, and then practiced his profession at Woodville, Mississippi, until the beginning of the Mexican War, in which he served as a 1st lieutenant in the 1st Mississippi Rifles. He was appointed United States district attorney for the southern district of Mississippi by President Buchanan, and held this post until 1861, when he recruited the Wilkinson Rifles and was elected its captain. He was elected colonel upon the organization of the 16th Mississippi Infantry at Corinth in June. He fought at First Manassas, Ball's Bluff (Leesburg), and in all the subsequent campaigns of the Army of Northern Virginia.

His promotion to brigadier general dates from November 1, 1862. His brigade later became a part of General Richard H. Anderson's division of the 3rd Corps. At Bristoe Station, on October 14, 1863, General Posey received a comparatively slight wound in the leg, which was not supposed to be serious at the time. However, infection soon set in, and he died in Charlottesville on November 13, 1863 in the home of Dr. Davis, a friend. He is buried on the grounds of the University of Virginia. (367)

John Smith Preston, a half-uncle by marriage and also the father-in-law of General Wade Hampton, was born at the Salt Works, near Abingdon, Virginia, April 20, 1809. (368) He attended Hampden-Sydney College, the University of Virginia, and Harvard, where he studied law. Beginning the practice of his profession at Abingdon, he later moved to Columbia, South Carolina, and subsequently for some years engaged in sugar planting in Louisiana. He returned to South Carolina in 1848, and served for eight years in the state senate. From 1856 to 1860 he lived abroad. An uncompromising secessionist, he headed the state's delegation to the Charleston Democratic convention of 1860. In the following year he was a commissioner to Virginia, and made an eloquent plea for the withdrawal of that state from the Union. As lieutenant colonel and assistant adjutant general he served on General Beauregard's staff during the reduction of Sumter and at the battle of First Manassas. He was promoted to colonel on April 23, 1863, and to brigadier general on June 10, 1864. Preston served in command of prison camps, conscript camps, and from July 30, 1863 until its discontinuance, as superintendent of the bureau of conscription in Richmond. After the war he lived in England until 1868, when he returned to the United States. At this time he made a speech at the University of Virginia, which because of its impassioned defense of the right of secession, received much criticism in the North. Completely unreconstructed until the end, he died in Columbia, South Carolina, May 1, 1881. General Preston was an orator of great force, and perhaps for this reason, his management of the unpopular conscript bureau was extremely able. He is buried in Columbia.

William Preston was born near Louisville, Kentucky, on October 16, 1816. He was educated in Kentucky and at Harvard, from which he received a law degree in 1838. He commenced practice in Louisville. At the beginning of the Mexican War he was appointed lieutenant colonel of the 4th Kentucky, with which he saw active service. Subsequently he was elected to both houses of the state legislature. In 1852 he went to Congress, and was defeated for re-election to a third term by General Humphrey Marshall. Appointed minister to Spain by President Buchanan in 1858, Preston was prominently engaged three years later in inducing his state to join the Confederacy. He served on the staff of his brother-in-law, General A. S. Johnston, with rank of colonel, until the latter's death at Shiloh. (369) Appointed brigadier general from April 14, 1862, he took part in the battles of Corinth, Murfreesboro, and Chickamauga. In 1864 he was appointed Confederate minister to the Imperial Mexican government, but he was unsuccessful in reaching Maximilian's court, and spent the last months of the war in the Trans-Mississippi Department. It is

sometimes stated that Preston attained the rank of major general in 1865; however, no record of such promotion is in existence. (370) He went to Mexico after the close of hostilities, and travelled to England and then to Canada before returning to Kentucky in 1866. A member of the lower house of the state legislature in 1868 and 1869, he attended the Democratic conventions of 1868 and 1880 as a delegate from his state. General Preston died in Lexington on September 21, 1887, and is buried in Louisville.

Sterling Price, "Old Pap," was born in Prince Edward County, Virginia, on September 20, 1809. He was educated at Hampden-Sydney College and afterwards studied law. About 1831 he

246

moved to Missouri with his parents and soon after purchased a farm in Chariton County which became his home. Price served six years in the legislature, and was speaker the last four. From 1844 to 1846 he was a member of Congress, and resigned in the latter year to participate in the Mexican War as colonel of the 2nd Missouri Infantry and brigadier general of volunteers. He was appointed military governor

of New Mexico by General S. W. Kearny, and later became governor of Missouri from 1853 to 1857. In March 1861 he was president of the state convention that opposed secession, and disagreeing with the extreme Unionists, he accepted command of the Missouri militia in May of that year. At the battle of Wilson's Creek he combined his forces with those of General Ben McCulloch to defeat the Federal General Lyon; he later captured the town of Lexington, with three thousand prisoners, but was forced to retreat into Arkansas by General S. R. Curtis. At the Confederate defeat at Elkhorn (Pea Ridge), Price and McCulloch by mutual agreement were under the command of Earl Van Dorn. After this battle Price accepted a Confederate commission as major general in the Provisional Army to rank from March 6, 1862. His campaign around Iuka and Corinth in October 1862 was unsuccessful; he also failed at Helena, Arkansas, the following year. In 1864 he aided Kirby Smith in repulsing Steele's Camden expedition. His raid through Missouri in September and October 1864, after initial successes, was finally turned back at Westport; and the end of the war found him in Texas with his command. After the collapse of Maximilian's Mexican Empire, where Price had gone following the Confederate surrender, he returned to Missouri in 1866, and died in St. Louis on September 29, 1867. He is buried in Bellefontaine Cemetery there.

Roger Atkinson Pryor was born near Petersburg, Virginia, July 19, 1828. He was educated in the schools of Nottoway County, and at the Classical Academy in Petersburg. He was graduated from Hampden-Sydney College in 1845 as valedictorian of his class and with considerable reputation as an orator. He then studied law at the University of Virginia and was admitted to the bar. By the outbreak of war in 1861 Pryor had had a notable career as lawyer, newspaper editor, and Congressman. He resigned from the House of Repre-

sentatives on March 3, 1861, Pryor is said to have declined the honor of firing the first shot at Fort Sumter. (371) He was elected to the Provisional Confederate Congress, but soon resigned to enter the army as colonel of the 3rd Virginia Infantry. Promoted brigadier general after the battle of Williamsburg (April 16, 1862), he led his brigade in the Seven Days, Second Manassas, and at Sharpsburg. In November of that year Pryor was given a small brigade and stationed south of James River. The following spring, for reasons which are not apparent in the records, but certainly at the instance of Longstreet and Lee, Pryor's regiments were separately reassigned, and he was left without a command. He resigned on August 18, 1863, and served thereafter without rank as a special courier attached to the cavalry. He was captured, November 27, 1864, and was confined in Fort Lafayette, not being released until a short time before the surrender. In September 1865 General Pryor went to New York, and became associated with the *Daily News;* the following year he was admitted to the state bar. During the remainder of a long life he practiced law, was a judge of the court of common pleas, and of the state supreme court, and for the last seven years, was a special referee of the appellate division of the court. He died in New York City on March 14, 1919, in his ninety-first year; he is buried in Princeton, New Jersey.

William Andrew Quarles was born near Jamestown, Virginia, July 4, 1825. He moved with his parents at the age of five to Christian County, Kentucky. After studying law at the University of Virginia, he was admitted to the bar in 1848, and commenced the practice of law in Clarksville,

248

Tennessee. A Pierce Elector in 1852, he was defeated for Congress in 1858, and meantime served as a circuit court judge, supervisor of banks for the state, and president of the Memphis, Clarksville, & Louisville Railroad. He also attended the Democratic conventions of 1856 and 1860 as a delegate from Tennessee. When the 42nd Tennessee Infantry was organized in 1861, Quarles was elected its colonel, and with it was captured at Fort Donelson. Upon his exchange he served for a time at Port Hudson in command of four consolidated Tennessee regiments. His command was later transferred to General Joseph E. Johnston's army during the Vicksburg campaign. Promoted brigadier general to rank from August 25, 1863, he took a gallant part in the Atlanta campaign and in Hood's Tennessee invasion. At the battle of Franklin he was wounded and again captured. Paroled on May 25, 1865, he returned to his home and resumed his profession. In 1875 General Quarles was elected to a seat in the Tennessee senate, and in 1880 and 1884, was a delegate to the Democratic National conventions. His death occcurred at the home of a daughter in Logan County, Kentucky, December 28, 1893; he is buried in Christian County. (372)

Gabriel James Rains was born in Craven County, North Carolina, June 4, 1803. He received a common-school education, and was graduated from West Point in the class of 1827. From then un-

249

til his resignation, on July 31, 1861, he had a most distinguished career in the United States Army. He was brevetted major for gallantry against the Seminoles, and achieved the regular rank of lieutenant colonel of the 5th Infantry on June 5, 1860. Meantime he had done considerable experimenting with explosives. On September 23, 1861 Rains was appointed as a brigadier in the Provisional Confederate Army, and assigned to the command of a brigade under D. H. Hill in the Department of the Peninsula. Falling back from Yorktown before McClellan's advance in the spring of 1862, he originated the anti-personnel mine, which he sowed in the roads in large quantities, causing not a few Union casualties. This hitherto unknown mode of warfare excited much comment and criticism from Federals and Confederates alike. General Longstreet forbade its further employment as "not proper." By the end of the war, however, even its most violent opponents were converted to its use. (373) Rains' last field service was at Seven Pines, where he was severely castigated by Hill. (374) Assigned as first superintendent of the volunteer and conscript bureau in December 1862, he was relieved in May of the following year. (375) He was occupied during the balance of the war arranging mine and torpedo defenses for such threatened points as Richmond, Charleston, and Mobile. He then resided in Atlanta for a time, and from 1877 to 1880, was a clerk in the quartermaster department at Charleston. He died in Aiken, South Carolina, August 6, 1881, and is buried in St. Thaddeus Cemetery.

James Edwards Rains was born at Nashville, Tennessee, April 10, 1833. He was graduated from Yale Law School at the age of twenty-one, and began practice in Nashville. In 1858 he was elected city attorney, and served also as associate editor of the Nashville *Banner.* He was in 1860 elected district attorney general for the counties of Davidson, Williamson, and Sumner. Enlisting as a private in the 11th Tennessee Infantry at the outbreak of the Civil War, he was elected and commissioned colonel of the regiment on May 10, 1861. During the winter of 1861-62 Rains occupied Cumberland Gap, and was finally flanked out of his position in June 1862. When Kirby Smith advanced into Kentucky he left Stevenson's division, including a brigade under Rains, to operate against the Federal General Morgan in the Gap. For his services in forcing Morgan northward Rains was promoted brigadier general on November 4, 1862. He was assigned to John P. McCown's division of Lieutenant General Hardee's corps dur-

ing the battle of Murfreesboro. General Rains occupied the extreme left of the Confederate line on December 31, 1862, and was almost instantly killed by a Minié ball while leading his men against a Federal battery. According to tradition, his last words were: "Forward my brave boys, forward!" (376) First buried on the battlefield, General Rains was removed in 1888 to Mt. Olivet Cemetery, Nashville, where his remains now lie.

Stephen Dodson Ramseur was born at Lincolnton, North Carolina, May 31, 1837. He entered the freshman class at Davidson College in that state at the age of sixteen, but left in 1855 to accept an appointment to West Point, from which he was graduated in 1860. Resigning on April 6, 1861, he entered the service of the Confederacy as captain of the Ellis Light Artillery, a Raleigh battery, with which he reported to General Magruder at Yorktown in the spring of 1862. That April he was elected colonel of the 49th North Carolina, a regiment he led with distinction during the Seven Days; he was severely wounded at Malvern Hill. Promoted brigadier general on November 1, 1862 to succeed General George B. Anderson, who had been mortally wounded at Sharpsburg, Ramseur again took the field before Chancellorsville. He fought gallantly there (and was again wounded), and in the subsequent combats of the 2nd Corps. A third time wounded at Spotsylvania Court House, he accompanied General Early to the Shenandoah, and

was promoted major general the day after his twenty-seventh birthday—the youngest West Pointer to attain that rank in the Confederate Army. (377) At the battle of Cedar Creek, October 19, 1864, after participating in the initial Confederate success, he was shot through both lungs while attempting to stem Sheridan's counterattack. He fell into the hands of the enemy, and was taken to Sheridan's headquarters, "Belle Grove," near Meadow Mills, where he died the following morning surrounded by his former friends and classmates at the Military Academy. Married less than a year, he had received word only the night before the battle of the birth of a daughter. His body was taken to Lincolnton for burial.

George Wythe Randolph was born at "Monticello"—the home of his maternal grandfather, Thomas Jefferson — near Charlottesville, Virginia, on March 10, 1818. At the age of thirteen he was appointed a midshipman in the navy, and served at sea for the next six years. He entered the University of Virginia in 1837, and in 1839 resigned from the navy. He also studied law and began practicing in Albemarle County. In 1850 he moved to Richmond. He organized the Richmond Howitzers after the John Brown raid, and served as one of Virginia's peace commissioners to Washington in 1861. Randolph commanded the Howitzers on the Peninsula that same summer, and was present at Big Bethel as General Magruder's chief of artillery. Promoted brigadier general to rank from February 12, 1862, he accepted the war portfolio in the Confederate Cabinet the following month. Since President Davis was in effect his own secretary of war, even in the matter of detail appointments, the position was little more than a clerkship, and Randolph resigned on November 15, 1862. It was soon discovered that he was suffering from tuberculosis, and he went to France for his health, ultimately resigning his army commission on December 18, 1864. After the war he returned to Virginia, but failed to recover. He died at "Edgehill," a family estate near Charlottesville, on April 3, 1867. He is buried at "Monticello."

Matt (378) **Whitaker Ransom,** an elder brother of General Robert Ransom, was born in Warren County, North Carolina, October 8, 1826. He was graduated from the University of North Carolina in 1847, and having studied law in his senior year, was at once admitted to the bar. A Whig

Presidential Elector in 1852, he represented his county in the lower house of the legislature from 1858 to 1861. In the latter year he was chosen one of three commissioners from North Carolina to the Confederate government at Montgomery. Enlisting as a private, he was almost immediately commissioned lieutenant colonel of the 1st North Carolina state troops, and subsequently colonel of the 35th North Carolina Infantry. This regiment was a part of his brother's brigade, which he later commanded. His rank of brigadier general dated from June 13, 1863. General Ransom took part in the battles of Seven Pines, the Seven Days, Sharpsburg, Fredericksburg, Plymouth, Weldon, Suffolk, and the siege of Petersburg. He was three times wounded. He finally surrendered his command at Appomattox, and at the close of the war, returned to North Carolina and resumed his law business. He meantime farmed his wife's plantation on Roanoke River. Elected to the United States Senate in 1872, he served continuously until 1895, at which time he was appointed minister to Mexico by President Cleveland. He died near Garysburg, North Carolina, October 8, 1904, and is buried on his plantation in Northampton County.

Robert Ransom, Jr. was born in Warren County, North Carolina, February 12, 1828, and was graduated from West Point in 1850. After service mainly on the frontier, he resigned his commission to enter Confederate service. He became a captain in the Regular Army, and colonel of the First North Carolina Cavalry, Provisional Army, also known as the 9th North Carolina Volunteers. Promoted brigadier general to

rank from March 1, 1862, he commanded a brigade under General Longstreet in the Seven Days battles, in the Maryland campaign, and at Fredericksburg. Subsequently transferred to North Carolina, and promoted major general to rank from May 26, 1863, he defended the Weldon railroad and then was given charge of the district which embraced the Appomattox and Blackwater Rivers. He later commanded in Richmond, and then in East Tennessee. After assisting General Beauregard at Drewry's Bluff against Butler, he commanded Jubal Early's cavalry for a time during the raid on Washington. He was compelled to retire on account of illness in the fall of 1864 and saw no further active service. After the war he had various employ-

ment, finally accepting a government post as civil engineer at New Bern, North Carolina. He died at New Bern, January 14, 1892, and is buried there. He was a younger brother of General Matt W. Ransom.

Alexander Welch Reynolds was born in Clarke County, Virginia, in April 1816. (379) He was graduated from West Point in 1838, saw some action against the Seminoles, and did a tour of garrison duty. In 1847 he was transferred to the quartermaster department. Eight years later he was dismissed from the service for failure to explain alleged discrepancies in his accounts. He was restored in 1858, and continued in service until he was dropped, October 4, 1861, for having "absented himself from duty." (380) Meantime he had

been appointed a captain in the Regular Confederate service as early as March of that year, (381) and on July 10, 1861 was commissioned colonel of the 50th Virginia Infantry. He served with John B. Floyd in Western Virginia in 1861-62, with Kirby Smith at Knoxville, and in 1863, was captured and paroled (and later exchanged) at Vicksburg. He was promoted brigadier general from September 14, 1863. He took part in the battle of Chattanooga, and his brigade was in Carter L. Stevenson's division of Hardee's corps during the Atlanta campaign. He sustained a wound at New Hope Church. In the last months of the war he was in North Alabama and Middle Tennessee. In 1869 he entered the service of the Khedive of Egypt in company with a group of ex-Union and Confederate officers, with rank of colonel, and served in various staff capacities under General W. W. Loring. He died in Alexandria, Egypt, on May 26, 1876. The consular section archives, U. S. State Department, record Reynolds' interment in Alexandria and contain a list of funeral and burial expenses. Correspondence with the U. S. Consulate and the Egyptian Government, however, has failed to pinpoint the grave. There is a stone to his memory in the cemetery of Saint James the Less, in Philadelphia, his wife's home. (382)

Daniel Harris Reynolds, a native of Ohio, was born at Centerburg, December 14, 1832. He attended Ohio Wesleyan University at Delaware, with General Otho F. Strahl. Later he entered the law school at Somerville, Tennessee, and was graduated and admitted to the bar in 1858. He removed to Lake Village, Arkansas, that year. In 1861 he raised a company for Confederate service, and served with it, as captain, in the battle of Wilson's Creek. While his company was a part of the 1st Arkansas Mounted Rifles, Reynolds was successively promoted major, lieutenant colonel, and after the battle of Chickamauga, colonel of the regiment. Reynolds acquired an enviable reputation for his leadership of the 43rd—which, incidentally, fought dismounted after the early part of the war. He was repeatedly

255

commended by his superiors, and was commissioned brigadier to rank from March 5, 1864. He led his new command through the Atlanta campaign, into Tennessee with Hood, and through the Carolinas. He was so badly wounded at Bentonville as to necessitate the amputation of one of his legs. Paroled at Charlottesville, Virginia, on May 29, 1865, General Reynolds returned to Arkansas and resumed his law practice. He served one term in the Arkansas state senate (1866-67), after which he resided in Lake Village until his death there on March 14, 1902. He is buried in Lake Village Cemetery. (383)

Robert Vinkler Richardson was born in Granville County, North Carolina, on November 4, 1820, but was taken early in life to Hardeman County, Tennessee, where he received his education. He was admitted to the bar, and moved to Memphis in 1847, where he practiced his profession. He also associated himself in business with the future Confederate generals, N. B. Forrest and Gideon J. Pillow. He served under the latter during the early part of the war, and subsequently recruited the 12th Tennessee Cavalry (1st Tennessee Partisan Rangers), and was elected its colonel. He was present at Shiloh and Corinth, and was attached to Forrest's forces with a much-

decimated command in the fall of 1863. On December 3 of that year he was appointed brigadier general; however, after being duly confirmed, the records exhibit that his nomination was returned by the Senate at the request of President Davis on February 9, 1864. Thereafter he and his regiment were attached to the command of General James R. Chalmers, with whom he seemingly operated until the close of the war. Upon the cessation of hostilities he went abroad for a time, and then returned to Memphis to engage in levee and railroad building, again being associated with General Forrest. While traveling in the interest of a projected railroad, he stopped for the night of January 5, 1870 at a tavern in the village of Clarkton, Dunklin County, Missouri. Here he was mortally wounded by an unknown assailant, who fired a charge of buckshot at him from behind a wagon in the yard of the inn. He died early the next morning, and was buried in Elmwood Cemetery, Memphis. (384)

Roswell Sabine Ripley, a native of Ohio, was born at Worthington in Franklin County, March 14, 1823, and was graduated from the U. S. Military Academy at the age of twenty, standing seventh in a class of thirty-nine. He was twice brevetted for gallantry in the Mexican War, of which he wrote a two-volume history shortly after its conclusion. Ripley— who was a nephew of General James W. Ripley, chief of ordnance of the U. S. Army from 1861 until his retirement in 1863 —married into the Middleton family of Charleston, South Carolina, in 1852. The following year he resigned his army commission to engage in business there. In 1860, as a lieutenant colonel of the state forces, he occupied Fort Moultrie after its evacuation by Major Robert Anderson, and also Fort Sumter, after its fall in April 1861. Appointed brigadier general in the Confederate service on August 15, 1861, he was in command of South Carolina until his relief the following year by General Pemberton. Ripley was a skillful and competent field officer but forever at odds with both his superiors and subordinates, including Generals Coop-

er, Beauregard, and Pemberton, when in departmental command. He was given a brigade in D. H. Hill's division, and fought throughout the Seven Days, and was severely wounded at Sharpsburg. Again on duty in South Carolina during 1863 and 1864, he was ordered to General J. E. Johnston's army in the spring of 1865, and joined it the day of the battle of Bentonville. At the termination of hostilities General Ripley went to England and engaged in a manufacturing venture, which soon failed. Thereafter his residence was in Charleston, but he spent much of his time in New York City, where he died on March 29, 1887. He is buried in Charleston.

John Selden Roane was born in Wilson County, Tennessee, January 8, 1817. Educated at Cum-

257

an opponent of secession. However, on March 20, 1862 he was appointed a Confederate brigadier, and he subsequently took an honorable part in the battle of Prairie Grove under General Hindman, who had superseded him in command of the District of Arkansas. Thereafter he served in Arkansas, Louisiana, and Texas until the end of the war, principally in garrison and on detached duty. Paroled at Shreveport, Louisiana, June 11, 1865, General Roane retired to his home at Pine Bluff, Arkansas, where he died on April 8, 1867. He is buried in Little Rock.

berland College in Kentucky, he followed an elder brother to Arkansas, and in 1844 was elected to the state legislature, and became its speaker. In 1846 he went to Mexico as lieutenant colonel of Colonel Archibald Yell's regiment of Arkansas volunteers. After Colonel Yell's death at Buena Vista, he succeeded to the command. He subsequently fought a duel with General (then Captain) Albert Pike over the conduct of his (Roane's) command at Buena Vista — both contestants escaped unwounded. Elected governor of Arkansas in 1849, he served until 1852. His administration was notable for his advocacy of a state system of roads and educational facilities. Roane does not seem to have been among the first to spring to arms in defense of the South, and was known as

William Paul Roberts, the youngest general officer in Confederate service, (385) was born in Gates County, North Carolina, July 11, 1841. At the age of nineteen he enlisted in the

19th North Carolina Volunteers (later the 2nd North Carolina), and was promoted through grades from junior 2nd lieutenant to major. Meantime he made an enviable record in North Carolina, and after the fall of 1862, with the Army of Northern Virginia. Commissioned colonel in June 1864, Roberts fought with great distinction at Reams' Station, where his dismounted regiment made a gallant charge on the Federal rifle pits. On February 23, 1865, he was appointed brigadier general to rank from February 21, and assigned to the command of a brigade in W. H. F. Lee's division. He was virtually overwhelmed at Five Forks, where his slender command was opposed to greatly superior Federal forces. He was paroled at Appomattox Court House and returned home. In 1875 he represented Gates County in the constitutional convention, and the following year, he was elected to the state legislature. From 1880 to 1888 he was state auditor. He died in Norfolk, Virginia, March 28, 1910, and is buried in Gatesville, North Carolina. The story goes that Robert E. Lee presented his own gauntlets to Roberts on the occasion of his being commissioned brigadier. (386)

Beverly Holcombe Robertson was born at "The Oaks," Amelia County, Virginia, June 5, 1827,

and was graduated from West Point in the class of 1849. Almost his entire old army service was with the 2nd Dragoons on the frontier. A part of the time he was under the command of Colonel (later Brigadier General) Philip St. George Cooke, U.S.A., the father-in-law of Jeb Stuart, who commended him repeatedly in dispatches. Robertson was dismissed from the U. S. Army on August 8, 1861, "having given proof of his disloyalty." (387) This charge was amply supported in Union eyes by the fact that he had been appointed a captain in the Confederate adjutant general's department to rank from March 16, 1861, (388) and was soon after elected colonel of the 4th Virginia Cavalry, C.S.A. (389) With this regiment he took part in Jackson's Valley

259

campaign of 1862, and after the death of Turner Ashby, commanded Jackson's cavalry. He was promoted brigadier general on June 9, 1862. Joining the Army of Northern Virginia in August, he served under Stuart in the Second Manassas campaign. Subsequently he was ordered to North Carolina. He returned to Virginia in May 1863 to operate with the main army during the Gettysburg campaign. At the time, Stuart's principal force was making the still-controversial flank march around the Army of the Potomac. Distrusted by Stuart as being "troublesome," and criticized during the movement into Pennsylvania, General Robertson was relieved and transferred to South Carolina, where he remained until the evacuation of the District on the approach of Sherman. (390) Some time after the war he removed to Washington and engaged in the insurance business. He died there in his eighty-fourth year, November 12, 1910. He was buried in Amelia County, Virginia. (391)

Felix Huston Robertson was the last survivor of the general officers of the Confederacy, (392) and the only native Texan to achieve a wreath around his stars. He was born at Washington, Texas, on March 9, 1839, the son of General Jerome B. Robertson. He attended Baylor

University when the school was located at Independence, Texas. He was appointed to West Point in 1857, but resigned on January 29, 1861 to offer his services to the new Confederacy. Commissioned 2nd lieutenant of artillery on March 9, 1861, he took part in the reduction of Sumter; then served at Pensacola on the staff of General Gladden; and, at Shiloh, commanded a battery with the rank of captain. He distinguished himself at Murfreesboro; he was there promoted major, and led a battalion in Longstreet's corps at Chicka-mauga. In January 1864 he was again promoted (to lieutenant colonel), and placed in command of the artillery of Wheeler's cavalry corps, with which he served during the Atlanta campaign. Promoted brigadier general on July 26, 1864, he served for a time as Wheeler's chief of staff; he then led a brigade, and later a division of cavalry, until he was severely wounded at Buckhead Creek near Augusta, Georgia, on November 29, 1864. He saw no further active service, but in April 1865 was sent by General Howell Cobb to treat for the surrender of the city of Macon with his old West Point associate, Major General James H. Wilson, U.S.V. For reasons not made apparent in the records the Confederate Senate consistently refused to confirm General Robertson at any grade from major to brigadier. His nomination to the last-named rank was rejected on February 22, 1865. After the war he returned to Texas, ultimately settling in Waco, and studying law. At the time of his death there, April 20, 1928, he had been for many years dean of the local bar. He is buried in Waco.

Jerome Bonaparte Robertson, "Polly," the father of General Felix H. Robertson, was born in Woodford County, Kentucky, March 14, 1815. Left penniless at an early age by the death of his father, he was apprenticed for some years to a hatter. Afterwards he studied medicine and was graduated from Transylvania University in 1835. Removing to Texas the following year, he saw some service in the army of the then Republic, and subsequently

settled in Washington County, where he practiced his profession for thirty-four years. Meantime he became renowned as an Indian fighter. He was also a member of both houses of the Texas legislature, and a delegate to the secession convention of 1861. He entered the Confederate Army as a captain in the 5th Texas Infantry; and was promoted lieutenant colonel in November 1861, colonel on June 1, 1862, and brigadier general on November 1, 1862. He led his regiment in the Seven Days battles, and was wounded at Second Manassas, and again at Gettysburg while in command of the Texas Brigade. Accompanying General Longstreet to the West, he fought at Chickamauga and in the Knoxville campaign, and subsequently was transferred to

Texas (393) to assume command of the reserve corps of the state. The balance of his war service was in the Trans-Mississippi. Returning to his home in Independence, Texas, General Robertson practiced medicine for a time, and in 1874 became superintendent of the state bureau of immigration. Five years later he moved to Waco, and interested himself in railroad building in West Texas. His death occurred at Waco on January 7, 1891, and he is buried there.

Philip Dale Roddey was born at Moulton, Lawrence County, Alabama, on April 2, 1826. (394) He had little or no formal schooling. For some years he worked as a tailor; he served as sheriff

of Lawrence County; and was then engaged in steamboating on the Tennessee River. He organized a cavalry company in 1861, and was elected its captain. During the first years of the war, he was employed in semi-independent scouting missions. Commissioned colonel in December 1862, Roddey recruited and organized the 4th Alabama Cavalry, and served during the balance of the war under both Forrest and Wheeler, mainly in North Alabama. He was promoted to brigadier general on August 3, 1863. Sometimes in a subordinate capacity and sometimes alone he made a number of important raids. He was active in the Atlanta campaign, and in Hood's subsequent Tennessee invasion. In the spring of 1865 he stood with Forrest at Selma in a last desperate effort to stem the invasion of the Federal General James Harrison Wilson. After the collapse of the Confederate lines, he and Forrest escaped by swimming the Alabama River under cover of darkness. Finally paroled on May 17, 1865, he engaged in business in New York, and became interested in a patent pump. While in England negotiating the sale of the patent General Roddey died in Westminster Hospital, London, of uremia, July 20, 1897. (395) He is buried in Greenwood Cemetery, Tuscaloosa, Alabama.

Robert Emmett Rodes was born at Lynchburg, Virginia, on March 29, 1829. After graduation from the Virginia Military Institute in 1848, he continued as assistant professor there until 1851, when he resigned to engage in the profession of civil engineering. At the outbreak of war (396) Rodes entered the Confederate Army as colonel of the 5th Alabama Infantry. His conduct at First Manassas soon won for him a brigadier's commission (October 21, 1861). He was severely wounded at Seven Pines, and resumed his command before he was well, in order to take part in the battle of Gaines's Mill. As a result he sustained a long illness. He particularly distinguished himself later at South Mountain and Sharpsburg; and on D. H. Hill's being sent to North Carolina in January 1863, he was assigned to command Hill's division. He was promoted major general for his services at Chancellorsville, where he led the van of Jackson's famous flank march. Rodes was also at the head of his division successively at Gettysburg, the Wilderness, and Spotsylvania. Transferred to the Shenandoah Valley with the 2nd Corps in June 1864, he participated in the subsequent movements of that command. He was mortally wounded at Winchester on September 19, 1864, while directing a counterattack which was substantially responsible for extricating the Confederate forces from that battlefield. He is buried in the city of his birth.

Lawrence Sullivan Ross was born at Bentonsport, Iowa, September 27, 1838. His parents took him to Texas while he was an infant. He was graduated from Wesleyan University, in Florence, Alabama, in 1859. He had spent his vacations in service against the Comanches, and in the latter year was made captain of a company of Texas Rangers. Since he had rescued the celebrated Cynthia Ann Parker in one engagement, and killed the chief Peta Necona in single combat in another, Ross had made a lasting reputation on the front-

1875; and a state senator in 1881 and 1883. He was then elected governor in 1887 and overwhelmingly re-elected two years later. From 1891 until his death he served as president of the Agricultural and Mechanical College of Texas at College Station, where he died, January 3, 1898. At that time he was probably the most popular private citizen in the state, known from one end to the other as "Sul" Ross. He is buried in Waco, Texas. (397)

ier when he entered Confederate service as a private. Promoted colonel of the 6th Texas Cavalry on May 14, 1862, he took part in the battle of Corinth in October, and particularly distinguished himself during the subsequent retreat from that place. He was appointed brigadier general to rank from December 21, 1863. He fought under and was universally commended by such officers as J. E. Johnston, Van Dorn, Hardee, Forrest, S. D. Lee, and W. H. Jackson. With a record of 135 battles and engagements, and 5 horses shot from under him, he returned home in 1865, penniless. At first he commenced farming in the valley of the Brazos. In 1873 he was elected sheriff of McLennan County; he was a member of the constitutional convention in

Thomas Lafayette Rosser was born in Campbell County, Virginia, October 15, 1836. The family emigrated to the Sabine River country of Texas in 1849. Appointed to West Point in 1856, at that time a five-year course, Rosser resigned on April 22, 1861, two weeks before he would have been graduated. He

was appointed a 1st lieutenant in the Regular Confederate service, and assigned as instructor to the Washington Artillery of New Orleans. He commanded a company of this regiment at First Manassas. After being wounded at Mechanicsville, he was made colonel of the 5th Virginia Cavalry, at the instigation of Jeb Stuart. He was wounded at Kelly's Ford, but continued to lead the 5th Virginia with brilliant success until he was promoted brigadier to rank from September 28, 1863. Rosser succeeded Beverly Robertson in command of the Laurel Brigade, and continued to win honors in the Overland campaign of 1864. In October 1864 he assumed command of Early's cavalry in the Shenandoah, and was promoted major general from November 1. He was defeated by Custer at Woodstock and Cedar Creek, and after two successful raids into West Virginia, he returned in the spring of 1865 to the Petersburg lines. He participated in the battle of Five Forks and the retreat to Appomattox, where, refusing to surrender, he cut his way out. However, he was captured, and paroled early in May. After the war he acquired considerable means as chief engineer of the Northern Pacific and Canadian Pacific Railroads. He later settled near Charlottesville, Virginia, as a gentleman farmer. On June 10,

1898 President McKinley appointed Rosser a brigadier general of U. S. Volunteers, and he donned the uniform he had put off thirty-seven years before. Honorably mustered out on October 31, 1898, he died at Charlottesville, March 29, 1910, and is buried in Riverview Cemetery.

Daniel Ruggles, a native of Massachusetts, was born at Barre, January 31, 1810, and was graduated from West Point in the class of 1833. He served in the Seminole War of 1839-40, and won the brevets of major and lieutenant colonel for gallant and meritorious conduct at Churubusco and Chapultepec during the war with Mexico. Meantime he had married into a Virginia family. He resigned from the U. S. Army on May 7, 1861, and commanded the state forces on the Rappahannock River line at the commencement of hostilities. Commissioned brigadier general on August 9, 1861, he was engaged at Corinth, before the battle of Shiloh, in receiving and assigning the troops forwarded there for Albert Sidney Johnston's army. During the battle he led the first division of Bragg's corps. Despite Grant's uncharitable opinion, substantially expressed in the words "if Ruggles is in command at Corinth, now is the time to attack," (398) he rendered good service and aided in the assault which caused the surrender of Prentiss' division. Thereafter his duties were largely administrative. He exercised district and departmental command at various points, and was ultimately assigned to duty as commissary general of prisoners on March 30, 1865. (399) After the war General Ruggles resided continuously in Fredericksburg, Virginia, except for four years spent managing a ranch in Texas. He was a member of the Board of Visitors to the Military Academy in 1884. He died at Fredericksburg in his eighty-eighth year, on June 1, 1897, and is now buried there.

Albert Rust was born in Fauquier County, Virginia, in 1818. (400) Emigrating to Arkansas about the year 1837, he settled in Union County, where he

studied law and was admitted to the bar. He served in the state legislature from 1842 to 1848, and from 1852 to 1854. In 1854 he was elected to Congress. He was defeated for re-election in 1856, but ran again in 1858 and was successful, serving until March 3, 1861. As colonel of the 3rd Arkansas Infantry, a regiment which he had recruited, he took part in the Cheat Mountain campaign in Western Virginia under General Robert E. Lee in the autumn of 1861. He served under Stonewall Jackson the following winter, and was appointed brigadier general to rank from March 4, 1862. After participating in the battle of Corinth the next October, he was sent back across the Mississippi in April 1863 with orders to report to General Sterling

Price. Thereafter he served under General Hindman in Arkansas, and under Generals Pemberton and Richard Taylor in Louisiana. His fortune swept away by the war, General Rust removed from his former home at El Dorado, Arkansas, to a farm on the north side of the Arkansas River in the vicinity of Little Rock, where he died on April 4, 1870. Although contemporary newspaper accounts of the funeral record that he was buried in Mount Holly Cemetery, Little Rock, (401) his grave cannot now be identified. No less an authority than the *Biographical Directory of the American Congress* states he was interred at El Dorado, but this is incorrect.

Isaac Munroe St. John was born at Augusta, Georgia, November 19, 1827. He moved with his parents to New York City, and was educated at the Poughkeepsie (N. Y.) Collegiate School and at Yale, from which he graduated in 1845. He first studied law, and then engaged in newspaper work in Baltimore. In 1848 he gave up journalism to become a civil engineer, and was associated with the Baltimore & Ohio Railroad, and from 1855 to 1861 with the Blue Ridge Railroad in Georgia and South Carolina. Enlisting as a private in the Fort Hill Guards of South Carolina, he soon became John B. Mag-

ruder's chief engineer at Yorktown, Virginia. In February 1862 he was commissioned captain of engineers. In October of that year, with rank of major of artillery, St. John was placed in charge of the Nitre Corps (subsequently the Nitre and Mining Corps), and was promoted lieutenant colonel and colonel in 1863. In this capacity he rendered invaluable service in producing desperately needed ordnance supplies. On February 16, 1865, by special act of Congress, he was made brigadier general and commissary general to supersede General Northrop. Paroled at Thomasville, Georgia, he returned to his profession of civil engineering. He was again connected with various railroads, and for two years with the city of Louisville, Kentucky, as chief engineer. At the time of his death at White Sulphur Springs, West Virginia, April 7, 1880, General St. John was in charge of the mining and engineering department of the Chesapeake & Ohio. (402) He is buried in Hollywood Cemetery, Richmond.

John Caldwell Calhoun Sanders was born at Tuscaloosa, Alabama, April 4, 1840, and grew up at Clinton, Greene County, whence he entered the state university in 1858. At the outbreak of war he left the university to enlist in a company of the 11th Alabama Infantry, of which he was elected captain. The first engagement in which the regiment took part was that of Seven Pines. In the ensuing Seven Days battles Sanders was severely wounded at Frayser's Farm, but returned to duty on August 11 to take command of the regiment. He was formally promoted to colonel after Sharpsburg, at the age of twenty-two. (403) He then fought with great gallantry at Fredericksburg, Salem Church, Gettysburg, and in the Overland campaign of 1864. At the battle of Spotsylvania he led Perrin's brigade after the latter's fall, and for his services in the Confederate assault to retake the "Mule Shoe," he was commissioned brigadier general from May 31, 1864. He was then assigned to the command of Cadmus M. Wilcox's old brigade of

Alabama regiments. General Sanders was later conspicuous during the opening operations of the siege of Petersburg, and particularly so in the battle of the Crater, where his brigade was a part of Mahone's division. On August 21, 1864, in one of the engagements on the Weldon railroad, he was shot through the thighs, the ball severing both femoral arteries. In a few minutes he bled to death. He is buried in Hollywood Cemetery, Richmond. (404)

Alfred Moore Scales was born at Reidsville, North Carolina, November 26, 1827, and was educated at Caldwell Institute, Greensboro, and at the state university. After studying law and commencing practice at Madison, he was solicitor of

Rockingham County, and was four times a member of the legislature. He was also a Representative in Congress from 1857 to 1859, and the following year was Presidential Elector on the Breckinridge ticket. Volunteering as a private in 1861, he was at once elected captain of Company H, 13th North Carolina, and succeeded W. D. Pender as colonel of the regiment in October. He participated in the Peninsular campaign of 1862, the Seven Days, and Fredericksburg, and was wounded at Chancellorsville. He was promoted brigadier general to rank from June 13, 1863. Again severely wounded on the first day at Gettysburg, he rode south in the same ambulance with Pender. Scales was left at Winchester, where he recovered. He took part in the

1864 campaign, but he was on sick leave in the closing months and does not seem to have been formally paroled. The records exhibit only that he applied for amnesty at Raleigh on June 22, 1866. (405) Resuming law practice in Greensboro, General Scales continued to be active politically. He served in the legislature from 1866 to 1869, and again in Congress from 1875 to 1884. In the latter year he was elected governor of North Carolina and held office for four years. He died at Greensboro on February 8, 1892, and is buried there.

Thomas Moore Scott, born in 1829, was a native of Georgia, and was probably born in Athens. He went to New Orleans as a young man, but later returned to Georgia, and for some years resided in La Grange. At the outbreak of the Civil War, Scott was engaged in farming in Claiborne Parish, Louisiana. On August 13, 1861 he enlisted in the 12th Louisiana Infantry, then being organized at Camp Moore. Of this regiment he was at once elected colonel, and accompanied it to Columbus, Kentucky. The 12th Louisiana was present at the battle of Belmont, although it was not actively engaged, and subsequently formed part of the garrison of Island No. 10, and in April 1862 of Fort Pillow under General John B.

Villepigue. The regiment also saw duty in the Port Hudson area during late 1862 and early 1863. It was a part of W. W. Loring's division at the battle of Baker's Creek in the Vicksburg campaign, and joined the forces of General Joseph E. Johnston in their operations. Scott then remained in Mississippi until his command accompanied General Leonidas Polk to Dalton, Georgia, in 1864. He distinguished himself in the ensuing Atlanta campaign, and was promoted brigadier general from May 10, 1864. He led his brigade in Hood's ill-fated Tennessee campaign, and was severely wounded at the battle of Franklin in November by the explosion of a shell. He apparently saw no further service, since no

record of his final capture or parole has been found. Returning to Louisiana, he again engaged in farming near Homer, and for some years operated a sugar plantation on the Gulf Coast. He died in New Orleans on April 21, 1876, and was buried in Greenwood Cemetery. (406)

William Read Scurry was born in Gallatin, Tennessee, February 10, 1821. (407) He went to Texas at the age of sixteen and settled in San Augustine. Upon the outbreak of the Mexican War he enlisted as a private in the 2nd Texas Mounted Volunteers. After gallant service he was mustered out at Monterey as major of the regiment. (408) In 1859 he was appointed commis-

sioner from Texas to fix the Texas-New Mexico boundary; also, he was a member of the secession convention of 1861. He entered the Confederate Army as lieutenant colonel of the 4th Texas Cavalry, and the year following was under the command of General H. H. Sibley in the attempted Confederate occupation of New Mexico Territory. He saw action both at Valverde and at Glorieta Cañon. His role in the latter engagement was rendered more important by Sibley's absence — the general was supposedly under a doctor's care at the time. (409) Scurry was promoted brigadier general to rank from September 12, 1862. On January 1, 1863, when General Magruder made his successful attack on and recapture of Galveston, Scurry commanded the land forces employed. In 1864 he participated with his brigade in the Red River campaign and was present at the battles of Mansfield and Pleasant Hill against Banks. After Banks' retreat became known, Scurry's command was immediately transferred to oppose Steele's advance; and at the battle of Jenkins' Ferry, April 30, 1864, he was mortally wounded. Refusing to be taken to the rear, where the surgeons might well have saved his life, he bled to death on the battlefield. (410) He is buried in the Texas State Cemetery at Austin.

Claudius Wistar Sears, a native of Massachusetts, was born in Peru, November 8, 1817, and was graduated from West Point in 1841. He resigned the year following to become a teacher. After a short period as instructor at St. Thomas's Hall, Holly Springs, Mississippi, he served as professor of mathematics at the University of Louisiana (now Tulane) from 1845 to 1859. Meantime he married into a Southern family from Houston, Texas. Returning to St. Thomas's as president, he presided until 1861, when he enlisted in the 17th Mississippi Infantry and was elected captain of Company G. Later commissioned colonel of the 46th Mississippi, he served at Chickasaw Bayou against Sherman and at Port Gibson in May 1863. Cap-

271

tured and paroled at Vicksburg, he was not exchanged for several months. He returned to his command early in 1864 and was appointed brigadier general to rank from March 1. Joining the Army of Tennessee at Resaca, Georgia, in May, Sears participated in the Atlanta campaign until disabled by illness. He was subsequently with General S. G. French in the desperate fight at Allatoona and accompanied Hood into Tennessee. During the battle of Nashville, while observing the enemy through his glass, a shell killed his horse and carried away one of his legs. (411) Taken to the rear, he was captured near Pulaski a few days later and was not paroled until June 23, 1865. The same year General Sears was elected to the chair of mathematics at the University of Mississippi, a post he continued to occupy until 1889. He died at Oxford, Mississippi, February 15, 1891, and is buried there. (412)

Paul Jones Semmes was born at Montford's Plantation, Wilkes County, Georgia, June 4, 1815. He attended the University of Virginia, (413) and returned to Georgia to become a banker and planter near Columbus. He also actively interested himself in the state militia, serving as captain of the Columbus Guards from 1846 until 1861. At the outbreak of the Civil War Semmes was

elected colonel of the 2nd Georgia Infantry and took his regiment to Virginia. Promoted brigadier general the following spring, to rank from March 11, 1862, he participated in Magruder's defense of Yorktown and Williamsburg, and also served in Magruder's division at the battle of Seven Pines. During the Seven Days battles his command was attached to McLaws' division of Longstreet's corps, with which he later rendered gallant service at Crampton's Gap and Sharpsburg. His brigade aided in the defense of Marye's Heights at the battle of Fredericksburg, and was present with McLaws at Salem Church during the Chancellorsville campaign. During Longstreet's attack against the Round Tops on the second day at Gettysburg, General Semmes was mortally wounded (July 2,

1863). Conveyed across the Potomac in an ambulance to Martinsburg, (West) Virginia, before the retreat of the main army, he died there on July 10, and was temporarily buried. His remains were later interred in Linnwood Cemetery, Columbus, Georgia. (414)

Jacob Hunter Sharp was born at Pickensville, Alabama, February 6, 1833. He was taken in infancy by his parents to Lowndes County, Mississippi. He attended the University of Alabama in 1850-51. He studied law, was admitted to the bar, and commenced practice in Columbus, Mississippi. Enlisting in 1861 as a private in the 1st Battalion Mississippi Infantry (later part of the 44th Mississippi), he was elected captain and fought at

Shiloh, in the Kentucky campaign, and at Murfreesboro. He was promoted colonel b e f o r e Chickamauga and led the 44th there and during the subsequent Chattanooga campaign. In the course of the Atlanta campaign (July 26, 1864) he was promoted brigadier general to supply the place of G e n e r a l William F. Tucker, who had been disabled by wounds. Thereafter he led his brigade with marked gallantry in Hood's Tennessee expedition and during the campaign of the Carolinas. He apparently fought his last battle at Bentonville, since no record of his personal parole at Greensboro has been found. (415) After the war General Sharp resumed his law practice, purchased the Columbus (Miss.) *Independent,* and became president of the Mississippi Press Association. He was active in the white supremacy movement during Reconstruction days; and was a member of the legislature from 1886 to 1890, being at one time speaker of the house. He died at Columbus on September 15, 1907, and is buried there. (416)

Joseph Orville Shelby was born in Lexington, Kentucky, December 12, 1830, and was educated by his step-father and at Transylvania University. He engaged in the manufacture of rope, first at Lexington and later at Waverly, Missouri. Eventually he became one of the wealthiest and most

273

influential citizens of the state. He led a band of pro-slavery Kentuckians in the Missouri-Kansas "war" of the late 1850's. At the outbreak of the Civil War he organized a cavalry company and enlisted under the banner of the Confederacy. Usually attached to the forces of General Sterling Price, Shelby was active in almost every campaign of the war west of the Mississippi River. He fought at Carthage, Wilson's Creek, Elkhorn, Helena, Camden, and in both of Price's Missouri raids, as well as in scores of minor actions. His reputation west of the river compared favorably with that of Bedford Forrest in the east, and earned him a contemporary renown in the area of almost equal distinction. He was appointed brigadier general to rank from December 15, 1863. (417) After the collapse of the Confederacy, and without waiting for his personal parole, General Shelby with a few of his command buried their battleflag in the Rio Grande and then crossed into Mexico to ally themselves with either the party of the Emperor Maximilian or his opponent, General Juarez. Following a rather confused series of negotiations, and the downfall of Maximilian, Shelby returned to Missouri to reconstruct his career. Enormously popular in the state, he refused all political offers until 1893 when President Cleveland appointed·him U. S. marshal for the Western District. While holding this office he died at Adrian, Missouri, February 13, 1897; he is buried in Kansas City.

Charles Miller Shelley was born in Sullivan County, Tennessee, December 28, 1833. He was taken by his parents in 1836 to Talladega, Alabama, where he grew up to follow his father's profession of architect and builder. A lieutenant of the Talladega Artillery in 1861, he spent six weeks at Fort Morgan; and upon the reorganization of his company into infantry, as a part of the 5th Alabama, he was elected captain. He was present in Virginia during the campaign of First Manassas. In January 1862 he recruited the 30th Alabama and was commissioned its colonel. He fought in Bragg's Kentucky in-

vasion, at Port Gibson, and at Vicksburg, where he was captured. Upon his exchange he joined the Army of Tennessee with his command and took part in every battle from Chattanooga to the final surrender at Greensboro. He was appointed brigadier general from September 17, 1864. In the famous assault on the Federal works at Franklin, Shelley's brigade lost 432 killed and wounded out of 1100 present for duty. Shelley himself escaped unhurt, although his horse was killed under him and his uniform was pierced by bullets. After spending a year in Louisiana post bellum, General Shelley returned to Alabama, and in 1874 was elected sheriff of Dallas County. Thereafter he served four consecutive terms in Congress as a Democrat, two of which were contested by his opponents. He then became fourth auditor of the Treasury by appointment of President Cleveland. The last years of his life were spent in promoting the industrial interests of Birmingham, Alabama, where he died on January 20, 1907. He is buried in Talladega. (418)

Francis Asbury Shoup, a native of Indiana, was born at Laurel, Franklin County, March 22, 1834. (419) He was educated at Asbury College (now De Pauw University) and at West Point, from which he was graduated in 1855. Shoup resigned from the army in 1860 to study law and to be admitted to the Indianapolis bar. The following year he went to Florida and gained admission to the St. Augustine bar. There ap-

pears to have been no reason for his adherence to the newly-formed Confederacy other than admiration for the Southern people he had known in the old army. At any rate, he soon volunteered and was appointed lieutenant of artillery, and in October 1861 was promoted major. He fought at Shiloh, as chief of artillery to General Hardee; and was assistant adjutant general to General Hindman at Prairie Grove. Commissioned brigadier general to rank from September 12, 1862, Shoup commanded a Louisiana brigade at Vicksburg, where he was captured. After his exchange he served as chief of artillery to General Joseph E. Johnston in the Atlanta campaign. When Johnston was superseded by Hood, Shoup became Hood's chief of staff. He was elected to the chair of mathematics at the University of Mississippi at the close of the war. In 1868 he took Episcopal orders and assumed also the duties of rector of St. Peter's Parish in Oxford. The following year he went to Sewanee as professor of mathematics and chaplain. Leaving in 1875, he served as rector of several churches, north and south. He returned to Sewanee in 1883, where as professor of mathematics, physics, and engineering, he remained until his death, September 4, 1896, at Columbia, Tennessee. He is buried at Sewanee.

Henry Hopkins Sibley was born at Natchitoches, Louisiana, May 25, 1816, and was graduated from West Point in the class of 1838. His service in the ante-bellum U. S. Army was extensive. It ranged from participation in the Seminole War of 1838-39 to duty in the Utah expedition against the Mormons. Brevetted for gallantry in Mexico, he resigned his commission on May 13, 1861, the same day he was promoted major of the 1st U. S. Dragoons. Three days later he was commissioned colonel in the Confederate Army, and on June 17, brigadier general. Sibley's only important Civil War service, during which his alleged predilection for the bottle was widely publicized, (420) was as commander of the expedition designed to secure New Mexico to the Confederacy.

After the battles of Valverde and Glorieta Cañon he was forced to retreat, since he could not subsist his command off the country. Under incredible hardships he reached El Paso in May 1862, and subsequently retired to San Antonio. Thereafter his career was beset with numerous misfortunes. Charges were twice preferred against him. Kirby Smith reported in March 1865 that he was without a command and not on duty. (421) At the close of the war General Sibley went abroad, and from 1869 to 1873 was a general of artillery in the Egyptian Army. Subsequently returning to the United States, he lectured on his Egyptian experiences. He spent his last years in ill health and comparative poverty, and died at Fredericksburg, Virginia (August 23, 1886), where he is buried. His name is associated with the Sibley tent, his invention, which was much used during the first years of the war by both armies but was later discontinued.

James Phillip Simms was born at Covington, Georgia, January 16, 1837. At the outbreak of the Civil War he was practicing law in that city. The date of his enlistment in the Confederate Army is in doubt. He first appears in the records as nominated to the grade of major, 53rd Georgia Infantry, on September 24, 1862. (422) The first field serv-

ice of this regiment had been during the Seven Days battles as a part of General John B. Magruder's command. Simms was presumably present with the 53rd at Second Manassas and Sharpsburg. He fought at Fredericksburg as colonel in command, (423) and his regiment captured the colors of the 2nd Rhode Island at Salem Church the following May. (424) Simms participated in the Gettysburg campaign, accompanied Longstreet to the West and was present at Knoxville, and fought throughout the Overland campaign of 1864. Transferred to the Shenandoah Valley in Kershaw's division, he commanded Goode Bryan's brigade after the latter's resignation in September, and was greatly distinguished at Cedar Creek. Returning to Petersburg, he took part in the siege of that fall and winter. He was

277

promoted to brigadier general from December 8, 1864. During the retreat from Richmond he was captured, along with his division commander and a number of other general officers, at Sayler's Creek, on April 6, 1865. He was released from Fort Warren on July 24. (425) General Simms then returned to Covington, where he resumed his law practice and resided until his death, May 30, 1887. (426) In 1865-66 and again in 1877 he was a member of the Georgia state legislature. He is buried in Covington.

William Yarnel Slack was born in Mason County, Kentucky, August 1, 1816. (427) When Slack was three years of age his father moved to Boone County, Missouri, and settled near Columbia, where Slack received his education and eventually studied law. He later moved to Chillicothe, Missouri, to commence practice. (428) Having served as captain of the 2nd Missouri Volunteers under Sterling Price in the war with Mexico, he resumed his profession after fourteen months in the army. In 1861 he was appointed brigadier general of the Missouri State Guard by Governor Claiborne F. Jackson. He fought at Carthage and Springfield and was severely wounded in the hip at the latter battle, but recovered to rejoin his command in October. On March 7, 1862, at the battle of Elkhorn, General Slack was again struck by a rifle ball only

an inch from his old wound. He was taken to a house a mile east of the battlefield and seemed to improve for a few days, but due to fear of capture, he was again moved to Moore's Mill, located about seven miles farther east. Here his condition rapidly deteriorated and he died early on the morning of March 21. First buried in the yard, his remains in 1880 were re-interred in the Confederate Cemetery at Fayetteville, Arkansas. (429) General Slack was posthumously promoted brigadier general in the Confederate service on April 17 to rank from April 12, and was duly confirmed by the Senate. There is a possibility that, due to the withdrawal of the Confederate forces from the vicinity of the battlefield, the news of his death had not reached Richmond. (430)

James Edwin Slaughter, a great-nephew of President James Madison, (431) was born in June 1827 on his father's estate, in the center of what was later to become the battlefield of Cedar (Slaughter's) Mountain. (432) He attended Virginia Military Institute in 1845-46, but withdrew to accept a commission in the U. S. Army at the outbreak of the Mexican War. Thereafter he remained in the army until 1861, when he was dismissed as 1st Lieutenant, 1st Artillery, on May 14. (433) Commissioned a captain of artillery in the Confederate service, he served on Bragg's staff at Pensacola, and was promoted major in November. On the following March 8 he was appointed brigadier general in the Provisional Army and assigned as assistant inspector general to General A. S. John-ston, with whom he served at Shiloh. Performing the same duties for the latter's successors, Generals Beauregard and Bragg, he continued through the Kentucky campaign, and was then given line command at Mobile. In April 1863 he went to Galveston as chief of artillery to General Magruder and later acted as his chief of staff. General Slaughter commanded at the last engagement of the war between Union and Confederate troops near Brownsville on May 12, 1865. At the close of hostilities he lived several years in Mexico. He returned to Mobile to engage in civil engineering and to serve for a time as postmaster. Finally removing to New Orleans, he died while on a visit to Mexico City, January 1, 1901, (434) and is buried there.

Edmund Kirby Smith, (435) called "Seminole" at West Point, was born at St. Augustine, Florida, on May 16, 1824, the son of New England parents. He obtained his early education at Benjamin Hallowell's preparatory school in Alexandria, Virginia, and was graduated from West Point in 1845. Commissioned in the infantry, he won the brevets of 1st lieutenant and captain for gallantry at Cerro Gordo and Contreras in the Mexican War. From 1849 to 1852 he was assistant professor of mathematics at West Point. Later he served in the Indian campaigns on the

Texas frontier. As major of the 2nd Cavalry in 1861, Smith refused to surrender Fort Colorado (in Texas) to the Texas militia under Ben McCulloch and expressed his readiness to fight to hold it. Nevertheless, he resigned his commission on April 6, when Florida seceded from the Union. He entered Confederate service as a lieutenant colonel and served in the Shenandoah under J. E. Johnston. On June 17, 1861 he was commissioned brigadier general in the Provisional Army and was severely wounded at First Manassas the following month. He was promoted major general on October 11, 1861, and in 1862 was in command of the District of East Tennessee. Smith participated in Bragg's invasion of Kentucky and won a decisive victory at Richmond, August 30, 1862. He became lieutenant general from October 9, 1862. From 1862 to 1865 he was in command of the Trans-Mississippi Department, and received the permanent rank of general in the Provisional Army on February 19, 1864. (436) In the spring of 1864 his army repelled the Red River expedition of General N. P. Banks. Smith was almost the last Confederate general in the field, but in a hopelessly isolated situation, he finally surrendered his troops to General E. R. S. Canby on May 26, 1865. After the war General Smith was for two years president of the Pacific and Atlantic Telegraph Company. Subsequently he was president of the Western Military Academy at Nashville, and chancellor of the University of Nashville; and from 1875 until his death, was professor of mathematics at the University of the South. The last survivor of the full generals of the Confederacy, he died at Sewanee, Tennessee, March 28, 1893, and is buried there.

Gustavus Woodson Smith was born at Georgetown, Kentucky, on either November 30 or December 1, 1821, (437) and was graduated from West Point in 1842. By profession an engineer, his varied career prior to the Civil War included service in Mexico, where he was thrice brevetted; duty at the Military Academy as an instructor; and work on the construction of forti-

fications. He resigned in 1854 to become a civil engineer. The outbreak of hostilities found him street commissioner of New York City and prominent in Democratic political circles. Commissioned major general in the Confederate Army on September 19, 1861, he commanded a wing of the Army of Northern Virginia during the Peninsular campaign. He was in chief command for a few hours after General Joseph E. Johnston was wounded at Seven Pines. He also served as Secretary of War *ad interim* in November 1862, and resigned his major generalcy the following January because of the promotion over his head of a number of officers junior in rank. (438) He was then appointed a major general of Georgia militia by Governor Joseph E. Brown. General Smith organized the state

forces and fought them with marked efficiency, particularly on the Chattahoochee before the battle of Atlanta, and on the fortified line at Savannah. Surrendering at Macon, April 20, 1865, the General was for some years superintendent of an iron-works at Chattanooga, Tennessee, and insurance commissioner of Kentucky from 1870 to 1876. He then moved to New York City, where he resided until his death, June 24, 1896. He published several works on the Mexican and Civil Wars, notably *Confederate War Papers,* and *The Battle of Seven Pines.* (See Bibliography ## 96, 259.) He is buried in New London, Connecticut.

James Argyle Smith was born in Maury County, Tennessee, July 1, 1831, (439) and was graduated

from the United States Military Academy in the class of 1853. He saw routine frontier service in the 6th Infantry, and resigned his commission on May 9, 1861 to join the Confederate service. He was appointed a captain of infantry in the Regular Army, and was soon promoted major and assistant adjutant general to General Leonidas Polk. At Shiloh he was lieutenant colonel of the 2nd Tennessee Infantry, where he was commended by his brigade commander, Colonel (later General) Preston Smith. Promoted colonel, he commanded the 5th Confederate Infantry at Perryville, Murfreesboro, and Chickamauga, after which and upon the repeated recommendations of his superiors, he was commissioned brigadier general to rank from September 30, 1863. He took a gallant part in the Atlanta campaign, in which he was painfully wounded. He led his brigade into Tennessee under Hood, and after the death of Cleburne at Franklin, commanded that officer's division at Nashville. While leading part of the remnant of Cheatham's corps in the Carolinas, General Smith was paroled at Greensboro on May 1, 1865. He then settled in Mississippi as a farmer. In 1877 he was elected superintendent of public education of the state, an office in which he served for many years. He died at Jackson, Mississippi, December 6, 1901, and is buried there.

Martin Luther Smith, a native of New York state, was born at Danby, Tompkins County, September 9, 1819, where his father had moved from Maine. He was graduated in 1842 at West Point —a class which furnished no less than nine general officers to the Confederate Army and thirteen to the Union from a total of fifty-six men. He was commissioned in the topographical engineers. Smith's old army career was almost entirely spent in the South, where in 1846 he married a girl from Athens, Georgia. He was brevetted for meritorious conduct while mapping the valley of Mexico City during the war of 1846-48. His "associations, feelings and interests" (440) compelled his resignation from the United States service on April 1, 1861 and his resolve to ally himself with the Confederacy. Com-

missioned major in the corps of engineers at the beginning of hostilities, he was soon promoted colonel of the 21st Louisiana Infantry. However, his forte was engineering. He was appointed brigadier general on April 11, 1862, and major general, November 4, 1862; and was given an important part in the planning and construction of the defenses of New Orleans and Vicksburg. However, he commanded troops at both places. A paroled prisoner of war for seven months after the surrender of Vicksburg, he was subsequently chief engineer of the Army of Northern Virginia and later of the Army of Tennessee. In the closing months of the war he prepared the defenses at Mobile under the supervision of General Beauregard. Surviving the surrender only a few months, he died in Savannah, July 29, 1866. He is buried in Athens.

Preston Smith was born in Giles County, Tennessee, December 25, 1823. He obtained his early education in the country schools of the neighborhood and attended Jackson College at Columbia. He then studied law, and after admission to the bar, moved first to Waynesboro and ultimately to Memphis. In 1861 he was commissioned colonel of the 154th Tennessee, a militia regiment which was mustered into Confederate service under its old state designation. While leading the 154th he was s e v e r e l y wounded at Shiloh. He was attached to Cleburne's division of General Kirby Smith's command during the invasion of Kentucky, in command of a brigade. After the wounding of Cleburne at Richmond, Kentucky, Smith commanded the division. He was promoted brigadier general on October 27, 1862. The following year he took into the battle of Chickamauga a brigade of four Tennessee regiments and a battalion in General B. F. Cheatham's division of General Leonidas Polk's corps—the corps that was intended to form the right wing of the army. In the course of an attack launched at dark on the night of September 19, 1863, General Smith unwittingly rode into the front of a Federal detachment, which recognizing him as a Confederate officer, fired a volley that mortally wounded him and killed his aide outright. Transported to the rear, he died less than an hour later. (441) His body was first taken to Atlanta and buried; some years later it was re-interred in Elmwood Cemetery, Memphis. (442)

Thomas Benton Smith was born at Mechanicsville, Tennessee, February 24, 1838. After securing his early education in the schools of the neighborhood, he attended Nashville Military Institute for four years. There seems to be no basis for the statement that he subsequently attended West Point for a year. (443) He worked in the shops of the Nashville & Decatur Railroad for a time. At the beginning of the war he was elected 2nd lieutenant of Company B, 20th Tennessee. He took part in the battles of Mill Springs and Shiloh, and was elected colonel of the regiment upon its reorganization in May 1862. Severely wounded at Murfreesboro, he fought at Baton Rouge, Chickamauga, and throughout the Atlanta campaign. He was promoted to brigadier general from July 29, 1864. During the battle of Nashville, General Smith and most of his command were captured. While being conducted to the rear, an unarmed prisoner of war, he was wantonly and repeatedly struck over the head with a sword by Colonel William Linn McMillen of the 95th Ohio Infantry. (444) General Smith was taken to a Federal field hospital, where it was found that his brain was exposed, and his death was anticipated momentarily. However, he recovered temporarily, only to spend the last forty-seven years of his life in the state asylum at Nashville. After working as a brakeman and conductor for various railroads, and running unsuccessfully for Congress in 1870, he was admitted to the hospital in 1876, dying there at the age of eighty-five on May 21, 1923. He is buried in Mount Olivet Cemetery in Nashville.

William Smith was born at "Marengo" in King George County, Virginia, September 6, 1797. He received his early education in Virginia and Connecticut. He

studied law and in 1818 began practice in Culpeper, Virginia. Nine years later he began a mail-coach service, and by 1834 was operating daily postal service from Washington, D. C. to Milledgeville, then the capital of Georgia. From the rapid expansion of this route and the resultant extra mail payments Smith derived his sobriquet, "Extra Billy." In the years between 1836 and the outbreak of the Civil War, Smith served five years in the Virginia senate, five terms in Congress, and one term as governor of his state. Becoming colonel of the 49th Virginia Infantry in 1861, he fought at First Manassas and was elected to the First Regular Confederate Congress. He attended sessions between campaigns, but ultimately resigned in 1863. Taking part in the Peninsular campaign, the Seven Days battles, Second Manassas, Sharpsburg, and Gettysburg, he was five times wounded. He was promoted brigadier general from January 31, 1863, and major general from August 12. On the following January 1, General Smith was again inaugurated governor of Virginia, serving until the end of the war. The remainder of his life was spent in farming on his estate, "Monterosa," near Warrenton, where he died in his ninetieth year, May 18, 1887. At the age of eighty he was elected to the Virginia house of delegates and served from 1877 to 1879. Smith liked to indulge his well-known aversion to the "spit-and-polish" West Point tradition: he was seen at least once during a battle topping his uniform with a high-crowned beaver hat, and since the weather was inclement, carrying a blue cotton umbrella. (445). He is buried in Hollywood Cemetery, Richmond.

William Duncan Smith was born in Augusta, Georgia, July 28, 1825, and was graduated from West Point in 1846. He fought in many of the battles of the Mexican War and was severely wounded at Molino del Rey. From 1859 to 1861 he was on leave of absence in Europe, and on January 28 of the latter year, resigned his commission of captain, Second Dragoons, to enter

Confederate service. First commissioned colonel of the 20th Georgia Infantry on July 14, 1861, he was promoted brigadier general to rank from March 7, 1862, and ordered to report to General John C. Pemberton, then in command of the Department of South Carolina and Georgia. In June, Smith was placed in command of the District of South Carolina, with headquarters at Charleston. On the sixteenth of that month he led one wing of General "Shanks" Evans' forces at the battle of Secessionville, South Carolina—an affair which resulted in a complete victory for the Confederates. Smith had by this time exhibited considerable ability both as a desk commander and in the field; and William Porcher Miles went so far as to urge his

appointment to supersede Pemberton. However, he shortly contracted yellow fever and died at Charleston on October 4, 1862, at the early age of thirty-seven. He is buried in the City Cemetery of Augusta. (446)

Gilbert Moxley Sorrel, a brother-in-law of General W. W. Mackall, was born at Savannah, Georgia, February 23, 1838. (447) In 1861 he was a clerk in the banking department of the Central Railroad of Georgia and a private in the Georgia Hussars, a Savannah militia company. After witnessing the bombardment of Fort Sumter and taking part in the capture of Fort Pulaski, Sorrel determined to go to Richmond and "get into the fight." Attached to General Longstreet's staff as captain and volunteer

aide-de-camp, he was present at First Manassas. From then until his chief's wounding at the Wilderness, Sorrel was constantly at Longstreet's side. He was promoted through grades to lieutenant colonel and chief of staff of the 1st Corps, and was present at every engagement of that command. At the Wilderness he was detailed to lead the troops which rolled up the left of the Federal II Corps. On October 27, 1864 he was appointed brigadier general and placed in command of a brigade of Georgia regiments in Mahone's division of the 3rd Corps. He was wounded in the leg near Petersburg, and was shot through the lung at Hatcher's Run in February 1865. He was at Lynchburg en route back to his command when he learned of the surrender of Appomattox. (448) After the war General Sorrel was a merchant at Savannah and later was connected with a steamship company. He died near Roanoke, Virginia, August 10, 1901, but is buried in Savannah. Sorrel wrote *Recollections of a Confederate Staff Officer* (see Bibliography # 97).

Leroy Augustus Stafford was born at "Greenwood," near Cheneyville, Rapides Parish, Louisiana, April 13, 1822. Educated in Kentucky and Tennessee, he returned home to become a planter; and in 1845 he was elected sheriff of his parish. He

served as a private in the Rapides Volunteers during the Mexican War. After its mustering out he was in the command of Ben McCulloch. At the outbreak of war in 1861 he was one of the most prominent and affluent planters of his region. He aided in recruiting the Stafford Guards, and was elected its captain. The company was mustered into Confederate service as Company B of the 9th Louisiana Infantry, with Stafford as lieutenant colonel. Promoted colonel to succeed Richard Taylor in October 1861, he took part in Jackson's Valley campaign the following spring, the Seven Days battles, Cedar Mountain, Second Manassas, Harpers Ferry, and Sharpsburg. In October 1862 his regiment was transferred to General Harry Hays' brigade, and fought in that command at Fredericksburg, Chancellorsville, and Gettysburg. Commissioned brigadier general on October 8, 1863, Stafford was assigned to the command of the 2nd Louisiana Brigade, Stonewall Division, and led it at Mine Run. On the first day of the battle of the Wilderness, May 5, 1864, he was mortally wounded while "leading his command with conspicuous valor," to quote from General Lee's report. (449) Three days later he succumbed in the Spottswood Hotel, Richmond, and was first buried in Hollywood Cemetery. His remains were moved in 1866 to "Greenwood," his ancestral home. (450)

Peter Burwell Starke, a brother of General William E. Starke, was born in Brunswick County, Virginia, in 1815. (451) As a young man he and his brothers operated a stage line from Lawrenceville to Petersburg via Boydton. He removed to Bolivar County, Mississippi, in the 1840's. He was an unsuccessful candidate for Congress in 1846, but later served in the lower house of the state legislature from 1850 to 1854, and was a member of the senate from 1856 to 1862. Commissioned colonel of the 28th Mississippi Cavalry on February 24, 1862, he was mainly employed in the defense of Vicksburg until it capitulated. He was attached to the forces of General Joseph E. Johnston toward the close of the campaign. He served in the brigade of General Frank C. Armstrong in the Atlanta campaign, and was promoted brigadier general from November 4, 1864. Thereafter, he was under Forrest in Hood's Tennessee campaign, and in the last months of the war, under General Chalmers in Mississippi. From 1866 to 1872 General Starke was a member of the board of Mississippi levee commissioners; and was also appointed for one term as sheriff of Bolivar County. Since all of the children of his first marriage had died soon after the war, he returned to Virginia in 1873 and settled in his native county near Lawrenceville. He died there on July 13, 1888, and is buried in an unmarked grave on what was formerly the farm of his second wife's family. (452)

288

William Edwin Starke, like his younger brother, General Peter B. Starke, was born in Brunswick County, Virginia, in 1814. After operating in early life a stage line with his brothers, he became most successful as a cotton broker in Mobile and New Orleans. He had been living in the latter city for many years when the Civil War broke out. Serving as aide-de-camp to General R. S. Garnett in the disastrous Western Virginia campaign of 1861, in which his chief was killed, he was soon commissioned colonel of the 60th Virginia Infantry. With this command he served for a time under Generals Floyd and Wise. During the battles of the Seven Days his regiment was in Field's brigade of A. P. Hill's division, and his gallant conduct was twice commended. Promoted brigadier general on August 6, 1862, he

was present at Second Manassas, and after the wounding of General Taliaferro, commanded the Stonewall Division of Jackson's corps. Thereafter he accompanied Jackson in the Maryland campaign and took part in the capture of Harpers Ferry. He arrived at Sharpsburg a day early, on September 16, 1862. Here he was again in command of Jackson's old division following the retirement from the field of General J. R. Jones. Starke was struck three times, early on the 17th, and survived for only about an hour. His remains were conveyed to Richmond, where he now lies buried in Hollywood Cemetery. (453)

William Steele, a native of Albany, New York, was born May 1, 1819. His father was a New Englander and his mother from Florida. He was graduated from West Point in the class of 1840, and received the brevet of captain for gallantry in the battles of Contreras and Churubusco. Much of Steele's service had been in Texas, and he married into a family from that state in 1850. He resigned on May 30, 1861, and was appointed colonel of the 7th Texas Cavalry. During Sibley's New Mexico expedition he commanded in the Mesilla area and was promoted brigadier general to rank from September 12, 1862. He was in command of Indian Territory in 1863, and had

George Hume "Maryland" Steuart was born at Baltimore, Maryland, August 24, 1828. He was graduated from West Point when he was but nineteen years of age, though he stood thirty-seventh in a class of thirty-eight members. (455) After routine cavalry service on the frontier he resigned his commission on April 22, 1861, and was appointed captain of cavalry in the Regular Confederate Army. Upon t h e formation of the 1st Maryland Infantry Steuart became its lieutenant colonel, and after First Manassas succeeded Arnold Elzey as colonel. Promoted brigadier general to rank from March 6, 1862, he commanded a brigade of four Virginia regiments and his old Maryland regiment in Ewell's division during the Valley campaign of that spring. He

charge of the Galveston defenses the following year. He then fought under General Richard Taylor in the Red River campaign and was complimented for his conduct at Pleasant Hill. After the death of General Thomas Green at Blair's Landing, he commanded Green's cavalry division for a time, as senior brigadier, until superseded by Major General John A. Wharton. After the war General Steele settled in San Antonio as a commission merchant. He moved to Austin in 1873 and was appointed adjutant general of the state, serving in that post for six years during the administrations of Governors Coke and Hubbard. He died at San Antonio on January 12, 1885, and is buried in Oakwood Cemetery, Austin. (454)

was seriously wounded at Cross Keys and disabled for some time. At Gettysburg he led a brigade in Edward Johnson's division of the 2nd Corps, and continued in command thereof until he and most of the division were captured in the "Mule Shoe" at Spotsylvania, early. in the morning of May 12, 1864. After his exchange he was assigned a brigade in Pickett's division north of the James, which he subsequently led at the battle of Five Forks and during the Appomattox campaign. After the war General Steuart took up residence on a farm in Anne Arundel County, Maryland. He died at South River, Maryland, November 22, 1903. For many years he served as commander of the Maryland division of the United Confederate Veterans. He is buried in Green Mount Cemetery, Baltimore.

Clement Hoffman Stevens, the son of an officer in the United States Navy, was born in Norwich, Connecticut, August 14, 1821. The family shortly moved to Florida and then to Pendleton, South Carolina, the state of his mother's birth. Stevens served for several years at sea as secretary to his kinsmen, Commodores William Shubrick and William Bee. He entered the Planters and Mechanics Bank in Charleston in 1842, and was cashier of the institution at the outbreak of

the Civil War. Something of an inventor, Stevens planned and later constructed what was perhaps the first armored fortification, a battery on Morris Island, Charleston Harbor, which was faced with railroad iron. He was severely wounded at First Manassas while serving as aide to his brother-in-law, General Barnard E. Bee, who was killed. Soon he was elected colonel of the 24th South Carolina, which he commanded at the battle of Secessionville. Attached to Gist's brigade in the Vicksburg campaign, he was subsequently transferred to the Army of Tennessee and was again badly wounded at Chickamauga. He was eulogized by General Gist as "the iron-nerved," and termed by his men "Rock" Stevens. He was promoted brigadier general to rank from January 20, 1864, and assigned to the command of a brigade in W. H. T. Walker's division. This he led with great gallantry and distinction during the Atlanta campaign, until he was fatally wounded at the battle of Peach Tree Creek, July 20, 1864. He died in Atlanta on July 25, and was buried in Pendleton, South Carolina.

Walter Husted Stevens was born at Penn Yan, New York, August 24, 1827. He was graduated fourth in the class of 1848 at the U. S. Military Academy, and was commissioned in the corps of engineers. His old army service was almost entirely in Louisiana and Texas. This fact added to his marriage to a sister of General Louis Hébert of Louisiana, had made him completely South-

ern in sentiment. In 1861 he submitted his resignation, which, however, was not accepted; and he was dismissed on May 2, 1861, on a technicality. (456) Appointed a captain of engineers in the Regular Confederate Army, he was engineer officer to General Beauregard at First Manassas. He was promoted to major and acted as chief engineer of the Army of Virginia, under General Joseph E. Johnston in Northern Virginia and during the Peninsular campaign. Upon the accession of General Lee to command, Stevens, having been promoted colonel, was placed in charge of the Richmond defenses, which he enlarged and strengthened. Appointed chief engineer of the Army of Northern Virginia, he received the rank of brigadier general from August 28, 1864. Stevens was supposedly the last uniformed man to cross Mayo's Bridge on the night of the evacuation of Richmond. (457) Paroled at Appomattox, he went to Mexico and became superintendent and engineer of the Imperial Railroad, a line designed by Maximilian to run from Vera Cruz to Mexico City. He died in Vera Cruz on November 12, 1867, at the early age of forty. He is buried in Hollywood Cemetery, Richmond.

Carter Littlepage Stevenson was born near Fredericksburg, Virginia, September 21, 1817. He

was graduated from West Point in 1838, and served on the frontier and in the Mexican War with the 5th Infantry. Because of an oversight by his commanding officer in forwarding his resignation, he was dismissed from the United States Army on June 25, 1861, "it having been ascertained, to the satisfaction of the War Department, that he had entertained and expressed treasonable designs against the Government of the United States." (458) He entered Confederate service as major of infantry in the Regular Army and colonel of the 53rd Virginia. Upon the recommendation of General Beauregard he was promoted brigadier general from February 27, 1862 and ordered to the West. He commanded the force which compelled the withdrawal of the Federal General Morgan from Cumberland Gap. He served with General Kirby Smith in the Kentucky campaign, and was promoted major general from October 10, 1862. Active in the Vicksburg campaign in command of a division in Pemberton's army, he was captured at the termination of the siege, paroled, and later exchanged. General Stevenson was then present at every battle of the Army of Tennessee from Chattanooga to Bentonville, with the exception of Franklin. Here, Stevenson's division and that of General H. D. Clayton were left on the south side of Duck River to demonstrate against Schofield while Hood executed his flank march with the rest of the army. Paroled at Greensboro, North Carolina, May 1, 1865, he was a civil and mining engineer until his death in Caroline County, Virginia, August 15, 1888. He is buried in Fredericksburg.

Alexander Peter Stewart, "Old Straight" to his men, was born in Rogersville, Tennessee, October 2, 1821. He was graduated from West Point in 1842 and resigned in 1845 to become an educator. From that time until the outbreak of the Civil War he occupied the chair of mathematics and natural and experimental philosophy at Cumberland University, at Lebanon, Tennessee, and at Nashville Uni-

versity. Although a strong anti-secessionist Whig in politics, he soon volunteered for the South. The first months of his Confederate service were spent in organizing camps of instruction. After commanding the heavy artillery and water batteries at Belmont, Missouri, he was appointed brigadier general, November 8, 1861, and assigned to a brigade in General Leonidas Polk's command. He fought gallantly in all the battles of the Tennessee Army. He was promoted major general to rank from June 2, 1863, and lieutenant general on June 23, 1864, when he succeeded to the command of Polk's corps. This he led to the end, being finally paroled with General Johnston's army at Greensboro in May 1865. First resuming his pro-

fessorship at Cumberland University, he later engaged in business in St. Louis from 1870 to 1874. In the latter year he was elected chancellor of the University of Mississippi, a post which he held until his resignation in 1886. General Stewart later was appointed a commissioner of the Chickamauga and Chattanooga National Military Park, serving until his death in Biloxi, Mississippi, August 30, 1908. He is buried in St. Louis.

Marcellus Augustus Stovall (459) was born in Sparta, Georgia, September 18, 1818. He attended school in Massachusetts. In 1835, at the age of seventeen, he enlisted in the Richmond Blues of Augusta, Georgia, for service in the Seminole uprising of that year. In 1836 he was appointed to the United States Military

Academy, but remained only one year because of illness. After a tour of Europe he returned to Augusta, and in 1846 settled on an estate near Rome in Floyd County. Captain of the Cherokee Artillery in 1861, he was made colonel of artillery in the state militia, and in October lieutenant colonel of the 3rd Georgia Battalion of infantry, in the Provisional Army. He was stationed in East Tennessee for a time and accompanied Kirby Smith into Kentucky. Afterwards he was attached to the Army of Tennessee, then under the command of General Bragg. He was also present at Murfreesboro. For his services at Chickamauga he was warmly commended by General Breckinridge. His promotion to brigadier dated from January 20, 1863. Thereafter he fought gallantly in the Atlanta campaign, accompanied General Hood into Tennessee, and with the remnant of the army, joined General Johnston in the Carolinas. Paroled on May 9, 1865, General Stovall returned to Augusta and engaged in cotton brokerage and the manufacture of fertilizers, organizing and operating the Georgia Chemical Works. He died at Augusta on August 4, 1895, and is buried there.

Otho French Strahl was born on June 3, 1831 at McConnelsville, Morgan County, Ohio. He at-tended Ohio Wesleyan University at Delaware with the future Confederate brigadier, Daniel H. Reynolds. He later studied law with Reynolds at Somerville, Tennessee, and was admitted to the bar in 1858. At the outbreak of the Civil War he was practicing in Dyersburg. Entering Confederate service as a captain of the 4th Tennessee Volunteer Infantry in May 1861, Strahl was promoted lieutenant colonel early the following year. He fought at Shiloh and Murfreesboro, and was promoted to colonel in January 1863. On July 28, 1863 he was further promoted to brigadier general and assigned to the command of a brigade in Cheatham's division of Polk's corps, which he led with marked gallantry at Chickamauga. In the Chattanooga campaign his command was in A. P. Stewart's division of Breckinridge's corps. During the Atlanta campaign Strahl's brigade was again under Cheatham in Hardee's corps, and continued under Cheatham (in John C. Brown's division) during Hood's invasion of Tennessee. At the bitter, hand-to-hand struggle of Franklin, on November 30, 1864, General Strahl was one of six Confederate general officers who were mortally wounded. Standing in the ditch outside the Federal works, he was handing up guns to his riflemen posted to fire down into the enemy on the inside when he was struck. His last words, in answer to the question of one of his men, (460) were: "Keep on firing." First buried at St. John's Church, Ashwood, Tennessee, his remains were removed to Dyersburg about 1900. (461)

James Ewell Brown "Jeb" Stuart was born in Patrick County, Virginia, February 6, 1833, and was graduated from West Point in 1854. Most of his service in the old army was with the 1st Cavalry on the Kansas frontier. In October 1859 he was aide to Robert E. Lee in the capture of John Brown at Harpers Ferry. When Virginia seceded he resigned his lieutenancy to enter Confederate service as colonel of the 1st Virginia Cavalry. He was assigned to J. E. Johnston in the Shenandoah and became famous almost at once for his exploits.

At First Manassas in July he fought gallantly, and was promoted brigadier on September 24, 1861. Before the Seven Days battles he was ordered by Lee to reconnoiter McClellan's right flank; he obtained the information in daring fashion by riding completely around McClellan's army. Promoted major general on July 25, 1862, he was placed over the Cavalry Division (later Corps) of the Army of Northern Virginia — a command he held until his death. He proved himself a premier intelligence officer, combining the highest skill and intrepidity; the only controversial items on his record sprang from the boldness that marked his every undertaking. In a raid on General Pope's communications he not only seized a large quantity of stores but also obtained documents giving the strength and disposition of the Union forces. In August 1862 he performed brilliantly in the action leading up to and during the battle of Second Manassas. In the Maryland campaign he detained the enemy at Crampton's Gap until Lee was ready to meet McClellan's army. At Fredericksburg Stuart's horse artillery rendered valuable service in checking the attack on Stonewall Jackson's corps. He moved with Jackson at Chancellorsville in the famous flank attack on General Hooker. In this battle Stuart was given command of the 2nd Corps after both Jackson and A. P. Hill had been wounded. One of Stuart's fiercest engagements took place at Brandy Station before the Gettysburg campaign. He was absent on a raid during the march into Pennsylvania — this owing to ambiguous instructions from Lee and Longstreet which gave Stuart considerable latitude of action; and he did not arrive on the field of Gettysburg until the battle had opened. Had the "eyes of the army" been present during the campaign, it is generally supposed that the conduct of operations would have been measurably different on the part of Lee. Certainly the engagement would not have been fought where it was. Continuing to distinguish himself through the winter of 1863-64, Stuart was mortally wounded on May 11, 1864, after having intercepted Sheridan's raid at Yellow Tavern in front of Richmond. He died the following day in the Confederate capital and is buried in Hollywood Cemetery there. Like his intimate friend, Stonewall Jackson, General Stuart soon became a legendary figure, ranking as one of the great cavalry commanders of America. His death marked the beginning of the decline of the superiority which the Confederate horse had enjoyed over that of the Union. Stuart was a son-in-law of Brigadier General Philip St. George Cooke of the Federal service; his wife's brother was Brigadier General John Rogers Cooke of the Confederacy.

William Booth Taliaferro was born at "Belleville," Gloucester County, Virginia, December 28, 1822. He was graduated from the College of William and Mary in 1841, and then studied law at Harvard. Commissioned as a captain of infantry in the United States Army on February 23, 1847, he was mustered out at the end of the Mexican War as major, 9th Infantry. He represented his county in the house of delegates from 1850 to 1853, was a Buchanan Elector in 1856, and commanded the Virginia militia at the time of John Brown's raid on Harpers Ferry. Taliaferro was for a time on the Peninsula as major general of

militia in the early days of the Civil War, and then, as colonel of the 23rd Virginia Infantry, was with General R. S. Garnett in Western Virginia. Serving under Stonewall Jackson the following winter, he was promoted brigadier general to rank from March 4, 1862. He took part in the Valley campaign and the subsequent movements of Jackson's command, until he was seriously wounded at Groveton. After the battle of Fredericksburg he was ordered to General Beauregard at Charleston, his subsequent military career being in South Carolina, Georgia, and Florida. He was paroled at Greensboro on May 2, 1865 as a major general; however, there exists no record of his formal promotion, and as late as April 4, 1865 he officially signed himself "Briga-

dier-General, Commanding.' (462) Following the war General Taliaferro again served in the legislature (1874-79), was judge of the Gloucester County Court (1891-97), and was at various times a member of the board of visitors of V.M.I., William and Mary, and other institutions in the state. He died on his estate, "Dunham Massie," in Gloucester County, February 27, 1898, and is buried in Ware Church Cemetery.

James Camp Tappan, the son of parents from Newburyport, Massachusetts, was born in Franklin, Tennessee, September 9, 1825. Educated at Exeter Academy in New Hampshire and at Yale, from which he was graduated in 1845, he studied law in Vicksburg, Mississippi,

and was admitted to the bar in 1846. Removing to Helena, Arkansas, he served two terms in the legislature of that state, the last as speaker. He was also elected a circuit court judge. His New England antecedents notwithstanding, Tappan promptly offered his services to the Confederate cause, and in May 1861 was commissioned colonel of the 13th Arkansas. He was commended by General Leonidas Polk for his dispositions at the battle of Belmont, and led his regiment at Shiloh where it participated in repeated charges on the celebrated "Hornets' Nest." Colonel Tappan then took part in Bragg's invasion of Kentucky and fought at Richmond and Perryville. Appointed brigadier general on November 5, 1862, he was transferred to the Trans-Mississippi Department. In 1863 he commanded a brigade under General Sterling Price. He fought with great credit at Pleasant Hill in the Red River campaign of 1864 against Banks, and his division (Churchill's) was thereafter immediately sent against Steele. He participated in the battle of Jenkins' Ferry and took part in Price's last raid into Missouri. Returning to Helena after the war, General Tappan resumed his law practice and again served in the legislature, twice declining the Democratic nomination for governor. At the time of his death in Helena,

March 19, 1906, he had been for many years dean of the Arkansas bar. He is buried in Maple Hill Cemetery. (463)

Richard Taylor, son of President Zachary Taylor and brother of Jefferson Davis' first wife, was born at "Springfields," a family estate near Louisville, Kentucky, on January 27, 1826. Much of his early life was spent in frontier posts while his father was an army officer. He later studied in Europe, and after transferring from Harvard to Yale, was graduated from the latter institution in 1845. For a time he was his father's military secretary during the Mexican War. He established himself as a sugar planter in Louisiana in 1850; then became interested in politics, and served from 1856 to 1861 in the state senate. Appointed colonel of the 9th Louisiana Infantry at the outbreak of hostilities, Taylor arrived at the field of First Manassas on the night of the battle. He was promoted brigadier general on October 21, 1861, and major general on July 28, 1862. He served under Jackson in the Valley campaign of 1862 and in the Seven Days battles before Richmond, and was assigned to command the District of West Louisiana that summer, an area in which he made a notable record with a paucity of troops and supplies. His most celebrated achievement was the complete repulse of Banks' Red River expedition at Mansfield and Pleasant Hill in the spring of 1864. Prevented from following up his advantage by what he deemed to be the incredible stupidity of his superior, General Kirby Smith, (464) Taylor asked to be relieved of his command. He was, nevertheless, promoted lieutenant general to rank from April 8, 1864, and assigned the Department of Alabama and Mississippi. He surrendered in May 1865 the last of the Confederate forces east of the Mississippi. After the war he was a leading advocate of leniency toward the Southern states, interceding with President Johnson on behalf of Jefferson Davis, and appealing for a less severe application of the Reconstruction Acts. He died in New York City, April 12, 1879, and is buried in Metairie Cemetery, New Orleans. (See Bibliography # 100.)

Thomas Hart Taylor was born July 31, 1825 at Frankfort, Kentucky, and was educated at Kenyon College, Ohio, and Centre College in his native state. Serving in the Mexican War in the 3rd Kentucky Infantry, of which he became 1st lieutenant, he had a varied business career thereafter, which included driving two herds of cattle to California. Hastening to enlist in 1861, Taylor was appointed captain of infantry, C.S.A., and lieutenant colonel, 1st Kentucky Infantry, in the Provisional Army; he was nominated colonel to rank from October 14, 1861. After some service in the Peninsular campaign, the 1st Kentucky, one of the twelve-months regiments, was mustered out in the summer of 1862. Taylor reported to Kirby Smith in East Tennessee and commanded a brigade in Stevenson's division at Cumberland Gap and in Kentucky. While serving as provost marshal on General Pemberton's staff at Vicksburg, he was captured and paroled, and after his exchange, commanded the District of South Mississippi and East Louisiana. Later he was provost marshal on General S. D. Lee's staff. Toward the end of the war he was post commander at Mobile. Taylor had been appointed, November 4, 1862, as a brigadier general; however, the records exhibit that President Davis failed then to nominate him to the Senate at that grade. (465) After the war General Taylor engaged in business at Mobile until 1870, when he returned to Kentucky. For five years he was a deputy U. S. marshal, and also served a total of eleven years as chief of police of Louisville. He died there on April 12, 1901, and is buried in the State Cemetery at Frankfort. (466)

James Barbour Terrill, a brother of the Federal General William R. Terrill who was killed at the battle of Perryville in 1862, was born in Bath County, Virginia, February 20, 1838. Graduated from the Virginia Military Institute in 1858, he studied law in Lexington and

was practicing in Warm Springs at the outbreak of war. He was elected major of the 13th Virginia in May 1861, and served at First Manassas, in Jackson's Valley campaign of 1862, during the Seven Days battles, and at Cedar Mountain, Second Manassas, Sharpsburg, and Fredericksburg. Meanwhile he was promoted lieutenant colonel, and then colonel of his regiment to rank from May 15, 1863. The latter promotion came after the battle of Chancellorsville. General Early said of his command that it "was never required to take a position that they did not take it, nor to hold one that they did not hold it." After fighting at Gettysburg and in the subsequent operations of the 2nd Corps in 1863, Terrill's 13th Virginia entered the campaign of 1864 as a part of

Pegram's brigade of Early's division. It took a gallant part in the battles of the Wilderness and Spotsylvania Court House. At the beginning of the engagements which terminated with the repulse of Grant at Cold Harbor on June 3, 1864, Terrill was killed at Bethesda Church on May 30, 1864. Already nominated to the Confederate Senate as a brigadier general to rank from May 31, 1864, he was confirmed as such on the same day, the date of his appointment being June 1, 1864. He was buried by the enemy near the spot where he fell. (467)

William Terry was born in Amherst County, Virginia, August 14, 1824. He attended a neighborhood "old field-school," and was graduated from the University of Virginia in 1848. He then taught school and studied law, was admitted to the bar, and commenced practice in Wytheville, Virginia. At times he edited the local *Telegraph*. A militia lieutenant at Harpers Ferry at the time of John Brown's raid in 1859, he entered the Confederate Army at the same grade in the 4th Virginia Infantry. After serving at First Manassas he was promoted major in 1862 and fought during the Seven Days battles and in the campaign of Second Manassas. He was wounded in the latter battle. Promoted colo-

nel in September 1863, and brigadier general to rank from May 19, 1864, Terry took a most gallant part in the subsequent battles and engagements of the Army of Northern Virginia from Fredericksburg to the attack on Fort Stedman on March 25, 1865. Here he was severely wounded for the third time during the war. Upon the cessation of hostilities he again took up his law practice at Wytheville, and was twice elected to Congress in later years, serving from 1871 to 1873 and from 1875 to 1877. He was also a delegate to the Democratic National Convention of 1880. General Terry was drowned on September 5, 1888, while attempting to ford Reed Creek near his home during a freshet. He is buried in Wytheville.

William Richard Terry was born at Liberty, Virginia, March 12, 1827. Graduated from the Virginia Military Institute in 1850, and later from the University of Virginia, he was a merchant in his home town when he entered the Confederate Army as captain of a cavalry company from Bedford County. His conduct at First Manassas won for him, in September 1861, the commission of colonel of the 24th Virginia Infantry, succeeding Jubal Early. Wounded at the battle of Williamsburg, he was back to lead his regiment at Second Manassas and in the subsequent operations of Pickett's division. He was promoted brigadier general to rank from May 31, 1864. Terry was wounded, in all, seven times during the war, the last occasion being at Dinwiddie Court House on March 31, 1865, immediately before the battle of Five Forks. Another of his wounds was sustained in the celebrated charge on the third day at Gettysburg. Following the war General Terry served eight years as a member of the Virginia senate; he was superintendent of the penitentiary, and from 1886 to 1893 of the Confederate Soldiers' Home in Richmond. He was also a member of the board of visitors of V.M.I. in 1873. Paralyzed by a stroke for some years, he died at Chesterfield Court House, Virginia, on March 28, 1897. He is buried in Hollywood Cemetery, Richmond. (468)

Allen Thomas, a brother-in-law of Lieutenant General Richard Taylor, (469) was born in Howard County, Maryland, December 14, 1830. Graduated from Princeton in 1850, he studied law, was admitted to the bar, and practiced in Howard County for a time. After his marriage he removed to Louisiana, where he became a planter. At the beginning of the Civil War he organized an infantry battalion of which he became major; when it was expanded into the 29th Louisiana Infantry, Thomas was appointed colonel to rank from May 3, 1862. Serving during the Vicksburg campaign, notably at Chickasaw Bluffs, he was cap-

tured at the termination of the siege, and after his parole, carried General Pemberton's report to Richmond. He was assigned later to collect and organize paroled prisoners west of the Mississippi. He was promoted brigadier general from February 4, 1864, and assigned to his brother-in-law's department in command of five Louisiana regiments and a battalion. He later succeeded to the command of the division upon General Polignac's departure for Europe. General Thomas had a varied and distinguished career after the war as planter, Presidential Elector, professor (and member of the board of supervisors) at Louisiana State University, coiner of the New Orleans branch mint, and U. S. consul and minister to Venezuela. He declined a Congressional nomination in 1876. From 1889 until 1907 his resi-

dence was Florida; in the latter year he moved to a plantation he had bought at Waveland, Mississippi, dying there on December 3. He is buried in the family vault of his wife at Donaldsonville, Louisiana.

Bryan Morel Thomas, a native of Georgia, was born near Milledgeville on May 8, 1836. He first attended Oglethorpe University; then entered West Point in 1854. After graduation he was commissioned in the 8th Infantry, from which he later transferred to the 5th Infantry. Resigning from the old army on April 6, 1861, he was appointed a lieutenant in the Regular Confederate service and took a commendable part in the battle of Shiloh on the staff of General Withers, discharging the duties of chief of ordnance and artillery. He continued to serve on Withers' staff

304

in the Kentucky campaign and at Murfreesboro. Upon the recommendation of General Leonidas Polk he was promoted colonel and placed in command of a regiment of reserve cavalry in General James H. Clanton's brigade in Alabama. On August 4, 1864 Thomas was commissioned brigadier general. Thereafter he led a mixed brigade of Alabama infantry, cavalry, and artillery in the Department of the Gulf, until he was captured at Fort Blakely on April 9, 1865. After his release General Thomas was a planter in Dooly and Whitfield counties, Georgia; a deputy U. S. marshal; and in 1884 established a private school. From 1891 until his death in Dalton, July 16, 1905, he served as superintendent of public schools of that city. He is buried in Dalton. (470)

Edward Lloyd Thomas was born on March 23, 1825 in Clarke County, Georgia, and was graduated from Emory College in 1846. He served in the war with Mexico as a 2nd lieutenant of Georgia mounted volunteers (Newton County Independent Horse). (471) Subsequently he declined a commission in the regular army and returned to his plantation. On October 15, 1861 he was appointed colonel of the 35th Georgia Infantry, a regiment he had recruited by authorization of President Davis. Leading this

command at Seven Pines and during the Seven Days battles, he was wounded at Mechanicsville, and after his recovery, fought in every major engagement of the Army of Northern Virginia with the exception of Sharpsburg. (At the time he was detached at Harpers Ferry paroling prisoners.) He was himself paroled at Appomattox on April 9, 1865. He had been a brigadier since November 1, 1862, and might have succeeded to the command of Pender's division after Gettysburg, had the unit not contained two brigades from North Carolina and one from South Carolina. General Lee felt that dissatisfaction might be caused by the promotion of a Georgian. (472) General Thomas resided on his estate after the war, until in 1885 he was appointed by President Cleveland to an office in the Land Department and subsequently in the Indian Bureau. He died at South McAlester, Indian Territory (now Oklahoma) on March 8, 1898, and is buried in Kiowa, Oklahoma.

Lloyd Tilghman was born at Rich Neck Manor, near Claiborne, Md., Jan. 18, 1816. Graduated from West Point in 1836, he resigned from the army the same year. From then until the outbreak of the Civil War, he was continuously employed as construction engineer on a number of railroads in the South, save for a period during the war with Mexico when he served on General Twiggs' staff and was captain of the Maryland and District of Columbia battalion of volunteers. Having made his residence in Paducah, Kentucky, since 1852, Tilghman entered the Confederate Army from that state in 1861. In February of the year

following he was charged with the inspection of Forts Henry and Donelson, and was in command of the former. He had noted its defective location prior to the Federal attack, but he nonetheless made a gallant defense and only surrendered the work to Grant after having sent the main portion of his troops to Donelson. A brigadier from October 18, 1861, he was not exchanged until the fall of 1862, when he took command of the 1st Brigade of General Loring's division in Van Dorn's Army of the West. Tilghman fought at Corinth, and during the retreat of the army from Holly Springs to Grenada, was in command of the rear guard. On May 16, 1863, while directing the fire of his artillery in the battle of Baker's Creek (Champion's Hill), he was struck in the chest by a shell fragment, which passed through his body. He is buried in Woodlawn Cemetery, New York, N. Y. (473)

Robert Augustus Toombs, usually known as "Bob" Toombs, was born in Wilkes County, Georgia, July 2, 1810. Withdrawing from the University of Georgia as the result of a prank, he was graduated from Union College (Schenectady, N. Y.) in 1828; and was admitted to the bar in 1830. He soon became not only wealthy but also politically prominent. Besides accumulating a substantial fortune in land and slaves, he

served in the Georgia legislature, in both houses of the Federal Congress, and as a delegate from Georgia to erect the new Confederate government. He missed by a hair being chosen President of the Confederate States instead of Jefferson Davis. (474) Accepting the portfolio of state with some reluctance, he served until July 19, 1861, when he was appointed brigadier general in the Provisional Army. He had meantime been elected to the Confederate Congress. Toombs' army career showed that he had some capacity, but he was inclined to be at odds with his superiors over old army discipline and procedure. He once remarked that the epitaph of the Confederate Army should be: "Died of West Point." He fought on the Peninsula and in the Seven Days, and was with

his brigade in the campaign of Second Manassas. He distinguished himself in the defense of Burnside's bridge at Sharpsburg, where he was wounded. Desiring promotion and failing to obtain it, he resigned on March 4, 1863. He spent the balance of the war in criticizing Davis and the Richmond administration. However, he saw some further military service during Sherman's advance through Georgia. Fleeing abroad to escape arrest in 1865, he returned in 1867 and again became a power in Georgia politics, although he never applied for pardon as a means of regaining his citizenship. As a consequence, he held no public office. General Toombs died in Washington, Georgia, on December 15, 1885, and is buried there.

Thomas Fentress Toon was born in Columbus County, North Carolina, June 10, 1840. On May 20, 1861, while in his senior year at Wake Forest College, he enlisted in the Columbus Guards No. 2, a company which later became a part of the 20th North Carolina. He returned to college immediately after his enlistment and was graduated in June. The same month he was elected 1st lieutenant of his company, and the following month, captain. Toon was wounded seven times during the war, and fought with conspicuous gallantry at Seven

such he continued through the balance of the Shenandoah campaign and in the Petersburg defenses. On March 25, 1865, during the assault on Fort Stedman, he received his last and most serious wound, which incapacitated him for further duty. General Toon resided in Columbus County, North Carolina, for some twenty-five years after the war, removing to Robeson County in 1891. At the turn of the century he was elected state superintendent of public instruction, and died at Raleigh on February 19, 1902. He is buried in Oakwood Cemetery. (476)

Pines, in the Seven Days, at South Mountain, and at Fredericksburg. Elected colonel of the 20th North Carolina on February 26, 1863—with his seniors waiving their rights to promotion —he led the regiment during Jackson's celebrated flank attack at Chancellorsville, at Gettysburg, and in the Mine Run campaign. After the battles of the Wilderness and Spotsylvania—in the latter of which General R. D. Johnston was wounded—Toon was promoted brigadier general from May 31, 1864. He commanded the brigade during Early's advance on Washington and in the battle of the Monocacy. However, in August, when General Johnston returned to command, Toon reverted to his former rank of colonel. (475) As

Edward Dorr Tracy was a native of Macon, Georgia, born on November 5, 1833. (477) By profession a lawyer, he removed to Huntsville, Alabama, in the

late 1850's. In the election of 1860 he stumped Northern Alabama in behalf of the Breckinridge ticket, having been selected as an alternate Elector for the state at large. At the commencement of the war he was chosen captain of a company from Madison County which became part of the 4th Alabama Infantry. Declining appointment as major of the 12th Alabama, he fought with the 4th at First Manassas, and on October 12, 1861, became lieutenant colonel of the 19th Alabama, whose colonel was Joseph Wheeler, later major general. He was at Shiloh, where he had a horse killed under him, and he subsequently went into East Tennessee with John P. McCown's division. He was recommended for promotion by Kirby Smith, his commission of brigadier general being dated August 16, 1862. Early in 1863 General Tracy's brigade of five Alabama regiments was sent to the Vicksburg theatre and reached Port Gibson, Mississippi, in time to take part in the battle of May 1. Of approximately 1500 officers and men present for duty equipped, the brigade sustained losses of 272 killed, wounded, and captured. Among the casualties was Tracy, who "fell near the front line, pierced through the breast, and instantly died without uttering a word." These words were reported by one of his regimental commanders, Colonel (later Brig-

adier General) Isham W. Garrott, who was himself killed six weeks after. General Tracy's remains were conveyed to Macon and there buried.

James Heyward Trapier was born at "Windsor," on Black River, near Georgetown, South Carolina, November 24, 1815. Graduated third in the class of 1838 at the U. S. Military Academy, he was commissioned into the corps of engineers, and performed the duties of that branch (mainly in the Northern states) until his resignation from the army in 1848. From then until the outbreak of the Civil War he resided on his plantation in South Carolina, and was also active in the militia. Trapier aided in the construction of the batteries in Charleston harbor, serv-

ing under General Beauregard with the ranks of captain and major. On October 21, 1861 he was promoted brigadier general and assigned to command the District of Eastern and Middle Florida. He was relieved from this post the following spring to command for a time a division under General Braxton Bragg at Corinth. Trapier's military accomplishments seem to have left something to be desired: he was alike condemned by the Florida state convention and subsequently by General Bragg as being unfit for command. (478) After the autumn of 1862 he held a succession of inferior posts in South Carolina until the close of the war. He survived only a few months, dying at the home of a friend near Georgetown, South Carolina, on December 21, 1865. (479) He is buried in the yard of the Church of St. George, Winyah, at Georgetown.

Isaac Ridgeway Trimble was born in Culpeper County, Virginia, May 15, 1802. He was graduated from West Point at the age of twenty and served for ten years in the old army as a lieutenant of artillery. He resigned in 1832 to enter the field of railroad development and spent the intervening years of his life, until 1861, as engineer for a succession of Eastern and Southern roads then being constructed. Meantime he identified himself

almost completely with the state of Maryland. At the outbreak of war he engaged in the burning of bridges north of Baltimore, so as to prevent the passage of Federal troops to Washington. He went to Virginia in May 1861 and accepted a commission as colonel of engineers in the state forces, and was at first detailed to construct the defenses of Norfolk. On August 9, 1861 he was appointed a brigadier general in the Provisional Army and assigned to the command of a brigade in Ewell's division, which he led with great distinction in the Valley campaign of 1862, the battles of the Seven Days, Cedar Mountain, and during the capture of Manassas Junction by Jackson. Severely wounded a few days later at the battle of Second Manassas, he returned to the army in time to participate in

Pickett's charge at Gettysburg, where he lost a leg and was captured. Not exchanged until February 1865, he was unable to rejoin the army prior to its surrender. Trimble was appointed major general to rank from January 17, 1863, and was perhaps Maryland's most distinguished soldier in the War between the States. He survived it many years and made his home in Baltimore, where he died January 2, 1888, in his eighty-sixth year. He is buried there in Green Mount Cemetery.

William Feimster Tucker was born in Iredell County, North Carolina, May 9, 1827, and was graduated from Emory and Henry College in Virginia at the age of twenty-one. The same year he moved to Houston, Mississippi. He was elected probate

judge of Chickasaw County, Mississippi, in 1855. He then studied law, was admitted to the bar, and was practicing his profession when the war broke out in 1861. Entering Confederate service as captain of Company K, 11th Mississippi Infantry, he fought at First Manassas in General Barnard E. Bee's brigade. Shortly thereafter Tucker's company was transferred to the West and incorporated into the 41st Mississippi of which he was commissioned colonel on May 8, 1862. He led his new regiment with great gallantry at Perryville, Murfreesboro, Chickamauga, and Chattanooga; and was promoted brigadier general to rank from March 1, 1864. In the course of the ensuing Atlanta campaign, General Tucker was so severely wounded at Resaca on May 14 as to be incapacitated for further field duty. In the closing weeks of the war he commanded the District of Southern Mississippi and East Louisiana. Returning to Chickasaw County, he resumed his former profession and was a member of the legislature in 1876 and 1878. He was assassinated on September 14, 1881 at Okolona, Mississippi, allegedly by two men hired for the deed by one Shaw, against whom General Tucker had a case pending for misappropriation of guardianship funds. He is buried in Okolona. (480)

David Emanuel Twiggs, the oldest officer of the old army to take up arms for the Confederacy, was born in Richmond County, Georgia in 1790. (481) He had a long and distinguished career in the United States service. Commissioned a captain in the 8th Infantry on March 12, 1812, he took a gallant part in our second war with England. He was promoted to major of the 28th Infantry in 1814. At the outbreak of the Mexican War he had attained the rank of colonel of the 2nd Dragoons, and almost at once, was promoted brigadier general. For his services in that conflict, particularly at the storming of Monterey, he received the brevet of major general and the presentation of a sword by resolution of Congress. On December 31, 1860 Twiggs was one of the four general officers of the line on the army roster, the others being Winfield Scott, John E. Wool, and William S. Harney. At the time he was in command of the Department of Texas. His Southern sympathies soon after induced him to surrender the military forces and stores under his command to Colonel (later General) Ben McCulloch, representing the state of Texas, an act for which he was dismissed from the United States service on March 1, 1861. On May 22 following, he was appointed major general in the Provisional Army of the Confederacy, the senior officer of that grade, and assigned to command the District of Louisiana. Too old for active field service, his infirmities soon compelled his virtual retirement, and he died near Augusta, Georgia, on July 15, 1862. General Twiggs' daughter was the wife of Colonel A. C. Myers, Quartermaster General of the Confederate Army. He is buried on the property where he was born.

Robert Charles Tyler stated his age as twenty-eight when he enlisted as a private in Company D, 15th Tennessee Infantry, on April 18, 1861. He is supposed to have been "born and reared" in Baltimore, although nothing positive is known of his early career until 1856, when he was embarked on the first expedition to Nicaragua of the filibuster, Wil-

liam Walker. In 1860 Tyler was not with the ill-fated Walker on the latter's second Nicaraguan expedition, but was apparently employed then in Baltimore; he later removed to Memphis, Tennessee. After enlistment his promotion in the Confederate Army was rapid. First a regimental quartermaster, he commanded the 15th Tennessee at the battles of Belmont and Shiloh with rank of lieutenant colonel; upon the reorganization of the regiment at Corinth, he was elected its colonel. He was wounded at Shiloh, and acted for a time as General Bragg's provost marshal during the invasion of Kentucky in the fall of 1862. Thereafter, Tyler was at the head of his regiment during the subsequent campaigns of the Tennessee Army, until he was so

badly wounded at Missionary Ridge as to cause amputation of one of his legs. While convalescing the following spring he was commissioned brigadier general to rank from February 23, 1864, although he does not seem ever to have rejoined the main army. Posted to duty at West Point, Georgia, Tyler was present there during most of the winter of 1864-65. On April 16, 1865, with a handful of extra-duty men, militia, and soldiers en route to rejoin their commands, he defended a small earthwork on the west side of town against a full brigade of Federal cavalry, part of the corps of Major General James H. Wilson. In the course of the storming of the work, called Fort Tyler, he was killed by a sharpshooter, and was buried in West Point. (482)

Robert Brank Vance, an elder brother of Governor (and Senator) Zebulon Vance of North Carolina, was born in Buncombe County on April 24, 1828. After attending the common schools of the district, he engaged in mercantile and agricultural pursuits, and served for some years as clerk of the court of pleas and quarter sessions. Recruiting in 1861 a company known as the "Buncombe Life Guards," he was elected its captain; and upon the formation of the 29th North Carolina Infantry, he was elected colonel. Sent to East Tennessee,

he took part with his regiment in the defense of Cumberland Gap and accompanied Kirby Smith into Kentucky. After the death of General James E. Rains at Murfreesboro, Vance then commanded the brigade for a time, until he came down with typhoid fever. While still ill he was promoted brigadier general to rank from March 4, 1863, and upon his recovery, was assigned to duty in Western North Carolina. In this region he was captured on January 14, 1864, at Crosby Creek, and was not released for exchange from Fort Delaware until March 10, 1865. After the war General Vance was six times elected to Congress, serving from 1873 to 1885. For the next four years he was assistant commissioner of patents in Washington. He was also a member of the

state house of representatives from 1894 to 1896. He died near Asheville, North Carolina, on November 28, 1899, in the county of his birth. He is buried in Riverside Cemetery, Asheville.

Earl Van Dorn was born near Port Gibson, Mississippi, on September 17, 1820. He was graduated fifty-second in a class of fifty-six members at the Military Academy in 1842 (James Longstreet stood fifty-fourth). He saw service in the Indian campaigns and was brevetted captain and major for gallantry in the Mexican War. By 1861 he had attained the regular rank of major in the celebrated 2nd United States Cavalry, whose field officers at the outbreak of the Civil War were Albert Sidney John-

ston, colonel; Robert E. Lee, lieutenant colonel; and George H. Thomas and Van Dorn, majors. Upon Van Dorn's resignation on January 31, 1861, Edmund Kirby Smith was appointed in his stead and served until he also resigned to join the South. Van Dorn was commissioned colonel and, on June 5, 1861, brigadier general in the Confederate service, and was assigned to Texas, where some of the Union forces surrendered to him. On September 19, 1861 he was promoted major general and transferred to Virginia. He was made commander of the Army of the West in the Trans-Mississippi theater the following January, where he fought and lost the battle of Elkhorn (Pea Ridge). He was subsequently transferred to the Army of Mississippi, with headquarters at Vicksburg. After his defeat at Corinth by W. S. Rosecrans he was superseded by General John C. Pemberton and placed in charge of Pemberton's cavalry. His most noteworthy achievement thereafter was the destruction, in December 1862, of Grant's supply depots at Holly Springs, Mississippi. This action temporarily disrupted Grant's projected operations against Vicksburg. He was assassinated in his headquarters at Spring Hill, Tennessee, May 7, 1863, (483) by a Dr. Peters, who alleged as a justification for his act that Van Dorn had "violated the sanctity of his home." Van Dorn's partisans termed the deed a cold-blooded murder for gain. (484) General Van Dorn is buried in Port Gibson, Mississippi.

Alfred Jefferson Vaughan, Jr., was born in Dinwiddie County, Virginia, May 10, 1830, and was graduated from the Virginia Military Institute in 1851. A civil engineer, he was a deputy U. S. surveyor in Southern California for a time. Later he was private secretary to Alfred Cumming of Georgia (uncle of General Alfred Cumming, C.S.A.), who was engaged in making a treaty with the Indians of the upper Missouri River on behalf of the Northern Pacific Railroad. After living on a farm in Marshall County, Mississippi, where he had settled in 1856, Vaughan

entered Confederate service as captain of the Dixie Rifles of Moscow, Tennessee. He had previously been unable to secure arms for a company he had recruited in Mississippi. Soon elected lieutenant colonel of the 13th Tennessee Infantry (and later colonel), he fought in every battle of the West under Generals Leonidas Polk, Sidney Johnston, Bragg, and J. E. Johnston from Belmont to an affair at Vining Station, Georgia, during the Atlanta campaign, where his leg was blown off by a shell. (485) He had previously had eight horses killed under him, but personally escaped unscathed until the incident referred to. Vaughan had been commissioned brigadier general to rank from November 18, 1863, and at the time he was wounded, he was in command of General Preston Smith's old brigade. After the war he returned to Mississippi, where he engaged in farming until 1872, and became prominent in the Grange movement. Removing to Memphis in that year, General Vaughan was elected clerk of the criminal court of Shelby County and re-elected in 1882. In 1897 he became commander of the Tennessee Division, United Confederate Veterans, a post which he held until his death in Indianapolis, Indiana, October 1, 1899. He is buried in Memphis.

316

John Crawford Vaughn was born in Roane County, Tennessee, on February 24, 1824. (486) As a captain in the 5th Tennessee Infantry he saw service in the Mexican War, from which he returned to become a merchant in his native town. Happening to be in Charleston, South Carolina, in April 1861, he witnessed the bombardment of Fort Sumter. He hastened home to recruit a regiment for the Confederate cause in an area which was virtually a stronghold of Union sentiment. Mustered into service as colonel of the 3rd Tennessee Infantry at Lynchburg, Virginia, June 6, 1861, he was ordered to report to General Joseph E. Johnston at Harpers Ferry, and the month following took part in the battle of First Manassas. Commissioned brigadier general to rank from September 22, 1862, he fought in the Vicksburg campaign and was surrendered with his brigade on July 4, 1863, when the city capitulated. During the 1864 operations in the Shenandoah, he commanded a cavalry brigade. He was at the battle of Piedmont and with General Early in the march on Washington, and was wounded near Martinsburg, (West) Virginia. After his recovery he was in command in East Tennessee and, upon the surrender of Lee, joined the forces of Joseph E. Johnston in North Carolina. Vaughn's brigade formed part of Jefferson Davis' escort during the latter's flight south. Vaughn himself was paroled at Washington, Georgia, on May 9, 1865. After the war he lived alternately in Brooks County, Georgia, and in Monroe County, Tennessee, serving one term as presiding officer of the Tennessee senate. He died near Thomasville, Georgia, September 10, 1875, and is buried in that city.

John Bordenave Villepigue, a South Carolina native of French descent, was born at Camden, July 2, 1830, and was graduated from West Point in the class of 1854. His career in the old army was mainly spent with the 2nd Dragoons in Kansas, Nebraska, and Utah. Resigning on March 31, 1861, he was first appointed a captain of artillery in the Regu-

lar Confederate service, and shortly thereafter colonel of the 36th Georgia Infantry, Provisional Army. Severely wounded while commanding the defense of Fort McRee in Pensacola harbor, he was much eulogized by General Braxton Bragg, of whom he seems to have been an especial favorite, and on whose staff he served for a time as chief of engineers and artillery. He then commanded at Pensacola and later at Mobile before being ordered to join Bragg at Corinth, with rank of brigadier general from March 13, 1862. Since General Beauregard deemed him "the most energetic young officer available," he was assigned to command at Fort Pillow on the Mississippi, where he conducted a stubborn and skillful defense against greatly superior Federal

317

land and naval forces. Finally ordered to retire, he blew up his fortifications and brought off his men. He afterwards commanded a brigade under General Van Dorn at Corinth and was again commended for efficient performance. Unfortunately for the Confederacy, General Villepigue soon after fell a victim to "fever," and died at Port Hudson, Louisiana, on November 9, 1862. He is buried in the town of his birth.

Henry Harrison Walker was born at "Elmwood," Sussex County, Virginia, October 15, 1832, (487) and was graduated forty-first in the class of 1853 at West Point. (John B. Hood stood forty-fourth on the roster of fifty-two.) His principal service in the ante-bellum army was in the Kansas "war" between the adherents of the pro- and anti-

slavery factions. He resigned on May 3, 1861, and was appointed a captain of infantry in the Regular Confederate States Army; he was subsequently elected lieutenant colonel of the 40th Virginia Infantry. Twice wounded at Gaines's Mill in the battles of the Seven Days, he was commended by both his brigade and division commanders, Generals Field and A. P. Hill. After being for some time in charge of a convalescent camp, he was appointed brigadier general on July 1, 1863, and took part in the action of Bristoe Station and the Mine Run campaign of that year. General Walker was again wounded during the battle of Spotsylvania Court House in May 1864. (488) After his recovery he served on court-martial duty in Richmond, and during the closing weeks of the war, in guarding the Richmond & Danville Railroad. (489) On April 10, 1865 Jefferson Davis, learning of the surrender at Appomattox, dispatched Walker, with the troops at Danville, to Joseph E. Johnston's army in North Carolina. (490) He was, however, paroled at Richmond on May 7, 1865. (491) After the war General Walker took up residence in Morristown, New Jersey, and he was for many years an investment broker. He died at Morristown on March 22, 1912, and is buried there in Evergreen Cemetery.

James Alexander Walker was born near Mt. Sidney, Augusta County, Virginia, on August 27, 1832. He was dismissed from the Virginia Military Institute in his senior year on charges preferred by Stonewall Jackson, then a professor at the Institute. He challenged Jackson to a duel, although the two did not meet. (492) After some eighteen months with the Covington & Ohio Railway, now the Chesapeake & Ohio, Walker studied law and was graduated from the University of Virginia. He settled in Pulaski County, and later entered Confederate service as captain of the Pulaski Guard. He was ordered to Harpers Ferry under the command of his old antagonist. Soon made lieutenant colonel of the 13th Virginia Infantry, he succeeded A. P. Hill as its colonel, upon the latter's promotion to brigadier in February 1862. Walker rapidly made a reputation as a desperate fighter and took part in almost every battle and engagement of the 2nd Corps from the Valley campaign of 1862 to Appomattox. He was severely wounded at Spotsylvania. At the special request of Jackson, who had come to have a high regard for him, he was promoted brigadier general from May 15, 1863, and given command of the old Stonewall Brigade. He was in divisional command at the surrender. General Walker then returned to Pulaski County and put in a crop of corn with two mules he had brought home from the army. Resuming his law practice, he was elected to the house of delegates in 1871 and lieutenant-governor of the state five years later. Splitting with the Democratic party over the "free-trade" policy of Cleveland, he became a Republican, and as such, was twice elected to Congress, serving from 1895 to 1899. He died in Wytheville, Virginia, October 20, 1901, (493) and is buried there.

John George Walker was born in Cole County, Missouri, July 22, 1822. He received his early education at the Jesuit College in St. Louis. Commissioned directly into the United States Army in 1846, he served during the war with Mexico and had attained the rank of captain by the

time he resigned, on July 31, 1861, (494) to enter Confederate service. He was immediately commissioned major of cavalry in the Regular Army, and after being appointed lieutenant colonel of the 8th Texas Cavalry, was made brigadier general on January 9, 1862. (495) He distinguished himself with the Army of Northern Virginia through the Maryland campaign, and was promoted major general on November 8, 1862. His division of two brigades took possession of Loudoun Heights in the operations against Harpers Ferry in September of that year, and subsequently rendered gallant service during the battle of Sharpsburg. At this juncture he was transferred to the Trans-Mississippi Department, where he assumed command of the

Texas infantry division. After participating in the Red River campaign, he relieved General Richard Taylor in the District of West Louisiana. At the close of the war he was in command of a division in the District of Texas, New Mexico, and Arizona, his troops being at the time composed of Steele's, Bee's, and Bagby's cavalry divisions, Cooper's Indians, and Slaughter's brigade. He went to Mexico without waiting for his personal parole at the termination of hostilities. (496) In later life he served as U. S. consul general at Bogota, Colombia, and as special commissioner to the South American republics on behalf of the Pan-American Convention. He died at Washington, D. C., July 20, 1893, and was buried in Winchester, Virginia.

Leroy Pope Walker was born in Huntsville, Alabama, on February 7, 1817. After attending the University of Alabama for a time, he left to study law and was admitted to the bar in 1837. He soon became prominent politically. He served a number of terms in the state legislature, was a judge of the circuit court, a delegate to the Nashville Convention of 1850, and Presidential Elector for the state at large in 1848, 1852, and 1856. Walker was closely identified with Alabama's secession movement and was chairman of the state's dele-

judge of a military court in North Alabama. (497) He resumed his law practice in Huntsville after the war, and became president of the state constitutional convention of 1875, and a delegate at large to the Democratic National Conventions of 1876 and 1884. He is buried in Huntsville, where he died on August 22, 1884.

Lucius Marshall Walker, a nephew of President James K. Polk, and brother-in-law of General Frank C. Armstrong, (498) was born at Columbia, Tennessee, on October 18, 1829. Graduated from West Point in the class of 1850, he resigned two years later to enter the mercantile business at Memphis, where he was residing in 1861. Walker

gation to the Charleston and Richmond Democratic conventions of 1860. Because of this background—as well as for geographical reasons—he became the Confederacy's first Secretary of War on February 21, 1861. However, he lacked administrative experience and failed to cope with the tremendous tasks of the department. Having aroused more than a little criticism in Congress, he resigned on September 16. The following day he was appointed a brigadier general in the Provisional Army. Serving in garrison command at Mobile and then Montgomery, he failed to secure field duty and resigned his commission on March 31, 1862. From April 6, 1864 until the close of the war, he served with rank of colonel as presiding

went into the Confederate Army as lieutenant colonel of the 40th Tennessee Infantry, of which he was made colonel on November 11, 1861 and assigned to command of the post at Memphis. He was promoted brigadier general to rank from March 11, 1862. On account of illness he was not present at Shiloh, but was later at Corinth and took part in the retreat to Tupelo and the engagement at Farmington. He incurred the displeasure of Braxton Bragg, who informed Richmond that Walker was not a "safe" man "to intrust with any command," (499) and later approved his application for a transfer west of the Mississippi. Reporting to Kirby Smith in March 1863, he was given command of a cavalry brigade and participated in Sterling Price's attack on Helena. Subsequently he fell out with General John S. Marmaduke, who had allegedly reflected unfavorably on Walker's courage. Despite Price's efforts to prevent a duel the event was arranged—"pistols at ten paces to fire and advance." At sunrise on the morning of September 6, 1863, at Little Rock, Arkansas, the antagonists met and General Walker fell mortally wounded. He died the following day (500) and is buried in Memphis. (501)

Reuben Lindsay Walker was born on May 29, 1827, at Logan, Albemarle County, Virginia,

and was graduated from the Virginia Military Institute in 1845. After following the profession of civil engineering for a time, he became a farmer in New Kent County. At the beginning of the Civil War he was assigned as commander of the Purcell Battery, with which he reached the field of First Manassas in time to shell the retreating Federals. Promoted major on March 31, 1862, and subsequently lieutenant colonel and colonel, he served as chief of artillery, first of A. P. Hill's division, and then of the 3rd Corps until the surrender at Appomattox. He is said to have never had a day's leave of absence save during the battles of the Seven Days, when he was ill in Richmond. He was promoted brigadier general of artillery to rank from February 18, 1865, after compiling a record of sixty-three battles and engagements. He returned to farming after the war, removing to Selma, Alabama, in 1872. Here, he was for two years superintendent of the Marine & Selma Railroad. He returned to Virginia in 1876 and was employed by the Richmond street railways and as construction engineer of the Richmond & Alleghany Railroad. After superintending the construction of an addition to the Virginia State Penitentiary, General Walker was appointed construction superintendent of the Texas State Capitol and resided in Austin from 1884 to 1888. He died on his farm in Fluvanna County, Virginia, June 7, 1890, and was buried in Hollywood Cemetery, Richmond.

William Henry Talbot Walker was born in Augusta, Georgia, November 26, 1816, and was graduated from West Point in the class of 1837. His career in the old army was both varied and distinguished. After sustaining a desperate wound in service against the Seminoles, he resigned from the army in 1838, but was reappointed in 1840. He was brevetted major and lieutenant colonel for his conduct in the Mexican War, where he was again wounded so gravely that he was given up by the surgeons. (502) Despite his wounds and

general poor health—it was said that he could rarely sleep except in a sitting posture — (503) Walker was one of the most experienced officers in the army when he resigned his major's commission on December 20, 1860. Appointed a brigadier in the Confederate service on May 25, 1861, he was stationed successively at Pensacola and in Northern Virginia. He resigned on October 29, ostensibly because of his health but more probably from dissatisfaction, for he was at once commissioned major general of Georgia state troops. He was appointed brigadier general in the Confederate Army to rank from February 9, 1863; soon afterwards he was promoted major general to rank from May 23, at the instance of General Joseph E. Johnston, who pro-

323

nounced Walker the only officer in his command competent to lead a division. He took part in the Vicksburg campaign under Johnston and commanded the Reserve Corps at Chickamauga. At the battle of Atlanta, on July 22, 1864, during Hardee's attack on the Federal left in front of the city, General Walker was instantly killed by a picket of the Federal 16th Corps. (504) He is buried in Augusta, Georgia.

William Stephen Walker was born on April 13, 1822, in Pittsburgh, Pennsylvania. (505) He was reared by his uncle, Senator Robert J. Walker of Mississippi (also a native of Pennsylvania), who was President Polk's Secretary of the Treasury. After attending school in Georgetown,

D. C., he took part in the Mexican War as a 1st lieutenant. He was brevetted captain for gallant and meritorious conduct at Chapultepec and honorably mustered out on August 31, 1848. Upon the expansion of the regular army in 1855 he was commissioned as captain of the 1st Cavalry, with which he served until his resignation, on May 1, 1861, to cast his lot with the South. Nominated a captain of infantry in the Regular Confederate Army on March 16, 1861, as from Florida, (506) he was first employed in mustering troops into Confederate service. Later he became colonel and acting inspector general of the Department of South Carolina and Georgia. He was in charge of a number of different districts in the state of South Carolina in 1862 and 1863, (507) and was promoted brigadier general on October 30, 1862. Commanding at Kinston, North Carolina, in April 1864, he was soon after called to assist General Beauregard in the defense of Petersburg. Here, on May 20, he was wounded and captured, and his foot amputated. (508) Exchanged in the fall of the year, he was in command in North Carolina when the war ended. General Walker thereafter made his home in Georgia. He died in Atlanta on June 7, 1899, and is buried there in Oakland Cemetery.

William Henry Wallace was born in Laurens District, South Carolina, March 24, 1827, and was graduated from South Carolina College in 1849. He was successively a planter, newspaper publisher, and lawyer. As a member of the legislature in 1860 he supported the call for a secession convention. At the expiration of his term he enlisted as a private in Company A, 18th South Carolina. Of this regiment he was elected lieutenant colonel in May 1862, and led it to Virginia shortly after the Seven Days battles. During the Second Manassas campaign the colonel of the 18th (509) was killed on August 30, 1862. Wallace succeeded him to rank from the same day, although not formally nominated to the Senate until June 10, 1864. (510) Meantime

he fought at South Mountain and Sharpsburg in "Shanks" Evans' brigade, returning with this unit to South Carolina where he took part in the defense of Charleston. In the spring of 1864 the brigade, under General Stephen Elliott, Jr., was ordered to Petersburg. In the battle of the Crater, on July 30, four companies of the 18th were blown up in the mine explosion. Promoted brigadier general on September 20, Wallace led the brigade through the last forlorn winter and on the retreat to Appomattox, where he was paroled on April 9, 1865. Subsequently he devoted himself to his law practice and the care of his plantation. He was one of the few Democrats elected to the state legislature in 1872; he was twice re-elected. In 1877 he was chosen circuit judge, an office which he filled until his retirement in 1893. General Wallace died on March 21, 1901, in Union, South Carolina, and is buried there.

Edward Cary Walthall was born on April 4, 1831, in Richmond. Virginia. He moved with his parents to Holly Springs, Mississippi, when he was ten, and was educated there at St. Thomas Hall. Later he studied law and was admitted to the bar in 1852. Four years afterwards he was elected district attorney and re-elected in 1859. Elected 1st lieu-

tenant of the Yalobusha Rifles in 1861, which became part of the 15th Mississippi, he shortly became lieutenant colonel of the regiment. He took a most commendable part in the disastrous engagement of Mill Springs (Fishing Creek) in January 1862. On April 11, 1862 he was elected colonel of the 29th Mississippi, which he commanded at Corinth and in the Kentucky campaign. Absent from the battle of Murfreesboro because of illness, he was promoted brigadier to rank from December 13, 1862, and fought gallantly at Chickamauga and Chattanooga. During the latter campaign he commanded the Confederates in the so-called "Battle above the Clouds" — which was neither a battle nor fought above the clouds. (511) In this engagement Walthall's thin skirmish line was notably distinguished, and its commander sustained a painful wound in the foot. Walthall fought with his customary steadfastness in the Atlanta campaign, and was promoted to major general from July 6, 1864. He went with Hood into Tennessee and had two horses killed under him at Franklin. Selected to command the rear guard in the retreat from Nashville the following month, General Walthall accompanied the remnant of the Army of Tennessee to the Carolinas, and was paroled at Greensboro on May 1, 1865. He resumed his law practice and became a leader in the movement to overthrow the carpetbag regime in Mississippi. He was appointed to the United States Senate, serving almost continuously from 1885 until his death in Washington, April 21, 1898. He is buried in Holly Springs.

Richard Waterhouse was born on January 12, 1832, in Rhea County, Tennessee, son of an elder Richard Waterhouse, with whom he has at times been confused. (512) After running away from home when still a boy, to engage in the Mexican War, he removed with his parents to San Augustine, Texas, in 1849, and there assisted the elder Waterhouse in the mercantile business. Soon after the outbreak of the Civil War he was instrumental

in recruiting the 19th Texas Infantry in and around Jefferson, Texas. On May 13, 1862 he was commissioned its colonel, serving during that year and the next under Generals Hindman and Holmes in Arkansas, and in Louisiana under General Richard Taylor. He was present at the engagement of Milliken's Bend in the command of General Henry E. McCulloch and was commended by his superior. Later he fought in Scurry's brigade at Mansfield and Pleasant Hill during the Red River campaign. For his services he was "assigned to command" as a brigadier general by Kirby Smith to date from April 30, 1864. He was subsequently officially appointed by President Davis to take rank from March 17, 1865,

and was confirmed the following day by the Confederate Senate. (513) After the war he resided in San Augustine and in Jefferson, apparently engaging in land speculation, a universal occupation of the place and time. In the course of a trip to Waco, in March 1876, he fell down stairs in a local hotel and dislocated his shoulder. Two days later, on March 20, he died of pneumonia. (514) He is buried in Jefferson. (515)

Stand Watie, a three-quarter-blood Cherokee Indian, was born December 12, 1806, near the site of the present city of Rome, Georgia. He learned to speak English at a mission school, and became a planter and assisted in the publication of the Cherokee newspaper, the *Phoenix.* In 1835

he and others signed the treaty by which the remaining Cherokee in Georgia agreed to their removal to what is now Oklahoma. This act split the Indians into two factions and made Watie the leader of the minority or treaty party. At the beginning of the Civil War the Cherokee attempted unsuccessfully to remain neutral, but ultimately divided along the same lines as before. The majority declared for the Union and the minority group under Watie pledged allegiance to the Confederacy. Watie raised a company early in 1861; he was later in the year appointed colonel of the 1st Cherokee Mounted Rifles, and brigadier general to rank from May 6, 1864. The Indians were engaged in the battles of Wilson's Creek and Elkhorn, and were principally used in raids and as skirmishers in the Territory and along its borders. It was found that, although excellent soldiers in a sudden offensive dash, they exhibited considerable reluctance to stand up to artillery fire. (516) General Watie's personal courage was unquestioned and he fought bravely to the end, supposedly not surrendering until June 23, 1865. After the war he resumed the life of a planter and also engaged in various business enterprises. He died at his home on Honey Creek, in what is now Delaware County, Oklahoma, September 9, 1871. He is buried in Old Ridge Cemetery there. (517)

Thomas Neville Waul was born on January 5, 1813, (518) in Sumter District, South Carolina. He attended South Carolina College until his junior year. After teaching school for a time in Florence, Alabama, he studied law in Vicksburg, Mississippi, and was admitted to the bar in 1835. Soon after, he removed to Gonzales County, Texas, where he established a plantation and also practiced his profession. An unsuccessful Democratic candidate for the United States Congress in 1859, he was elected to the Provisional Congress of the Confederacy in 1861 and served until the erection of the permanent government. He recruited Waul's Texas Legion in 1862,

and was commissioned its colonel on May 17. He was surrendered with his command at Vicksburg in July 1863, and was promoted after his exchange to brigadier general from September 18, 1863. In the Red River campaign of 1864 he commanded a brigade in General John G. Walker's division at Mansfield and Pleasant Hill. Later he was transferred to Arkansas to oppose Steele, and fought at the battle of Jenkins' Ferry. Immediately upon the close of hostilities in 1865, General Waul was elected to the first Texas reconstruction convention. Thereafter he practiced law in Galveston, and in later life retired to a farm in Hunt County, near Greenville, where he died on July 28, 1903, in his ninety-first year. Leaving no blood relatives, General Waul was the last of his line. He is buried in Fort Worth, Texas. (519)

Henry Constantine Wayne was born in Savannah, Georgia, on September 18, 1815. He received his early education in the schools of Northampton and Cambridge, Massachusetts. In 1834 he was appointed to West Point and was graduated in 1838 as a 2nd lieutenant in the 4th Artillery. He transferred to the quartermaster's department in 1846 with rank of staff captain; he was brevetted major for gallantry at the battles of Contreras and

Churubusco in Mexico. During the 1850's Wayne was engaged in procuring camels in Africa and testing in the southwestern United States their adaptability for use as a means of army transportation. He resigned from the old army on December 31, 1860, and upon the secession of Georgia, he was appointed adjutant and inspector general of the state by Governor Joseph E. Brown. On December 16, 1861 Wayne was commissioned a brigadier general in the Provisional Army of the Confederate States. However, four days after being ordered to Joseph E. Johnston at Manassas Junction (January 7, 1862), he resigned his Confederate commission. He then served until the end of the war in his former capacity. He was for a time directly in command of the Georgia militia, until relieved by General G. W. Smith in September 1864. At the close of hostilities General Wayne resumed residence in Savannah, where he was in the lumber business from 1866 to 1875. He died there on March 15, 1883. In 1850 he published *Sword Exercises Arranged for Military Instruction*. He is buried in Laurel Grove Cemetery, Savannah. (520)

David Addison Weisiger was born on December 23, 1818, at "The Grove," in Chesterfield County, Virginia. During the war with Mexico he served as 2nd lieutenant of Company E, 1st Virginia Volunteers. Afterwards he entered business in Petersburg. As a captain of Virginia militia he was officer of

the day at the hanging of John Brown in 1859. Two years later, as a major of the 4th Virginia Battalion Militia, he was on duty at Norfolk. Entering the Confederate Army as colonel of the 12th Virginia Infantry, on May 9, 1861, he served on the lower Peninsula until the spring of 1862, when his regiment was attached to the Army of Northern Virginia in General William Mahone's brigade. With this command he fought at Seven Pines, during the Seven Days battles, and at Second Manassas, where he was dangerously wounded and disabled until the following July. At the Wilderness, on May 6, 1864, he succeeded Mahone in command of the brigade, and was commissioned brigadier with temporary rank from May 31. Subsequently he was placed on the permanent list to date from July 30. This was a recognition of his distinguished services at the battle of the Crater, where he and Mahone led the Confederate counterattack and were largely responsible for the complete victory that followed. He was again wounded in this battle. (521) Paroled at Appomattox on April 9, 1865, General Weisiger returned to Petersburg and became cashier of a bank. He later engaged in business in Richmond, and died there on February 23, 1899. He is buried in Petersburg. (522)

Gabriel Colvin Wharton was born on July 23, 1824, in Culpeper County, Virginia. He was graduated second in the class of 1847 at the Virginia Military Institute. (523) He then took up the profession of civil engineering and spent a number of years before the Civil War in Arizona, where he had mining interests. Elected major of the 45th Virginia Infantry in July 1861, he became colonel of the 51st Virginia the following month. He led this regiment in General John B. Floyd's Western Virginia campaign of that summer and fall. Escaping with Floyd from Fort Donelson in February 1862, he was transferred east. He served under Generals Loring and Samuel Jones, again in the western part of Virginia, and was promoted to brigadier general

from July 8, 1863. He was in temporary command of the Valley District, and was with General Longstreet in East Tennessee in the winter and spring of 1863-64. He commanded his brigade at New Market and in the pursuit of Hunter; and also fought with it under General Early in the Shenandoah campaign and in the raid on Washington. His command was overwhelmed and dispersed at Waynesboro in March 1865. He was finally paroled at Lynchburg on June 21. (524) At the close of the war General Wharton took up residence in Radford, Virginia, where he lived for more than forty years. Elected several times to the state senate, he devoted much time to the development of mining in the state, and died in Radford on May 12, 1906. He is buried there in the family cemetery. (525)

John Austin Wharton was born near Nashville, Tennessee, July 3, 1828. (526) Moving early with his father to Texas, he was educated there and at South Carolina College. Wharton was admitted to the bar in Brazoria, Texas, and practiced there until the outbreak of the Civil War, when he was elected a member of the secession convention. He joined Colonel B. F. Terry's Texas Rangers (8th Texas Cavalry) as a captain of one of its companies. He became its com-

On April 6, 1865 General Wharton was killed in a quarrel with Colonel George W. Baylor of the 2nd Texas Cavalry. Having differed over "military matters," the two officers met in the rooms of General Magruder in a Houston hotel. According to Baylor's account, General Wharton had slapped his face and called him a liar; whereupon Baylor shot and killed Wharton. The general was later found to have been unarmed. (528) He is buried in Austin. (529)

mander after the death of Colonel Terry and Lieutenant Colonel Lubbock; and led it at Shiloh with great distinction. He sustained a wound at Shiloh, but recovered in time to participate in the Kentucky campaign of 1862. He was promoted brigadier general on November 18, 1862. Serving under Forrest and Wheeler and again distinguishing himself at Murfreesboro and Chickamauga, he was named major general to rank from November 10, 1863. The following year he was assigned to the command of the cavalry in General Richard Taylor's department. He took part in the closing scenes of the Red River campaign, during which his cavalry harried Banks after the latter's defeat. (527) For the remainder of the war he served in the Trans-Mississippi.

Joseph Wheeler was born at Augusta, Georgia, September 10, 1836. He was graduated from West Point in 1859, and resigned his 2nd lieutenant's commission in the Mounted Rifles on April 22, 1861. Twenty-one months later he was a Confederate major

general and in command of all the cavalry in the Army of Tennessee at the early age of twenty-six. Initially commissioned a 1st lieutenant of artillery, he was on September 4, 1861 appointed colonel of the 19th Alabama Infantry, with which he fought at Shiloh. Soon after, he was transferred to the mounted arm, and on July 13, 1862 Bragg made him chief of cavalry of the Army of Mississippi. From that time until the close of the war he was almost constantly engaged in battle. Three times wounded himself, thirty-six staff officers fell by his side, and sixteen horses were shot under him. His exploits were second only to those of Bedford Forrest. Promoted brigadier general on October 30, 1862, and major general from January 20, 1863, (530) he commanded the cavalry during Bragg's invasion of Kentucky, at Murfreesboro, and in the Chattanooga campaign. During the Atlanta campaign he was again active and made several raids on Sherman's communications. In opposing Sherman's advance to Savannah, he was less successful. His command came to be much criticized for lack of discipline, both there and in the later campaign of the Carolinas, where he was superseded as chief of cavalry by Lieutenant General Wade Hampton. Following his capture in Georgia in May of 1865,

Wheeler was released from Fort Delaware on June 8. He resided for a time in New Orleans after the war, and moved to Wheeler, Alabama, in 1868. In 1881 he was elected for the first time to Congress, serving in all eight terms. A major general of U. S. Volunteers in the Spanish-American War, he was retired as a brigadier general of the regular army on September 10, 1900. General Wheeler died in Brooklyn, New York, January 25, 1906, and is buried in Arlington.

John Wilkins Whitfield was born March 11, 1818, in Franklin, Tennessee, and educated in the local schools. During the Mexican War he served as captain of the 1st, and lieutenant colonel of the 2nd, Tennessee Infantry. About 1853 he moved to Independence, Missouri, and

for the next several years was an Indian agent in Missouri and Arkansas. Upon the establishment of Kansas Territory, he was elected its delegate to Congress, serving until 1857. Afterwards he was register of the land office at Doniphan, Kansas, until 1861. Whitfield entered the Confederate Army as major of the 4th Battalion Texas Cavalry. Later he became colonel of the 27th regiment, and fought at Pea Ridge (Elkhorn) in 1862, and at the battle of Iuka under General Sterling Price, where he was painfully wounded. Attached to General Earl Van Dorn's command in the spring of 1863, he was commissioned brigadier general on May 9. He was under Joseph E. Johnston in the Vicksburg campaign of that year, and later commanded a brigade under General W. H. Jackson in Mississippi. Apparently without a command at the end of the war, General Whitfield was paroled at Columbus, Texas, on June 29, 1865. (531) Thereafter he made his home in Lavaca County, Texas, which he represented in the state legislature. He died near Hallettsville, October 27, 1879, and is buried in Hallettsville Cemetery.

William Henry Chase Whiting was born in Biloxi, Mississippi, on March 22, 1824. He attained the highest grades ever made· up to that time at West Point, from which he was graduated in 1845. (532) Thereafter he supervised river and harbor improvements and the construction of fortifications in California and the South. Entering Confederate service as a major of engineers, he soon joined General Joseph E. Johnston's Army of the Shenandoah as chief engineer and arranged its transfer to First Manassas. He was there promoted brigadier general on the field by President Davis, to rank July 21, 1861. Commanding a division, he participated in the battle of Seven Pines, in the Valley campaign under Jackson, and in the Seven Days around Richmond. After Malvern Hill, Whiting was ordered to Wilmington, North Carolina, where he developed Fort Fisher at the mouth of Cape Fear River into the strongest fortress in the Confederacy. He was appointed major general on April 22, 1863. For a brief interlude in the summer of 1864 he was at Petersburg. Here, his failure to get his command into action at Port Walthall Junction, during the movement which bottled up the Federal General Butler, earned him the accusation of being under the influence of whiskey or narcotics. The rest of his war service was in North Carolina. Fort Fisher was finally taken on January 15, 1865, after a prolonged naval bombardment and a land assault, (533) and after the Wilmington garrison, under General Bragg, had failed to lend proper support. Whiting was severely wounded and made a prisoner of war. He was conveyed to Fort Columbus in New York Harbor, (534) where he died of his wounds on March 10, 1865. He is buried in Oakdale Cemetery, Wilmington, North Carolina.

Williams Carter Wickham was born on September 21, 1820, at Richmond, Virginia. He was educated at the University of Virginia, and after being admitted to the bar in 1842, he practiced law for a time, and became a planter. In 1849 he was elected to the house of delegates and was in 1859 sent to the state senate. Meantime

he was for many years presiding justice of the Hanover County court. Although a Union man in principle, he took his militia company, the Hanover Dragoons, into Confederate service immediately upon the secession of his state. He was present at the battle of First Manassas, and was commissioned lieutenant colonel of the 4th Virginia Cavalry in September 1861. He was promoted to colonel in August 1862. His army career was connected uninterruptedly with Stuart's Cavalry Corps. Wounded at Williamsburg and again during the Maryland campaign, he remained with the army until the fall of 1864, although he had been elected to the Second Regular Confederate Congress shortly after the battle of Chancellorsville. He was appointed briga-

335

dier general to rank from September 1, 1863. His last active service was with Early in the Shenandoah Valley. General Wickham resigned his commission on November 9, 1864, and took his seat in Congress, where he remained until the end of the war. Formerly a Whig, he espoused the Republican party in 1865, and from 1871 to his death was chairman of the board of supervisors of Hanover County. At the same time he was markedly successful in business as president of the Virginia Central Railroad and later of the Chesapeake & Ohio. In 1880 he declined the secretaryship of the navy offered him by President Hayes, and the year following he refused the Republican nomination for governor. For the last five years of his life he was again a member of the state senate. He died in Richmond on July 23, 1888, and is buried in Hanover County, Virginia.

Louis Trezevant Wigfall was born near Edgefield, South Carolina, April 21, 1816. He was educated at the University of Virginia and South Carolina College, graduating from the latter in 1837. He was admitted to the bar in 1839. An intransigent secessionist as early as 1844, he moved to Marshall, Texas, in 1848; served in both houses of the state legislature; and in December 1859 was elected to the

United States Senate. Here he hurled defiance in the face of his Northern adversaries and was instrumental in the defeat of the Crittenden compromise. At all times he advocated the withdrawal of the Southern states and the formation of a Confederacy. He was ultimately expelled from the Senate on July 11, 1861. He had meantime been present at the bombardment of Sumter, serving as an aide to General Beauregard. At the time, his visit to the fort to demand its surrender advertised him as something of a military hero. Already a member of the Provisional Congress, he was commissioned colonel of the 1st Texas Infantry on August 28, 1861. On October 21 following, President Davis appointed him brigadier general in the Provisional Army. In command for a time of the Texas Brigade, General Wigfall resigned on February 20, 1862, to take a seat in the Confederate Senate, where he remained until the war's end. A violent partisan of Joseph E. Johnston and bitter opponent of the President's conduct of the war, he worked unceasingly to undermine the chief executive's powers. He was largely responsible for the passage of the bill which made Lee the General in Chief of the armies of the Confederacy in the closing weeks. Escaping to England in 1865, he returned to the United States in 1872 and took up residence in Baltimore. Two years later he removed again to Galveston, Texas, where he died on February 18, 1874, a month after his arrival. He is buried in the Episcopal Cemetery in Galveston.

Cadmus Marcellus Wilcox, a native of Wayne County, North Carolina, was born May 29, 1824, but grew up in Tipton County, Tennessee. He attended the University of Nashville before his appointment to West Point in 1842. He was graduated and commissioned in 1846. His record in the Mexican War was most gallant, and he received the brevet of 1st lieutenant at Chapultepec. He published *Rifles and Rifle Practice* in 1859. On June 8, 1861 he resigned, and fought at First Manassas as colonel of the

9th Alabama Infantry. He was promoted to brigadier general on October 21, 1861. From then until the surrender at Appomattox, Wilcox was present with the Army of Northern Virginia at virtually all of its major battles. He was made major general after the Gettysburg campaign to rank from August 3, 1863, and assumed command of Pender's old division. Although his conduct was uniformly reliable and his dispositions skillful, perhaps his most notable contribution to the cause was his last-ditch defense of Fort Gregg on the Petersburg lines on April 2, 1865. Wilcox's support enabled Longstreet to get into position to cover the army's retreat westward. After the war, General Wilcox settled in Washington, and in 1886 was appointed by President Cleveland chief of the railroad division of the Land Office, a position he retained until his death on December 2, 1890. General Wilcox was universally esteemed in the North as well as in the South. Four of the pallbearers at his funeral were former general officers of the United States Army and four were erstwhile general officers of the Confederacy. He is buried in Oak Hill Cemetery in Washington.

John Stuart "Cerro Gordo" Williams was born near Mount Sterling, Kentucky, July 10, 1818, and graduated from Miami University at Oxford, Ohio, in 1839. Admitted to the bar the following year, he commenced practice in Paris. Kentucky. During the Mexican War he served first as captain of an independent company attached to the 6th U. S. Infantry, and later as colonel of the 4th Kentucky Volunteers. His dashing conduct won for him the sobriquet by which he was afterwards known. A member of the Kentucky legislature in 1851 and 1853, Williams was originally an anti-secessionist. However, he disliked the idea of coercion on the part of the national government, and he ultimately entered the Confederate Army as colonel of the 5th Kentucky Infantry on November 16, 1861. Promoted brigadier general to rank from April 16, 1862, he served under Humphrey Marshall in Eastern

Kentucky and Southwestern Virginia. After Marshall's resignation Williams commanded the Department of East Tennessee in the fall of 1863, opposing the advance of Burnside to Knoxville. He was relieved in November at his own request, but he continued to operate in the area, and aided in defeating a Federal attack on the salt works at Abingdon, Virginia. During 1864 he was attached to the Army of Tennessee in Wheeler's Cavalry Corps. However, his brigade became separated from the main command during the raid into Tennessee in August 1864; (535) and Williams was again employed in Southwestern Virginia until the end of the war. Becoming a farmer at Winchester, Kentucky, he was returned to the legislature in 1873 and 1875. He

338

was an unsuccessful candidate for governor in the latter year. In 1878 he was elected to the United States Senate, but was defeated for re-election six years later, and resumed farming. He died at Mount Sterling, July 17, 1898, and is buried in Winchester.

Claudius Charles Wilson was born in Effingham County, Georgia, October 1, 1831. Educated at Emory College in Oxford, Georgia, from which he was graduated in 1851, he read law and gained admission to the Savannah bar the year following. In 1859 he was elected solicitor-general for the eastern circuit of Georgia, but resigned in 1860. Wilson was residing in Chatham County at the outbreak of war. He entered the Confederate Army as captain of Company I, 25th Georgia Infantry, a regiment of which he was elected and commissioned colonel on September 2, 1861. After being equipped and drilled, his command served throughout 1862 at various points on the South Carolina and Georgia coasts. In 1863 it was attached to the forces under Joseph E. Johnston in the Vicksburg campaign, and following the surrender of Vicksburg, was ordered to Georgia. At the battle of Chickamauga Colonel Wilson commanded a brigade in W. H. T. Walker's reserve corps, and so distinguished was his conduct that he was recommended for

promotion to brigadier general. Unfortunately, he was soon attacked by camp fever, from which he died at Ringgold, Georgia, November 27, 1863. Eleven days previously his promotion to the grade of brigadier had been announced, and he was posthumously confirmed as such by the Confederate Senate on February 17, 1864. He is buried in Bonaventure Cemetery, Savannah. (536)

Charles Sidney Winder, a native of Maryland, was born in Talbot County on October 18, 1829. (537) He was a graduate of the United States Military Academy in the class of 1850. En route to Panama on a troop ship in the year 1854, he showed such heroism during a hurricane in the At-

ginia regiments he led throughout the celebrated Shenandoah Valley campaign of 1862. Subsequently he accompanied Jackson to Richmond, where he took a most gallant part in the battles of the Seven Days, and was prominent in the attack at Gaines's Mill. In the preliminaries to the campaign of Second Manassas, and while commanding Jackson's division (Stonewall himself was in command of the corps), Winder was frightfully mangled by a shell at Cedar Mountain on August 9, 1862, and died within a few hours. General Winder was one of the most capable officers in the army, and his loss was officially lamented by both Generals Lee and Jackson in their reports. He is buried at Wye House near Easton, Maryland. (538)

John Henry Winder was born in Somerset County, Maryland, February 21, 1800, and was graduated from West Point at the age of twenty. He was later an instructor of tactics there when Jefferson Davis was a cadet. Resigning in 1823, he was reappointed to the army four years later, and was brevetted major and lieutenant colonel for gallant and meritorious conduct during the Mexican War. He resigned his commission as major, 3rd Artillery, on April 27, 1861; and was appointed brigadier general in the Provisional Confederate Army on June 21, and made pro-

lantic that he was promoted captain on March 3, 1855, supposedly the youngest at that time in the United States service. He resigned his commission on April 1, 1861, and was appointed a major of artillery in the Regular Confederate Army to rank from March 16. After taking part in the reduction of Fort Sumter in Charleston Harbor, he was commissioned colonel of the 6th South Carolina Infantry on July 8. The same month, he reached the battlefield of First Manassas with his regiment too late to take part in the engagement. He was promoted brigadier general in the Provisional Army to rank from March 1, 1862 and was assigned to the command of what later became known as the "Stonewall Brigade" in Jackson's division. This brigade of five Vir-

charges were utterly without foundation. Winder adopted every means at his command to assure that the prisoners received the same ration as did Confederate soldiers in the field, scanty as that allotment was. His task was rendered almost impossible by the refusal of the Federal government to effect an exchange. Weighed down by the fatigue and anxiety of his duties, he died at Florence, South Carolina, on February 7, 1865, (539) and is buried in Green Mount Cemetery, Baltimore. (540)

Henry Alexander Wise was born on December 3, 1806, at Drummondtown, Virginia. He was graduated at Washington College, Pennsylvania, in 1825; and three years later opened a law office in Nashville, Tennessee, where he practiced for a time before returning to Virginia in 1830. An aggressive champion of states' rights, he was elected to Congress in 1833 as a Jacksonian Democrat, but later turned Whig and supported the Harrison - Tyler ticket of 1840. He declined the navy portfolio proffered him by President Tyler and was rejected by the Senate as minister to France, but he was from 1844 to 1847 minister to Brazil. Again becoming a Democrat, he supported both Pierce and Buchanan, and from 1856 to 1860 was governor of Virginia. At the outbreak of the Civil War, although

vost marshal of Richmond. This office made him not only responsible for the prison camps in the vicinity, but also for the arrest and return of deserters, and for the maintenance of order in a city swelled to more than twice its normal size by the war. At one period the fixing of commodity prices for the inhabitants of the Confederate capital also devolved upon him. On November 21, 1864 he assumed the duties of commissary general of prisoners east of the Mississippi. His earlier police powers had made him generally unpopular in Richmond. However, the opprobrium heaped upon him by loyal Confederates was nothing compared to the execrations of the Northern press and public, who accused him of deliberately starving Union prisoners of war. The

mond and wrote *Seven Decades of the Union,* which he published in 1872. Never seeking amnesty or the restoration of his civil rights, he died at Richmond on September 12, 1876, and is buried in Hollywood Cemetery. His brother-in-law was Major General George Gordon Meade, U. S. A., the Union hero of Gettysburg.

Jones Mitchell Withers was born in Madison County, Alabama, January 12, 1814. He was graduated from the U. S. Military Academy in the class of 1835, but resigned the same year to study law. The year following he served as a volunteer during the Creek uprising. Subsequently he practiced his profession, engaged in cotton factoring, and was active in the Alabama state militia, making his residence in Tuscaloosa and Mobile. At the outbreak of the war with Mexico, Withers was reappointed in the United States Army as lieutenant colonel of the 13th Infantry, and was later promoted colonel of the 9th; but he again resigned at the termination of hostilities. From that time until the beginning of the Civil War he was a merchant in Mobile. He was mayor of that city from 1858 to 1861 and also served in the state legislature. Entering the Confederate Army as colonel of the 3rd Alabama Infantry, he was promoted brigadier general on July 10, 1861, and major general from April 6,

past middle age and totally without military training, he volunteered and was appointed a brigadier general on June 5, 1861. At the head of the Wise Legion and other troops, he fought in the West Virginia campaign under Robert E. Lee; again in North Carolina; under Beauregard in the defense of Charleston; and in Florida. From May 1864 to the end he was on the Petersburg lines, at Drewry's Bluff, and in Richard H. Anderson's corps in the defense of Richmond. The day following the battle of Sayler's Creek and two days prior to the surrender at Appomattox, General Lee placed Wise in divisional command, although he was never formally appointed major general. (541) After the war he practiced law in Rich-

1862. He was first in command of the Mobile defenses; he then fought at Shiloh at the head of two brigades; took part in the Kentucky invasion; and at Murfreesboro was highly commended by both Generals Bragg and Leonidas Polk. Succeeded in divisional command in August 1863 by General Hindman, he subsequently was in charge of the reserve forces of Alabama until the end of the war. Thereafter he was a cotton broker, editor of the Mobile *Tribune*, (542) again mayor of Mobile in 1867, city treasurer in 1878-79, and later a claim agent in Washington. General Withers died at Mobile on March 13, 1890, (543) and is there buried in Magnolia Cemetery.

William Tatum Wofford was born in Habersham County,

Georgia, June 28, 1824. (543A) He was educated in the local schools and at Gwinnett County Manual Labor School. Afterwards he studied law, was admitted to the bar, and began practice in Cassville, Georgia. He served as captain of a battalion of Georgia mounted volunteers in the Mexican War. From 1849 to 1853 he occupied a seat in the legislature, edited for a time the Cassville *Standard*, and as a member of the state convention of 1861, voted against secession. He soon was in the army as colonel of the 18th Georgia Infantry, and after being briefly employed in North Carolina, took part in the 1862 campaign around Richmond in Hood's Texas Brigade. At Second Manassas, South Mountain, and Sharpsburg he commanded

the brigade as senior colonel. At Fredericksburg the 18th was in T. R. R. Cobb's brigade; and Wofford succeeded Cobb after the latter's death there. He was officially promoted to brigadier general from January 17, 1863. Thereafter General Wofford was continuously with the 1st Corps of the Army of Northern Virginia—first under McLaws, and later Kershaw — at Chancellorsville, Gettysburg, Knoxville, in the Overland campaign of 1864, and in the Shenandoah. On January 23, 1865, at the request of Governor Brown, he was assigned to command of the Department of North Georgia. He was paroled at Resaca on May 2, 1865. Forthwith elected to the national House of Representatives, he was refused his seat by the Republican radicals. During the remainder of his life General Wofford w a s active in railroad organization and in civic matters, serving as trustee of several educational institutions and as a member of the state constitutional convention of 1877. He died near Cass Station, Georgia, May 22, 1884, and is buried in Cassville Cemetery.

Sterling Alexander Martin Wood, a native of Alabama, was born March 17, 1823, at Florence. He obtained his early education in that city. Graduating from the Jesuit College of St. Joseph's at Bardstown, Kentucky, in 1841, he studied law and commenced practice first in Murfreesboro, Tennessee, and later in Florence. He was solicitor of the fourth judicial circuit of Alabama from 1851 to 1857. In the latter year he was elected to the legislature; and in 1860, as editor of the Florence *Gazette,* he strongly supported John C. Breckinridge for the presidency. He entered the Confederate Army as captain of the Florence Guards. Upon the organization of the 7th Alabama Infantry, Wood was elected its colonel on May 18, 1861. He served with this regiment at Pensacola until February 1862, when he was ordered to take his command to the army being concentrated under General Albert Sidney Johnston in Kentucky. He had meantime been promoted brigadier general on January 7.

After fighting bravely at Shiloh, he headed the 4th Brigade of Buckner's division at Perryville and was badly wounded by a shell fragment. At Murfreesboro and at Chickamauga his brigade was in Cleburne's division. For some reason not readily apparent in the records, Cleburne, in his official report of the latter battle, omitted mention of Wood while praising his other brigade commanders. (544) At any rate, Wood resigned his commission on October 17, 1863, and was not again in service during the war. Going to Tuscaloosa, where his family had taken refuge, General Wood resumed the practice of law and was again a member of the legislature in 1882-83. A member of the law faculty of the University of Alabama in 1889-90, he was also attorney for the Alabama Great Southern Railway from its beginning until his death at Tuscaloosa on January 26, 1891. He is buried in Tuscaloosa. (545)

Ambrose Ransom "Rans" Wright was born on April 26, 1826, at Louisville, Jefferson County, Georgia. He read law under the tutelage of Governor and Senator Herschel V. Johnson —who later became his brother-in-law—and was admitted to the bar. He became quite prominent politically, though he ran unsuccessfully for the Georgia legislature and for Congress. He was a

Fillmore Elector in 1856. A supporter of Bell and Everett in 1860, and Georgia commissioner to Maryland in 1861, he was commissioned colonel of the 3rd Georgia Infantry on May 18, 1861, and served in North Carolina and Georgia until the summer of 1862. He was promoted brigadier on June 3, 1862, and sent to Virginia. Wright's Georgians made a distinguished record in the Army of Northern Virginia from the Seven Days battles to the siege of Petersburg, and Wright was badly wounded at Sharpsburg. As of November 26, 1864 Wright was named major general and ordered to Georgia, where he exercised command until the end of the war. In 1863 he had been elected to the Georgia state senate and president of that body *in absentia*. Resuming his law practice after the termination of hostilities, he purchased the Augusta *Chronicle and Sentinel* in 1866, and in 1871 was defeated for the Democratic nomination to the U. S. Senate. The following year General Wright was a delegate to both the state and national Democratic conventions and was elected to the national House of Representatives, but died at Augusta, Georgia, December 21, 1872, before taking his seat. At a special election to fill the vacancy Alexander H. Stephens was elected his successor. (546) General Wright is buried in City Cemetery, Augusta. (547)

Marcus Joseph Wright was born at Purdy, Tennessee, June 5, 1831, and was educated in the local academy. After studying law, he removed to Memphis, where he became clerk of the common law and chancery court. For some years previous to the Civil War, Wright had been lieutenant colonel of the 154th Tennessee militia regiment. He was mustered into the service of the Confederacy with this regiment, which was re-named the 154th Senior Tennessee Infantry. After acting as military governor of Columbus, Kentucky, until its evacuation, he fought at Belmont and was wounded at Shiloh. During Bragg's invasion of Kentucky in 1862 he was on the staff of General Cheatham and took part in the battle of Perryville. Pro-

moted brigadier general from December 13, 1862, he led General D. S. Donelson's old Tennessee brigade at Chickamauga and in the Chattanooga campaign. He later commanded the post and District of Atlanta, the post at Macon, and at the end of the war, the District of North Mississippi and West Tennessee. Paroled at Grenada, Mississippi, on May 19, 1865, he returned to his law practice in Memphis, where for some time he also acted as assistant purser of the United States Navy Yard. In 1878 General Wright was made agent for the collection of Confederate records in connection with the monumental official U. S. government publication, *War of the Rebellion: Official Records of the Union and Confederate Armies* (see Bibliography #13). He worked at this task until his retirement in June 1917, and made invaluable contributions to this primary source of the history of the war. He also wrote prolifically for magazines and published a number of books of a historical nature. General Wright died in Washington, D. C., in his ninety-second year, December 27, 1922. He is buried in Arlington.

Zebulon York, a native of Avon, Franklin County, Maine, was born October 10, 1819. He was educated at Wesleyan Seminary at Kent's Hill, Maine; at Transylvania University, Kentucky; and at the University of Louisiana (now Tulane), from which he was graduated in law. He then went to Vidalia, Louisiana, where he soon became the leading attorney of the parish and accumulated a large fortune in cotton planting. At the outbreak of the Civil War he and his partner were reputed to own six plantations, with 1,700 slaves and an annual production of 4,500 bales; they were also said to pay the largest realty taxes in the state. Organizing a company of the 14th Louisiana Infantry, York was successively elected its major, lieutenant colonel, and colonel; and fought with the regiment on the Peninsula and throughout the Seven Days battles. After the campaigns of Second Manassas, Maryland, and Fredericksburg, he was on re-

cruiting duty in Louisiana during the Chancellorsville campaign, but again led his regiment at Gettysburg. During the Virginia campaign of 1864 he was promoted brigadier general from May 31, 1864, and was given command of the remnant of Hays' and Stafford's old Louisiana brigades. Gallantly leading his troops in the Shenandoah Valley during that summer and autumn, his left arm was so badly shattered by a shell at the battle of Winchester on September 19 as to necessitate amputation. Upon his recovery, he was engaged in recruiting for his brigade from among the foreign-born prisoners of war held in Confederate prison camps. (548) Paroled on May 6, 1865, in North Carolina, he was financially ruined by the course of events. In his later

347

years he operated the York House in Natchez, Mississippi, where he died on August 5, 1900, and where he is buried. (549)

Pierce Manning Butler Young was born on November 15, 1836, (550) at Spartanburg, South Carolinà, but moved with his parents as a small boy to Bartow County, Georgia. Obtaining his early training at the Georgia Military Institute, he secured an appointment to West Point in 1857, but resigned upon the secession of Georgia a few months before he would have been graduated. Appointed a 2nd lieutenant of artillery in the Regular Confederate service, on March 16, 1861, Young rose rapidly to lieutenant colonel of Cobb's Legion and the command of its cavalry. He was attached

to General Wade Hampton's brigade of Stuart's Cavalry Corps, and was distinguished for "remarkable gallantry" in the Maryland campaign. He was promoted to brigadier general to rank from September 28, 1863, having been commissioned colonel from November 1, 1862. During part of 1864 he commanded Hampton's old division, and in November was sent to Augusta, Georgia, to collect troops and to aid in the defense of the city, then being threatened by Sherman. He was subsequently promoted temporary major general to rank from December 30, 1864, and under the command of Hampton, resisted Sherman's advance through the Carolinas. General Young became prominent politically after the war and served five terms (or parts of terms) as a Democrat in Congress, from 1868 to 1875, during the turbulent Reconstruction period. A delegate to the Democratic National Conventions of 1872, 1876, and 1880, he also held several consular and diplomatic posts proffered by both Republican and Democratic presidents. He died in New York City, July 6, 1896, and is buried in Cartersville, Georgia, near his old plantation.

William Hugh Young was born in Booneville, Missouri, January 1, 1838. His parents took him to Texas in infancy, and the family resided first in Red River, and

later in Grayson, county. He received a good education at Washington College, Tennessee; at McKenzie College, Texas; and at the University of Virginia, which last he attended from 1859 to 1861. (551) In September 1861 he returned to Texas and recruited a company for Confederate service. He was elected captain of this unit, which became part of the 9th Texas Infantry. After the battle of Shiloh he was promoted colonel of the regiment. He fought with great gallantry at Perryville, Murfreesboro (where he was wounded), in the Vicksburg campaign under Joseph E. Johnston (during which he was again wounded), and at Chickamauga, where he received yet another wound. In the Atlanta campaign the 9th Texas was in General M. D.

Ector's brigade; at Kennesaw Mountain, Young suffered two more wounds but continued in command and was made brigadier general from August 15, 1864, to succeed Ector after the latter was disabled. On the subsequent march into Tennessee General Young's left foot was all but shot off during the attack on the Federal forts at Allatoona, Georgia, and he fell into the hands of the enemy. He was not released from Johnson's Island, Ohio, until July 24, 1865. After that time he was a prominent lawyer and real estate operator in San Antonio, Texas, until his death on November 28, 1901. (552) He is buried in Confederate Cemetery, San Antonio.

Felix Kirk Zollicoffer was born on May 19, 1812, in Maury County, Tennessee. He received a rather scant education, and at the age of sixteen, he entered newspaper work in Paris, Tennessee. He served one year in the Seminole uprising of 1836 as a lieutenant of volunteers. Upon his return, he steadily forged ahead in the field of journalism, and at the same time became a political power in the state. His occupation of the minor offices of adjutant general and state comptroller (1845-49) and state senator (1849-52) were a small indication of the influence of a man who was able to carry Tennessee for the Whig candidate,

General Winfield Scott, in the Presidential campaign of 1852 and to secure his own election to Congress at the same time. He served until 1859, having declined to run for a fourth term. A strong supporter of the Bell-Everett ticket in 1860 and a member of the "peace conference" in Washington the following year, Zollicoffer accepted a commission as brigadier general in the Provisional Confederate States Army on July 9, 1861. As department commander, he went to East Tennessee in an effort to mollify the strong Union sentiment in the area. His miltiary dispositions were, unhappily, less well-conceived than his political strategy. In the face of positive suggestions to the contrary from General Albert Sidney Johnston, he moved his force to the Kentucky side of the Cumberland River (553) prior to the arrival of his immediate superior, General George B. Crittenden. With the river at their back and with notice of the approach of a Federal column under General George H. Thomas, Crittenden was left with no choice but to advance and attack. In the ensuing sharp encounter at Mill Springs (Fishing Creek) on January 19, 1862, General Zollicoffer was instantly killed by a volley from a Union regiment, into the van of which he had ridden unaware. He is buried in City Cemetery, Nashville.

APPENDICES

APPENDIX I

TRANS-MISSISSIPPI OFFICERS ASSIGNED TO DUTY

The following were "assigned to duty" as general officers in orders from Headquarters, Trans-Mississippi Department, on the dates shown, but were not appointed as such by President Davis:

Arthur P. Bagby, Colonel, 7th Texas Cavalry, assigned as brigadier general, April 13, 1864, to date March 17, 1864; assigned as major general, May 16, 1865.

Horace Randal, Colonel, 28th Texas Cavalry, assigned as brigadier general, April 13, 1864, to date April 8, 1864.

William H. King, Colonel, 18th Texas Infantry, assigned as brigadier general, April 16, 1864, to date April 8, 1864.

Xavier B. De Bray, Colonel, 26th Texas Cavalry, assigned as brigadier general, April 13, 1864.

Robert P. Maclay, Major of Artillery, assigned as brigadier general, May 13, 1864, to date April 30, 1864

B. Frank Gordon, Colonel, 5th Missouri Cavalry, assigned as brigadier general, May 16, 1865.

Sidney D. Jackman, Colonel, 7th (Jackman's) Missouri Infantry, assigned as brigadier general, May 16, 1865.

Levin M. Lewis, Colonel, 16th Missouri Infantry, assigned as brigadier general, May 16, 1865.

Alexander W. Terrell, Colonel, Terrell's Texas Cavalry, assigned as brigadier general, May 16, 1865.

APPENDIX II

CAMPAIGNS AND BATTLES CITED
(Note: Skirmishes are marked with an asterisk)

Abingdon, Virginia, June 20, 1864

Allatoona, Georgia, October 5, 1864

Alleghany Summit, West Virginia, December 13, 1861

Antietam, *see* Sharpsburg

Appomattox campaign, Virginia, March 29-April 9, 1865

Appomattox Court House, Virginia, surrender at, April 9, 1865

Arkansas Post, Arkansas, January 10-11, 1863

Atlanta, Georgia, July 22, 1864; evacuated by Confederates under Hood, September 1, 1864

Atlanta campaign, Georgia, May-September, 1864

Baker's Creek (Champion's Hill), Mississippi, May 16, 1863

Ball's Bluff (Leesburg), Virginia, October 21-22, 1861

Bath, West Virginia, January 3-4, 1862

Baton Rouge, Louisiana, operations about, July 27-August 6, 1862

"Battle Above the Clouds" (Lookout Mountain), Tennessee, November 24, 1863

Bean's Station, Tennessee, December 14, 1863

Belmont, Missouri, November 7, 1861

Bentonville, North Carolina, March 19-21, 1865

Berryville, Virginia, September 3-4, 1864

Bethel (Bethel Church, Big Bethel, Great Bethel), Virginia, June 10, 1861

Bethesda Church, Virginia, May 30-31, 1864; June 1-3, 1864

Big Bethel, *see* Bethel

Blair's Landing, Louisiana, April 12-13, 1864

Bluff Spring, Florida, March 25, 1865

Booneville, Mississippi, captured, May 30, 1862

Boonsboro, *see* South Mountain

Brandy Station (Beverly Ford, Fleetwood), Virginia, June 9, 1863

Brices Cross Roads, Mississippi, June 10, 1864

Bristoe Station, Virginia, October 14, 1863

*Brownsville, Texas, last engagement of the war at, May 12, 1865

Buckhead Creek, Georgia, November 28-29, 1864

Buckland Mills, Virginia, October 19, 1863
Buffington's Island, Ohio, July 19, 1863
Camden expedition, Arkansas, March 23-May 3, 1864
Carolinas campaign, January 1-April 26, 1865
Carthage, Missouri, July 5, 1861
Cedar Creek (Bell Grove), Virginia, October 19, 1864
Cedar Mountain (Cedar Run Mountain, Slaughter Mountain, Southwest Mountain), Virginia, August 9, 1862
Chambersburg, Pennsylvania, burned, July 30, 1864
Chancellorsville, Virginia, May 2-4, 1863
Chantilly (Ox Hill), Virginia, September 1, 1862
Charleston, South Carolina, bombardment of, August 21, 1863; December 31, 1863
Charlestown, West Virginia, October 18, 1863
Chattanooga, Tennessee, November 23-25, 1863
Chattanooga campaign, Tennessee, August-November, 1863
Cheat Mountain campaign, West Virginia, September 11-17, 1861
Chickahominy, *see* Cold Harbor
Chickamauga, Georgia, September 19-20, 1863
Chickamauga campaign, Georgia, August 16-September 22, 1863
Chickasaw Bayou, Mississippi, December 27-28, 1862
Chickasaw Bluffs, Mississippi, December 29, 1862
Cloyd's Mountain, Virginia, May 9, 1864
Cold Harbor (Gaines's Mill, Chickahominy), Virginia, June 27, 1862
Cold Harbor, Virginia, June 3, 1864; vicinity of, May 31-June 12, 1864
Columbia, Tennessee, in front of, November 24-27, 1864
Corinth, Mississippi, October 3-4, 1862
Corrick's Ford, West Virginia, July 13, 1861
Cosby Creek, Tennessee, January 14, 1864
Crampton's Gap, *see* South Mountain
The Crater, Virginia, July 30, 1864
Cross Keys, Virginia, June 8, 1862
Cumberland Gap, Tennessee, evacuated by Federals, Septemper 17, 1862
Dalton, Georgia, May 9-13, 1864; surrendered, October 13, 1864
*Devall's Bluff, Arkansas, July 6, 1862
Dinwiddie Court House, Virginia, March 31, 1865

Dranesville, Virginia, November 26-27, 1861; December 20, 1861

Drewry's Bluff, Virginia, May 12-16, 1864

Dumfries (Quantico Creek), Virginia, October 11, 1861

Dumfries, Virginia, December 12, 1862; December 27, 1862

Durham Station, North Carolina, surrender of J. E. Johnston at, April 26, 1865

Egypt, Mississippi, December 28, 1864

Elkhorn (Pea Ridge), Arkansas, March 6-8, 1862

Elkhorn Tavern, *see* Elkhorn

Ezra Church, Georgia, July 28, 1864

*Falling Waters, Maryland, July 14, 1863

Farmington, Mississippi, May 9-10, 1862

Farmville, Virginia, April 7, 1865

Fisher's Hill, Virginia, September 22, 1864

Fishing Creek, *see* Mill Springs

Five Forks, Virginia, April 1, 1865

Fort Blakely, Alabama, April 2-9, 1865

Fort Donelson, Tennessee, siege and capture of, February 12-16, 1862

Fort Fisher, North Carolina, bombardment of, December 24-25, 1864; bombardment and capture of, January 13-15, 1865

Fort Gregg (Petersburg lines), Virginia, April 2, 1865

Fort Harrison, Virginia, September 29-30, 1864

Fort Hatteras, North Carolina, August 28-29, 1861

Fort Henry, Tennessee, January 17-22, 1862

Fort Hindman (Arkansas Post), Arkansas, January 4-17, 1863

Fort Jackson, Louisiana, bombardment and surrender of, April 18-28, 1862

Fort McRee, in Pensacola Harbor, Florida, November 22, 1861; January 1, 1862

Fort Morgan, Alabama, August 9-23, 1864

Fort Moultrie, South Carolina, occupied by Federals, February 18, 1865

Fort Pillow, Tennessee, April 14-June 5, 1862; captured by Confederates, April 12, 1864

Fort St. Philip, Louisiana, capture of, April 18-28, 1862

Fort Sanders, Tennessee, November 29, 1863

Fort Stedman, in front of Petersburg, Virginia, March 25, 1865

Fort Sumter, South Carolina, bombardment of, April 12-13, 1861
Fort Tyler, near West Point, Georgia, April 16, 1865
Fox's Gap, *see* South Mountain
Franklin, Tennessee, November 30, 1864
Frayser's Farm (White Oak Swamp), Virginia, June 30, 1862
Fredericksburg (Marye's Heights), Virginia, May 3-4, 1863
Fredericksburg, Virginia, December 13, 1862
Front Royal, Virginia, May 23, 30, 31, 1862
Fussell's Mill, Virginia, August 13-20, 1864
Gaines's Mill, *see* Cold Harbor
Galveston, Texas, attack on blockade fleet at, January 1, 1863
Gettysburg, Pennsylvania, July 1-3, 1863
Gettysburg campaign, Pennsylvania, June-July, 1863
Glorieta Cañon, New Mexico, March 26-28, 1862
Grand Gulf, Mississippi, March 31, 1863
Greensboro, North Carolina, J. E. Johnston surrendered at, April 26, 1865
Groveton (Manassas Plains), Virginia, August 29, 1862
Grubbs Crossroads, Kentucky, August 21, 1864
Harpers Ferry, West Virginia, September 12-15, 1862
*Harrisonburg, Pennsylvania, June 6, 1862
Hatcher's Run, Virginia, February 5-7, 1865
Helena, Arkansas, January 1, 1863; July 4, 1863
*High Bridge, Virginia, April 6-7, 1865
Holly Springs, Mississippi, July 1, 1862; November 13, 28, 1862; December 20, 1862
Island No. 10, Tennessee, capture of, April 7-8, 1862
Iuka, Mississippi, September 19, 1862
Jackson, Mississippi, capture of, July 10, 1863
Jenkins' Ferry, Arkansas, April 30, 1864
Jonesboro, Georgia, August 31-September 1, 1864
Kelly's Ford (Fair Gardens), Tennessee, January 27, 1864
Kelly's Ford, Virginia, December 20-22, 1862; November 7, 1863
Kennesaw Mountain, Georgia, June 10, 1864; July 3, 1864
Kentucky campaign, August-October, 1862
Kernstown, *see* Winchester
Kinston, North Carolina, January 25, 1863; expedition, June 20-23, 1864

Newburgh, Indiana, capture of, July 18, 1862
Newtonia, Missouri, September 30, 1862
Olustee, Florida, February 20, 1864
Overland campaign, Virginia, Summer, 1864
Paducah, Kentucky, capture of, March 25, 1864
Payne's Farm, Virginia, November 27, 1863
Pea Ridge, *see* Elkhorn
Peach Orchard, Virginia, June 29, 1862
Peachtree Creek, Georgia, July 20, 1864
Peninsular campaign, Virginia, April-July, 1862
Pennsylvania campaign, *see* Gettysburg campaign
Pensacola, Florida, evacuated by Confederates, May 9-12, 1862; evacuated by Federals, March 20-24, 1863
Perryville, Kentucky, October 7-8, 1862
Petersburg, Virginia, assault on lines of, June 15-18, 1864
Petersburg, Virginia, siege of, June 15, 1864-April 2, 1865
Piedmont, Virginia, June 5, 1864
Pine Mountain, Georgia, June 14, 1864
Pittsburg Landing, *see* Shiloh
Pleasant Hill, Louisiana, April 9, 1864
Plymouth, North Carolina, April 17-20, 1864
Port Gibson, Mississippi, May 1, 1863
Port Hudson, Louisiana, siege of, May 21-July 8, 1863
Port Republic, Virginia, June 8-9, 1862
Port Royal (Port Royal Ferry), South Carolina, January 1, 1862; June 6, 1862; July 4, 1862
Port Royal Bay (Forts Walker and Beauregard), South Carolina, November 7, 1861
Port Walthall Junction, Virginia, May 6-7, 1864
Prairie Grove, Arkansas, December 7, 1862
Princeton, West Virginia, September 16, 1861; May 15-17, 1862
Rappahannock Bridge, Virginia, October 22, 1863
Reams' Station, Virginia, August 25, 1864
Red River campaign, Louisiana, March 10-May 22, 1864
Resaca, Georgia, May 14-15, 1864
Rich Mountain, West Virginia, July 11, 1861
Rich Mountain campaign, West Virginia, *see* Western Virginia campaign
Richmond, Kentucky, August 30, 1862
Richmond, Virginia, siege of, June 19, 1864-April 3, 1865
Romney, West Virginia, January 10, 1862

Romney expedition, West Virginia, December 1861-January 1862

Salem Church, Virginia, May 3-4, 1863

Savage's Station, Virginia, June 29, 1862

Savannah campaign, Georgia, November 15-December 21, 1864

Sayler's Creek, Virginia, April 6, 1865

Secessionville, South Carolina, June 16, 1862

Selma, Alabama, April 2, 1865

Seven Days battles, Virginia, June 26-July 2, 1862. *See* Cold Harbor, Frayser's Farm, Malvern Hill, Meadow Bridge, Peach Orchard, Savage's Station

Seven Pines (Fair Oaks), Virginia, May 31-June 1, 1862

Sharpsburg (Antietam), Maryland, September 17, 1862

Shenandoah Valley campaign, Virginia, Early's, June-November, 1864

Shenandoah Valley campaign, Virginia, Jackson's, April-June, 1862

Shiloh (Pittsburg Landing), Tennessee, March 16, 1862; April 6-7, 1862

*Smithburg, Tennessee, July 4, 1863

South Mountain, Maryland, September 14, 1862

Spanish Fort, Alabama, siege and capture of, March 27-April 8, 1865

Spotsylvania Court House, Virginia, May 8-21, 1864

Spring Hill (Thompson's Station), Tennessee, November 29, 1864

Springfield, *see* Wilson's Creek

Suffolk, Virginia, expedition against and siege of, April 11-May 4, 1863

Telford's Depot, Tennessee, September 8, 1863

Tennessee campaign, Hood's, November-December, 1864

Thoroughfare Gap, Virginia, August 28, 1862; October 17-18, 1862

Tullahoma campaign, Tennessee, June 23-July 7, 1863

Tupelo, Mississippi, May 5, 1863; July 14-15, 1864

Valverde, New Mexico, February 21, 1862

Vicksburg, Mississippi, bombardment of, June 28, 1862

Vicksburg campaign, Mississippi, December 20, 1862-January 3, 1863; siege, May 19-July 4, 1863

Walthall's Junction, *see* Port Walthall Junction

Washington, D. C., Early at Fort Stevens near, July 11-12, 1864

Waynesboro, Virginia, June 10, 1864; September 29, 1864; March 2, 1865

Weldon Railroad, Virginia, August 18-21, 1864

Western Virginia campaign, June 25-July 17. 1861

Westport, Missouri, October 21-23, 1864

White Oak Swamp, *see* Frayser's Farm

Wilderness, Virginia, May 5-7, 1864

Wilderness campaign, Virginia, May-June, 1864

Williamsburg, Virginia, May 5, 1862

Williamsport, Maryland, July 6, 1863

Wilmington, North Carolina, occupied by Federals, February 22, 1865

Wilson's Creek (Springfield), Missouri, August 10, 1861; October 25, 1861

Winchester (Kernstown), Virginia, March 22-23, 1862; July 24, 1864

Winchester (Opequon), Virginia, September 19, 1864

Winchester, Virginia, May 25, 1862

Woodstock, Virginia, April 1-2, 1862; September 23, 1864

Yellow Tavern, Virginia, May 11, 1864

Yorktown, Virginia, siege of, April 5-May 4, 1862

NOTES

WHERE an officer's career has been wholly reconstructed from published and generally accessible works, the sources are not given in these notes. In such cases the reader will understand that the subject's life is treated *in extenso* in one or more such standard reference biographies as *Dictionary of American Biography, Cyclopedia of American Biography, Confederate Military History,* and so on. However, newspapers, manuscripts, obscure books, and information secured from descendants or other individuals are always cited. Notes are also given in those instances in which the author's research had led him to differ from previously published accounts.

Most publications are cited in abbreviated form—by the last name of the author or editor, by short title, or by initials.

The following works are referred to by initials:

B.D.A.C.—*Biographical Directory of the American Congress, 1774-1949.*

C.A.B.   —*Appleton's Cyclopedia of American Biography.*

C.V.   —*Confederate Veteran Magazine.*

D.A.B.   —*Dictionary of American Biography.*

J.C.S.C. —*Journal of the Congress of the Confederate States of America, 1861-1865.*

L.F.O.   —*List of Field Officers . . . in the Confederate States Army, 1861-1865.*

L.S.O.   —*List of Staff Officers of the Confederate States Army, 1861-1865.*

M.G.O.   —*Memorandum Relative to the General Officers . . . of the Confederate States, 1861-1865.*

O.R.   —*War of the Rebellion . . . Official Records of the Union and Confederate Armies.*

S.H.S.P. —*Southern Historical Society Papers.*

Note: The italicized number that appears first in a citation corresponds to the number of the appropriate entry in the Bibliography, where the full name of the author, title. and facts of publication may be found.

(1) An interesting article by a Southern editor dealing with this subject is Edward A. Pollard, "The Confederate Congress," *Galaxy Magazine,* VI (December 1868), 749.

(2) Dallas *Morning News,* April 21, 1928.

(3) *116. Stickles,* 423.

(4) From a sketch by his son-in-law in *19. C.V.,* XXII, 389.

(5) Nashville *Daily American,* March 29, 1893, quoted in *22. D.A.B.*

(6) *9. M.G.O., passim.*

(7) *Ibid.,* 5 and n., *30; 6. J.C.S.C.,* 716 ff. The Confederate States Congress adjourned for the last time on March 18, 1865.

(8) *13. O.R.,* XLVI, Pt. 2, pp. 1268-75.

(9) *Ibid.,* XLVII, Pt. 3, pp. 732-36.

(10) *Ibid.,* XLVII, *passim.*

(11) *6. J.C.S.C.,* III, 522, 544, 674-75; *298. Rowland,* VI, 160.

(12) On April 30, 1862 McLaws' division of four brigades reported an effective strength of 11,803 *(13. O.R.,* XI, Pt. 3, pp. 479-80). On March 1, 1865 the 2nd Corps reported 532 officers and 7508 men present for duty *(ibid.,* XLVI, Pt. 1, pp. 388-89).

(13) Letter in the author's possession.

(14) *268. Freeman,* I, 261 and n.

(15) Neither appears in *9. M.G.O.*

(16) The President had agreed to appoint Harris a brigadier general upon the occasion of his trip south in 1864 but refused to do so on the spot. Colonel Harris died before Davis returned to Richmond (see *111. Roman,* II, 276-77). Time ran out on the gallant Munford and Douglas, although both adopted the title post bellum.

(17) See *9. M.G.O.,* upon which the list of officers in this book is based, and which has been compared with the manuscript registers of appointments to the Confederate Army, in the National Archives, Washington.

(18) Robert C. Tyler, whose only known occupation after joining the Walker expedition in 1860 was that of "clerk" *(Baltimore City Directory* of 1860). See Note 482.

(19) Gibbon was actually born in Pennsylvania, although he was taken to Charlotte, North Carolina, in infancy and was reared there.

(20) Hood reverted to his permanent rank of lieutenant gen-

362

eral, P.A.C.S., after stepping down as commander of the Army of Tennessee.

(21) In accordance with a ruling by Attorney General George Davis, all officers confirmed by the Provisional Congress had to be reconfirmed by the Regular Congress. Only Cooper, R. E. Lee, J. E. Johnston, and Beauregard were thus reconfirmed as Generals, Regular Army, A. S. Johnston having been killed and Bragg being confirmed in his place by the Regular Congress. No other names on the regular roster were submitted for reconfirmation.

(22) See 22. *D.A.B.* and 4. *Heitman.*

(23) This order was published in book form with illustrations by Charles H. Wynne of Richmond in 1861, by authority of General Cooper.

(24) Since a number of the pictures postdate the war, the generals will sometimes appear as older men in civilian dress. The reader should also be aware that uniforms have in some instances been added by a zealous photographer of a later day.

(25) Adams' sketch in 22. *D.A.B.,* taken largely from an obituary in the New Orleans *National Republican,* June 14, 1872, is notably inaccurate in many respects. He gave his age as twenty-nine and the state of his birth as Kentucky in the 1850 Federal census of Hinds County, Mississippi. When paroled on May 9, 1865 he stated his age to be forty-three. His mother was the daughter of Daniel Weisiger, a Kentucky pioneer; and his father, U. S. District Judge George Adams, resided continuously in Frankfort from 1811 until 1825, when the family moved to Natchez. General Adams was married twice and left at least four surviving children. Information herein from: a son, Colonel D. W. Adams, Old Fort, North Carolina; Mississippi Department of Archives and History; Kentucky Historical Society, Frankfort; Western Kentucky State College, Bowling Green; 9. *M.G.O.; 13. O.R.; 6. J.C.S.C.*

(26) Probably at St. Joseph's College, now St. Joseph Preparatory School.

(27) The others were A. L. Long and R. L. Walker. See 9. *M.G.O.*

(28) See sketch by D. S. Freeman in 22. *D.A.B.*

(29) It is not shown by 6. *J.C.S.C.* that General Allen's nomination to the grade of major general was acted upon by the Senate prior to final adjournment, although he stated in an autobiographical sketch in 19. *C.V.,* II, 324, that he was confirmed in March 1865. The nomination, dated March 13, was received by the Senate on the 14th

and referred to the Committee on Military Affairs the same day. There it apparently remained until final adjournment on the 18th.

(30) *314. Hill,* II, 60 n.

(31) Authority of Mr. Franklin Garrett, Atlanta, Georgia; *19. C.V.,* IX, 418 gives March 3, 1824, cited in *22. D.A.B.* Also see *32. Northen.*

(32) *22. D.A.B.* and *4. Heitman.*

(33) See his autobiography in *299. S.H.S.P.,* XXIV, 57; also *1. B.D.A.C. 22. D.A.B.* gives February 12.

(34) *268. Freeman,* III, 721.

(35) Spelling of middle name on authority of Georgia Historical Society. *4. Heitman* renders it as "Houston."

(36) Sketch of General S. R. Anderson is taken mainly from the minutes of a "Meeting of Citizens to Take Action on the Death of General Anderson" (Tennessee Historical Commission). Additional data was kindly supplied the author by Mr. S. A. Weakley of Nashville, a grandson.

(37) Middle name, "Jay," on authority of Princeton University Library, Princeton, New Jersey.

(38) Contrary to *189. Evans,* he did not graduate from or attend West Point. See *21. Cullum* and *35. Register of Graduates, U.S.M.A.*

(39) *13. O.R.,* XXXVIII, Pt. 5, p. 953. He was exchanged on the 3rd *(19. C.V.,* VII, 364).

(40) *13. O.R.,* XLII, Pt. 2, p. 1189.

(41) *299. S.H.S.P.,* XXXVII, 145.

(42) *Ibid.,* 150. The author of this account was a captain in the 38th Virginia of Armistead's brigade and frequently quotes Colonel Rawley W. Martin of the 53rd Virginia, who fell by the side of Armistead, but later recovered.

(43) Scullyville, once the old Choctaw agency, is in Sequoyah County, Oklahoma, some nineteen miles southwest of Fort Smith, Arkansas, on U. S. Route 271. The agency building was still standing in 1952. Armstrong's father, an officer in the regular army, was agent for the Choctaws at the time.

(44) This phase of Armstrong's career seems to have been generally overlooked by historians. He accepted promotion to the grade of captain on June 6, 1861 *(4. Heitman),* and commanded a company of the 2nd U. S. Dragoons at First Manassas on July 21, 1861 *(13. O.R.,* II, 393). On August 10, 1861 he was serving as volunteer aide-de-camp on the staff of General Ben McCulloch at the battle of Wilson's Creek *(ibid.,* III, 107). Three days later his resignation was accepted by the U. S. War Department. Why he and certain other officers were

permitted to resign without prejudice at this late date is one of the minor mysteries of the war.

(45) The best account of Armstrong's ante- and post-bellum careers is contained in a series of articles which appeared in the *Chronicles of Oklahoma,* a publication of the Oklahoma Historical Society, during 1952 and 1953, and which confirm his middle name as "Crawford." Also see *22. D.A.B.*

(46) The most complete life is *108. Avirett.* The author was chaplain of Ashby's old regiment.

(47) Date of birth from *189. Evans.* According to a thumbnail sketch in the *Southern Bivouac* (February 1885), he was born May 23, 1825.

(48) This data and place and date of birth courtesy of Mrs. William Baldwin Shearon, Nashville, Tennessee, niece of General Baldwin by marriage, who knew personally the General's widow. According to his obituary in the Mobile *Register and Advertiser,* February 21, 1864, General Baldwin was born "at Sumterville, Sumter District, S. C., on the 27th of August, 1827." For obvious reasons Mrs. Shearon's statement, taken from family records, has been preferred. The author here is especially indebted to Mrs. Frank M. Drake, President, United Daughters of the Confederacy chapter, Columbus, Mississippi, for her assistance.

(49) Barry has no sketch in *189. Evans* or other biographical dictionary. Much of the data here is taken from Dr. James Sprunt, *Chronicles of the Cape Fear River,* 305 (New Hanover Historical Commission, Wilmington, North Carolina). Year of birth (obtained from Barry's tombstone) is at variance with the *Alumni History of the University of North Carolina,* which recites June 21, 1840.

(50) See *13. O.R.,* XXXVI, Pt. 2 for a full discussion of Barton's relief from command by Ransom, and his regimental commanders' expressions of confidence in him.

(51) Fredericksburg (Virginia) *Free Lance,* April 12, 1900, which after giving an account of his funeral, states he was buried in the City Cemetery next to his brother, W. S. Barton. According to *22. D.A.B.,* he is buried in Arlington.

(52) Apparently based on a statement in *189. Evans* to the effect that Battle, while in the hospital in Richmond, was advised by Lieutenant Colonel H. L. Clay of the Adjutant General's Department "that his commission as major-general, dating from the battle of Winchester, had been forwarded to the army." If so, it was not entered

on the manuscript registers of appointments to the army, now in the National Archives, which are the source of *9. M.G.O.*

(53) He was assigned by Secretary of War Floyd on January 23 and relieved by Floyd's successor, Joseph Holt, on the 28th, establishing an all-time record for brevity of tenure in the office. Beauregard later claimed his removal largely arose from Holt's animosity toward Senator John Slidell of Louisiana, Beauregard's brother-in-law, something of an absurdity in view of the attendant circumstances. See *110. Basso,* 61.

(54) This episode has been largely blinked by historians of the Army of Northern Virginia, presumably in an effort to maintain Lee's infallibility. But see *111. Roman,* II, chapters 36 and 37. Documents quoted therein appear in *13. O.R.* Colonel Roman was inspector general on Beauregard's staff and one of the three officers sent by Beauregard to Lee (then north of the James) to plead for reinforcements. At this point neither Lee nor the Richmond authorities could be made to realize that Grant was moving his army over the river, and that a large part of it was already confronting Beauregard's handful in front of Petersburg. The lines ultimately occupied by Beauregard remained relatively stable until the evacuation in April 1865.

(55) Authority of Miss Nora M. Davis, Troy, South Carolina. *16. C.A.B.*: August 8, 1824; *22 D.A.B.*: February or March 1824; *189. Evans:* 1823; *41. Wright:* 1835. According to *21. Cullum,* he was "aged 37" at the time of his death.

(56) *71. Haskell.* On the authority of Major Thomas G. Rhett, assistant adjutant general to General J. E. Johnston at First Manassas, who was with Bee almost from the time he was shot until he died, and others, Colonel Haskell makes the categorical statement that Bee angrily denounced Jackson for "standing like a stone wall" and allowing his and Colonel Francis S. Bartow's brigades to be sacrificed. Also see *268. Freeman,* I, Appendix V, for a full discussion of the incident, including the version of Colonel Haskell.

(57) See report of General Richard Taylor, *13. O.R.,* XXXIV, Pt. 1, pp. 580-81, which characterizes Bee's conduct at Monett's Ferry, Louisiana, as exhibiting "great personal gallantry, but no generalship." However, Kirby Smith, perennially at odds with Taylor, defended Bee *(ibid,* 615). Also see John A. Wharton to Bee *(ibid).* General John G. Walker was also severely critical of Bee *(ibid,* XLI, Pt. 2. pp. 1066-67).

(58) Bee was paroled at Columbus, Texas, on June 26, 1865 as a major general *(9. M.G.O.)*; however, as late as May 16, 1865 he was referred to as "Brigadier-General" *(13. O.R.,* XLVIII, Pt. 2, p. 1309), and was not included in the list of promotions made by General Kirby Smith on the same day *(ibid,* 1307).

(59) Information as to certain facts courtesy of Mrs. D. C. Farnham of San Francisco, a granddaughter.

(60) Place of Benton's birth can only be conjectured from contemporary letters written to his father (Missouri Historical Society, St. Louis). His mother was a resident of Franklin, Tennessee, at the time of her marriage. Date of birth courtesy same source as above; other data from University of Mississippi Library and Mississippi Department of Archives and History.

(61) Many sources erroneously state that Benton was mortally wounded on July 28, 1864 (by implication during the attack of S. D. Lee's corps at Ezra Church on that day). However, Benton's old brigade was under the command of W. F. Brantley all day on the 28th *(13. O.R.,* XXXVIII, Pt. 3, p. 799). The author is indebted to Mr. Craig Mathews of Dalton, Georgia, and Mr. Lewis H. Beck of Griffin, Georgia, for establishing the correct dates as herein given.

(62) New Orleans *Daily Picayune,* June 22, 23, 1891.

(63) See *23. Eliot,* 302. Unpublished Confederate correspondence in the National Archives, Washington, indicates that the authorities were considering "dropping" Blanchard in March 1865.

(64) *48. Boggs* also gives a sketch of his life ante and post bellum.

(65) Information as to certain facts from papers by his daughter (State Historical Society of Missouri, Columbia). See *19. C.V.,* XVI, 159, and XXI, 564, for details of his death, burial, and reburial.

(66) See *114. Seitz* for a sympathetic and sometimes apologetic treatment.

(67) University of Mississippi Library, authority of a son. However, in a letter written on October 10, 1863 (National Archives) he stated he was fifty-nine.

(68) General St. John R. Liddell in the *Southern Bivouac* (February 1886), p. 533.

(69) See *308. Rowland,* I, 293, and *17. Biographical and Historical Memoirs of Mississippi,* I, 420-22.

(70) See the extended account of his assassination in the Jackson (Mississippi) *Semi-Weekly Clarion,* November 18, 1870. Information as to certain facts from a great-niece,

Mrs. M. F. Clegg, Houston, Texas, and from Mr. Ned Lee, Editor, *Webster Progress,* Eupora, Mississippi.

(71) A list of Confederate officers captured at Sayler's Creek, published in the New York *Herald* on April 9, 1865, does not include the name of General Brevard *(19. C.V., XXVIII, 215).*

(72) Information on General Brevard's life before and after the war was kindly furnished the author by the Florida State Library Board and by Mrs. E. M. Brevard of Tallahassee.

(73) The vote was two yeas, eighteen nays *(6. J.C.S.C., IV, 577).* The only affirmative votes were cast by Senators G. A. Henry of Tennessee and R. M. T. Hunter of Virginia, both administration stalwarts.

(74) Much of the data herein is by courtesy of General Cobb's grandson, Mr. Howell Cobb Erwin, Athens, Georgia, whose father was General Browne's attorney and probated his will. Browne gave his age as forty-seven in the 1870 Federal census. Research in Ireland and England has proved disappointing. Although the general is said to have been a nephew of the "Earl of Sligo," the present Marquess of Sligo can find no record of a Browne connection among his forebears. Nor has the British War Office in London any record of Browne's Crimean service (or other service) in Her Majesty's Army.

(75) Augusta (Georgia) *Chronicle,* August 18, 1885.

(76) Georgia Department of Archives and History, Atlanta.

(77) *116. Stickles.* Also see *22. D.A.B.,* etc. His son, Lieutenant General Simon Bolivar Buckner, Jr., U.S.A., was killed in Okinawa in 1945.

(78) Major Generals John Buford and Napoleon Bonaparte Buford. See *22. D.A.B.* for confirmation of spelling of first name, "Abraham," and not "Abram" as sometimes rendered.

(79) Courtesy of Kentucky Historical Society.

(80) *1. B.D.A.C., 189. Evans.*

(81) *19. C.V.,* XL, 435.

(82) *299. S.H.S.P.,* XXXI, 68 ff.

(83) *13. O.R.,* XXIV, Pt. 3, pp. 560, 562.

(84) See *33. Owen.* Information as to certain facts courtesy of Alabama Department of Archives and History, Montgomery.

(85) Jackson acted as the elder Carroll's second in a duel with Jesse Benton, brother of Thomas Hart Benton and uncle of General Samuel Benton (q.v.). See *293. James,* 150-54.

(86) *13. O.R.,* XX, Pt. 2, pp. 417, 508; and X, Pt. 2, p. 379.

(87) Much confusion exists as to the dates of Carroll's birth

and death. His headstone recites "1813-1866." According to a certified copy of his burial certificate (in the author's possession) he died at the age of "57 years." Records in the possession of his descendants are scanty in regard to Carroll, although voluminous on his father, and on his son, William Henry, Jr.

(88) This was the old "Tennessee" brigade of General M. J. Wright which Carter directed until assigned to the command of General George Maney's brigade after Jonesboro. See Notes 315 and 316.

(89) He relieved Brigadier General George Maney on the night of August 31, 1864. Cheatham was at the time in command of Hood's old corps. See *13. O.R.*, XXXVIII, Pt. 3, pp. 708, 712.

(90) Information on General Carter ante bellum by courtesy of his granddaughter, Mrs. William T. Bailey of Nashville.

(91) The "Spring Hill Affair" has provoked as much controversy as any incident of the Civil War, being touched off by the posthumous publication of *73. Hood,* which gives Hood's version. Cheatham's reply may be found in *299. S.H.S.P.,* IX, 524-41. Contemporary reports of the campaign are in *13. O.R.,* XLV, Pt. 1; correspondence relating thereto, *ibid.,* Pt. 2. For an impartial analysis see *243. Hay* and *211. Horn.* Cheatham, who had the last word (since Hood was dead), seems to have a better documented case, although no one has been able to explain the exact cause or causes of the failure. It will forever remain as one of the great might-have-beens of the war. Also see *19. C.V.,* XVI, 25-41.

(92) Date of birth courtesy of the Adjutant General, Washington, D. C.

(93) Contrary to both *16. C.A.B.* and *189. Evans,* Chilton did not "resign" in 1864. See *13. O.R.,* Ser. 4, III, 268. For evidence that he was still on duty in the Adjutant General's Department as late as February 20, 1865, see *ibid.,* Ser. 1, XLIX, Pt. 1, p. 999. *9. M.G.O.* and *41. Wright* do not record where or when he was paroled; he probably accompanied General Samuel Cooper to North Carolina and was embraced by the terms of the Sherman-Johnston convention.

(94) The father was T. A. R. Nelson, who had acted as one of Andrew Johnson's counsel in the course of the President's impeachment, and was at the time of Clanton's death a justice of the Tennessee supreme court. The reasons for the assassination, which stemmed from the bitter sentiment which divided Tennessee during the war, are ably

discussed in the East Tennessee Historical Society's *Publications* (1955) by Allen J. Going.

(95) Exact date of birth courtesy of Mrs. Walter Sillers, Sr., Rosedale, Mississippi from General Clark's tombstone.

(96) The other was Prince de Polignac.

(97) In a memorial to the Confederate Congress read by Cleburne to the regimental commanders and general officers of the Army of Tennessee on January 2, 1864 *(183. Dubose,* 256 ff.).

(98) Date of birth from *1. B.D.A.C.; 41. Wright* gives the 22nd.

(99) Cobb had deserted the Democratic party in 1850 to join with the antislavery Whigs in upholding the compromise measures of that year. This act undoubtedly insured his name's being discarded at Montgomery in 1861. See *291. Hendrick,* 96-97.

(100) A degree of mystery surrounds Colston's antecedents. It seems reasonably certain that Dr. Raleigh T. Colston was not his father; the latter's wife, a native Frenchwoman, denied on her deathbed that she was his mother. See *16. C.A.B.* for an account of the circumstances of his birth. Also see *20. Couper,* IV, 10.

(101) *13. O.R.,* XLIII, Pt. 1, p. 579.

(102) Dates of birth and death from Atlanta *Journal,* May 21, 1894, and General Cook's tombstone (courtesy of Mr. Craig Mathews, Dalton, Georgia), both of which are at variance with *1. B.D.A.C.* and *22. D.A.B.*

(103) Stuart married Cooke's sister, Flora, in 1855 *(22. D.A.B.).*

(104) The Cooke family was still further divided by the marriages of the other two daughters. Maria married Assistant Surgeon Charles Brewer, U.S.A., later a Confederate surgeon; Julia, Brevet Brigadier General Jacob Sharpe, U.S.V. See *181. Thomason,* 28, 64.

(105) Dates of birth and death on authority of Mr. P. St. George Cooke, Richmond, Virginia, courtesy of Mr. John R. Peacock, High Point, North Carolina.

(106) For much of the data on the life of General D. H. Cooper the author is indebted to Mr. R. T. C. Head of San Francisco, a great-grandson. Information as to certain facts courtesy of a grand-niece, Mrs. Martha H. Curtis, Galveston, Texas, and the Oklahoma Historical Society, Oklahoma City.

(107) *21. Cullum* states he died "aged 81." All other authorities, however, including his nephew, General Fitzhugh Lee, agree he was born in 1798. See a sketch by the latter in *299. S.H.S.P.,* III, 269-76.

(108) It may be of interest that his eldest daughter, Maria,

was the wife of General Frank Wheaton, U.S.A., of Rhode Island.

(109) That General Cooper spontaneously made delivery of the records of his office to the U. S. government, as stated in *22. D.A.B.*, is somewhat debatable. In a letter written in 1869 the General set forth that the records "were unfortunately captured" at Charlotte, North Carolina *(299. S.H.S.P.*, VII, 290). Cooper was paroled at Charlotte on May 3, 1865 *(9. M.G.O.* and *41. Wright).*

(110) *19. C.V.*, XVII, 425.

(111) *22. D.A.B.*, citing Raleigh *News and Observer*, December 27, 28, 1919; *19. C.V.*, XXVIII, 45. *1. B.D.A.C.* gives the year 1831.

(112) *211. Horn,* 68.

(113) Crittenden was made to bear the onus of the Fishing Creek disaster, and was freely characterized as a "common drunkard," being "in a beastly state of intoxication" (at the time of the battle), having committed as well "the greater sins of treason, treachery and cowardice," and being, in short, a "besotted inebriate" *(ibid.,* 70). That some factual basis may have existed for at least certain of these allegations is demonstrated by Hardee's arrest of Crittenden at Iuka, Missississippi, on April 1, 1862, for drunkenness *(ibid.,* 446, n. 43; and *13. O.R.*, X, Pt. 2, p. 379). He was subsequently declared by Bragg to be unsuited for a responsible position *(211. Horn,* 158; *13. O.R.*, XVII, Pt. 2, p. 673).

(114) *28. The Land We Love,* V, 97.

(115) No positive verification of his middle name can be found. "Brevard" is suggested by two independent sources, one being a great-nephew, Mr. Shelby Myrick, Savannah, Georgia.

(116) Date of birth from document in National Archives, Washington, D. C.

(117) Unpublished records in the National Archives, Washington, D. C., courtesy of Mr. Rex Magee, Chevy Chase, Maryland.

(118) San Francisco *Examiner*, March 5, 1899.

(119) See *299. S.H.S.P.*, XXVIII, 299; and *6. J.C.S.C.* The vote was eleven to six for rejection, and two days later, thirteen to six for reconsideration and confirmation. T. R. R. Cobb asserted to his wife, on the authority of General William M. Browne, then one of the President's aides, that reconsideration was obtained by the promise of the Athens, Georgia, postmastership to oppositionist senators.

(120) See sketch in *Florida Law Journal* (February 1949), by

his granddaughter, which is inaccurate as to the date of his death. The date herein was obtained from grave-marker and from the Alexandria (Va.) *Gazette*, March 11, 1898.

(121) According to his daughter, the late Mrs. Frank P. Christian of Lynchburg, Virginia, General Dearing was accidentally shot by one of his own men.

(122) The author is indebted to Mrs. Martha Rivers Adams, Lynchburg, Virginia, for a sketch of Dearing's life which appeared in the Lynchburg *News* (presumably in 1933) ; also to the General's grandson, Mr. G. Lynch Christian of Lynchburg.

(123) *22. D.A.B.* and *189. Evans* err in stating that Deas's mother was a sister of General James Chesnut, Jr. She was, in fact, General Chesnut's aunt, a sister of his father, Colonel James Chesnut, Sr. See *316. Kirkland-Kennedy*, Pt. 2, 376-77. The Deas family removed to Alabama out of the elder Deas's pique at having been defeated for the South Carolina senate in 1832 by his brother-in-law, James Chesnut, Sr. *(ibid.,* 377).

(124) Place of birth (in New Jersey) on authority of Virginia State Library, Richmond (based upon an annotated copy of *41. Wright).*

(125) Dates of birth and death from his gravestone in St. Paul's Churchyard, Alexandria, Virginia, courtesy of Mr. Bert Sheldon, Washington. Also see *19. C.V.,* XVIII, 508.

(126) Date of death on authority of *1. B.D.A.C.* and General Dibrell's tombstone.

(127) His father, Colonel John Dockery, was a resident of Montgomery County in 1830; his mother, Ann Mask, was presumably a daughter of Pleasant M. Mask of the same county. Date of birth from Dockery family Bible in the possession of Mrs. Walter Browning of Indianapolis. Also see Natchez *Democrat,* March 2, 1898. The sketch of Dockery in *189. Evans* is lacking in detail and entirely omits mention of his services at Vicksburg. For other facts the author is indebted to Mrs. Dan McDonald of Pine Bluff, Arkansas, a niece, and to Mrs. Nettie W. Alexander, Dallas, Texas.

(128) *317. Clayton,* 396.

(129) *23. Eliot,* 328.

(130) The name is variously spelled "Dunovant" and "Dunnovant." However, he seems to have signed himself "Dunovant." See *7. L.F.O.,* 38.

(131) *2. General Orders, C.S.A.,* 110 ff.

(132) Longstreet's acceptance of the inevitable, and his open espousal of Republicanism, added to criticisms made by him of General Lee, resulted in a series of vitriolic articles

from the pen of Early. Since the latter was a more able disputant (albeit a less able commander), Early was generally conceded to have had the better of an argument which redounded to the credit of neither man. Such feuds were painfully frequent in the post-war years.

(133) See *323. Johnson* for an account of his career.

(134) "Address delivered by Hon. Wm. Henry Trescot in the House of Representatives of South Carolina, September 8, 1866"; also *28. The Land We Love,* IV, 453, and grave marker.

(135) Which was that of his paternal grandmother *(22. D.A.B.).*

(136) On March 7, 1863 General R. E. Lee recommended Elzey to be chief of artillery of the Army of Northern Virginia, "if his health and habits do not interfere." See *77. Lee,* 78. The ultimate appointment—presumably due to Elzey's slow recovery from the frightful skull wound sustained at the battle of Gaines's Mill—went to William N. Pendleton, whom Lee had suggested for direction of the guns of the 2nd Corps *(ibid.,* 79). Elzey was assigned as chief of artillery, Army of Tennessee, on September 8, 1864, and relieved from duty on February 17, 1865 *(13. O.R.,* XXXVIII, Pt. 5, p. 1031, and XLVII, Pt. 2, p. 1208.)

(137) For his part in which, he received the thanks of the Confederate Congress on December 17, 1861 *(6. J.C.S.C.).*

(138) *1. B.D.A.C.* is here followed as to year of birth, since it agrees with date on General Featherston's tombstone. *D.A.B.* gives 1819. *16. C.A.B., 41. Wright,* and *189. Evans* give various dates.

(139) *39. Association of Graduates, U.S.M.A.*

(140) *23. Eliot,* 335; *13. O.R.,* XLVII, Pt. 2, pp. 1004, 1012, 1027-28, 1127.

(141) *19. C.V.,* XVIII, 427, as to place of burial.

(142) Data herein largely from *The United Daughters of the Confederacy Magazine* (July 1951). According to *19. C.V.,* XVIII (1910), p. 250, he was originally buried in Fernandina. Presumably his remains were later moved to Jacksonville.

(143) Place of burial on authority of Colonel Thomas Spencer, Atlanta.

(144) *19. C.V.,* XV, 488; *21. Cullum; 189. Evans.* See *13. O.R.,* XLI, Pt. 1, pp. 105, 108-109, 120-21, for the seeming unpopularity of Forney in the Trans-Mississippi Department; also see Kirby Smith to John G. Walker, *ibid.,* XLVIII, Pt. 1, p. 1442.

(145) First buried in Elmwood Cemetery, the remains of both Forrest and his wife were re-interred in 1905 under an equestrian statue in Forrest Park, Memphis.

(146) February 16, 1864. The vote was eighteen (unanimous) against confirming *(6. J.C.S.C.,* III, 781) . See *13. O.R.,* XXX, Pt. 2, pp. 607-38, for Frazer's defense of his action at Cumberland Gap.

(147) Information as to certain facts courtesy of General Frazer's daughter, Mrs. Mary Frazer Vincent, Pittsford, New York.

(148) *189. Evans,* IX (Missouri) , 79.

(149) *9. M.G.O.* and *41. Wright.* Captain W. Gordon McCabe, adjutant of Pegram's artillery battalion, writing in *299. S.H.S.P.,* XXX, 53, states in reference to General Frost's separation from Confederate service: "deserted and dropped."

(150) Data from Texas State Historical Association.

(151) The inscription on General Gardner's gravestone in St. John's Cathedral Cemetery records that he was "aged 50 yrs. 3 mos." at the time of his death. His father took up residence in New York City in 1818 *(22. D.A.B.).*

(152) Baptismal Register of St. John's Cathedral, Lafayette, Louisiana.

(153) See sketch of Charles K. Gardner in *22. D.A.B.*

(154) Inscription from his tombstone.

(155) Memphis *Commercial Appeal,* June 17, 1901; *189. Evans.*

(156) See *27. Johnson* for an extended sketch.

(157) Authority of Virginia State Library, Richmond.

(158) A number of accounts of the death of Garnett are in existence, none too circumstantial. The most credible (although not set down until 1915) is that by Private R. H. Irvine, Company I, 19th Virginia, who was acting as one of Garnett's couriers on July 3. See *19. C.V.,* XXIII, 391. It is entirely possible that the General's remains now rest in "Gettysburg Hill," Hollywood Cemetery, Richmond, Virginia, where the supposed Virginia dead from the battlefield were re-interred in 1872 and 1873 *(299. S.H.S.P.,* XXXIII, 27) .

(159) Although the name has been almost universally rendered as "Carrick's" for the past ninety-two years in all published accounts of the engagement, the ford was named after the nearby family of William Corrick. The West Virginia historical marker at the ford properly spells the name "Corrick's." (From a photograph in possession of the author courtesy of Mr. Ken McClain, publisher of the Parsons (West Virginia) *Advocate,* who advises that the name has always been locally known as "Corrick.") Garnett was actually killed at an unnamed ford about a half-mile north of Corrick's *(13. O.R.,* II, 285 ff). Corrick's Ford is located some four miles south of the present town

of Parsons, Tucker County, West Virginia.

(160)   Garnett had married Marianne Nelson of New York in 1857. She died the year after and was buried in her father's lot in Brooklyn. After temporary interment in Green Mount Cemetery, Baltimore, the remains of Garnett were removed to the Nelson lot in August 1865.

(161)   Extended correspondence with members of the Garrott family has failed to establish the month and day of the General's birth.

(162)   General Garrott's widow told her daughter-in-law that he was buried "under the window of a friend's house in Vicksburg,' and that his remains were never subsequently removed (from a letter in the author's possession). The exact location of the grave does not seem to be known.

(163)   Birthplace authority of Messrs. Ernest and Paul Girardey, French cousins of the General, courtesy Mr. Craig Mathews, Dalton, Georgia. His father was a resident of St. Amarin prior to emigrating in 1842. Exact date of birth from a letter written by the General to his wife on his twenty-fifth birthday. The letter is in possession of his grandson, Mr. L. G. Smith, Pelham Manor, New York.

(164)   Major General Charles W. Field in *299. S.H.S.P.,* XIV, 552-54.

(165)   For the sketch the author is indebted for many facts to General Gist's great-niece, Mrs. W. Bedford Moore, Jr.. Columbia, South Carolina.

(166)   General Gladden's great-granddaughter, Mrs. G. Price Russ, Jr., Mobile, Alabama, is authority for much of the information.

(167)   *19. C.V.,* XXVIII, 133; *203. Clark,* III, 405. Other sources vary widely. Extensive research by Mrs. W. B. Wingo of Norfolk, Virginia, has failed to establish anything more circumstantial.

(168)   *9. M.G.O., 41. Wright.*

(169)   *13. O.R.,* XLII, Pt. 3, p. 1200.

(170)   In a list of Confederate officers captured at Sayler's Creek appears "Maj. J. M. Goggin" *(19. C.V.,* XXVIII, 215, quoting the New York *Herald,* April 9, 1865).

(171)   For much of the data the author is indebted to General Goggin's grandson, Mr. J. M. Goggin, El Paso, Texas.

(172)   See *127. Cowles;* also *299. S.H.S.P.,* XXIX, 139 ff.

(173)   The most conclusive evidence that Gordon was not a lieutenant general is to be found in the articles of surrender signed at Appomattox Court House, wherein his signature appears as "J. B. Gordon, Maj.-Gen." *(19. C.V.,* V, 405).

(174) Courtesy New York Historical Society.

(175) Granbury's tombstone, first erected at his grave in Columbia, and subsequently moved with his remains to Texas, is incorrect as to his birthplace and the spelling of his surname (Granberry). Information on which sketch herein is based was obtained from an article in the Granbury (Texas) *News,* November 30, 1893, contributed by his sister, Mrs. A. D. Moss of Brownwood, Texas.

(176) New Orleans *Daily Picayune,* December 13, 1892.

(177) *118. Brown,* 531-33.

(178) New Orleans *Daily Picayune,* October 23, 28, 29, 1861.

(179) Much of the data courtesy of a great-grandson, Mr. W. F. G. McMurry, St. Charles, Missouri. The Historian of the Vicksburg National Military Park states General Green was first buried on the George Marshall plot in the city cemetery there. However, the present custodian of the cemetery is unable to say whether his remains were later moved, and if so, where.

(180) See *19. C.V.,* XV, 78-81, for a sketch of Green. Although sometimes referred to as a major general in the *O.R.,* no record of his promotion to that grade, either by President Davis or by Kirby Smith, can be found.

(181) Authority of Mr. Richard L. Dunlap, Jr., Paris, Tennessee, courtesy of Mrs. George Smith, Bisbee, Arizona.

(182) Some data on General Greer by courtesy of his granddaughter, Miss Anna H. Smith, Marshall, Texas.

(183) See *19. C.V.,* XXII, 125, 463 ff., and XXVIII, 12; also *22. D.A.B.*

(184) Month and day of birth authority of Dr. Neill W. Macaulay, Columbia, South Carolina.

(185) From a biographical sketch furnished by a son to the Ohio University Alumni Association, Athens, Ohio, to which the author is indebted for a copy.

(186) See *16. C.A.B.; 68. Grimes; 203. Clark,* V, 648; *19. C.V.,* VII, 557; and Professor Manly Wade Wellman in *True Crime Detective* (Summer 1953), pp. 87-102.

(187) At the time of the actual surrender General Hagood was in South Carolina attempting to collect the absentees of his command. See *68. Hagood,* 365 ff., which includes a sketch of his life.

(188) *Southern Bivouac* (March 1885), 295.

(189) *19. C. V.,* XXXVII, 312.

(190) *Ibid.,* XVII, 349.

(191) *323. Johnson,* from which information for sketch herein was obtained.

(192) Middle name and month and day of death authority of a great-grandson, Professor Guy B. Harrison, Jr., Baylor

University, Waco. Other data courtesy of Texas State Historical Society and Texas State Library, Austin.

(193) Ante- and post-bellum careers from *323. Johnson.*

(194) *1. B.D.A.C.* gives "Steubenville, Ohio"; *132. Drake* gives "Youngstown" (Ohio).

(195) Authority of a daughter, Miss Ann C. Hawes, Fort Thomas, Kentucky, courtesy Mr. Craig Mathews, Dalton, Georgia.

(196) Date of death from copy of death certificate in the author's possession. *41. Wright* and *21. Cullum* give November 2.

(197) Information as to ante- and post-bellum careers from *19. C.V.,* VII, 418.

(198) According to the Quartermaster General's Office of the Army, Hébert's place of burial is as stated; however, the grave marker furnished by this agency's Memorial Division in 1935 has never been placed and was recently (1954) in the possession of his great-grandson, Mr. Harris W. Champagne, Breaux Bridge, Louisiana, with whom the author has corresponded, and who has diligently sought for years to establish his great-grandfather's last resting place.

(199) Same comment as 198 above.

(200) Authority of Dr. R. Gerald McMurtry, Fort Wayne, Indiana.

(201) *268. Freeman,* II, 507.

(202) San Francisco *Daily Alta California,* February 1, 1875; unpublished records in the National Archives, Washington.

(203) *Ibid.;* also Federal census of 1870, city of Norfolk, Virginia.

(204) Letter in the National Archives, Washington.

(205) *Ibid.;* records in the U. S. Naval Academy Library, Annapolis, Maryland.

(206) *189. Evans.*

(207) *8. L.S.O.*

(208) *7. L.F.O.*

(209) *189. Evans.*

(210) *9. M.G.O., 41. Wright.* Confirmed February 17, 1864.

(211) *13. O.R.,* LII, Pt. 2, p. 542.

(212) Letter, dated February 16, 1865 (National Archives).

(213) *9. M.G.O., 41. Wright.*

(214) Norfolk *Journal,* various editions during 1870, 1871, and 1872; Norfolk *Landmark,* January 7, 1874, quoting San Francisco *Examiner;* San Francisco *Daily Alta California,* February 1, 1875. *189. Evans* and certain lists of surviving Confederate generals published in *299. S.H.S.P.,* XXVII,

424, and XX, 37, are totally inaccurate as to Higgins post-bellum career and date of death.

(215) *299. S.H.S.P.,* III, 171, and IV, 126; *101. Taylor,* 92-93.

(216) *268. Freeman,* III, 240-47.

(217) *13. O.R.,* XXV, Pt. 2, p. 810.

(218) Mr. Thomas J. Barnes, McMinnville, Tennessee, and *210. Head.*

(219) *268. Freeman,* I, 17-18. At the time Hill was colonel of the 1st North Carolina, and nominally subject to the orders of General John B. Magruder, commanding at Yorktown.

(220) On June 27, 1864 he was "wounded and his sight impaired for several months" *(19. C.V.,* XXXVIII, 102).

(221) See *9. M.G.O.; 41. Wright; 6. J.C.S.C.,* III, 809, and IV, 535. The vote on the second nomination was eighteen to two against confirming. On March 14, 1865 his nomination to be Second Auditor of the Treasury was also rejected by the Senate. On June 10, 1864 he was confirmed by the same body as colonel and assistant adjutant general *(ibid.).*

(222) *9. M.G.O.* and *41. Wright.*

(223) Place and date of death courtesy of Mr. C. B. Searcy, Longwood, Florida.

(224) Month and day of birth on authority of *Southern Historical Research Magazine* (April 1936). Other data from Miss I. Hogg, Houston, Texas, a granddaughter; *19. C.V.,* XV, 379; *323. Johnson; 321. Handbook of Texas.*

(225) Raleigh *Observer,* June 22, 1880, quoted in *22. D.A.B.* For a contemporary view of Holmes' Confederate career see *314. Hill, passim.*

(226) The name is not infrequently misspelled "Owensville," as on Hood's first gravestone in Lafayette Cemetery No. 1, New Orleans, as well as on his present tomb in Metairie Cemetery there.

(227) Although New Orleans experienced more than three thousand deaths from yellow fever in 1878, the following year but six were recorded, three of them in the Hood household. See *136. Dyer,* 318. (Incidentally, Dr. Dyer has kindly advised the author that the date of Hood's birth as given in this biography is a typographical error.)

(228) Date of death from *34. V.M.I. Register.*

(229) Date of birth from *22. D.A.B.,* which cites *Men of Mark in Virginia* and *38. Tyler.* Other sources, including *1. B.D.A.C.,* vary.

(230) Date of birth from tombstone.

(231) See *268. Freeman,* III, 83-86, 171, 198, 201 for the reasons for Iverson's transfer from the A.N.V. These references make it plain that the direction of his brigade at Chan-

cellorsville and Gettysburg was not up to Lee's expectations.

(232)   *19. C.V.,* XVII, 623. (This article is in error.)

(233)   The most extensive sketch is to be found in *318. Moore.*

(234)   *189. Evans* and *22. D.A.B.* are in error as to the dates of both of H. R. Jackson's appointments as brigadier in Confederate service. See *9. M.G.O.* and *41. Wright.*

(235)   *268. Freeman,* I, 513, 516, 523-24, 528, 562-64, 574-80; *71. Haskell,* 16.

(236)   *268. Freeman,* II, 669.

(237)   *22. D.A.B.* and *19. C.V.,* XI, 232.

(238)   This was the corps of Lieutenant General Polk, later A. P. Stewart's.

(239)   *22. D.A.B.,* citing Nashville *American,* March 31, 1903.

(240)   Their great-grandfather, John Jackson, emigrated from England to the United States in 1748. See *137. Dabney.*

(241)   *189. Evans* states he attended Virginia Military Institute; however, his name does not appear in *34. V.M.I. Register.*

(242)   See his memoirs, *213. Johnson.* Exact date of death and place of burial from copy of death certificate in the author's possession.

(243)   Date of death from his tombstone. Other sources vary widely.

(244)   His tombstone recites the dates "April 16, 1816-Feb. 22, 1873." However, as the Richmond *Dispatch* in its issue of March 4 states he died on March 2, the latter date has been preferred, even though the same article gives the date of his birth as "May 12, 1816." *38. Tyler* agrees with dates of birth and death given herein.

(245)   *143. Johnston,* 497, quoted in *211. Horn,* 105.

(246)   *66. Grant,* I, 360.

(247)   Although it is not so stated in his obituary in *19. C.V.,* XIX, 41, he was for some years engaged in expanding the subscription list of the *299. S.H.S.P.,* being frequently mentioned in the latter publication as its "General Agent," and reported therein as travelling throughout the Southern states, making addresses, and so on.

(248)   Johnston contended that he was the senior in grade to resign from the U. S. Army for Regular Confederate service; Davis' rejoinder set forth that Johnston's rank derived from the staff rather than from the line. For an extended discussion of this unfortunate dispute, see *74. Johnston* and *53. Davis.* The partisans of both men argued the question endlessly; secondary sources are numerous. After considerable study it is the author's opinion that Davis' position was technically well taken, despite the untoward results.

(249) *215. Lewis,* 652.

(250) *189. Evans* errs in stating that he was "included in the surrender at Appomattox." See *13. O.R.,* XLVII, Pt. 2, p. 1354. *9. M.G.O.* and *41. Wright* are authority for place and date of Johnston's parole. See *19. C.V.,* XXVIII, 110, for an obituary.

(251) *22. D.A.B.*

(252) Since known as "Burnside's Bridge"; in recent years it has carried heavy truck traffic from Sharpsburg to Boonsboro, Maryland.

(253) *268. Freeman,* III, 350 n. Contrary to *21. Cullum,* Jones was not killed at Spotsylvania Court House on May 10, 1864. See Ewell's report in *13. O.R.,* XXXVI, Pt. 1, p. 1070, quoted by Dr. Freeman.

(254) *268. Freeman,* II, 665; *13. O.R.* XXV, Pt. 1, pp. 1005, 1025.

(255) *13. O.R.,* XXV, Pt. 2, p. 810.

(256) *9. M.G.O.* and *41. Wright.*

(257) Photostatic copy (in possession of the author by courtesy of Mr. J. R. Peacock, High Point, North Carolina) of "Autograph Book" collected at Johnson's Island in 1864 by Lieutenant Colonel Howell Webb, 11th Tennessee Infantry; and *13. O.R.,* XLVI, Pt. 3, p. 787.

(258) *9. M.G.O.* and *41. Wright.*

(259) Although nominated to the Confederate Senate on September 19, 1862, consideration was postponed "till the next session of Congress" on October 13, 1862. The matter was here seemingly allowed to drop. *6. J.C.S.C.* discloses no further consideration of the nomination. *9. M.G.O.* and *41. Wright* recite that the appointment was "not acted upon by the Senate for two sessions."

(260) *21. Cullum* errs in stating he died in Pennsylvania. Dates of birth and death from his tombstone in Hollywood Cemetery, and *38. Tyler,* which confirms place of death.

(261) See *19. C.V.,* XI, 266, for further details of General Jones' career.

(262) As to the date of Kelly's mortal wounding the author must disagree with the conclusions of Miss Maud McLure Kelly (no relation) in her fine sketch of Kelly which appeared in *The Alabama Historical Quarterly* (Spring 1947), wherein she states that the General was mortally wounded at Franklin on August 20, 1864. On that date Wheeler's command (which included Kelly's division) was at Stewart's Landing on the Little Tennessee River southwest of Knoxville, after which Wheeler was compelled by high water to go above Knoxville to cross the Holston and French Broad Rivers, before starting west.

Wheeler in his report *(13. O.R.,* XXXVIII, Pt. 3, p. 958) states he did not leave the Tennessee & Georgia Railroad until the 20th. On September 2 the command fought an engagement near Franklin with the Federal forces under General L. H. Rousseau, in which action Kelly unquestionably sustained his fatal wound. See Rousseau's report in *13. O.R.,* XXXVIII, Pt. 2, p. 911; and *197. Annals of the Army of Tennessee* (which gives a day-by-day chronology of the movements of Wheeler's command). The *O.R.* include no mention of a shot being fired at Franklin on August 20, 1864.

(263) Courtesy of Miss Maud McLure Kelly on authority of the U. S. War Department.

(264) Spelling of middle name on authority of Mr. John R. Peacock, High Point, North Carolina.

(265) Cleburne's corps commander, William J. Hardee, was Kirkland's wife's uncle.

(266) There is some confusion as to the spelling of Law's middle name, since even his death certificate renders it "McIver"; however, "McIvor" accords with existing family records.

(267) Maine Bureau of Vital Statistics.

(268) From August 3, 1861 until November 11, 1861, with rank of major, he was acting chief of the engineer bureau in Richmond *(13. O.R.,* Ser. 4, I, 531, 1176).

(269) New York *Herald,* September 29, 1866, and *21. Cullum.* All available evidence points to what is now Niagara Falls, Ontario, which from 1856 to 1881 was called Clifton (Mr. D. C. Patten, city clerk of Niagara Falls, to the author, February 25 and March 5, 1954).

(270) *43. Alexander,* 485. In this and subsequent pages Alexander makes plain his dislike for Leadbetter, commenting acidly that he "being the oldest military engineer in the Confederate service, was supposed to be the most efficient."

(271) His father, Edmund Jennings Lee, was presumably a first cousin of Robert E. Lee. See *169. Lee* for details of Edwin G. Lee's career.

(272) Dates of birth and death from tombstone.

(273) *13. O.R.,* XLIII, Pt. 2, p. 926.

(274) He was the son of Sidney Smith Lee, his mother being a sister of the wife of General Cooper. Mrs. Lee and Mrs. Cooper were sisters of U. S. Senator James M. Mason of Virginia, later one of the putative Confederate emissaries to the Court of St. James.

(275) W. H. F. Lee and R. F. Hoke were both appointed major generals on April 23, 1864, Lee to rank from date of

appointment, Hoke from April 20. Lee was born May 31, 1837, Hoke on May 27 of the same year. See *9. M.G.O., 22. D.A.B.,* etc.

(276) See *189. Evans; 16. C.A.B.; 299. S.H.S.P.,* XVII, 61; and *313. Henderson,* II, 813, for his career.

(277) *203. Clark,* III, 284.

(278) Courtesy of Colonel W. J. Morton, former Librarian, U. S. Military Academy.

(279) See Liddell's Ms *War Record* (Confederate Memorial Hall, New Orleans) ; New Orleans *Republican,* February 16, 18, 20, 1870; New Orleans *Picayune,* February 16, 18, 20, 1870.

(280) Dates of birth and death from his tombstone in Thorn-rose Cemetery, Staunton, Virginia, courtesy of Miss Margaret Lynn Templeton, a descendant. See Richmond *Dispatch,* November 13, 1886 for other details of his career.

(281) *299. S.H.S.P.,* XXIX, 212-15; *19. C.V.,* XVIII, 427.

(282) *22. D.A.B.* is here followed; the author of Long's sketch therein obtained certain facts from the General's daughter.

(282 A) Another of Sumner's daughters married E. E. McLean, graduated from West Point, 1842; later major and quartermaster, C.S.A. *(174. Noll,* 176) . Both sons, however, adhered to the Union, later rising to high rank.

(283) No completely adequate war time biography of Longstreet has, in the author's opinion, been written. An excellent account of his post-war career is in *157. Sanger-Hay,* Pt. 2, written by Mr. Thomas R. Hay, Locust Valley, New York.

(284) Incredible as it may seem, the average age of the other eighteen colonels of the line in 1860 was sixty-six. Eight of the eighteen were in their seventies and one (Colonel William Whistler of the 4th Infantry) was eighty. Loring, aged forty-two, was nine years younger than Colonel Philip St. George Cook of the 2nd Dragoons.

(285) Loring entered Egyptian service as a *Lewan Pacha* (brigadier general) , and was subsequently promoted *Féreek Pacha* (major general) . Meantime he won the orders of "The Osmanli" and "Grand Officer of the Medjidieh" *(81. Loring,* 448) .

(286) He came from a long line of distinguished Bostonians; his birth in Washington was occasioned by his father, Dr. Joseph Lovell, being Surgeon General of the Army. Mansfield Lovell's wife, Emily, daughter of Colonel Joseph Plympton of the U. S. Infantry, was also of New England descent. Lovell's decision to cast his lot with

the South may be accounted for by his long-time association with General G. W. Smith (q.v.).

(287) *13. O.R.,* XXXII, Pt. 2, pp. 563-64; XXXVIII, Pt. 5, p. 892; XLVI, Pt. 3, p. 1339; XLVII, Pt. 2, p. 1454. He was included in the Sherman-Johnston convention of April 26, 1865, but his personal parole has not been found *(9. M.G.O.* and *41. Wright).*

(288) Sketch of General Lyon is mainly taken from *304. Baker* and *305. Battle,* both by courtesy of the Kentucky Historical Society. Also see *19. C.V.,* XV, 560.

(289) *22. D.A.B.*

(290) In the author's possession.

(291) *210. Head.*

(292) *19. C.V.,* XXVI, 404.

(293) Authority of Mr. J. A. Sharp, Sevierville, Tennessee, a great-great-nephew.

(294) His evacuation of New Madrid was strongly criticized. General Beauregard later termed the operation "the poorest defense made by any fortified post during the whole course of the war" *(211. Horn,* 144, quoting from *111. Roman,* I, 358). Also see, *13. O.R.,* XVII, Pt. 2, p. 651.

(295) Court-martialed at Shelbyville, Tennessee, March 16, 1863; found guilty, and sentenced to be suspended from rank, pay, and emoluments for six months *(2. General Orders, C.S.A.,* No. 83, June 13, 1863).

(296) *23. Eliot,* 385.

(297) *13. O.R.,* XLIX, Pt. 1, pp. 334-35.

(298) Arkansas *Democrat,* January 22, 1879.

(299) *19. C.V.,* XII, 68.

(300) He was ranked only by Alexander R. Lawton of Georgia in the list of brigadiers. See *9. M.G.O.* and *41. Wright.*

(301) Sketch of H. E. McCulloch from *323. Johnson; 19. C.V.,* III, 189; *189. Evans;* Austin (Texas) *Daily Statesman,* March 13, 1895.

(302) Year of birth from *16. C.A.B.* Extensive research has failed to develop a more exact date.

(303) Places and dates of birth and death authority of the late Mr. Louis C. Mackall, Garden City, New York, compiler of a family genealogy. The author is also indebted, for his assistance, to Mr. Kenneth W. Mackall, Cicero, New York.

(304) McLaws' wife was a first cousin both of Jefferson Davis' first wife and of her brother, Lieutenant General Richard Taylor.

(305) For an extended treatment of the Longstreet-McLaws controversy, see *268. Freeman,* III, 290 ff.

(306) See *19. C.V.,* XI, 265-66.

(307) *Ibid,* VII, 368.

(308) See *159. Stedman* and *19. C.V.,* VII, 397.

(309) Contrary to *22. D.A.B.* and other sources, he was born as herein stated, based upon his age in years, months, and days when admitted to the University of Virginia and to West Point. For this and details of Magruder's marriage the author is indebted to Mr. Thomas R. Hay, Locust Valley, New York.

(310) Appointed June 1, 1864 to rank from date; declined June 7 *(9. M.G.O.* and *41. Wright).*

(311) C. C. Pearson, *The Readjuster Movement in Virginia* (1917), quoted in *22. D.A.B.* The latter work is in error as to the date of Mahone's promotion to brigadier general. See *9. M.G.O.* and *41. Wright.*

(312) Authority of a niece, Mrs. A. H. Bishop, Fayette, Missouri.

(313) Eliza Chalmers, daughter of Dr. John G. Chalmers, a former secretary of the treasury of the Texas Republic.

(314) The author is also greatly indebted to Mr. and Mrs. C. E. Denny of Fayette, Missouri, for data on General Major.

(315) Inferentially from his own report and that of his successor in command of Cheatham's division, Brigadier General John C. Carter *(13. O. R.,* XXXVIII, Pt. 3, pp. 708, 712). None of the tables of organization in the *O.R.* show Maney present after August 31, 1864.

(316) *9. M.G.O.* and *41. Wright.* No source can be found which renders any account of Maney's services after the battle of Jonesboro. He may have remained with the army in a staff capacity, as he was reported (by a Federal officer) to have been seen at Dalton, Georgia, in October, when Hood's forces were en route to Tennessee *(13. O.R.,* XXXIX, Pt. 1, p. 723). His old brigade was subsequently commanded by General Carter (killed at Franklin), and by Colonel Hume R. Feild.

(317) *9. M.G.O.* and *41. Wright.* Confirmed March 18, 1865, the last day on which the Confederate Senate was called to order.

(318) *9. M.G.O.* and *41. Wright.*

(319) *6. J.C.S.C.*

(320) Supporters of the claims of other states to these honors are referred to Martin's sketch in *22. D.A.B.,* which cites numerous North Carolina authorities. That Martin was a superlatively able quartermaster and commissary is beyond question.

(321) *9. M.G.O., 41. Wright, 6. J.C.S.C.*

(322) No obituary of General Martin appeared in *19. C.V.* at the time of his death.

(323) *13. O.R.,* XXXIV, Pt. 3, p. 828.

(324) *9. M.G.O., 41. Wright.* Nor is there any record of nomination to the Senate in *6. J.C.S.C.*

(325) See *162. Goolrick* and *21. Cullum.*

(326) For sketches of General Miller's life the author is indebted to the Florida State Library Board, Tallahassee. Date of death and place of burial on authority of Mr. Craig Mathews, Dalton, Georgia.

(327) Exact date of death and place of burial courtesy Alabama Department of Archives and History.

(328) *323. Johnson, 41. Wright.*

(329) *13. O.R.,* XXXI, Pt. 3, p. 852. After (and before) his resignation—mainly due to the execrable index of the *O.R.*—he has been confused with other "John C. Moore's."

(330) *9. M.G.O., 41. Wright.*

(331) *9. M.G.O., 41. Wright;* balance of sketch of General Moore from *189. Evans.* Manchester was in 1865 a suburb of Richmond.

(332) Day of death and place of burial from Confederate Museum, Richmond, authority of Bureau of Vital Statistics, Richmond, and Shockoe Cemetery.

(333) See *164. Swiggett.*

(334) Nelson's career has been pieced together from several sources: *321. Handbook of Texas* (incorrect in some particulars) ; *302. Garrett; 324. Texas Memorial History; 189. Evans; 222. Stuart; 19. C.V.,* XX, 216; *4. Heitman,* etc. The author owes a special debt to the Archives Division of the Texas State Library. The General died in a camp two miles from Austin, Arkansas, later named "Camp Nelson" in his honor *(198. Blessington,* 44).

(335) His mother was Claudia Margaret Bellinger.

(336) *6. J.C.S.C.*

(337) See *77. Lee* for details of this rather obscure series of events. O'Neal's nomination was not submitted to the Senate. Both *9. M.G.O.* and *41. Wright* are authorities for the cancellation of the appointment.

(338) The author is here indebted to Mrs. Walter Stokes, Jr., of Nashville, for a sketch of her grandfather written by William S. Speer and published in 1888 by Albert B. Tavel of Nashville.

(339) *13. O.R.,* LIII, 975.

(340) *Ibid.,* XXXIV, Pt. 3, p. 823; *9. M.G.O.; 41. Wright.*

(341) See *311. Conrad,* V, 68-69, and *310. Bay* for slightly varying accounts of General Parsons' death and burial (cour-

tesy State Historical Society of Missouri, Columbia).

(342) The author is here indebted to Mr. C. D. Mussey of McAllen, Texas, and Mr. Virgil Lott of Roma, Texas, for their original research on this problem.

(343) See Lexington (Virginia) *Gazette,* February 2, 9, 1944, and *166. Paxton,* edited by Paxton's son. The latter work was kindly loaned to the author by Mr. Frank Paxton, Jr., Kansas City, Missouri, a great-grandson of General Paxton.

(344) *16. C.A.B.; 41. Wright; 189. Evans; 34. V.M.I. Register; 19. C.V.,* XII, 293; and *299. S.H.S.P.,* XXXVI, 285-353.

(345) Date from Peck family Bible, courtesy of Mr. Craig Mathews, Dalton, Georgia.

(346) *199. Booth.*

(347) *9. M.G.O., 41. Wright.*

(348) Madison Parish, Louisiana, courthouse records.

(349) See *9. M.G.O.; 41. Wright; 268. Freeman,* III, 629.

(350) He had been seriously wounded in the leg at the Wilderness the previous May.

(351) See *167. Pemberton,* by his grandson of the same name, for an extended discussion of Pemberton's reasons for joining the Confederacy.

(352) See *169. Lee.*

(353) Greenwood (South Carolina) *Index Journal,* August 3, 1949, courtesy of Dr. N. W. Macaulay, Columbia, South Carolina.

(354) His wife was Emeline Butler, daughter of former governor Pierce M. Butler of South Carolina, who was killed at Churubusco in the Mexican War, while commanding the Palmetto Regiment of South Carolina volunteers. According to family records, Perrin was 1st lieutenant of Company D of this regiment; however, *4. Heitman* lists him as a 2nd and 1st lieutenant of the 12th U. S. Infantry. He may have first been in the volunteers before accepting a U. S. commission.

(355) His mother's maiden name was Nancy Flank, authority of Mrs. Mary T. Moore, Librarian, Western Kentucky State College, Bowling Green, to whom the author is also indebted for the exact date of Perry's birth and the place of his burial. *22. D.A.B.* recites only the year of his birth, and incorrectly renders his middle name as "Flake."

(356) *268. Freeman* records that Pettigrew was mortally wounded "shortly before midnight" on the night of July 13-14, citing Heth's report *(13. O.R.,* XXVII, Pt. 2, p. 640) as authority. Examination of this report makes it seem certain that Pettigrew could not have been wounded

much before noon of the 14th. Additional testimony may be found *ibid.*, Pt. 1, pp. 94, 990, and in *203. Clark*, II, 375-76.

(357) Interestingly enough, Pickett was appointed to West Point at the instance of Abraham Lincoln by the latter's former law partner, Congressman John T. Stuart of Illinois (*299. S.H.S.P.*, XXIV, 151).

(358) Arising out of a territorial dispute in Puget Sound in 1859.

(359) Lieutenant Colonel John C. Haskell, a veteran of the charge, later testified that the commander and his personal staff went no farther than the Codori farm buildings. He further states that neither Pickett nor his staff received a scratch in the charge (*71. Haskell*, 34-35). Haskell commanded a battalion of 1st Corps artillery at Gettysburg. Also see *203. Clark*, II, 44. Nonetheless, it should be pointed out that Pickett's personal courage was proved on too many occasions to be called into question on this evidence.

(360) *150. Freeman*, IV, 112, 445-46. General Lee had earlier requested Pickett to destroy all copies of the latter's Gettysburg report, presumably because of reflections made by Pickett on the troops which were his supports in the assault of July 3. The relations of Lee and Pickett post bellum were markedly strained.

(361) See *22. D.A.B.* and *19. C.V.*, XXXIX, 218.

(362) *13. O.R.*, Ser. 4, III, 1082.

(363) *Daily Arkansas Gazette* (Little Rock), October 10, 1878, cited in *22. D.A.B.*

(364) From a biographical sketch by his son-in-law in *19. C.V.*, XXII, 389, which is also authority for the correct spelling of his full name and title. General Lunsford L. Lomax had died on May 28 in Washington.

(365) The source references for this controversy between two of President Davis' close friends and supporters are numerous. For an impartial discussion see *211. Horn*, 282 ff.

(366) Atlanta *Constitution*, April 30, May 3, 1945.

(367) See *27. Johnson* for an extended sketch of Posey's career.

(368) He married Harriet, half-sister of Hampton's father. Their second daughter, Margaret, was Hampton's first wife (*130. Wellman*).

(369) General Johnston's first wife was Henrietta Preston (*19. C.V.*, VI, 105-106).

(370) There is no record in *9. M.G.O., 41. Wright,* or *6. J.C.S.C.* of his promotion.

(371) See Lieutenant General Stephen D. Lee in *299. S.H.S.P.,*

XI, 501-502, for what should be a resolution of this celebrated debate as to who fired the first shot at Fort Sumter.

(372) Middle name on authority of Mr. William A. Quarles, Clarksville, Tennessee; other details of sketch from *210. Head;* and facts regarding death and burial from Mr. Craig Mathews, Dalton, Georgia.

(373) See *268. Freeman,* I, 268-69, for a discussion of Rains' "land torpedoes."

(374) *Ibid,* 268. Dr. Freeman comments that Rains was "at heart a scientist, and was more interested in explosives than field command." The immediate cause of Hill's displeasure was Rains' alleged failure to deliver an attack in the vicinity of Casey's Redoubt on May 31, 1862.

(375) *13. O.R.,* Ser. 4, II, 241, 1074.

(376) See *19. C.V.,* XVI, 209, for an account of Rains' life by a nephew, which spells his middle name as herein. *16. C.A.B.* and *189. Evans* give "Edward."

(377) W. H. F. Lee, born the same day, did not attend West Point.

(378) *7. L.F.O.,* purportedly from a signature, renders his first name as "Matthew." *22. D.A.B.* and *1. B.D.A.C.:* "Matt." A post-bellum letter in the author's possession is merely signed "M. W. Ransom."

(379) Reynolds' parentage and early life are enigmatic. Most sources state he was born as recorded here. However, Clarke County was not set off from Frederick County until twenty years after his birth. His father is listed at various times in both counties. He recorded his age as seventeen years and three months upon his admission to West Point, July 1, 1833, which is at variance with all published sources.

(380) *21. Cullum.*

(381) National Archives, Washington.

(382) His son, Frank (or Francis) A. Reynolds, also a colonel in the Khedive's army, was graduated from West Point in the class of June 24, 1861. After assisting in drilling volunteers at Washington, he was dismissed from the U. S. service on July 16, 1861, "Having Tendered his Resignation in the Face of the Enemy." He was later lieutenant colonel of the 39th North Carolina Infantry, C.S.A., and after his post-bellum service in Egypt, died in Ilion, New York, on July 19, 1875, aged thirty-four *(21. Cullum,* No. 1965; *299. S.H.S.P.,* XXX, 76; *8. L.S.O.; 4. Heitman).*

(383) *16. C.A.B.; 19. C.V., II,* 3; and Mrs. Robert W. Reynolds, Lake Village, Arkansas, his daughter-in-law.

(384) For certain data on General Richardson the author is

indebted to Mr. R. E. Richardson, De Valls Bluff, Arkansas, a grandson; and to Mr. C. Moffett Moore of the Cossitt Library, Memphis, Tennessee. General Richardson's Civil War career has been mainly reconstructed from *13. O.R., 9. M.G.O., 7. L.F.O.,* and *6. J.C.S.C.* He was apparently, and unfortunately, overlooked by the editors of *189. Evans,* which carries no mention of his name. An account of his assassination appeared in the Memphis *Public Ledger,* January 11, 1870.

(385) Despite numerous claims on behalf of other officers put forth in the last ninety-odd years, this conclusion is inescapable from the now-known vital statistics.

(386) *189. Evans.*

(387) *21. Cullum.*

(388) *6. J.C.S.C.*

(389) *189. Evans.*

(390) See *268. Freeman,* III, 208-209, 210 n., for his differences with Stuart.

(391) *39. Association of Graduates, U.S.M.A.* (1911).

(392) See his obituary in the Dallas *Morning News,* April 21, 1928. Also see *13. O.R.; 189. Evans; 19. C.V.,* XXXVI, 365, and XXXIX, 341; *35. Register of Graduates, U.S.M.A.; 6. J.C.S.C.*

(393) Apparently with the tacit consent of Longstreet, Micah Jenkins, temporarily commanding McLaws' division of the 1st Corps, preferred charges against Robertson for alleged pessimistic remarks made in the course of an engagement at Bean's Station, in December, during the Knoxville campaign (*13. O.R.,* XXXI, Pt. 1, p. 470). Robertson had previously been suspended from command for alleged delinquency in the affair at Wauhatchie in October (*ibid.,* 466-67). His orders to assume command of the "reserve forces of the State of Texas" are in *ibid.,* XXXIV, Pt. 4, p. 692. If brought to trial on either specification, no record thereof has been found.

(394) Inscription on his tombstone. Most published sources give the year 1820 without month or day.

(395) "Entry of Death" in the author's possession. Inscription on tombstone: "July 19, 1897."

(396) He was at the time captain of the Warrior Guards of Tuscaloosa, Alabama (*299. S.H.S.P.,* XXIX, 282).

(397) See *22. D.A.B.;* and *19. C.V.,* II, 169, XI, 340, and XVIII, 317.

(398) *13. O.R.,* X, Pt. 2, p. 62.

(399) *Ibid.,* Ser. 4, III, 1177. On June 12, 1864 Lieutenant General Polk referred to him as "without employment" (*299. S.H.S.P.,* IX, 184-85). Also see Richmond *Times* and

Richmond *Dispatch,* June 2, 1897.

(400) *171. Rust.* Neither this source nor *1. B.D.A.C.* gives exact date of birth, nor does his granddaughter know it.

(401) See *Arkansas Gazette* (Little Rock), April 6, 7, 1870. Mrs. C. S. Woodward of Little Rock, who served twenty-one years as treasurer of the Mt. Holly Cemetery Association, states positively that Rust was buried there, but that his grave cannot be found (in a letter to the author, October 31, 1952).

(402) See *42. Yale Class History, 1845;* also *22. D.A.B.*

(403) Nominated to the Senate on April 24, 1863 *"vice* Col. G. Field, resigned 11 Sept. 1862" *(6. J.C.S.C.).* However, a roster of Longstreet's corps as of December 20, 1862 lists him as "Col. J. C. C. Sanders." Evidently the appointment had already been made.

(404) Exact location unknown.

(405) *9. M.G.O., 41. Wright.* Also see *189. Evans,* IV, 350. He was last shown to be in actual command of his brigade on January 31, 1865 *(13. O.R.,* XLVI, Pt. 2, p. 1182).

(406) Due to the destruction of family records in successive fires, General Scott's descendants, with whom the author has corresponded, possess little information. His father, George Scott, was born in Athens in 1800; his mother was Mary Anne Moore of Greene County, Georgia. Thomas Scott was admitted to the Masonic Order in New Orleans in 1852, and was married in La Grange, Georgia, in 1854, two of his children being born in La Grange in 1856 and 1857. The Federal census of 1860 finds him in Claiborne Parish, Louisiana. His Confederate career has been reconstructed from various sources, including *13. O.R., 189. Evans, 9. M.G.O.* and *199. Booth.* The *Daily Picayune* (New Orleans), April 22, 1876, and the New Orleans *Times,* April 22, 23, 1876, carry accounts of the somewhat unusual circumstances of Scott's death. The Louisiana Historical Society is authority for the place of his burial. For his post-bellum career and other facts the author is indebted to the General's great-niece, Miss Annie Claire Atkinson of Texarkana, Arkansas.

(407) *321. Handbook of Texas.*

(408) *19. C.V.,* XXXV, 372.

(409) *236. Eisenschiml-Long,* 94, 96; *312. Keleher,* 201, n. 31.

(410) *323. Johnson,* 245.

(411) *19. C.V.,* XI, 327.

(412) See *30. University of Mississippi Catalog,* 18-19, for a biography of Sears.

(413) *299. S.H.S.P.,* XXXIII, 54, lists him on the honor roll of the University of Virginia among 445 former students

who gave their lives during the Civil War, although he is not mentioned in *27. Johnson,* which purports to give biographical sketches of the same students—a strange omission, considering Semmes' rank.

(414) The author is indebted to both the Georgia Department of Archives and History and the Georgia Historical Society for data on General Semmes. His death and successive places of burial on authority of *194. Moore,* VII, 115, and Mr. Craig Mathews, Dalton, Georgia.

(415) *9. M.G.O., 41. Wright.*

(416) Much of the data on General Sharp was furnished the Mississippi Department of Archives and History by his daughter, Mrs. Mary Sharp Owens.

(417) On May 16, 1865 Shelby was promoted major general in orders from headquarters, Trans-Mississippi Department *(13. O.R.,* XLVIII, Pt. 2, p. 1307). Similar appointments, unsanctioned by Richmond, are treated in Appendix I.

(418) See *1. B. D. A. C.* and *189. Evans* for accounts of his career.

(419) According to *19. C.V.,* XI, 311, the monument to Shoup at Sewanee recites the year of his birth as 1835. All other sources, however, agree on 1834. See *22. D.A.B., 189. Evans, 16. C.A.B., 41. Wright,* etc.

(420) See Note 409 above.

(421) *23. Eliot,* 427; *13. O.R.,* XLVIII, Pt. 1 p. 1430.

(422) *6. J.C.S.C.* The Georgia Department of Archives and History advises the author that Simms was appointed assistant quartermaster of the 42nd Georgia on August 20, 1862.

(423) *13. O.R.,* XXI, 1070.

(424) In the campaign of Chancellorsville *(189. Evans).*

(425) *9. M.G.O., 41. Wright.*

(426) Dates of birth and death, etc. on authority of Georgia Department of Archives and History.

(427) State Historical Society of Missouri, Columbia.

(428) *28. The Land We Love,* VI, 357.

(429) *Ibid.,* and State Historical Society of Missouri, Columbia.

(430) *9. M.G.O., 41. Wright, 6. J.C.S.C.*

(431) His mother was Letitia Madison, a niece of the fourth President.

(432) Authority of Colonel William Couper, Virginia Military Institute, Lexington, Virginia. No more exact date of birth can be found.

(433) *4. Heitman,* who does not give the reason therefor.

(434) Washington (D. C.) *Evening Star,* January 4, 1901.

(435) The maiden name of General Smith's mother was Kirby. Sometime after the General's death, the family adopted

the hyphenated name, "Kirby-Smith." According to the General's daughter, Mrs. Randolph Buck, St. Augustine, Florida, the change of name took place about 1888. The General's name is sometimes spelled in this way, and he is thus indexed in *22. D.A.B.*

(436) The only appointment so made during the war. Hood's was a temporary appointment under a different law; the other full generals were of the Regular Confederate Army.

(437) Based upon his age in years, months, and days as given on his death certificate, courtesy of Mr. Craig Mathews, Dalton, Georgia.

(438) *I. e.,* the elevation of Longstreet, Kirby Smith, Jackson, *et al.* to the grade of lieutenant general.

(439) *39. Association of Graduates, U.S.M.A.*

(440) *22. D.A.B.,* quoting Senator David Yulee to Jefferson Davis, March 1, 1861.

(441) The attack in which Smith was mortally wounded was launched about 6:00 p.m. of the 19th. Smith lived less than an hour thereafter. See Cheatham's report in *13. O.R.,* XXX, Pt. 2, p. 79. *16. C.A.B.* erroneously states he was killed on the 20th.

(442) *25. Elmwood Cemetery.*

(443) *218. McMurray,* 393, and *318. Moore,* 144 are authorities for T. B. Smith's career ante and post bellum; he is not listed in *35. Register of Graduates, U.S.M.A.* He may have attended Nashville Military Institute, later the University of Nashville; see Nashville *Banner,* September 24, 1953.

(444) That it was this particular officer and not others of similar name who have been at various times blamed, was demonstrated by the author in an article published in the District of Columbia Civil War Round Table *News Letter* (November 1952).

(445) For an account of Smith's amusing eccentricities, see *268. Freeman,* I, 66 n., also *19. C.V.,* VIII, 161-64.

(446) Sketch of General W. D. Smith is reconstructed from the Charleston (South Carolina) *Daily Courier,* October 6, 1862; Georgia Historical Society; *21. Cullum;* and *189. Evans.*

(447) He was a grandson of Gilbert Moxley. Some sources erroneously give his first name as George, as does his obituary in the Savannah *Morning News,* August 12, 1901. His older sister married General Mackall. Date of birth from his tombstone.

(448) See *97. Sorrel* for his wartime career.

(449) *13. O.R.,* XXXVI, Pt. 1, p. 1038.

(450)   Sketch of General Stafford is mainly taken from *176. Stafford*, an account of his life written by his grandson.

(451)   Year of birth from his second marriage license, which, issued on March 11, 1873, recites he was fifty-eight. However, in February, 1865, he gave his age as fifty-one (document in National Archives, Washington).

(452)   The author is indebted to Mr. Robert B. Starke of Denver, Colorado, a grandson, and to Mr. W. Brooke Price of Lawrenceville, Virginia, for certain facts.

(453)   Richmond *Enquirer*, October 2, 1862, and Mr. W. Brooke Price of Lawrenceville, Virginia.

(454)   Courtesy of Brigadier General W. H. Martin, assistant adjutant general of Texas.

(455)   *21. Cullum*, No. 1405.

(456)   *Ibid.*, No. 1372.

(457)   *19. C.V.*, XXX, 250.

(458)   *21. Cullum*, No. 982.

(459)   Middle name on authority of his daughter, Mrs. Ernest M. North, Savannah, Georgia.

(460)   This was S. A. Cunningham, founder and for twenty years proprietor of *19. C.V.* See *ibid.*, IV, 300.

(461)   *189. Evans; 19. C.V.*, II, 3, IV, 299-300, VII, 460.

(462)   This officer appears to have been supernumerary and not on duty after the forces commanded by General Joseph E. Johnston were reorganized and consolidated on April 9, 1865, the remnant of his division being assigned to Major General Patton Anderson *(13. O.R.*, XLVII, Pt. 1, p. 1063). His parole as a major general may have been due to a clerical error. No promotions to any of the four grades of general officers were or could have been made after the evacuation of Richmond by the Confederate government on April 2, 1865. There exists no record of his appointment to the grade of major general on January 1, 1865, as set forth by *22. D.A.B., 189. Evans*. See *41. Wright, 9. M.G.O., 6. J.C.S.C.*, etc.

(463)   *19. C.V.*, XXXIX, 330; *189. Evans*.

(464)   For both sides of this celebrated controversy, see *13. O.R.*, XXXIV, Pts. I-IV; also *100. Taylor*, 176-95.

(465)   *9. M.G.O., 41. Wright*. This may have been due to the fact that he was not commanding troops from his own state, a *sine qua non* with Davis. "Organization of Troops in the District of the Gulf . . . March 10, 1865" *(13. O.R.*, XLIX, Pt. 1, p. 1046) lists him as "Col. Thomas H. Taylor"; same on November 20, 1864 *(ibid.*, XLV, Pt. 1, p. 1232). The Confederate War Department seems to have taken the position that he reverted to his former rank.

(466) For data on General T. H. Taylor the author is indebted to the Kentucky Historical Society, Frankfort.

(467) *34. V.M.I. Register; 189. Evans; 20. Couper*, III, 14. To Mrs. Maurice Moore, Lynchburg, Virginia, a cousin by marriage of General Terrill, the author is greatly indebted for data.

(468) See *19. C.V.*, V, 179, and XXXVI, 416; also *299. S.H.S.P.*, XX, 323-24.

(469) Their wives, the Misses Bringier of Louisiana, were sisters.

(470) *32. Northen* and Colonel Thomas Spencer, Atlanta. Also see *189. Evans.*

(471) Georgia Department of Archives and History and *4. Heitman.* Date of birth from *32. Northen*, III, 97.

(472) *268. Freeman*, III, 201.

(473) Kentucky Historical Society; *19. C.V.*, I, 274-75. The latter contains an interesting account of a "feud" existing between Generals Pemberton and Tilghman at the time of the latter's death. In this piece Pemberton is termed "pompous" and his dispatches "fulsome."

(474) *291. Hendrick,* 95-100.

(475) *9. M.G.O., 41. Wright.*

(476) See *203. Clark,* various volumes and pages, for Toon's career. Date of death and place of burial courtesy of Mr. John R. Peacock, High Point, North Carolina.

(477) *33. Owen* as to date of birth; other details from *189. Evans.*

(478) *13. O.R.*, XVII, Pt. 2, p. 673, and LIII, 216-17, 221-22.

(479) Places and dates of birth and death courtesy of a granddaughter, Miss Elizabeth Heyward Jervey, Charleston, South Carolina.

(480) Mississippi Department of Archives and History; and Miss Mattie Lee Buchanan of Okolona, a granddaughter. Also see *19. C.V.*, VI, 152, and XV, 516; *13. O.R.*, XLIX, Pt. 2, p. 407; *189. Evans.*

(481) The month and day of General Twigg's birth cannot be ascertained. Contrary to *22. D.A.B.* and other sources, he died on the date set forth here, as attested by documents filed in connection with the probate of his will in the Civil District Court of New Orleans (Docket No. 18,445).

(482) Tyler is by all odds the most enigmatic figure of the 425 generals of the Confederacy. The author has conducted exhaustive research in Maryland, Tennessee, and Georgia, without learning anything conclusive as to his antecedents or early life. Tradition has it that he was a cousin of General Bradley Tyler Johnson of Mary-

land (q.v.). If so, his grandmother was in all probability Polly Bond (Clagett) Tyler of Prince George's County. He seems not to have married, nor can he be connected with any of the numerous Tylers living in Baltimore in 1850 and 1860. An "R. C. Tyler, Clerk" is listed in the 1860 *Baltimore City Directory*, which is the only evidence the author has found of Tyler's connection with that city. Statements as to his birthplace in *41. Wright, 189. Evans*, and *318. Moore* seem to have been derived from an account in *19. C.V.*, IV, 381-82, written by W. J. Slatter of Winchester, Tennessee, who was apparently an army comrade of Tyler's in the early part of the war. His participation in the Walker expedition presumably derives from the same source. However, there is also evidence in the William Walker Papers (Callender I. Fayssoux Collection, Middle American Research Institute, Tulane University) that he was with Walker in Nicaragua as a 1st lieutenant of infantry as early as March 14, 1856. The same source definitely establishes his middle name as "Charles." A letter in the National Archives, dated 1862, recites that he was "a stranger in Tennessee." In his efforts to trace General Tyler's early career the author wishes to acknowledge his indebtedness to Mr. William N. Wilkins, Baltimore; Mr. William G. Smith, Washington; and Miss Helen A. Tyler, Hickman, Kentucky. The General's Confederate services are to be found in *189. Evans; 8. L.S.O.; 7. L.F.O.; 9. M.G.O.;* and *19. C.V.*, IV, 381-82. The most circumstantial account of the assault on Fort Tyler and of Tyler's death, written by Judge L. B. McFarland of Memphis, who acted as the General's adjutant on that day, is to be found in *19. C.V.*, XXIII, 353-55; also see *ibid.*, XV, 117, 237.

(483) Van Dorn's death is almost universally given as May 8. However, see J. E. Johnston to S. Cooper, May 7, 1863, in which the former reports Van Dorn's death "this morning" *(13. O.R.*, XXIV, Pt. 1, p. 214); Brigadier General W. H. Jackson in General Orders No. 1, May 7, assuming command after Van Dorn's death *(ibid.*, LII, Pt. 2, p. 467); and Jackson's announcement of Van Dorn's death at 1:00 p.m. "today," same date *(ibid.).*

(484) See *182. A Soldier's Honor* for the circumstances surrounding his death.

(485) *19. C.V.*, V, 567.

(486) Places and dates of birth and death from his tombstone in Laurel Hill Cemetery, Thomasville, Georgia.

(487) Authority of a certified copy of his death certificate, in the author's possession.

(488) His foot was amputated as a result *(268. Freeman,* III, 393).
(489) *102. Wise,* 412 ff.
(490) *298. Rowland,* VI, 543.
(491) *9. M.G.O., 41. Wright.*
(492) *20. Couper,* III, 179.
(493) Dates of birth and death from his tombstone in East End Cemetery, Wytheville, Virginia. A few sources recite slightly different dates.
(494) *4. Heitman.*
(495) *9. M.G.O., 41. Wright.* Walker's nomination as brigadier, dated December 11, 1861, was received by the Provisional Congress on the 13th. Confirmation followed on January 9, 1862 *(6. J.C.S.C.).* He was nominated as major of cavalry in the Regular Confederate service on December 21, 1861 to rank from March 16, 1861. Like similar appointments, there is no record of confirmation *(ibid.).*
(496) *9. M.G.O., 41. Wright.*
(497) *6. J.C.S.C.*
(498) His mother, Jane Maria Polk, was the President's sister. Walker's sister, Maria Polk Walker, married General Armstrong.
(499) *13. O.R.,* XX, Pt. 2, pp. 417, 508.
(500) *Ibid.,* XXII, Pt. 1, pp. 521-22, 525-26; and *19. C.V.,* XX, 418, for accounts of Walker's duel with Marmaduke, and his death.
(501) *25. Elmwood Cemetery.*
(502) *100. Taylor,* 22.
(503) *Ibid.*
(504) The most comprehensive and scholarly account of Walker's death is to be found in the Atlanta *Constitution* Sunday magazine of July 27, 1930, written by that eminent authority on the Atlanta campaign, Mr. Wilbur G. Kurtz of Atlanta, to whose untiring interest the author is much indebted for this and other information.
(505) Authority of his daughter, Mrs. Henry Peoples of Atlanta, courtesy Mr. Craig Mathews, Dalton, Georgia.
(506) *6. J.C.S.C.*
(507) *13. O.R.,* XIV, 493, 523, 587.
(508) *189. Evans,* which is notably inaccurate as to Walker's ante-bellum career, confusing him with Commodore William S. Walker of the U. S. Navy. For certain facts the author is indebted to Mr. Franklin Garrett of Atlanta.
(509) James M. Gadberry.
(510) *6. J.C.S.C.*
(511) For an exposé of this often-quoted myth, see *211. Horn,* 297-98. The author quotes General Grant: "There was

no such battle and no action even worthy to be called a battle on Lookout Mountain. It is all poetry." A fog from the Tennessee River bottom provided the celebrated "clouds."

(512) The only published account of the career of General Waterhouse which the author has been able to find is in *321. Handbook of Texas*. Therein the lives of Colonel Richard Waterhouse, Sr., and of his son, Brigadier General Richard Waterhouse, Jr., are telescoped and emerge as the life of the younger man. The elder Waterhouse, also a Mexican War veteran, was slain by robbers in his store at San Augustine, Texas, on December 31, 1863. The author is here much indebted to Mrs. Penelope J. Allen of Chattanooga, and to Mr. Palmer Bradley of Houston, Texas, for assisting in separating the identities of the two men. The various sources from which the author has reconstructed the career of General Waterhouse are too numerous to mention individually.

(513) *13. O.R.*, XXXIV, Pt. 3, p. 823; *9. M.G.O.; 41. Wright; 6. J.C.S.C.* He was confirmed on the last day on which the Confederate Senate convened.

(514) Houston *Telegraph*, March 21, 22, 24, 1876; Waco (Texas) *Daily Examiner*, March 21, 22, 1876.

(515) Oakwood Cemetery. His gravestone recites the dates "1833-1876," manifestly not those of his father, who was born in 1805 and died in 1863. See Note 512 above.

(516) *189. Evans.*

(517) Besides *22. D.A.B.*, which carries an account of Watie's life, the *Chronicles of Oklahoma* (a quarterly publication of the Oklahoma Historical Society) should be consulted for the relations between the United States and the Five Civilized Tribes before and after the Civil War.

(518) Authority of *19. C.V.*, III, 380; confirmed by University of South Carolina *Annual* for 1902.

(519) See both sources above; also obituary in the Dallas *Morning News*, July 29, 1903, for his career.

(520) *32. Northen, 21. Cullum, 9. M.G.O., 41. Wright*, Georgia Historical Society. There is no sketch of Wayne in *189. Evans.*

(521) For a discussion of the claims of Mahone and Weisiger for first honors at the Crater, see Richmond *Times*, February 26, 1899, and *299. S.H.S.P.*, XXVIII, 204-21.

(522) *19. C.V.*, VII, 362; Richmond *Times*, February 24, 1899. *189. Evans* erroneously refers to him as "Daniel Adams" Weisiger.

(523) *34. V.M.I. Register.*

(524) At Lynchburg. See *9. M.G.O., 41. Wright.*

(525) See *19. C.V.*, VIII, 320, and XIV, 318. Information as to certain facts from his grandson, Mr. W. R. Wharton, Jr. of New York City.

(526) Wharton's place and date of birth are variously recited. Data here from an article by William Wharton Groce, "Major-General John A. Wharton" in the *Southwestern Historical Quarterly* (January 1916), which conflicts with the inscription on his headstone in the State Cemetery, Austin, Texas (*19. C.V.*, XL, 96).

(527) He was assigned to command Taylor's cavalry after the death of General Thomas Green at Blair's Landing (*189. Evans*).

(528) *19. C.V.*, V, 530, and VI, 164.

(529) He was apparently first buried in Hempstead, Texas. See *ibid.*, XVIII, 317. For other details of Wharton's career see *ibid.*, XX, 216; *16. C.A.B.*; and *189. Evans*.

(530) For verification of the fact that Wheeler was not promoted a lieutenant general, see the author's analysis in the Introduction, and *299. S.H.S.P.*, XXXII, 41-42. Wade Hampton was unquestionably promoted lieutenant general (February 14, 1865) in order to rank Wheeler, whom he was to supersede, and who ranked Hampton as a major general by seniority (*9. M.G.O.*, *41. Wright*).

(531) *9. M.G.O.*, *41. Wright*. Whitfield's Confederate career after July 1, 1863 is most obscure. A few days prior he had been assigned by General W. H. Jackson to the command of one of his two brigades on special orders from the headquarters of General J. E. Johnston (*13. O.R.*, LII, Pt. 2, p. 497). Thereafter he disappears from the *O.R.* save for a brief mention by General W. T. Sherman, who reported his brigade on January 19, 1864 as being "on [its] old ground" near Yazoo City (*ibid.*, XXXII, Pt. 2, p. 146). *189. Evans* states that "through the whole of 1864 he commanded a brigade under Forrest and was in Mississippi when the war closed in 1865." However, he is not mentioned in *126. Wyeth* nor in *124. Henry*. During the Atlanta campaign Jackson's three brigades were commanded by Generals Armstrong, Ferguson, and Ross, the last of which contained Whitfield's old regiment, the 27th Texas Cavalry. See *1. B.D.A.C.* for a summary of his life.

(532) His grades were in fact not surpassed until the graduation of General Douglas MacArthur in 1903.

(533) For a scathing denunciation of Bragg's supineness on this occasion, see *299. S.H.S.P.*, X, 350-68, an article by Colonel William Lamb, who commanded the garrison at Fort Fisher. Bragg's defense of his operations is in

ibid., 346-49. Also see *13. O.R.,* XLVI, Pt. 1. p. 394 ff, for the official reports.

(534) On Governors Island, now known as Fort Jay.

(535) Wheeler makes no bones about criticizing Williams' performance on this occasion. See *13. O.R.,* XXXVIII, Pt. 3, p. 959.

(536) Data on General Wilson courtesy of the Georgia Department of Archives and History; Georgia Historical Society; also from *32. Northen, 189. Evans, 9. M.G.O.,* and *41. Wright.* His remains were removed to Bonaventure from Laurel Grove Cemetery, Savannah.

(537) *16. C.A.B.*

(538) See *268. Freeman,* II, 48, 49 and n., for an account of the various reburials of General Winder.

(539) No less than five different dates and places of death are given for Winder. The author, after carefully sifting the evidence, believes that the most reliable authority is Winder's adjutant, Captain W. G. Barth, who telegraphed General Cooper in Richmond on February 8, 1865 from Columbia, South Carolina: "Gen. Winder died last night at Florence, S. C." *(13. O.R.,* XLVII, Pt. 2, p. 1121). This conclusion, however, runs counter to the statement of General Winder's granddaughter, who states he died "in Columbia, S. C., in the railroad station." That he died in Florence is confirmed by the Charleston *Daily Courier,* February 9, 1865, which, however, recites a different day.

(540) General Winder was first buried in Columbia, his grave being carefully concealed to prevent desecration by Sherman's invaders.

(541) For an amusing account of Wise's activities while en route to Appomattox, see *102. Wise* and *268. Freeman,* III, 714 ff. Also see *299. S.H.S.P.,* XXV, 16 ff. Earlier in the war Wise had been peremptorily ordered to report at General Elzey's office in Richmond "as early as possible tomorrow morning." No doubt with tongue in cheek, he made his appearance at 5:50 a.m., and was referred to Elzey's residence, where he was told to report at the latter's office at 9:00 a.m. His orders were subsequently issued at noon. All this was sarcastically endorsed by Wise on the original order, of which a copy is in the author's possession.

(542) *United Daughters of the Confederacy Magazine* (July 1948), p. 18. Not stated elsewhere.

(543) *21. Cullum, 4. Heitman, 281. Miller.*

(543 A) Year from tombstone in Cassville Cemetery. Other sources recite 1823.

(544) See *13. O.R.,* XXX, Pt. 2 for the various reports pertaining to Cleburne's division at Chickamauga. The 16th Alabama of Wood's brigade apparently "acted badly" *(ibid.,* 162). It is possible that Cleburne came to the conclusion that Wood had lost control of his command during that sanguinary battle.

(545) Information from Miss Lilian Hill, Tuscaloosa, a granddaughter; *300. Brewer;* and *33. Owen,* courtesy of Mr. Rucker Agee, Birmingham. No precise reason can be assigned for Wood's resignation.

(546) *1. B.D.A.C.,* which has no sketch of Wright, since he did not take his seat.

(547) Day of birth and place of death authority of *303. Jones.* Other data from *32. Northen.*

(548) *13. O.R.,* Ser. 2, VIII, 178, 254; also Ser. 4, III, 825, 1029.

(549) The balance of General York's career is reconstructed from *189. Evans* and his obituary in the Natchez *Daily Democrat,* August 7, 1900.

(550) Some sources give the year of General Young's birth as 1839. However, upon the acceptance of his appointment to West Point in the spring of 1857, he gave his age as "twenty years and four months." Colonel Thomas Spencer of Atlanta also has kindly advised the author that a history of Bartow County, Georgia; Young's tombstone; and family records in the possession of Mrs. John L. Cummings of Cartersville, Georgia—all recite the year 1836. It is not improbable that the later date was advanced post bellum to support a claim that General Young was the youngest major general in Confederate service; although no evidence exists that General Young himself was a party to such an allegation. However, no other member of his class (or subsequent class) at the Military Academy attained such high rank in the Confederate Army.

(551) Courtesy of Mr. George O. Ferguson, Jr., Registrar, University of Virginia.

(552) See his obituary in *19. C.V.,* X, 31.

(553) He was subsequently given a direct order by Crittenden to cross back. See *211. Horn,* 67-68.

BIBLIOGRAPHY

I. WORKS OF BIOGRAPHICAL REFERENCE

A. Official Government Records

1. *Biographical Directory of the American Congress, 1774-1949*. Washington, D. C., 1950.
2. C. S. A. *General Orders from the Adjutant and Inspector General's Office, 1862-1863*. Richmond, 1864.
3. C.S.A. War Department. *Regulations for the Army of the Confederate States, 1863*. Richmond, 1863.
4. Heitman, Francis Bernard. *Historical Register of the United States Army, from its Organization, September 29, 1789 to September 29, 1889*. Washington, D. C., 1890. New and enlarged edition. 2 vols. Washington, D. C., 1903.
5. U.S.A. *Army Register of 1860*. (Executive Document, 36 Cong., 2 Sess., No. 54.) Washington, D. C., 1861.
6. U.S.A. *Journal of the Congress of the Confederate States of America, 1861-1865*. 7 vols. (Senate Document, 58 Cong., 2 Sess., No. 234.) Washington, D. C., 1904.
7. U.S.A. *List of Field Officers, Regiments, and Battalions in the Confederate States Army, 1861-1865*. Washington, D. C., n. d.
8. U.S.A. *List of Staff Officers of the Confederate States Army, 1861-1865*. Washington, D. C., 1891.
9. U.S.A. *Memorandum Relative to the General Officers Appointed by the President in the Armies of the Confederate States, 1861-1865*. Washington, D. C., 1905.
10. U.S.A. *Preliminary Report on the Eighth Census, 1860*. (Executive Document, 37 Cong., 2 Sess., No. 116.) Washington, D. C., 1862.

11. U.S. Navy Department. *The War of the Rebellion . . . Official Records of the Union and Confederate Navies.* 30 vols. and index. Washington, D. C., 1894-1922.

12. U. S. War Department. *War of the Rebellion . . . Atlas to Accompany the Official Records of the Union and Confederate Armies.* Compiled by Calvin D. Cowles. 175 plates. Washington, D. C., 1891-95. New edition. *Official Atlas of the Civil War.* Edited by Henry Steele Commager. New York: Thomas Yoseloff, Inc.: 1958.

13. U. S. War Department. *War of the Rebellion . . . Official Records of the Union and Confederate Armies.* 128 parts in 70 vols. Washington, D. C., 1880-1901.

14. U. S. War Department Library. *Bibliography of State Participation in the Civil War, 1861-66.* (War Department Document, No. 432.) 3rd edition. Washington, D. C., 1913.

B. Biographical Collections, Special Sources

15. [*Appleton's*] *American Annual Cyclopaedia and Register of Important Events.* 14 vols. New York, 1862-75.

16. *Appleton's Cyclopedia of American Biography.* 6 vols. New York, 1898.

17. *Biographical and Historical Memoirs of Mississippi.* 2 vols. Chicago, 1891.

18. Bradford, Gamaliel. *Confederate Portraits. Boston,* 1914.

19. *Confederate Veteran, The.* 40 vols., January 1893-December 1932. Nashville, 1893-1933. (Magazine founded and edited by Sumner A. Cunningham.)

20. Couper, William. *One Hundred Years at V.M.I.* Richmond: Garrett & Massie, Inc., 1939.

21. Cullum, George Washington. *Biographical Register of the Officers and Graduates of the U. S. Military Academy. . . .* Boston and New York, 1891. [The original edition in 3 vols. has been supplemented at 10-year intervals.]

22. *Dictionary of American Biography.* Edited by Allen Johnson, Dumas Malone, and Harris E. Starr. 20 vols. and supplement. New York: Charles Scribner's Sons, 1928-44. Also "Century Edition." 11 vols., 1946.

23. Eliot, Ellsworth. *West Point in the Confederacy.* New York: G. A. Baker & Co., Inc., 1941.

24. Eliot, Ellsworth. *Yale in the Civil War.* New Haven: Yale University Press, 1932.

25. Elmwood Cemetery Association of Memphis. *Charter, Rules, Regulations, and By-laws of the Elmwood Cemetery Association of Memphis.* Memphis, 1874.

26. Hesseltine, William B. *Confederate Leaders in the New*

South. Baton Rouge: Louisiana State University Press, 1950.

27. Johnson, John Lipscomb. *The University Memorial.* . . . Baltimore, 1871.

28. *Land We Love, The.* Charlotte, North Carolina, 1866-1869. (Magazine edited and published by Lieutenant General D. H. Hill.)

29. Mickle, William E. *Well Known Confederates and Their War Records.* New Orleans, 1907. Revised edition, 1915.

30. *Mississippi, University of, Historical Catalogue of the, 1849-1909.* Nashville, 1910.

31. *National Cyclopedia of American Biography.* 37 vols. New York, 1892-1951.

32. Northen, William J. (ed.). *Men of Mark in Georgia.* N.p., 1911.

33. Owen, Thomas M. *History of Alabama and Dictionary of Alabama Biography.* Chicago, 1921.

34. *Register of Former Cadets, Virginia Military Institute.* Roanoke, 1939.

35. *Register of Graduates and Former Cadets, United States Military Academy, 1802-1948.* New York: West Point Alumni Foundation, Inc., 1948.

36. Schaff, Morris. *The Spirit of Old West Point 1858-1862.* Boston, 1907.

37. Snow, William Parker. *Southern Generals, Their Lives and Campaigns.* New York, 1866.

38. Tyler, Lyon Gardiner (ed.). *Encyclopedia of Virginia Biography.* 5 vols. New York, 1915.

39. *U. S. Military Academy, The Annual Association of Graduates of the.* N.p., n.d.

40. Walker, Charles D. *Memorial, Virginia Military Institute.* . . . Philadelphia, 1875.

41. Wright, Marcus J. *General Officers of the Confederate Army.* . . . New York, 1911.

42. *Yale Class History of 1845.* New Haven, n.d.

II. PERSONAL NARRATIVES, DIARIES, LETTERS

43. Alexander, Edward Porter. *Military Memoirs of a Confederate.* New York, 1907.

44. Bartlett, Catherine T. *My Dear Brother.* Richmond: Dietz Press Inc., 1952.

45. Battle, Kemp Plummer. *Memories of an Old-Time Tar Heel.* Edited by William James Battle. Chapel Hill: University of North Carolina Press, 1945.

46. Blackford, Susan Leigh (comp.). *Letters from Lee's Army*. New York: Charles Scribner's Sons, 1947.

47. Blackford, William Wallis. *War Years with Jeb Stuart*. Foreword by Douglas Southall Freeman. New York: Charles Scribner's Sons, 1945.

48. Boggs, William Robertson. *Military Reminiscences of General Wm. R. Boggs*. Durham, North Carolina, 1913.

49. Borcke, Heros Von. *Memoirs of the Confederate War for Independence*. 2 vols. London, 1866. Reprint edition. New York: Peter Smith, 1938.

50. Brent, Joseph Lancaster. *Memoirs of the War Between the States*. N.p., 1940.

51. Browne, Junius H. *Four Years in Secessia*. Hartford, Connecticut, 1865.

52. Chestnut, Mary Boykin. *A Diary from Dixie*. Edited by Isabella D. Martin and Myrta Lockett Avary. New York, 1905. Revised and enlarged edition. Edited by Ben Ames Williams. Boston: Houghton Mifflin Company, 1949.

53. Davis, Jefferson. *The Rise and Fall of the Confederate Government*. 2 vols. New York, 1881. Memorial edition. Richmond: Garrett & Massie, Inc., 1938. New edition. New York: Thomas Yoseloff, Inc., 1958.

54. Dawson, Francis Warrington. *Reminiscences of Confederate Service, 1861-1865*. Charleston, 1882.

55. DeLeon, Thomas Cooper. *Four Years in Rebel Capitals*. Mobile, 1890.

56. Douglas, Henry Kyd. *I Rode with Stonewall*. Chapel Hill: University of North Carolina Press, [1940].

57. Duke, Basil Wilson. *Reminiscences of General Basil W. Duke, C.S.A.* New York, 1911.

58. Early, Jubal A. *A Memoir of the Last Year of the War for Independence in the Confederate States of America*. New Orleans, 1867.

59. Early, Jubal Anderson. *Autobiographical Sketch and Narrative of the War between the States*. With Notes by R. H. Early. Philadelphia, 1912.

60. Eggleston, George Cary. *A Rebel's Recollections*. New York, 1889. Reprint edition. Bloomington: Indiana University Press, 1958.

61. Fremantle, Arthur James Lyon. *Three Months in the Southern States, April-June, 1863*. London, New York, and Mobile, 1863. New edition published as *The Fremantle Diary*. Edited with Commentary by Walter Lord. Boston: Little, Brown and Company, [1954].

62. French, Samuel G. *Two Wars*. Nashville, 1901.

63. Gilmor, Harry. *Four Years in the Saddle*. New York, 1866.

64. Gordon, John B. *Reminiscences of the Civil War*. New York, 1903. Memorial edition. With an Introduction by Stephen D. Lee and "A Memorial Sketch of the Last Hours, Death and Funeral of General John B. Gordon" by Mrs. Frances Gordon-Smith, 1904.

65. Gorgas, Josiah. *Civil War Diary*. Edited by Frank Vandiver. Tuscaloosa: University of Alabama Press, 1947.

66. Grant, Ulysses Simpson. *Personal Memoirs of U. S. Grant*. 2 vols. New York, 1885. Second edition. Edited by Frederick D. Grant. New York, 1895. 1 vol. edition. Edited with Notes and an Introduction by E. B. Long. Cleveland: The World Publishing Company, [1952].

67. Grimes, Major General Bryan. *Extracts of Letters of Major General Bryan Grimes*. Pamphlet. Raleigh, 1883.

68. Hagood, Johnson. *Memoirs of the War of Secession*. Columbia, South Carolina, 1910.

69. Hamlin, Percy Gatling (ed.). *The Making of a Soldier*: *Letters of General R. S. Ewell*. Richmond: Whittet & Shepperson, 1935.

70. Harrison, Mrs. Burton. *Recollections Grave and Gay*. New York, 1911.

71. Haskell, John Cheves. *Memoirs*. [Unpublished manuscript in possession of Ezra J. Warner.]

72. Haywood, Marshall DeLancey. *John Branch, 1782-1863*. Raleigh, 1915.

73. Hood, John Bell. *Advance and Retreat: Personal Experiences in the United States and Confederate States Armies*. New Orleans: Published for the Hood Orphan Memorial Fund, 1880.

74. Johnston, Joseph E., *Narrative of Military Operations, Directed, During the Late War Between the States*. New York, 1874. Reprint edition. With an Introduction by Frank E. Vandiver. Bloomington: Indiana University Press, 1959.

75. Jones, John Beauchamp. *A Rebel War Clerk's Diary, at the Confederate States Capital*. 2 vols. Philadelphia, 1866. New and enlarged edition. Edited with an Introduction and Historical Notes by Howard Swiggett. 2 vols. New York: Barnes and Noble, 1935. New edition. Condensed and edited by Earl Schenck Miers. New York: Sagamore Press, 1958.

76. Kean, Richard Garlick Hill. *Inside the Confederate Government*: *The Diary of Richard Garlick Hill Kean*. Edited by Edward Younger. New York: Oxford University Press, 1957.

76a. Lane, Walter Paye. *The Adventures and Recollections*

of Walter P. Lane. . . . Marshall, Texas, 1887. 2nd edition, 1928.

77. Lee, Robert Edward. *Lee's Confidential Dispatches to Davis, 1862-1865*. New York, 1915. Edited with an Introduction and Notes by Douglas Southall Freeman. New edition. Edited with Additional Notes by Grady McWhiney. New York: G. P. Putnam's Sons, 1957.

78. Lee, Robert Edward [Jr.]. *Recollections and Letters of General Robert E. Lee*. New York, 1904.

79. Lomax, Elizabeth Lindsay. *Leaves from an Old Washington Diary, 1854-1863*. New York: E. P. Dutton & Company, 1943.

80. Longstreet, James. *From Manassas to Appomatox; Memoirs of the Civil War in America*. Philadelphia, 1896. Second edition, revised, 1903.

81. Loring, William Wing. *A Confederate Soldier in Egypt*. New York, 1884.

82. McKim, Randolph H. *A Soldier's Recollections*. New York, 1911.

83. Marshall, Charles. *An Aide-de-camp of Lee*. Edited by Sir Frederick Maurice. Boston: Little, Brown and Company, 1927.

84. Maury, Dabney Herndon. *Recollections of a Virginian*. New York, 1894.

85. Mosby, John S. *Mosby's War Reminiscences*. Boston, 1887. New edition. *The Memoirs of Colonel John S. Mosby*. Edited by Charles Wells Russell. Boston, 1917. Reprint edition. With an Introduction by Virgil Carrington Jones. Bloomington: Indiana University Press, 1959.

86. Mosgrove, George Dallas. *Kentucky Cavaliers in Dixie*: *Reminiscences of a Confederate Cavalryman*. Edited by Bell Irvin Wiley. Jackson, Tennessee: McCowat-Mercer Press, Inc., 1957.

87. Myers, Frank M. *The Comanches*: *A History of White's Battalion, Virginia Cavalry*. Baltimore, 1871. Reprint edition. Marietta, Georgia: Continental Book Company, 1956.

88. Noll, Arthur Howard (ed.). *Bishop Quintard's Memoirs of the War*. Sewanee, Tennessee, 1905.

89. Patrick, Robert Draughon. *Reluctant Rebel*: *The Secret Diary of Robert Patrick, 1861-1865*. Edited by F. Jay Taylor. Baton Rouge: Louisiana State University Press, 1959.

90. Poague, William Thomas. *Gunner with Stonewall*. Edited by Monroe F. Cockrell. With an Introduction by Bell Irvin Wiley. Jackson, Tennessee: McCowat-Mercer Press, Inc., 1957.

91. Pryor, Mrs. Roger A. *My Day: Reminiscences of a Long Life.* New York, 1909.

92. —— *Reminiscences of Peace and War.* New York, 1904.

93. Reagan, John H. *Memoirs, with Special Reference to Secession and the Civil War.* New York, 1906.

94. Russell, William Howard. *My Diary, North and South.* New York, 1863.

95. Semmes, Raphael. *Memoirs of Service Afloat.* Baltimore, 1869.

96. Smith, Gustavus W. *Confederate War Papers.* New York, 1884.

97. Sorrel, G. Moxley. *Recollections of a Confederate Staff Officer.* With an Introduction by John W. Daniel. New York, 1905. Reprint edition. Edited by Bell I. Wiley. Nashville: McCowat-Mercer Press, Inc., 1958.

98. Sterling, Ada (ed.). *A Belle of the Fifties, Memoirs of Mrs. Clay of Alabama.* New York, 1905.

99. Stiles, Robert. *Four Years Under Marse Robert.* New York, 1903.

100. Taylor, Richard. *Destruction and Reconstruction: Personal Experiences of the Late War.* New York, 1879. New edition. Edited by Richard B. Harwell. New York: Longmans, Green and Company, 1955.

101. Taylor, Walter H. *Four Years with General Lee.* New York, 1878.

102. Wise, John S. *The End of an Era.* Boston, 1900.

103. Withers, Robert E. *Autobiography of an Octogenarian.* Roanoke, 1907.

104. Wright, Mrs. D. G. *A Southern Girl in '61.* New York, 1905.

III. CONFEDERATE BIOGRAPHIES

105. *ALLEN, HENRY WATKINS.* Dorsey, Sarah A. *Recollections of Henry Watkins Allen.* New York, 1866.

106. *ANDERSON, RICHARD HERON.* Walker, C. Irvine. *The Life of Lieutenant General Richard Heron Anderson of the Confederate States Army.* Charleston, 1917.

107. *ASHBY, TURNER.* Ashby, Thomas A. *Life of Turner Ashby.* New York, 1914.

108. *ASHBY, TURNER.* Avirett, Dr. James B. *Memoirs of General Turner Ashby and His Compeers.* Baltimore, 1867.

109. *BATE, WILLIAM B.* Marshall, Park. *A Life of William B. Bate.* Nashville, 1908.

110. *BEAUREGARD, PIERRE GUSTAVE TOUTANT.*

Basso, Hamilton. *Beauregard.* New York: Charles Scribner's Sons, 1933.

111. *BEAUREGARD, PIERRE GUSTAVE TOUTANT.* Roman, Alfred. *The Military Operations of General Beauregard in the War Between the States, 1861 to 1865.* 2 vols. New York, 1884.

112. *BEAUREGARD, PIERRE GUSTAVE TOUTANT.* Williams, T. Harry. *P. G. T. Beauregard: Napoleon in Gray.* Baton Rouge: Louisiana State University Press, 1955.

113. *BENJAMIN, JUDAH P.* Meade, Robert Douthat. *Judah P. Benjamin, Confederate Statesman.* New York: Oxford University Press, 1943.

114. *BRAGG, BRAXTON.* Seitz, Don C. *Braxton Bragg.* Columbia, South Carolina: The State Company, 1924.

115. *BRECKINRIDGE, JOHN CABELL.* Stillwell, Lucille. *John Cabell Breckinridge.* Caldwell, Idaho: Caxton Printers, Ltd., 1936.

116. *BUCKNER, SIMON BOLIVAR.* Stickles, Arndt M. *Simon Bolivar Buckner.* Chapel Hill: University of North Carolina Press, 1940.

117. *BUTLER, MATTHEW CALBRAITH.* Brooks, Ulysses Robert. *Butler and His Cavalry in the War of Secession, 1861-1865.* Columbia, South Carolina, 1909.

118. *CABELL, WILLIAM LEWIS.* Brown, Alexander. *The Cabells and Their Kin.* Richmond, Virginia: Garrett & Massie, Inc., 1939. (This volume is also informative about John Cabell Breckinridge.)

119. *CHAMBERLAYNE, HAM.* Chamberlayne, C. G. (ed.). *Ham Chamberlayne, Virginian.* Richmond: Dietz Printing Company, 1932.

120. *DAVIS, JEFFERSON.* McElroy, Robert. *Jefferson Davis, the Real and the Unreal.* 2 vols. New York, 1937.

121. *EARLY, JUBAL A.* Bushong, Millard Kessler. *Old Jube, A Biography of Jubal A. Early.* Boyce, Virginia: Carr Publishing Company, Inc., 1955.

122. *EWELL, RICHARD STODDERT.* Hamlin, Percy Gatling. *"Old Bald Head": General R. S. Ewell.* Strasburg, Virginia: Shenandoah Publishing House, Inc., 1940.

123. *FORREST, NATHAN BEDFORD.* Henry, Robert Selph (ed.). *As They Saw Forrest: Some Recollections and Comments of Contemporaries.* Jackson, Tennessee: McCowat-Mercer Press, Inc., 1956.

124. *FORREST, NATHAN BEDFORD.* Henry, Robert Selph. *"First With the Most" Forrest.* Indianapolis: The Bobbs-Merrill Company, [1944].

125. *FORREST, NATHAN BEDFORD.* Lytle, Andrew

Nelson. *Bedford Forrest and His Critter Company.* New York: G. P. Putnam's Sons, 1931.

126. *FORREST, NATHAN BEDFORD.* Wyeth, John A. *Life of General Nathan Bedford Forrest.* New York, 1899.

127. *GORDON, JAMES B.* Cowles, William H. *The Life and Services of Gen'l James B. Gordon.* An address delivered in Raleigh, North Carolina, May 10, 1887. Pamphlet. N.p., n.d.

128. *GORDON, JOHN B.* Tankersley, Allen P. *John B. Gordon: A Study in Gallantry.* Atlanta: The Whitehall Press, 1955.

129. *GORGAS, JOSIAH.* Vandiver, Frank E. *Plowshares Into Swords: Josiah Gorgas and Confederate Ordnance.* Austin: University of Texas Press, 1952.

130. *HAMPTON, WADE.* Wellman, Manly Wade. *Giant in Gray: A Biography of Wade Hampton of South Carolina.* New York: Charles Scribner's Sons, 1949.

131. *HASKELL, ALEXANDER CHEVES.* Daly, Louise Haskell. *Alexander Cheves Haskell, The Portrait of a Man.* N.p., 1934.

132. *HATTON, ROBERT HOPKINS.* Drake, James Vaulx. *Life of General Robert Hatton.* Nashville, 1867.

133. *HELM, BEN HARDIN.* McMurtry, R. Gerald. *Ben Hardin Helm.* Chicago: Privately printed for the Civil War Round Table, 1943.

134. *HILL, AMBROSE POWELL.* Hassler, Warren W. *Lee's Forgotten General.* Richmond: Garrett & Massie, Inc., 1957.

135. *HILL, AMBROSE POWELL.* Schenck, Martin. *Up Came Hill.* Harrisburg: Stackpole Company, 1958.

136. *HOOD, JOHN BELL.* Dyer, John P. *The Gallant Hood.* Indianapolis: The Bobbs-Merrill Company, 1950.

137. *JACKSON, THOMAS JONATHAN.* Dabney, Robert Lewis. *Life and Campaigns of Lieut.-Gen. Thomas J. Jackson.* New York, 1866.

138. *JACKSON, THOMAS JONATHAN.* Davis, Burke. *They Called Him Stonewall: A Life of Lt. General T. J. Jackson, C. S. A.* New York: Rinehart and Company, 1954.

139. *JACKSON, THOMAS JONATHAN.* Henderson, G. F. R. *Stonewall Jackson and the American Civil War.* New impression. 2 vols. London, 1919. 1-vol. edition. New York: Grossett & Dunlap, Inc., n.d.

140. *JACKSON, THOMAS JONATHAN.* Tate, Allan. *Stonewall Jackson, the Good Soldier.* New York: Minton, Balch & Company, 1928. Paperback edition. Ann Arbor: University of Michigan Press, 1958.

141. *JACKSON, THOMAS JONATHAN.* Vandiver, Frank E. *Mighty Stonewall.* New York: McGraw-Hill Book Company, Inc., 1957.

142. *JENKINS, MICAH.* Thomas, John P. *Career & Character of General Micah Jenkins, C. S. A.* Pamphlet. Columbia, South Carolina, 1903.

143. *JOHNSTON, ALBERT SIDNEY.* Johnston, William Preston. *The Life of Albert Sidney Johnston.* New York, 1878.

144. *JOHNSTON, ALBERT SIDNEY.* Moore, Avery C. *Destiny's* Soldier. San Francisco, 1958.

145. *JOHNSTON, JOSEPH E.* Govan, Gilbert E., and James W. Livingood. *A Different Valor, The Story of General Joseph E. Johnston, C. S. A.* Indianapolis: The Bobbs-Merrill Company, Inc., 1956.

146. *JOHNSTON, JOSEPH E.* Hughes, Root W. *General Joseph E. Johnston.* "Great Commanders Series." New York, 1893.

147. *JOHNSTON, JOSEPH E.* Johnson, Bradley T. *A Memoir of the Life and Public Service of Joseph E. Johnston.* Baltimore, 1891.

148. *LEE, ROBERT EDWARD.* Davis, Burke. *Gray Fox: Robert E. Lee and the Civil War.* New York: Rinehart and Company, 1956.

149. *LEE, ROBERT EDWARD.* "A Distinguished Southern Journalist" [Edward A. Pollard]. *The Early Life, Campaigns, and Public Services of Robert E. Lee; With a Record of the Campaigns and Heroic Deeds of His Companions in Arms.* New York, 1871.

150. *LEE, ROBERT EDWARD.* Freeman, Douglas Southall. *Robert E. Lee: A Biography.* 4 vols. New York: Charles Scribner's Sons, 1934-1935. Pulitzer Prize Edition, 1936.

151. *LEE, ROBERT EDWARD.* Lee, Fitzhugh. *General Lee.* New York, 1894.

152. *LEE, ROBERT EDWARD.* Long, A. L. *Memoirs of Robert E. Lee.* New York, 1886.

153. *LEE, ROBERT EDWARD.* Maurice, Sir Frederick. *Robert E. Lee the Soldier.* Boston, 1925.

154. *LEE, ROBERT EDWARD.* Miers, Earl Schenck. *Robert E. Lee: A Great Life in Brief.* New York: Alfred A. Knopf, 1956.

155. *LEE, ROBERT EDWARD.* Snow, William Parker. *Lee and His Generals.* New York, 1867.

156. *LONGSTREET, JAMES.* Eckenrode, H. J., and Bryan Conrad. *James Longstreet, Lee's War Horse.* Chapel Hill: University of North Carolina Press, 1936.

157. *LONGSTREET, JAMES.* Sanger, Donald Bridgman and Thomas Robson Hay. *James Longstreet. I. Soldier,* by Donald Bridgman Sanger. *II. Politician, Officeholder, and Writer,* by Thomas Robson Hay. Baton Rouge: Louisiana State University Press, 1952.

158. *McCABE, WILLIAM GORDON.* Gordon, Armistead C. *Memories and Memorials of William Gordon McCabe.* 2 vols. Richmond: Old Dominion Press, Inc., 1925.

159. *MacRAE, WILLIAM.* Stedman, Charles M. *A Sketch of the Life and Character of General William MacRae.* Memorial Address Delivered May 10th, 1890, at Wilmington, North Carolina. N.p., n.d.

160. *MAHONE, WILLIAM.* Blake, Nelson Morehouse. *William Mahone of Virginia.* Richmond: Garrett & Massie, Inc., 1935.

161. *MALLORY, STEPHEN R.* Durkin, Joseph. *Stephen R. Mallory.* . . . Chapel Hill: University of North Carolina Press, 1954.

162. *MERCER, HUGH.* Goolrick, James T. *The Life of General Hugh Mercer.* N.p., 1906.

163. *MORGAN, JOHN HUNT.* Holland, Cecil F. *Morgan and His Raiders.* New York: The Macmillan Company, 1942.

164. *MORGAN, JOHN HUNT.* Swiggett, Howard. *The Rebel Raider: A Life of John Hunt Morgan.* Indianapolis: Bobbs-Merrill Company, Inc., 1934.

165. *MOSBY, JOHN S.* Jones, Virgil Carrington. *Ranger Mosby.* Chapel Hill: University of North Carolina Press, 1944.

166. *PAXTON, ELISHA FRANKLIN.* Paxton, John Gallatin (arr.). *Elisha Franklin Paxton.* N.p., 1905.

167. *PEMBERTON, JOHN CLIFFORD.* Pemberton, John C., III. *Pemberton: Defender of Vicksburg.* Chapel Hill: University of North Carolina Press, 1942.

168. *PENDER, WILLIAM DORSEY.* Montgomery, Walter A. *Life and Character of Major General W. D. Pender.* Raleigh, 1894.

169. *PENDLETON, WILLIAM NELSON.* Lee, Susan Pendleton. *Memoirs of William Nelson Pendleton, D. D.* Philadelphia, 1893.

170. *POLK, LEONIDAS.* Polk, William M. *Leonidas Polk: Bishop and General.* 2 vols. New York: Longmans, Green and Company, 1893. Reprinted, 1915.

171. *RUST, ALBERT.* Rust, Ellsworth Marshall. *Rust of Virginia, 1654-1940.* Washington, D. C.: Privately printed, 1940.

172. *SHELBY, JOSEPH ORVILLE.* Edwards, John N.

Shelby and His Men. Cincinnati, 1867.
173. *SHELBY, JOSEPH ORVILLE.* Flaherty, Daniel. *General Jo Shelby, Undefeated Rebel.* Chapel Hill: University of North Carolina Press, 1954.
174. *SMITH, EDMUND KIRBY.* Noll, Arthur Howard. *General Kirby Smith.* Sewanee, Tennessee, 1907.
175. *SMITH, EDMUND KIRBY.* Parks, Joseph Howard. *General Edmund Kirby Smith, C. S. A.* Baton Rouge: Louisiana State University Press, 1954.
176. *STAFFORD, LEROY AUGUSTUS.* Stafford, Dr. G. M. G. *General Leroy Augustus Stafford.* N.p., n.d.
177. *STEPHENS, ALEXANDER HAMILTON.* Abele, Rudolph R. Von. *Alexander H. Stephens, A Biography.* New York: Alfred A. Knopf, 1946.
178. *STEWART, ALEXANDER PETER.* Wingfield, Marshall. *General A. P. Stewart. . . .* Memphis: The West Tennessee Historical Society, 1954.
179. *STUART, JAMES EWELL BROWN.* Davis, Burke. *Jeb Stuart, The Last Cavalier.* New York: Rinehart and Company, Inc., 1957.
180. *STUART, JAMES EWELL BROWN.* McClellan, Henry Brainerd. *The Life and Campaigns of Major General J. E. B. Stuart.* Boston, 1885. Reprint edition. Edited by Burke Davis. Bloomington: University of Indiana Press, 1958.
181. *STUART, JAMES EWELL BROWN.* Thomason, John W., Jr. *Jeb Stuart.* New York: Charles Scribner's Sons, 1930.
182. *VAN DORN, EARL.* [Anon.]. *A Soldier's Honor.* London, New York, Montreal, 1902.
183. *WHEELER, JOSEPH.* Dubose, John Witherspoon. *General Joseph Wheeler and the Army of Tennessee.* New York, 1912.
184. *WHEELER, JOSEPH.* Dyer, John P. *"Fightin' Joe" Wheeler.* Baton Rouge: Louisiana State University Press, 1941.
185. *WISE, HENRY ALEXANDER.* Wise, Barton Haxall. *The Life of Henry A. Wise of Virginia.* New York, 1899.

IV. MILITARY ACCOUNTS

A. General

186. "A. K. M." [Alexander K. McClure]. *Annals of the War, Written by Leading Participants North and South.* Philadelphia, 1879.
187. *Battles and Leaders of the Civil War . . . being for the*

most part Contributions by Union and Confederate Officers. Based upon "The Century War Series." Edited by Robert Underwood Johnson and Clarence Clough Buel. 4 vols. New York, 1887-88. Reprint edition. With an Introduction by Roy F. Nichols. New York: Thomas Yoseloff, Inc., 1957. New and revised, 1-vol. edition. Edited by Ned G. Bradford. New York: Appleton-Century-Crofts, 1956.

188. Eisenschiml, Otto, and Ralph Newman. *The Civil War.* Vol. I: *The American Iliad;* Vol. II: *The Picture Chronicle.* New York: Grosset & Dunlap, Inc., 1956.

189. Evans, Clement Anselm (ed.). *Confederate Military History: A Library of Confederate States History.* 12 vols. Atlanta, 1899.

190. Foote, Shelby. *The Civil War; A Narrative:* Vol. I, *Fort Sumter to Perryville.* New York: Random House, Inc., 1958.

191. Harwell, Richard Barksdale (ed.). *The Confederate Reader.* New York: Longmans, Green & Company, Inc., 1957.

192. Hutchins, E. R. *The War of the 'Sixties.* New York, 1912.

193. Livermore, Thomas L. *Numbers and Losses in the Civil War in America, 1861-1865.* Boston, 1900. Reprint edition. Bloomington: Indiana University Press, 1957.

194. Moore, Frank (ed.). *The Rebellion Record: A Diary of American Events . . . .* With an Introduction by Edward Everett. 11 vols. and supplement. New York, 1861-68.

195. Oates, William C. *The War Between the Union and the Confederacy, . . .* New York, 1905.

196. Paris, Louis Phillipe Albert D'Orleans, Comte de. *History of the Civil War in America.* Authorized translation by Louis F. Fasistro. Edited by Henry Cappee and John P. Nicholson. 4 vols. Philadelphia, 1875-[88].

B. Units and Leaders

197. Annals of the Army of Tennessee and Early Western History. Nashville, April-December, 1878. (Magazine edited by Dr. Edwin L. Drake.)

198. Blessington, James P. *Campaigns of Walker's Texas Division.* New York, 1875.

199. Booth, Anoren B. (ed.). *Records of Louisiana Confederate Soldiers and Louisiana Confederate Commands.* 3 vols. New Orleans, 1920.

200. Brownlee, Richard S. *Gray Ghosts of the Confederacy:*

413

Guerrilla Warfare in the West, 1861-1865. Baton Rouge: Louisiana State University Press, 1958.

201. Buck, Irving A. *Cleburne and His Command*. New York, 1908. Reprint edition. Edited by Thomas Robson Hay. Nashville: McCowat-Mercer Press, 1958.

202. Caldwell, J. F. J. *The History of a Brigade of South Carolinians*. Philadelphia, 1866. Reprint edition. Marietta, Georgia: Continental Book Company, 1951.

203. Clark, Walter (ed.). *Histories of the Several Regiments and Battalions from North Carolina in the Great War, 1861-1865*. 5 vols. Raleigh, 1901.

204. Confederate, A. *The Grayjackets. . . .* Richmond, 1867.

205. Cooke, John Esten. *Stonewall Jackson and the Old Stonewall Brigade*. Edited by Richard Barksdale Harwell. Charlottesville: University of Virginia Press, 1954.

206. Dufour, Charles L. *Gentle Tiger*. Baton Rouge: Louisiana State University Press, 1957.

207. Duke, Basil Wilson. *Morgan's Cavalry*. New York, 1906.

208. [Hancock, R. R.]. *Hancock's Diary; or a History of the Second Tennessee Confederate Cavalry. . . .* Nashville, 1887.

209. Harrison, Walter. *Pickett's Men: A Fragment of War History*. New York, 1870.

210. Head, Thomas A. *Campaigns and Battles of the Sixteenth Regiment, Tennessee Volunteers*. Nashville, 1885.

211. Horn, Stanley F. *The Army of Tennessee: A Military History*. Indianapolis: The Bobbs-Merrill Company, 1941. New edition. Norman: University of Oklahoma Press, 1953.

212. Hunt, Aurora. *The Army of the Pacific. . . .* Glendale, California: Arthur H. Clark Company, 1951.

213. Johnson, Adam Rankin. *The Partisan Rangers*. Louisville, Kentucky, 1904.

214. Jones, Virgil Carrington. *Gray Ghosts and Rebel Raiders*. New York: Henry Holt and Company, 1956.

215. Lewis, Lloyd. *Sherman, Fighting Prophet*. New York: Harcourt, Brace and Company, 1932.

216. McCarthy, Carlton (ed.). *Contributions to a History of the Richmond Howitzer Battalion*. Four pamphlets. Richmond, 1883-1886.

217. McDonald, William N. *A History of the Laurel Brigade*. Baltimore, 1907.

218. McMurray, W. J. *History of the Twentieth Tennessee Regiment*. Nashville, 1904.

219. Mosby, John S. *Stuart's Cavalry in the Gettysburg Campaign*. New York, 1908.

220. Pickett, Lasalle Corbell. *Pickett and His Men.* Atlanta, 1899.

221. Ridley, Bromfield L. *Battles and Sketches of the Army of Tennessee.* Mexico, Missouri, 1906.

222. Stuart, B. C. *Texas Indian Fighters and Frontier Rangers.* Manuscript, Texas State Archives, Austin, Texas.

223. Sykes, E. T. *Walthall's Brigade.* Mississippi History Society Publications. Vol. I, "Centenary Series." N.p., 1916.

224. Thomas, Henry W. *A History of the Doles-Cook Brigade, Army of Northern Virginia, C.S.A.* Atlanta, 1903.

225. Thompson, Ed Porter. *History of the Orphan Brigade.* Louisville, 1898.

226. Wells, Edward L. *Hampton and his Cavalry in '64.* Richmond, 1899.

227. Williams, Alfred B. *Hampton and His Red Shirts.* Charleston: Walker, Evans, & Cogswell Company, 1935.

228. Williamson, James J. *Mosby's Rangers.* New York, 1896.

229. Wise, George. *History of the Seventeenth Virginia Infantry, C.S.A.* Baltimore, 1870.

230. Wise, Jennings Cropper. *The Long Arm of Lee.* 2 vols. Lynchburg, Virginia, 1915.

C. Battles and Campaigns

231. Beauregard, P. G. T. *A Commentary on the Campaign and Battle of Manassas.* New York, 1891.

232. Bigelow, John, Jr. *The Campaign of Chancellorsville.* New Haven: Yale University Press, 1910.

233. Bill, Alfred Hay. *The Beleaguered City: Richmond 1861-65.* New York: Alfred A. Knopf, 1946.

234. *Campaigns of the Civil War.* 13 vols. New York: Charles Scribner's Sons, 1881-1885.

235. Dowdey, Clifford. *Death of a Nation* [Gettysburg]. New York: Alfred A. Knopf, 1958.

236. Eisenschiml, Otto, and E. B. Long. *As Luck Would Have It.* Indianapolis: Bobbs-Merrill Company, Inc., 1948.

237. English Combatant, An. *Battlefields of the South from Bull Run to Fredericksburg.* 2 vols. New York, 1864.

238. Fiebeger, G. J. *Campaigns of the Civil War.* West Point, New York, 1910.

239. Goldsborough, William W. *The Maryland Line in the Confederate States Army.* Baltimore, 1869.

240. Gosnell, H. Allen. *Guns on the Western Waters.* Baton Rouge: Louisiana State University Press, 1949.

241. Gracie, Archibald. *The Truth about Chickamauga.* Boston, 1911.

242. Haskell, Frank Aretas. *The Battle of Gettysburg.* Madison: Wisconsin History Commission, 1910. New edition. Edited by Bruce Catton. Boston: Houghton Mifflin Company, 1958.

243. Hay, Thomas Robson. *Hood's Tennessee Campaign.* New York: Neale Publishing Company, 1929.

244. Heyward, Dubose, and Herbert Ravenel Sass. *Fort Sumter 1861-1865.* New York: Farrar & Rinehart, 1938.

245. Horn, Stanley F. *The Decisive Battle of Nashville.* Baton Rouge: Louisiana State University Press, 1956.

246. Johnson, John. *The Defense of Charleston Harbor.* Charleston, South Carolina, 1890.

247. Johnson, Ludwell H. *Red River Campaign: Politics and Cotton in the Civil War.* Baltimore: Johns Hopkins Press, 1958.

248. Jones, Samuel. *The Siege of Charleston.* New York, 1911.

249. Kerby, Robert Lee. *The Confederate Invasion of New Mexico and Arizona, 1861-1862.* Los Angeles: Westernlore Press, 1958.

250. Key, William. *The Battle of Atlanta and the Georgia Campaign.* New York: Twayne Publishers, 1958.

251. Lindsley, John Berrien (ed.). *The Military Annals of Tennessee.* Nashville, 1886.

252. Miers, Earl Schenck, and Richard A. Brown (eds.). *Gettysburg.* New Brunswick: Rutgers University Press, 1948.

253. Mitchell, Joseph B. *Decisive Battles of the Civil War.* New York: G. P. Putnam's Sons, 1955.

254. Monaghan, Jay. *Civil War on the Western Border.* Boston: Little, Brown and Company, 1955.

255. Norton, Oliver Willcox. *The Attack and Defense of Little Round Top.* New York, 1913.

256. Patch, Joseph Dorst. *The Battle of Ball's Bluff.* Edited by Fitzhugh Turner. With an Introduction by V. C. Jones. Leesburg, 1958.

257. Pratt, Fletcher. *Civil War on Western Waters.* New York: Henry Holt and Company, Inc., 1956.

258. Rice, DeLong. *The Story of Shiloh.* Pamphlet. N. p., n. d.

259. Smith, Gustavus W. *The Battle of Seven Pines.* New York, 1891.

260. Stackpole, Edward H. *Chancellorsville—Lee's Greatest Battle.* Harrisburg: Military Service Publishing Company, 1958.

261. ———. *Drama on the Rappahannock*: *The Fredericksburg Campaign*. Harrisburg: Military Service Publishing Company, 1957.

262. ———. *They Met at Gettysburg*. Harrisburg: Eagle Books, 1956.

263. Steele, Matthew Forney. *American Campaigns*. 2 vols. Harrisburg: Military Service Publishing Company, 1949.

264. Swanberg, W. A. *First Blood, The Story of Fort Sumter*. New York: Charles Scribner's Sons, 1958.

265. Tucker, Glenn. *High Tide at Gettysburg*. Indianapolis: The Bobbs-Merrill Company, Inc., 1958.

266. Turner, Edward Raymond. *The New Market Campaign*. Richmond, 1912.

D. Strategy and Command

267. Deaderick, Baron. *Strategy in the Civil War*. Harrisburg: Military Service Publishing Company, 1947.

268. Freeman, Douglas Southall. *Lee's Lieutenants: A Study in Command*. 3 vols. New York: Charles Scribner's Sons, 1942-1944.

269. Fuller, J. F. C. *Grant and Lee: A Study in Personality and Generalship*. 2nd edition. Bloomington: University of Indiana Press, 1957.

270. Liddell Hart, B. H. *Sherman: Soldier, Realist, American*. New York: F. Praeger Company, 1958.

271. Vandiver, Frank. *Rebel Brass: The Confederate Command System*. Baton Rouge: Louisiana State University Press, 1956.

272. Williams, Kenneth P. *Lincoln Finds a General: A Military Study of the Civil War*. 4 vols. New York: The Macmillan Company, 1949-56.

273. Williams, T. Harry. *Lincoln and His Generals*. New York: Alfred A. Knopf, 1952. Reprint edition. New York: Grosset & Dunlap, Inc., 1957.

E. Picture Books

274. Blay, John S. *The Civil War: A Pictorial Profile*. New York: Thomas Y. Crowell Company, 1958.

275. Buchanan, Lamont. *A Pictorial History of the Confederacy*. New York: Crown Publishers, Inc., 1951.

276. Donald, David, Hirst D. Milhollen, Milton Kaplan, and Hulen Stuart (eds.). *Divided We Fought: A Pictorial History of the War, 1861-1865*. New York: The Macmillan Company, 1952.

277. Johnson, Rossiter. *Campfires and Battlefields: A Pictorial Narrative of the Civil War*. Reprint edition. New York: Barnes & Noble, 1958.

278. Kredel, Fritz, and Frederick P. Todd. *Soldiers of the American Army*. Chicago: Henry Regnery Company, 1954.

279. Meredith, Roy. *Mr. Lincoln's Contemporaries*. New York: Charles Scribner's Sons, 1951.

280. Meserve, Frederick Hill, and Carl Sandburg. *The Photographs of Abraham Lincoln*. New York: Harcourt, Brace and Company, 1944.

281. Miller, Francis Trevelyan, and Robert S. Lanier (eds.). *The Photographic History of the Civil War*. 10 vols. New York, 1911. New edition. Edited by Henry Steele Commager. 5 vols. New York: Thomas Yoseloff, Inc., 1957.

V. BACKGROUND

282. Cole, Arthur C. *The Irrepressible Conflict, 1850-1865*. Vol. 7, "History of American Life Series." New York: The Macmillan Company, 1934.

283. Coulter, E. Merton. *The Confederate States of America, 1861-1865*, Vol. VII, *A History of the South*. Baton Rouge: Louisiana State University Press, 1950.

284. ———. *Travels in the Confederacy: A Bibliography*. Norman: University of Oklahoma Press, 1948.

285. Craven, Avery O. *Civil War in the Making, 1815-1860*. Baton Rouge: Louisiana State University Press, 1959.

286. ———. *The Growth of Southern Nationalism, 1848-1861*. Vol. VI, *A History of the South*. Baton Rouge: Louisiana State University Press, 1953.

287. Dowdey, Clifford. *The Land They Fought For: The South as the Confederacy, 1832-1865*. New York: Doubleday & Company, Inc., 1955.

288. Eaton, Clement. *History of the Southern Confederacy*. New York: The Macmillan Company, 1954.

289. Freeman, Douglas Southall. *A Calendar of Confederate Papers*. Richmond, 1908.

290. ———. *The South to Posterity: An Introduction to the Writing of Confederate History*. New York: Charles Scribner's Sons, 1939.

291. Hendrick, Burton J. *Statesmen of the Lost Cause; Jefferson Davis and His Cabinet*. Boston: Little, Brown and Company, 1939.

292. Henry, Robert Selph. *The Story of the Confederacy*. Indianapolis: The Bobbs-Merrill Company, Inc., 1931. New and revised edition. With a Foreword by Douglas Southall Freeman. New York: Grosset & Dunlap, Inc., 1954. Revised edition. Indianapolis: The Bobbs-Merrill Company, Inc., 1957.

293. James, Marquis. *The Life of Andrew Jackson*. Indianapolis: The Bobbs-Merrill Company, Inc., 1941.
294. Patrick, Rembert W. *Jefferson Davis and His Cabinet*. Baton Rouge: Louisiana State University Press, 1944.
295. Pollard, Edward A. *The Lost Cause*. New York, 1866.
296. Randall, James G. *Civil War and Reconstruction*. Boston: D. C. Heath and Company, 1953.
297. Richardson, James D. *A Compilation of the Messages and Papers of the Confederacy*. Nashville, 1906.
298. Rowland, Dunbar (ed.). *Jefferson Davis, Constitutionalist, His Letters, Papers and Speeches*. 10 vols. Jackson, Mississippi: Privately printed for the Mississippi Department of Archives and History.
299. *Southern Historical Society Papers, The*. 49 vols. Richmond: The Southern Historical Society, 1876-1943.

VI. STATE AND LOCAL HISTORY

ALABAMA
300. Brewer, Willis. *Alabama: Her History, Resources, War Record and Public Men*. Montgomery, 1872.

GEORGIA
301. Bryan, T. Conn. *Confederate Georgia*. Athens: The University of Georgia Press, 1953.
302. Garrett, Franklin. *Atlanta and Its Environs*. New York: Lewis Historical Publishing Co., 1954.
303. Jones, Charles E. *Georgia in the War, 1861-1865*. N. p., 1909.

KENTUCKY
304. Baker, Clausine R. *History of Caldwell County, Kentucky*. Madisonville, Kentucky, 1936.
305. Battle, J. H., W. H. Perrin, and G. C. Kniffin. *Kentucky: A History of the State*. Louisville, 1885.
306. Neuman, F. G. *The Story of Paducah*. Paducah, 1927.

LOUISIANA
307. Bragg, Jefferson Davis. *Louisiana in the Confederacy*. Baton Rouge: Louisiana State University Press, 1941.

MISSISSIPPI
308. Rowland, Dunbar (ed.). *Encyclopedia of Mississippi History*. Atlanta, 1907.
309. Sillers, Florence Warfield (Comp.). *History of Bolivar County, Mississippi*. Jackson, Mississippi: Herderman Brothers, 1948.

MISSOURI
310. Bay, Wm. Van Ness. *Reminiscences of the Bench and Bar Missouri*. St. Louis, 1878.

311. Conrad, Howard L. (ed.) . *Encyclopedia of the History of Missouri*. New York, 1901.

NEW MEXICO

312. Keleher, William A. *Turmoil in New Mexico, 1846-1868*. Santa Fe: Rydal Press, 1952.

NORTH CAROLINA

313. Henderson, Archibald. *North Carolina, The Old North State and the New*. Chicago, 1941.
314. Hill, Daniel Harvey. *North Carolina in the War Between the States*. 2 vols. Raleigh: Edwards & Broughton, 1926. (The author is the son of General Daniel H. Hill.)

SOUTH CAROLINA

315. Cauthen, Charles Edward. *South Carolina Goes to War*. Chapel Hill: University of North Carolina Press, 1950.
316. Kirkland, T. J., and R. M. Kennedy. *Historic Camden*. 2 vols. Columbia, South Carolina, 1926.

TENNESSEE

317. Clayton, William W. *History of Davidson County, Tennessee*. Philadelphia, 1880.
318. Moore, John Trotwood (ed.) . *Tennessee, The Volunteer State*. Chicago, 1923.
319. Sims, Carlton C. (ed.). *A History of Rutherford County* [Tennessee]. N. p., 1947.
320. Wright, Marcus J. (Comp.) . *Tennessee in the War, 1861-1865*. New York, 1908.

TEXAS

321. *Handbook of Texas*. Austin: Texas State Historical Society, 1952.
322. Henderson, Harry McCarry. *Texas in the Confederacy*. San Antonio: Naylor Company, 1955.
323. Johnson, Sid. S. *Texans Who Wore the Gray*. N.p., n. d.
324. *A Memorial and Biographical History of McLennan, Falls, Bell, and Coryell Counties, Texas*. Chicago, 1893.

420